AF553182

VISION, COURAGE AND SERVICE

Life and Times of
General T.N. Raina, MVC

Also by
Satish K. Issar

~

General S.M. Shrinagesh: Soldier, Scholar, Statesman

VISION, COURAGE AND SERVICE

Life and Times of General T.N. Raina, MVC

Brigadier Satish K. Issar, VSM, IA (Retd.)

Foreword by
General V.P. Malik, PVSM, AVSM (Retd.)
Former Chief of the Army Staff

www.visionbooksindia.com

www.visionbooksindia.com

A Vision Books Original

ISBN 10: 93-86268-51-5
ISBN 13: 978-93-86268-51-8

First Published in 2021 by
Vision Books Pvt. Ltd.
(Incorporating Orient Paperbacks and CARING Imprints)
24 Feroze Gandhi Road, Lajpat Nagar 3
New Delhi 110024, India.
Phone: (+91-11) 2984 0821 / 22
e-mail: visionbooks@gmail.com

Printed at
Thomson Press
B-315, Okhla Industrial Area, Phase 1
New Delhi 110020, India.

Contents

Part III

~

Invasion by the Dragon

Part IV

~

Higher Command, Staff Appointments and Birth of A New Nation

Part V

~

The Indian Army under General T.N. Raina, MVC

Part VI

~

Dedication to the Regiment

Part VII

~

Military and Diplomacy

Maps

List of Abbreviations

AC	Ashoka Chakra.
ADC	Aide de Camp.
AG	Adjutant General.
AGI	Army Group Insurance.
AHQ	Army Headquarters. The main headquarters of the Indian Army in New Delhi.
AIIMS	All India Institute of Medical Sciences.
ALG	Advance Landing Ground.
AMS	Assistant Military Secretary.
AOC	Army Ordinance Corps. Also, Air Officer Commanding, an appointment in IAF.
AOC-in-C	Air Officer Commanding-in-Chief.
APC	Armoured Personnel Carriers
ASC	Army Supply Corps.
AT	Animal Transport.
ATGM	Anti-tank wire-guided missile.
AWHO	Army Welfare Housing Organisation.
AWWA	Army Wives Welfare Association.
AVSM	Ati Vishisht Seva Medal.
AQMG	Assistant Quartermaster-General.
Bde	Brigade; a subordinate formation of a division.
BM	Brigade Major.
Bn	Battalion.
BGS	Brigadier General Staff.
Brig	Brigadier. Commander of a brigade or a senior staff officer. US usage refers to this rank as one-star (for

	the insignia worn). The holder is regarded as a General in US Army (and US Air Force), a practice that was discarded by the British in the 1920s.
C-in-C	Commander-in-Chief.
Cdr	Commander.
Cdt	Cadet.
Cdre	Commodore, a rank in Indian Navy, equivalent to Brigadier in Indian Army and Air Commodore in the Indian Air Force.
Capt	Captain.
Cav	Cavalry; usually a tank regiment, as in "7 Cav. Regt.", but can be a reconnaissance regiment with light armoured vehicles.
CB	Companion of the Most Honourable Order of the Bath.
CDS	Chief of Defence Staff.
CFL	Cease Fire Line established in Kashmir under UN supervision on 1st January 1949. Replaced by the Line of Control (LOC) as per Shimla Agreement, 1972.
CIE	Corps of Indian Engineers.
CILQ	Compensation in lieu of Quarters.
CO	Commanding Officer of a unit, i.e. an infantry battalion, artillery regiment, armoured regiment. Usually it was commanded by an officer of the rank of Lt Col which has now been upgraded to the rank of Colonel.
COAS	Chief of the Army Staff. A misnomer, as he is not just "chief" of the staff officers, but the commander of Indian Army.
COR	Colonel of the Regiment.
COS	Chief of Staff.
COSC	Chiefs of Staff Committee.
CMA	Corps Maintenance Area.
CNS	Chief of the Naval Staff. An officer of the rank of Admiral (Adm).

CAS	Chief of the Air Staff. An officer of the rank of Air Chief Marshal (ACM).
Col	Colonel.
Coy	Company.
CP	Central Provinces.
CPs	Check Posts.
CPI (M)	Communist Party of India (Marxist).
CPOs	Central police organizations. Raised by an act of Parliament for deployment on internal security police duties, at the direction of Ministry of Home affairs, Government of India, like Border Security Force (BSF), Central Reserve Police (CRPF), Central Industrial Force (CISF), Indo-Tibetan Border Police (ITBP), Special Security Force (SSF), and so on. Assam Rifles which was the only Para Military Force has now been absorbed as a CPO.
CAPF	Central Armed Police Force. Nomenclature of seven security forces in India under the authority of Ministry of Home Affairs (MHA). These are, Assam Rifles (AR), Border Security Force (BSF), Central Reserve Police Force (CRPF), Central Industrial Security Force (CISF), National Security Guard (NSG), Indo-Tibetan Border Police (ITBP), and Sashastra Seema Bal (SSB).
CI	Civil Internee (CI). After occupation of a territory by the invading nation / power during War, civilians of the captured territory were put in CI camps.
CSOs	Civilian Staff Officers.
D	Distinguished.
DAG	Deputy Adjutant General.
DAMS	Deputy Assistant Military Secretary.
DBO	Daulat Beg Oldi.
D.S.O.	Distinguished Service Order. A war time decoration in the British Indian Army awarded to officers for distinguished services.
DCOAS	Deputy Chief of the Army Staff.

DSSC	Defence Services Staff College.
Div	Division. A formation of, usually, three brigades (Bdes. q.v.). The smallest military formation capable of sustained independent operations, because it has extensive integral logistic support. An infantry division has only one tank regiment allocated but will have two or more infantry brigades; an armoured division will usually have two armoured brigades and one infantry brigade, usually mounted in armoured personnel carriers.
DMA	Department of Military Affairs.
DMI	Director Military Intelligence.
DMO	Director Military Operation.
ERE	Extra-Regimental Employment.
EME	Electrical and Mechanical Engineers. A supporting service of the fighting (combat) arms of Indian Army. It is responsible for the technical maintenance of all equipment, which it undertakes in barracks and in the field, for which it receives too little praise. For example, its technicians repair tanks in just as dangerous conditions as the forward troops.
FA	Faculty of Arts.
FC College	Forman Christian College.
Flt Lt	Flight Lieutenant
FM	Field Marshal.
FDL	Forward Defended Locality.
GHQ	General Headquarter.
GICO	General Intelligence Course.
GOC-in-C	General Officer Commander-in-Chief (usually a Field Army Commander).
Gen	General.
GOC	General Officer Commanding. In the Indian Army, typically, a Major-General commanding a Division and a Lt Gen commanding a Corps, respectively.

Gp	Group; as in "71 Mountain Brigade Group", which was a brigade allocated more than the normal amount of combat and logistic units. It could operate outside divisional command, reporting directly to the next higher HQ, if so ordered.
Gp Capt	Group Captain. A rank in the air force.
GPW	Great Paper Writer.
GTC	Gorkha Training Centre.
GC	Gentleman Cadet.
GSO-2	General Staff Officer-2
HAA	High Altitude Area.
Hav	Havildar.
HQ	Headquarter.
IA	Indian Army.
IAF	Indian Air Force.
IAS	Indian Administrative Service.
IAT	Institute of Armament and Technology.
IAUL	Indian Army Unattached List.
IALO	Indian Army Liaison Officer.
IB	Intelligence Bureau.
ICO	Indian Commissioned Officer.
ICS	Indian Civil Service. Re-designated after Independence of India as Indian Administrative Service (IAS).
ICU	Intensive Care Unit.
ICV	Infantry Combat Vehicle.
IDSA	Institute for Defence Studies and Analyses.
IDSM	Indian Distinguished Service Medal.
IDC	Imperial Defence College
ILP	Interim Location Plan.
IMS	Indian Medical Service which opened enrolment of Indian doctors during World War l and continued till World War 2.
IMTRAT	Indian Military Training Team.
IPS	Indian Police Service.
INC	Indian National Congress.

IALO	Indian Army Liaison Officer.
IMC	Indian Military College.
JC	Junior Commander.
IMA	Indian Military Academy.
J and K	Jammu and Kashmir.The erstwhile princely Kashmir State acceded to India on 26th October 1947. After the Indo-Pak War of 1947-48, a part of the state has remained under occupation of Pakistan (POK). J & K has been reorganised wef 5th August 2019 as Union Territories of J&K and Ladakh, respectively.
JCO	Junior Commissioned Officer. This rank includes Jemadars (now Naib Subedar), Subedars and Subedar Majors, who have the command responsibility of a platoon and in the past also held the appointment of second-in-command of rifle companies.
KBE	Knight (or Dame) Commander of the Most Excellent Order of the British Empire.
KCB	Knight (or Dame) Commander of The Most Honourable Order of the Bath.
KCIOs	King Commissioned Indian Officers.
KLP	Key Location Plan.
Kms	Kilometres.
KRAs	Key Result Areas.
KRC	Kumaon Regimental Centre.
LAC / LC	Line of (Actual) Control in Kashmir, established in 1949 and 1972, respectively.
LI	Light Infantry.
Lieut. / Lt	Lieutenant. A rank for subalterns.
LOC	Line of Communications, also Line of Control
LOH	Lady of the House.
Lt Col	Lieutenant-Colonel. An officer rank in the Indian Army. Earlier, lieutenant-colonels used to command of a battalion or similar-sized unit, or middle-ranking staff officer. This appointment was upgraded to the rank of Colonel.

Lt Gen	Lieutenant-General. Commander of a Corps, Field Army (Command) or a Principal Staff Officer (PSO) or Head of Arms and Services at AHQ. US convention of reference to this rank as a "Three-star General" has been caught on in other Armies, too.
LRF	Laser Range Finder.
MA	Military Assistant.
M.C.	Military Cross.
MAP	Medical Aid Posts
Maj	Major. A field officer rank.
Maj-Gen	Major-General. Commander of a Division (*see*, GOC), or senior staff officer. A "Two-star General" as explained above.
MMG	Medium Machine Gun.
MOH	Meat on Hoof.
MVC	Maha Vir Chakra. India's second highest military gallantry award given for "acts of conspicuous bravery".
MEA	Ministry of External Affairs.
MOD	Ministry of Defence.
MHA	Ministry of Home Affairs.
MTO	Mechanical Transport Officer.
NATO	The North Atlantic Treaty Organization (NATO) was founded in 1949 and is a group of 30 countries from Europe and North America that exists to protect the people and territory of its members.
Nb / Sub	Naib Subedar.
NDA	National Defence Academy.
NDC	National Defence College.
NEFA	North East Frontier Agency (re-designated as Arunanchal Pradesh).
NHTA	Naga Hills and Tuensang Area.
NNRC	Neutral Nations Repatriation Commission
NPC	New Pay Code.
NWFP	North West Frontier Province.
NCC	National Cadet Corps.
OCs	Officer Cadets.

OTS / OTA	Officer Training School / Officer Training Academy.
OBE	Order of the British Empire.
OHT	Other Hill Tribes.
Op	Operation.
ORBAT	Order of Battle.
ORs	Other Ranks.
PAF	Pakistan Air Force.
PAI Force	Persian and Iraq Force.
Para	Parachute Regiment.
PBG	President's Body Guard.
PGM	Precision Guided Munitions.
POK	Pakistan Occupied Kashmir.
POW	Prisoners of War (POW).
PPO	Pension Paying Office.
PPP	Pakistan People's Party.
PVC	Param Vir Chakra. India's highest gallantry award for "most conspicuous bravery in the presence of the enemy".
PM	Prime Minister.
PLA	People's Liberation Army.
PSO	Personal Staff Officer. A senior officer (Brigadier or above) appointed as adviser, confidante, filter, and organizer to a very senior officer, usually a General Officer Commander-in-Chief (GOC-in-C), or COAS. Principal Staff Officer. Heads of Branches at AHQ, e.g. AG, QMG, MGO, DCOAS, MS and so on. Personal Security Officer. A specially trained person in the art of providing physical security to high ranking officials and persons classified as of high security risk.
Pt.	Point, with reference to heights on map.
QMG	Quarter Master General.
QR	Qualitative Requirement.

R.I.A.F.	Royal Indian Air Force.
Regt.	Regiment. Units of armour and artillery are referred to as regiments; whereas infantry has regiments composed of many battalions. So, confusingly, are agglomerations of infantry battalions, e.g. the Kumaon Regiment, the Naga Regiment, and so on.
RMC	Royal Military College.
RMO	Regimental Medical Officer.
RPF	Railway Protection Force.
RSNDC	Royal Swedish National Defence College.
SAARC	South Asian Association for Regional Cooperation.
SD	Staff Duty.
SEATO	South East Asia Treaty Organisation.
SEAC	South East Asia Command. Created during 2nd World War for control of all operations in South East Asia, which was under the command of Admiral Lord Louis Mountbatten of Burma.
SSG	Special Services Group.
SI	Seriously ill.
SM	Sena Medal.
Sr DS	Senior Directing Staff.
TAR	Tibet Autonomous Region.
TEWT	Tactical Exercises without Troops.
UNCIP	United Nation Commission in India and Pakistan.
UNO	United Nations Organisation.
UNMOGIP	United Nations Military Observer Group in India and Pakistan.
UNSC	United Nations Security Council.
USI	United Service Institution of India.
UTC	University Training Corps, which was open to college students. After Independence, it has been replaced with National Cadet Corps (NCC).
V.C.	Victoria Cross. The highest British gallantry award.
VCOs	Viceroy Commissioned Officers.
VrC	Vir Chakra. A gallantry award.
YOs	Young Officers.

YNA	Yugoslav National Army.
Wg Cdr	Wing Commander.
2IC	Second-in-Command.
14 GTC	14 Gorkha Training Centre.

Foreword

The release of *Vision, Courage and Service: Life and Times of General T.N. Raina* coincides with two important events related to General Tapishwar Narain Raina, India's eighth Chief of the Army Staff: first, one hundred years of his birth and, second, the India-China face-off in Eastern Ladakh with Chushul bowl as its centre point. During the Sino-Indian war in 1962, General (then a Brigadier) Raina had stoutly defended the Chushul bowl against heavy attacks by the Chinese People's Liberation Army (PLA).

General Raina's biography is a classic tale of a military leader who was born in a humble middle class service (postal service) family and achieved greatness through sheer hard work, self-belief, opportunities and experience. From a University Training Corps cadet while studying for a Bachelor's degree in 1938, without attending military academies like the Royal Military College, Sandhurst or the Indian Military College, Dehradun, for formal pre-commission training, he rose to become Chief of the Indian Army and Chairman, Chiefs of Staff Committee. With his military experience of wars and peace and India's peculiar political and bureaucratic environment, General Raina developed a professional vision and perspective plan for the Indian Army and put that into practice when he became the Army Chief.

As an Emergency Commissioned officer, General Raina saw active service with his unit in the Middle East, Burma and the Far East in World War II. After Independence, he went through the usual command, staff and instructional appointments expected of a promising infantry officer. Despite a permanent disability of partial vision due to the loss of his right eye very early in his service, he never let it come in the way of his professional training and duties.

In 1962, when the Chinese PLA invaded Eastern Ladakh, most of the fighting took place around Chushul bowl on 18-19th November. As a resolute and determined Commander of 114 Infantry Brigade defending Chushul, then Brigadier Raina led his troops from the front, blunted the attack and gave a bloody nose to the Chinese PLA. In recognition of his "conspicuous courage and exemplary leadership in handling the brigade", the Government of India awarded him the Maha Vir Chakra, the nation's second highest gallantry award.

I saw Brigadier Raina for the first time soon thereafter. My battalion, 3 Sikh Light Infantry, had been airlifted to Ladakh in October 1962. It was deployed on the Darbuk-Chang La-Sakti-Karu approach leading to Leh and tasked to prepare defences between Chang La and Sakti. As a young Captain, I was holding Zingral Post at the Western end of Chang La when the cease fire brought an end to the 1962 Sino-India War. In April 1963, our Commanding Officer invited Brigadier Raina to the unit's Baisakhi celebration, which he accepted despite the long and arduous drive from Chushul to Sakti via Chang La. I was asked to escort him from Chang La to Sakti and then back the next day.

By now, Brigadier Raina was a much respected military leader having courageously defended Chushul bowl during the war. Escorting such a personality was a matter of much pride for me, then a starry-eyed young Captain. It was a great opportunity to watch him at close quarters, hear him speak and interact with junior officers and men.

One remembers General Raina as someone who spoke less but was a patient listener. He was a no-nonsense person on matters of military discipline, ethos and value system. One could even call him an introvert; shy of publicity and attention in the media, even within the military. No one had any doubt that he was an intellectual, and a deep thinking person.

In India's military history, due to human resource mismanagement and lack of strategic vision at the political level, the 1950s is considered a dark period for the armed forces which culminated in the traumatic experience of 1962 war. The war led to serious introspection in the Government of India and brought in necessary expansion, modernisation, hard training and greater professionalism in the armed forces.

During India-Pakistan war in 1971, General Raina commanded 2 Corps on the Eastern front (Khulna Sector) and later moved the Corps to the Western front. For his distinguished service during this war, he was awarded Padma Bhushan.

The post 1962 period of peace and wars (1965 and 1971) gave General Raina excellent experience and foresight for the higher military appointments which followed. It also enabled him to develop his own vision for the future of the Indian Army. By now he had also come to be known as a "soldier's soldier"; a sign of his rapport with the men he commanded and his concern for the ordinary soldier.

From General Raina's three years tenure as Chief of the Army Staff, there are three important ethical and visionary events that I wish to single out here.

First, within days of his taking over as Army Chief, General Raina had the courage to decline Prime Minister Indira Gandhi's request to associate the Indian Army with the enforcement of Emergency. It is a measure of the respect and regard in which he was held that the Prime Minister accepted the stance he took. He upheld the dignity and status of the appointment of Chief of the Army Staff and also ensured that Indian Army remains wedded to its apolitical ethos.

The second instance is of strategic relocation of field formations to enhance their ability to mobilise faster in the event of a war situation with Pakistan. General Raina ordered relocation of many Regimental Centres from their permanent locations in Punjab, Uttar Pradesh and Rajasthan to India's interior and moved field formations to those locations which were closer to their intended areas of operational deployment on the western borders. As expected, there was much resistance within the army and those who manage its defence budget. But General Raina was firm. He ensured time-bound implementation of this relocation plan.

The third instance, a visionary decision, is of setting up an Expert Committee to prepare a 25-year perspective plan (1975-2000) for the Indian Army. After evaluating national security threats, future battlefield and military strategy, the Committee was to determine the size of the army, suggest doctrinal and organisational changes and equipment philosophy to complement these changes. For this Committee, he did not select very senior officers but those who were talented, promising and distinguished, capable of preparing such a report and implementing the decisions during their tenures. Needless to say, the recommendations and implementation of this committee had a profound impact on the professional updating and modernization of the army.

Military life is always adventurous and often romantic. There is an interesting romance in this biography too. Young Raina, an Indian Army officer serving in Saigon in November 1945 met a young French girl Marie Antoinette (Ninette). Three months later, he proposed marriage to her and left for his next posting. Despite being oceans apart, and occurrence of many historic geo-political events in India and abroad, their love, and letters, kept them in touch with each other. After three years, Ninette sailed all alone from Marseille to India and the couple got married in an Officers Mess in Dehradun on 25th February 1949. Mrs. Raina's personal notes in this biography on her life with her husband, and in the military, are lucid, very interesting and often touching. They also reflect the love and strength of this lady who shared General Raina's life till his end.

The author of this book, Brigadier Satish Kumar Issar, VSM carries strong credentials in the writing of this biography He is from the Kumaon Regiment as was General Raina. When General Raina became a Corps Commander, he selected Brigadier Issar as Deputy Assistant Military Secretary, a part of his personal staff, and later as Military Assistant during his tenure as Chief of the Army Staff and Chairman, Chiefs of Staff Committee. In those appointments, Brigadier Issar remained very closely associated with General Raina, both in his office and at home with his family members. He is an experienced author having earlier written *The Illustrated History of Kumaon Regiment: The Images of Valour and Triumph*, followed by *A New Sunrise in the East: Story of The Naga Regiment*. Besides these two books, Satish Issar authored the biography, *General S.M. Shrinagesh: Soldier, Scholar, Statesman*, who was the first COAS of the Indian Army from the Kumaon Regiment.

This book on General Raina fulfils a major void which existed in the biographies of post-Independence military leaders who with their profound thinking and vision made substantial contribution to professionalism in India's armed forces and strengthened its ethos and value system. It makes a very useful contribution to the military history of India.

GENERAL V.P. MALIK, PVSM, AVSM (Retd.)
Former Chief of the Army Staff, Indian Army

Preface

This book was inspired by my admiration for General Tapishwar Narain Raina, an officer from the Kumaon Regiment who rose to become the eighth Chief of the Indian Army on 1st June 1975 at the age of 54 years and five months. A battle-hardened soldier, gentleman and visionary, he enjoyed the reputation of being a far-sighted military leader. Among other accomplishments, he enhanced the operational readiness of the army, improved the service conditions and introduced welfare schemes that the Indian Army continues to benefit from even today.

Tapishwar Narain ("Tappy") Raina joined the army as a second lieutenant during the Second World War and saw action both in the Middle East and in Southeast Asia. By the time he became a Lieutenant Colonel, Tappy Raina as he was popularly known, had already made a name for himself amongst his contemporaries both in the regiment and in the Army as being one of the ablest commanding officers. As a young officer in 15 Kumaon (Indore), I had heard of the various innovative methods introduced by him as CO 14 Kumaon (Gwalior) to train his battalion for war and peace. Considerable emphasis had also been placed on sporting activities. Such ventures were not restricted to 14 Kumaon (Gwalior) alone but were also extended to all the battalions of Kumaon Regiment. Thus numerous officers and jawans could benefit from the coaching camps he organised for basketball, athletics and swimming.

Tappy Raina was acknowledged to be professionally superior to most of his peers and not only had he earned an out of turn promotion to the rank of Brigadier but was also selected to command 114 Infantry Brigade. This brigade was operationally responsible for the defence of Ladakh, from the Karakoram Pass in the North to Demchok in the South, a frontage of nearly 480 kilometres. Here he earned laurels during the tenacious battle of Chushul in 1962. His stratagem and tactics were successful in defeating the Chinese PLA at a time when the Chinese Army was having virtually a free run into Indian territory elsewhere in the North East, the Chinese offensive in the Ladakh Sector, however, could not make headway and also proved very costly in losses for PLA forces.

Under Brigadier Raina's command, the unparalleled saga of sacrifice of the brave Ahirs of "C" Company, 13 Kumaon under Major Shaitan Singh at Rezangla, and of the plucky Gurkhas of 1/8 Gurkha Rifles under Major Dhan Singh Thapa on the other side of Spanggur Gap defending the Gurung Hill Complex including posts Sirjap I and II across the Pangong Tso is legendary. Both Major Shaitan Singh and Major Dhan Singh Thapa who fought to the last man and the last round were posthumously awarded India's highest gallantry award, Paramvir Chakra (PVC). Providentially, Major Dhan Singh Thapa was later found alive as a prisoner of war and repatriated back to India. For his exemplary leadership in the defence of Chushul, the gateway to Leh, government of India awarded Brigadier Raina the country's second highest gallantry award, the Maha Vir Chakra (MVC).

The Battle of Chushul of 1962 is of special relevance at the time of writing this book with the PLA of China once again engaged in a face-off with Indian Army in Eastern Ladakh since April 2020. Although the terrain and the two adversaries are the same, the force levels, resources and political will now are, however, much more balanced, if not in India's favour.

On promotion to the rank of Maj Gen, Tappy Raina was appointed General Officer Commanding of 25 Infantry Division, and he successfully implemented the terms of Tashkent Declaration signed at Tashkent in erstwhile USSR between Prime Minister Lal Bahadur Shastri and the Pakistani President, Field Marshal Ayub Khan in January 1966. Later, as General Officer Commanding 2 Corps, he took part in the war against Pakistan Army in East Pakistan in December 1971 which led to the creation of Bangladesh. His subsequent rise to become General Officer Commanding-in-Chief Western Command paved the way for him to be selected by the Indian Government as India's eighth Chief of the Army Staff. He thus became the third officer from Kumaon Regiment to attain this high rank and appointment.

I first met Lieutenant Colonel Raina in August 1962 at Chaubatia, a suburb of Ranikhet Cantonment, when he came to visit the newly raised 5th Battalion, Kumaon Regiment. I had been posted there as part of this newest battalion of the regiment from my parent battalion, 15 Kumaon (Indore). My first impression was that he was a man of the stature of Napoleon, with sharp features. In the course of conversation I gathered that both he and his French wife, Ninette, loved Ranikhet and the Kumaon hills, to which they were frequent visitors. Their son, Jyoti, and daughter, Anita, were in boarding school in Nainital.

It was on Brigadier Raina's recommendation that after the Sino-Indian conflict of 1962, the 7th and 14th battalions of the Jammu and Kashmir Militia were merged and reorganized into the regular Indian Army as Ladakh Scouts in June 1963. They were to be the eyes and ears of the army deployed operationally for the defence of Ladakh. In June 1963, I received my posting orders to report to Headquarters of Ladakh Scouts, then located at Phyang, near Leh. After seven days of acclimatisation, I was appointed Officer Commanding "F" Company which was operationally responsible for a vast area from Siachen in the west, Area Daulat Beg Oldi (DBC) and Depsang Plateau in the north and the Cheng Chenmo River in the east with Company HQ at Umlong, short of Saser Glacier. This Area was on the flank of 114 Infantry Brigade Sector which was still under the command of Brigadier Raina. Although I did not meet him in person during my nearly three-year tenure with Ladakh Scouts, I did visit HQ 114 Infantry Brigade in December 1963 after my visit to DBO / Depsang Plateau. Due to the closure of Saser La because of very heavy early snowfall, I could not return to my Company HQ along this route. Instead, along with four jawans of my company, I had to return to Nubra Valley, trekking along River Shyok, the old winter trade route. It took us eighteen days to walk from Sultan Chusku to Village Shyok. On reporting back at HQ Delta Sector, I submitted my detailed report to HQ 3 Mountain Division. I later learnt that this and some of my reports of Chinese activities in my area of operational responsibility, were read with interest even by Brigadier Tappy Raina, Commander 114 Infantry Brigade.

I met Major General Tappy Raina for the second time in 1968 while I was posted with 6 Kumaon in Area Kanzalwan in Gurais Sector (North Kashmir). He was then Chief of Staff at Headquarters 15 Corps. Area Kanzalwan was at a very high altitude and remained cut off from the rest of the Kashmir Valley for six to seven months in a year. Fresh vegetables would reach us only infrequently, delivered by Indian Air Force helicopters. General Raina, who visited frequently, always brought fresh vegetables, which was a welcome change to a diet based mostly on tinned rations. As officiating CO in the absence of Lieutenant Colonel M.K. Nair, who was away attending a 6-month course at the Infantry School, I had the opportunity to receive some guidance from General Raina whenever he visited us on professional and operational matters.

My close association with him, however, only began after my appointment as Deputy Assistant Military Secretary at HQ 2

Corps, then located at Kotkapura near Faridkot in Punjab, and later at Chandimandir, when Lieutenant General Raina was the GOC. I became his confidential staff officer. When General Raina received his promotion as GOC-in-C Western Command in October 1973, I accompanied him as his officiating Assistant Military Secretary and remained in this appointment till the arrival of Lieutenant Colonel R.N. Mahajan, VSM in January 1974. Exactly two years later while I was commanding 5 Kumaon I received posting orders to report to Chief of the Army Staff's Secretariat at New Delhi to relieve Lieutenant Colonel Ravi Mahajan, VSM who had been approved to be promoted to the rank of brigadier and posted as commander of an infantry brigade. I remained MA to the COAS for the remaining period of General Raina's tenure as Chief of the Army Staff and Chairman Chiefs of Staff Committee from January 1976 to May 1978.

Throughout my association with General Raina, I was always awed by his personal conduct, the scope of his knowledge, his impeccable character, the clarity of his mind, his foresight, vision and his sense of justice and fair play in both personal and professional life. A stickler for rules and discipline, he was, at the same time, compassionate, humane and deeply concerned about the welfare of all ranks and their families. He had an exterior of granite but a heart of wax. Here was a General Officer who was barely 54 years and 5 months old when he was selected to head one of the largest armies of the world. He held this appointment for a full tenure of three years and retired at the age of 57 years and 5 months.

This biography traces General Raina's upbringing, his motivation for choosing the army as a career, his achievements and also his contributions towards the growth of Indian Army. His most important contribution was his steadfast steering of Indian Army on an "Apolitical" path when the Emergency was imposed in India on 25th June 1975, within a month of his taking over as Chief of Army the Staff. This book also highlights values that remain forever relevant, particularly for the youth of our country: the realisation early in life of the value of hard work, higher knowledge, and following the righteous path. These are essential requisites for significant achievement in the life in any profession. What motivated the youth of General Raina's generation was a sense of adventure and an urge to follow a path different from that which most orthodox middle class families then normally encouraged. Pride in the uniform, the routine of training, punctuality and discipline were virtues that Tappy Raina imbibed when he was a member of the University Training Corps (UTC). These were precious lessons that remained with him throughout his life. Every officer commissioned in Indian Army takes an oath to place the nation first, the comfort and welfare of the men under his command next, and his own personal comfort and welfare last. Tappy Raina exemplified this motto throughout his career.

This book offers many relevant lessons and will prove particularly useful to all officers of the Indian Armed Forces, to civil bureaucrats dealing with defence matters, and to students of military science and history. It is a valuable study for officers of the armed forces on how to face professional challenges whether in peace or war. It also highlights how their administrative experience, operational skills and leadership qualities may be applied in the field of management, both in the military and civil society.

In the twenty-eight years of post-independence period, Tappy Raina's experience in the army convinced him that the military system in a democracy can and should be complementary to the civil system, and *vice-versa.* Two vital aspects that underlie the efficiency of the armed forces, namely training and discipline, enable them to invariably deliver whenever requisitioned to aid civil authority. However, the process of decision making when dealing with the civil establishment within the government had always been slow and time consuming. Also, important decisions were rarely recorded in detail and almost never made public. That is why on taking over as Chief of the Army Staff on 1st June 1975,

Tappy Raina knew exactly how to accelerate this process. Despite bureaucratic hurdles, he managed to get government approval on many operational and administrative decisions, some of which had remained pending since the time when he was Deputy Adjutant General at Army Headquarters in September 1970. He was also fully convinced of the close inter-relationship between the country's foreign and defence policies in the forging of bilateral relationships with other countries and strove to maintain a level of trust, confidence and understanding with the external affairs establishment ensuring a broad consensus on strategic objectives. The many exchanges of visits by heads of foreign armed forces, both from NATO and Warsaw Pact countries brought out his diplomatic skills. At the same time, the unresolved disputes with China on the demarcation of the boundary between the two nations, as also of Pakistan's claim on Kashmir led him, with his characteristic foresight, to constitute an Expert Committee to prepare a vision document for the Indian Army till the year 2000. The Indian Army today, and the several Chiefs of Staff who succeeded him, owe a great deal to the vision of General Raina.

General Raina was in favour of retaining a younger profile of the army to make it capable of operating in the high altitude, cold and mountainous terrain along India's long international borders. To maintain this younger profile, he proposed to the government to laterally induct army officers, JCOs and other ranks into central police organisations (CPOs) to boost their leadership, training and operational efficiency. Incidentally, when Tappy himself laid down his office as Chief of the Army Staff and Chairman Chiefs of Staff Committee on 31st May 1978, he was only 57 years and 5 months old.

Even after General Raina retired, the nation had great hopes of availing his services in different capacities. Despite being diagnosed with cancer, when he was in remission the government persuaded him to accept the appointment of High Commissioner of India in Canada, at a time when relations between the two countries were under strain because of India's nuclear test at Pokhran in 1974. Reluctantly, he accepted the new responsibility. Alas, after a hard battle against all odds and ill health, Tappy Raina died in harness, after smoothing out the wrinkles in Indo-Canadian relations.

BRIGADIER SATISH K. ISSAR, VSM, IA (Retd.)

House No. 34,
Sector 6,
Panchkula: 134109 (Haryana),
Tel: 0172-2583852.

Acknowledgements

At the time of his retirement, General Raina had thought of writing his autobiography. Unfortunately, this did not happen because of a serious setback to his health shortly after his retirement. Thus, this author, assisted by his dedicated team of Major Yogesh Prasad (former Joint Secretary, Cabinet Secretariat), Brigadiers Swatantra Kumar Sapru and Dara J. Govadia, researched the requisite material from published journals and books and through extensive interviews and data gathered from General Raina's peers, associates, and family. It is also based on the author's close association with the late General, supplemented by exhaustive notes on General Raina's personal life by the late Mrs. Ninette Raina and some valuable inputs by their daughter, Anita Raina Thapan and grand-son, Madhav Raina Thapan. These have been authenticated against other official documentation and published material. A great deal of valuable information was received from late Lieutenant General R.N. Mahajan, PVSM, VSM, who had a very close association with General Raina over nearly four decades. Lieutenant General Gurbaksh Lal Bakshi vividly recalled his experiences as a young officer in 14 Kumaon (Gwalior) when "Tappy" Raina was its CO.

I would like to mention the following in particular for their guidance and encouragement: Lieutenant Generals A.N. Vohra, J.F.R. Jacob, P.N. Kathpalia, D.D. Saklani and Surinder Nath Sharma, Major Generals Laxman Singh Lehl, B.K. Mehta, A.E. Joseph, A. Kaul, Gurdeep Singh, Brigadiers Teg Bahadur Kapur,

R.V. Jatar, Aapjit Anand, Brig P.N. Kaul, Colonel Narinder (Bull) Kumar and Lieutenant Colonel T.S. Pal.

Valuable material was provided to me by General V.P. Malik, Lieutenant Generals S.K. Sinha, Depinder Singh, S. Nambiar and Tej K. Sapru, Major Generals Jagjit Singh, B.P. Murgai, Ashok Krishna and as also Mr. Swarup Singh, son of late Major General Joginder Singh.

I would also like to express my gratitude to Lieutenant General Rana Pratap Kalita, UYSM, AVSM, SM, VSM, Colonel of the Kumaon and Naga Regiments, Maj Gen Nawnit Kumar, Brigadier Govind Singh Rathore, both former Commandants, and the present Commandant KRC, Ranikhet, Brig I.S. Samyal. I would also like to thank Colonels Ram Das Prabhu, former CO 5 Kumaon, and Kashyap Thakkar, CO 18 Kumaon, for their help and assistance whenever it was needed. I also express my appreciation and thanks to Colonel S.K. Sharma, former CO 1 Ladakh Scouts and latter Commandant Ladakh Scouts Training Centre, Leh, for his ready help in updating and assistance whenever needed.

Lastly, I owe it to my wife, Juliet C. Issar, our son Sunil and daughter Kavita Issar Batra and nephew, and Vikas Issar for their constant encouragement and support to keep me going on this task which I started in 2010, soon after the launch of the biography of another COAS, *General S.M. Shrinagesh: Soldier, Scholar and Statesman* in 2009. Due to a serious setback to Juliet's health, I had to put this work on hold in 2012. After her health attained some stability in early 2019, Juliet persuaded me to take up the unfinished task of compiling this biography of late General Tappy Raina.

The person, who originally suggested that I should write about the life and times of Gen Raina soon after I retired from Army on 31st January 1991, was my friend Kapil Malhotra. He was firm in his belief that such a book would be invaluable for future generations; this encouraged me to finally take up the writing of this book.

> *"Life is a journey: days-months-years go by! Time passes and leave behind memories that fill us with nostalgia. Turning through the pages of Time, we find the History of our heritage".*
>
> ~ Anon

Part I

Early Life

"It is only those who dare to sail, who reach the shore!"
~ Anon

Chapter 1

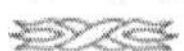

Early Life

While talent for music, dance, sports, mathematics and other domains of activity can be spotted in young children and nurtured from an early age, the qualities that make for a great leader are not always quite so apparent. Leadership, moreover, emerges from a combination of many factors in which personality traits is but one element. The childhood circumstances and environment also shape the outlook and attitude of a potential leader. All these characteristics are then put to test on life's stage; they are moulded and enhanced through challenging situations, tragedy, good fortune and other vagaries of life.

In this first section, through the early life of Tapishwar Narain Raina, we shall see what made him distinct to his family members and peers. There was no hint in those tender years of anything exceptional in the making, but there was, nevertheless, a certain predisposition that was to manifest more strikingly as life unfolded.

The Formative Years

The Rainas are Kashmiri Pandits, who were original inhabitants of Rainavari[1], situated twelve kilometres outside Srinagar, the capital

---

[1] It is believed that Kashmiri Pandits, who originally belonged to Rainavari, later settled down in the main city, Sri Nagar, came to be known as Rainas, and that Rainavari was the capital of the famous King Rana Datta 436 A.D.-497 A.D. There was also a large garden of this king situated at the site of present Rainavari ("vari" in Kashmiri means a garden).

of the former Kashmir *Riyasat* (State). Kashmiri Pandits a part of larger Shaivites Saraswat Brahmin community. Who were the main settlers in Kashmir Valley from time immemorial? After the advent of Muslim influence in the Kashmir valley, many Kashmiri Pandits were induced or forced for conversion to Islam faith. It is believed that during Emperor Aurangzeb's rule, numerous Kashmiri Pandits migrated from Kashmir due to persecution by the Mughal ruler. Many of those who stayed behind embraced Islam. Others moved away much later due to lack of economic opportunities and good education. Some settled in the neighbouring hill districts of undivided Punjab (now Himachal Pradesh), whilst others spread to the plains of Punjab, the Central Province (present Madhya Pradesh), Rajputana (present Rajasthan), and the United Province (present Uttar Pradesh). Some Raina families that continued to retain their links with Rainavari remained in Jammu District of Kashmir *Riyasat* (princely state). In all cases, children of these immigrants were encouraged to pursue higher education. Some took up medicine or science; others joined the civil services, or became teachers and lawyers.

The ancestors of Tapishwar Narain Raina, as per the existing family tree, can be traced to one Rishi Raina, who was the great-grandfather of Rai Sahib Pandit Anand Narain Raina, the father of General Raina. Anand Narain Raina started his career in the Royal Postal Service as a post master. It was there that he received the title of "Rai Sahib" in recognition of his devotion to duty.

This branch of the Raina family had settled in Jammu where Tapishwar Narain Raina was born on 21st January 1921. The family affectionately called him "Tapu". He was the youngest of the five children of Anand Narain and Mohini Raina (*nee* Bhan).

Tapu was barely a year old when his mother died while giving birth to a sixth child and the infant, named Karan, too, died a few months later. A similar tragedy had also struck Brij Narain Raina, the elder brother of Anand Narain as he, too, had become a widower with four children. The joint family thus consisted of Anand Raina with his five children and Brij Raina with his four children. It fell to Raj Rani Raina, the mother of Anand and Brij Raina, to bring up the nine motherless children. Tapu had a special affection for his paternal grandmother (*daadi*), Raj Rani. Later in life he often talked about her to his children. Besides giving him a lot of love he also maintained that he had never eaten more delicious food than that prepared by her! Neither of the two widowed brothers remarried.[2]

Family relationships were strong among the Rainas. When Tapu's maternal grandfather, passed away in 1937, his widow, Basso Bhan, was left all alone.[3] So she was taken into the joint family of the Rainas. The children now had both their grandmothers to care for them. When Raj Rani passed away and Basso Bhan was unable to manage the family alone, Tapu's uncle, Brij Narain, resigned from his transferable job in order to look after the family. Basso Bhan lived to a ripe old age and was taken care of by her grandson and Tapu's eldest brother, Suraj Narain Raina.

Being in a transferable job, Anand Raina was posted at various places in India, including Shimla (Simla), Lahore, Mumbai (Bombay) and Pune (Poona). So although the children began their education in Jammu, they eventually shifted to Ludhiana when Anand Raina was transferred there. Tapu was enrolled in Arya High School from where at the age of fifteen, in 1936, he passed his matriculation (class 10) examination. He then joined Government College at Ludhiana (affiliated to Punjab University, Lahore), from where he completed his F.A. (Faculty of Arts) degree in 1938.

After his father's transfer from Ludhiana, as Head Post Master, GPO, Lahore, Tapu joined Forman Christian College in Lahore, from where he graduated and earned a B.A. degree. He chose to do his M.A. in history. On most days, Tapu would cycle the ten miles (sixteen kilometres) to his college and back twice a day; in

---

[2] Ninette, who Tapu married years later, once innocently asked her husband why neither his father nor uncle had remarried. It would have made it easier to bring up the children. "He was shocked", said Ninette, and replied "Oh, no! That was not done in our family. One just remained faithful. Marriage is for eternity." That was Ninette's first glimpse of the values of her family-in-law.

[3] Tapu's mother Mohini Bhan was the only child of Bhishambar Nath Bhan, an advocate, and his wife Basso Bhan (*nee* Kunzru).

the morning for classes, and in the evening for military training in the University Training Corps.

From his very childhood, Tapu was on a different wavelength to the rest of his family. His adolescence was marked by restlessness and dissatisfaction with life. The family was modest, honest, hard-working and god-fearing; and life, on the whole, was austere, spartan and very disciplined. Being the youngest sibling, Tapu was often made to do much of the house work by his brothers, something that he resented throughout childhood. One of the things he disliked the most was that, even at the age of ten, he would be made to get up at 4 a.m. to milk the family buffalo, a task his elder brothers conveniently passed on to him. Tapu felt that, as the youngest member of the family, he was clearly the least important! Perhaps the family, too, found him a trial. His ideas were different, he was outspoken and, also, somewhat aloof. From her brothers-in-law Ninette learnt that as a child, Tapu was aggressive, strong-willed and very independent. Despite this, however, there was always a deep bond of affection and mutual respect among all members of the Raina family.

The family lived in a house built on a 4-*kanal* (one kanal equals 500 square yards) plot of land in a newly developed area of Lahore which became famous as Model Town. The area was developed by Lal Chand whose son, Captain Chaudhry Raghuvendra Singh, later became one of the biggest developers of the National Capital Region of Delhi. The Raina family thereafter made Lahore the base for the joint family even when Pandit Anand Raina was transferred again. After Partition, Anand Raina settled down in Ludhiana where he and his brother had jointly built a house during Anand Raina's earlier tenure in the city. This now became the family base, although by then the children were all settled and had moved to different parts of India.

While Tapu Raina was growing up in Lahore in the 1930s, his elder brothers and sisters were settling down in life. Suraj Narain Raina, the eldest sibling, married Uma Kaul in 1936 in Lahore. She was the grand daughter of Bal Kishen Kaul (1866-1937), the first doctor in the Kashmiri community, who was on the staff of Lahore Medical College. Tapu's eldest sister Saroopo was married in 1939 to Kishori Lal Tikku, and Khem, the second elder sister, was married in 1944 to Jiwan Zalpuri. Both weddings also took place in Lahore

Two friends of Tapu, who later became his colleagues in the army, also lived in Model Town, Lahore. They were Abhimanyu Vir Vohra (nicknamed Vir) and Vijay Chandra Khanna. While Vir Vohra was enrolled in Government College Lahore, Vijay Khanna, who was two years younger, was, like Tapu, a student of Forman Christian College (F.C. College). Vir Vohra and Vijay Khanna both followed Tapu in joining University Training Corps (UTC) and later also joined the army. Both, rose to become lieutenant generals in Indian Army.

Vir Vohra and Vijay Khanna recalled how they would often raid a nearby mango orchard during hot summer afternoons. Although they would urge Tapu to join them, he always refrained because he considered it improper. But he readily joined them for hockey, football or cycling.

Another amusing trick that they sometimes played was to sneak into the girls' compartment of the special university bus that used to take students from Model Town to their respective colleges in Lahore. The bus was so designed that the driver and conductor sat in the driver's cabin, next to which was the partitioned space, meant only for women students. The rear compartment of the bus was earmarked for male students. The number of boys, however, used to exceed the capacity and any late comers were accommodated in the girls' section. On many occasions, Tapu, Vir Vohra and Vijay Khanna would deliberately drag their feet and board the bus when the boys' section would already be full and the conductor would, therefore, allow the three of them to travel in the women's section.

In college, Tapu was fond of Urdu and Persian poetry. His personal lifestyle and beliefs, however, were regulated by the *Bhagavad Gita* which he had learnt by heart while still in school. As a college student, he became a member of the 4th (Lahore) Battalion, Punjab University Training Corps (UTC) from October 1938 to

March 1941. He received the following certificate in recognition of his performance in the UTC:

> Mr Tapishwar Narain Raina, B.A. has been a student of Forman Christian College since 1938. During this period I have known him personally both in class as well as a member of the University Training Corps; and it gives me pleasure to say that I knew Mr Raina as a young gentlemen, excellent in character and in manners, keen on his work, active and disciplined and entirely dependable.
>
> As a member of the college detachment of the UTC he won the "best recruit" cup for the year 1939-40, his first year in the UTC. As a member of the college Rifle Club he proved to be a steady and accurate shot. This year he shouldered further responsibilities as Vice-President of the College Rifle Club and as assistant in the UTC Detachment Office; for the latter he was awarded a cup. His work in both these offices has been entirely commendable.
>
> A young man of Mr Raina's attainments ought to fill with distinction any position of responsibility for which he is qualified.
>
> Signed:
Lieutenant,
4th (Lahore) Battalion UTC, & Professor
F.C. College, Lahore.

Chapter 2

Career in the Indian Army

In 1942, even as war clouds gathered over British India, the Quit India Movement of Indian National Congress, an agitation for freedom from British rule, also gained momentum. Indian Army units were already engaged in fighting in Europe and North Africa against the alliance of Nazi Germany and the Italians. When Japan too, became a threat in South East Asia, there was a sudden spurt in the demand for manpower, both officers and sepoys, for the Indian Army. Many college students were inspired to join the defence forces in India and Tapu did not remain unaffected by this. Lahore, the capital of undivided Punjab, was abuzz with a great deal of military activity. The cantonment had a large presence of personnel of the Royal Indian Army and Royal Indian Air Force (RIAF).

When Tapu announced to the family that he was going to join the army, it raised quite a storm. Imagine a deeply religious and peace loving family of Brahmins, orthodox in outlook, having a warrior in their midst! Moreover, joining the army meant crossing the seas as well, another taboo for Brahmins at that time. Ultimately, of course, the family had to let him go, wishing him well.

Tapu had first thought to join Royal Indian Air Force (RIAF). He even trained as a flight cadet for two months in the Air Wing of UTC and completed nineteen hours of flying at Lahore Flying Club during July-August 1941. But it was not to be, and his destiny pulled him to the Army instead. He was selected the same year as an officer cadet at Officers Training School (OTS), Mhow in Central Provinces (now Madhya Pradesh). His post-graduation in history, therefore, was never completed.

We must recall that Indians began to be enrolled as officers in the army only after World War I. Indian Army had been raised, trained and maintained by the British Government in India. During World War I (1914 to 1918), Indians could serve in Indian Army only in positions below those of officers. After World War I, a phase of Indianisation of the army commenced when British Government issued instructions in June 1918 for the selection of young Indians for entry into the Royal Military College (RMC), Sandhurst (UK). The annual intake was only ten candidates, in two batches of five each. Meanwhile, to improve the intake of Indian officers in Indian Army, an Indian Military College on the pattern of RMC, Sandhurst was inaugurated in Dehradun on 10th December 1932 by Field Marshal Sir Philip Chetwode[4], the then Commander-in-Chief of Indian Army.

With war clouds threatening the British colonies in Asia on several fronts, there was a growing need of additional officers. British Government thus set up officers training schools (OTSs). OTS Mhow was one such war time school to offer basic military and leadership training, by putting officer cadets (OCs) through an abridged course. Those who successfully completed the training were granted an emergency commission in Indian Army. The

---

[4] The central hall of the main building of Military College, Dehra Dun is named after Field Marshal Sir Philip Chetwode as Chetwode Hall. It was inaugurated on the penultimate day of the first term of the 1st Course of Gentlemen Cadets (GCs) on 10th December 1932. Field Marshal Chetwode laid down three golden principles that he felt must guide an officer of any national army. Ever since then, these principles became the motto of all GCs passing out of this institution, even today:

"THE SAFETY, HONOUR AND WELFARE OF YOUR COUNTRY COMES FIRST, ALWAYS AND EVERY TIME.

THE HONOUR, WELFARE AND COMFORT OF THE MEN YOU COMMAND, COMES NEXT.

YOUR OWN EASE, COMFORT AND SAFETY COMES LAST, ALWAYS AND EVERY TIME."

OTSs were able to supplement the existing intake at Royal Military College (RMC), Sandhurst and Indian Military College, Dehra Dun. To meet the shortfall of regular officers in Indian Army, the Indian Military College was renamed as Indian Military Academy (IMA), to cater for the shorter training of additional gentleman cadets.

The rapid expansion of the army from approximately 200,000 to 20,00,000 forced Government of India to cast the recruitment net wide. The myth of martial classes was broken and new classes were recruited. This also applied to the officer cadre that grew from about 1,000 before World War 2, to 15,740 by end of the War. The force became truly an Indian Army, representing all areas and classes of the vast country.

Tapu Raina joined OTS Mhow in September 1941, and was assigned to No. 1 Platoon of "A" Company. Officer Cadets (OCs) where J.F.R. Jacob[5] and Ralengnao Kathing[6] were some of his

[5] When the liberation of East Pakistan took place in 1971, Tappy Raina was General Officer Commanding 2 Corps in the rank of Lieutenant General while Jacob was Chief of Staff, HQ Eastern Command in the rank of Major General. When Tappy Raina assumed the appointment of COAS Indian Army with the rank of General, Lieutenant General Jacob became General Officer Commanding-in-Chief Eastern Command, Calcutta (now Kolkata).

[6] Major Ralengnao Kathing, popularly known as "Bob" to his hordes of admirers must surely rate among the tallest nationalists of the North East. A Naga (Tangkhul) from the tribal district of Ukhrul, Bob had many firsts to his credit. In his richly endowed life, Bob was a teacher, a soldier, a bureaucrat, a minister and, finally, a diplomat. Among the numerous honours he received in his lifetime, the prominent ones were: Member of the British Empire (MBE) and Military Cross (MC). Later, the Indian Government awarded him the Padma Shree. It was apt that Major Ralengnao Kathing got commissioned into the 19 Hyderabad Regiment (present Kumaon Regiment), as the latter has had an almost umbilical relationship with the region. Judging by any yardstick, Bob must surely occupy a prominent place in the Regiment's "Roll of Honour" which contains some of the Indian Army's greatest names.

course mates. On completion of the training, Tapu was selected to join the infantry's 19 Hyderabad Regiment, and was granted King's Emergency Commission as second lieutenant on 12th April 1942. His course mate, J.F.R. Jacob, was selected for Regiment of Royal Artillery, and had to undergo additional training in gunnery at Artillery School, Deolali[7] (now in Maharashtra). Jacob was granted emergency commission in the Royal Regiment of Artillery as second lieutenant in September 1942, five months after Tapu Raina was commissioned.

Like all newly commissioned young officers, Second Lieutenant Tapishwar Narain Raina reported to 19 Hyderabad Regiment Training Centre (10 /19 Hyderabad Regiment), at Agra Cantonment[8]. In the army, his nickname eventually became Tappy. However, to family and old friends he always remained Tapu. The training battalion to which he was assigned was commanded by Lieutenant Colonel C.J. Attfield. Thereafter, Tapu attended and qualified in the Company Weapons Course at Infantry School, Saugor (27th July-17th August 1942) and Field Camouflage Course at Kirkee, near Poona (now Pune).

Later, he was posted to 2nd Battalion, 19 Hyderabad Regiment which was also at Agra but was preparing to move to the Palel Sector in Burma. Within a couple of months, however, he was transferred to the 1st Battalion, 19 Hyderabad Regiment, which was then serving in Iraq as part of the Persian and Iraq Force (PAI Force).

A brief history of 19 Hyderabad Regiment at this point would be useful for the reader.[9]

---

[7] The Artillery School had moved from Kakul (now in Pakistan) to Deolali in 1940.

[8] With the re-designation of 19 Hyderabad Regiment as The Kumaon Regiment on 27th October 1945, the Training Centre at Agra was renamed as The Kumaon Regimental Centre (KRC). After India's independence the KRC moved to Ranikhet in the Kumaon hills (now in Uttrakhand state).

[9] See *Valour Triumphs: A History of the Kumaon Regiment,* Major K.C. Praval.

19 Hyderabad Regiment

19 Hyderabad Regiment was born in the Deccan Plateau in the closing decades of 18th century as part of the army of the Nizam[10] of Hyderabad. The Nizam's descendants ruled that state until its merger with the Indian Union in 1948. The first Nizam (Governor) of the Deccan, Mir Qamar-ud-din, had been appointed by the eighth Mughal Emperor Jahandar Shah in 1713. However, a series of weak rulers resulted in the rapid disintegration of the Mughal Empire and most provincial governors became independent rulers. This brought them into direct contact with the British and the French who were then struggling to establish their commercial and political interests in India.

Mir Qamar-ud-din founded the Asaf Jahi dynasty and he and his successors retained the title of "Subahdar", or Governor. Qamar-ud-din was an astute general and a born leader but his immediate successors lacked his qualities. It was their constant struggle for supremacy with other contending powers in southern India that led to the creation of military units from which the Hyderabad Regiment, now Kumaon Regiment is descended.

Russell Brigade

In 1811, Henry Russell became the British Resident at the court of the Nizam of Hyderabad and undertook the reorganisation of Nizam's forces. The only troops of the Nizam that Russell speaks well of in one of his reports were two "regular" battalions belonging to Muhammad Salabat Khan, the Subahdar of Berar. It is from Muhammad Salabat Khan's corps that the present 4th and 5th battalions of the Kumaon Regiment are descended.

In 1812, because of a mutiny in two infantry regiments of the Nizam's forces, the Nizam was induced by the Resident, Henry Russell, to sanction the raising of two battalions of regular infantry that were to be equipped and disciplined like the sepoys of the East India Company's army. These two battalions came to be

---

[10] Nizam in Urdu means Governor. Under the later Mughal emperors, the Nizam was nominally their vassal.

known as the Russell Brigade in March 1813. Both eventually became part of Kumaon Regiment.[11] These battalions were raised and commanded by British officers while the junior ranks and sepoys were Indian. The battalions were equipped with a certain amount of artillery from the Company's stocks, and salaries for the personnel were also paid from the Resident's treasury.

[11] Both battalions formed part of the Kumaon Regiment till 15th April 1952, when the 1st Battalion left the fold to join the newly raised Parachute Regiment, as 3rd Battalion, The Parachute Regiment. The 2nd Battalion, The Russel Brigade, continued as the Kumaon Regiment Centre, located at Ranikhet.

Chapter 3

Second World War (1939-1945)

Tapu Raina joined the army during a period of dramatic events in different parts of the world which had a direct bearing on the British Indian Army.

Hitler had taken over as chancellor of Germany in 1933. His expansionist ambitions led to the annexation of Austria in 1938, Czechoslovakia in March 1939 and an attack on Poland on 1st September of the same year. At this, Britain declared war against Germany on 3rd September 1939, which in turn led to the start of the Second World War. That same day, Lord Linlithgow, the Viceroy of India (1936-1944), declared that India, too, was at war.

The Indian National Congress Party that was in power in eight out of eleven provinces of India, objected to such an important declaration being made without British government even consulting a single Indian leader. As a consequence, the Indian National Congress (INC) governments resigned and declared that they would not co-operate with the government. Subsequently, on 8th August 1942 the Congress party launched the Quit India Movement, demanding that the British quit India and grant freedom to the country. This boycott did not have much impact on the actual conduct of the War, except that it may have affected some recruitment to the officer rank.

At the start of the Second World War, the British Middle East Command stretched from Persian Gulf to Egypt, and thence along the coast of North Africa. In June 1939, General (later Field

Marshal) Lord Archibald Percival Wavell[12] was appointed General Officer Commanding-in-Chief, Middle East Command. The major threats to his theatre of command came from the Italians in Libya and in East Africa which included Ethiopia, Somaliland and Eritrea. Italy had declared war on Britain on 8th June 1940 and this war was fought between the two colonial powers in Egypt, Sudan and Libya.

As events in North Africa were unfolding, the area of Persia (now Iran) and Iraq had also become active. In March 1941, a pro-German group seized power in Iraq but with the help of British Indian troops the previous government was reinstated on 30th April 1941. In June 1941, the Germans invaded Russia and it became imperative for the British to secure Iran as a gateway to Russia especially since Emperor Shah Reza I of Iran was pro-Germany. Syria was secured in June 1941, and on 25th August of the same year the Russians and British jointly invaded Persia.

The 8 Indian Division and 10 Indian Division from Iraq formed the British complement of the invading force. Although no actual operations took place in Syria, Iraq or Persia thereafter, six infantry divisions and one armoured division were deployed in the area for most of the war, doing very little.

The Persia and Iraq Force (PAI Force)

In the middle of March 1943, Lieutenant Tapu Raina was transferred from 2/19 Hyderabad Regiment to 1st Battalion (Russel's), 19 Hyderabad Regiment (1/19 Hyderabad), which was operationally deployed in Iraq as part of the PAI Force. Lieutenant Colonel R.C. Muller was the commanding officer. The battalion had only recently returned to Iraq after a tour of duty in Palestine and Egypt.

---

[12] In 1941, Lord Wavell was appointed as Commander-in-Chief, India, followed by his elevation in January 1943 to the rank of Field Marshal. When Lord Linlinthgow retired as Viceroy in the summer of 1943, Field Marshal Wavell was chosen to replace him, and he remained the Viceroy of India from October 1943 to January 1947.

It was while he was with a detachment at Dibia (Iraq), that Tapu was wounded in a grenade-throwing accident on 12th March 1944, He suffered multiple injuries on both thighs and eventually lost one eye[13]. Major R.R. Muirhead, a senior major in the battalion, took it upon himself to inform Tapu's father, Rai Sahib Pandit Anand Narain Raina[14] about the grenade accident involving his son.

Tapu's wounds were severe, but good care by competent army doctors, combined with the deep concern, affection and constant encouragement from fellow officers from his battalion, kept his morale high. His fellow officers were in constant touch with Tapu's family, keeping them updated with the state of his health. Captain U.C. Pant, an Indian officer of the 1/19 Hyderabad Regiment, who was slightly senior to Tapu also wrote to the family. A copy of some these letters are reproduced below.

Letter 1

Major R. R. Muirhead

1/19 Hyderabad Regiment,
C/O PAI Force,
15th March 1944.

Dear Mr. Raina,

You will have had news of your son's accident with a bomb. I have visited him in hospital and he is quite cheerful. The Surgical Specialist, who is looking after him, expects that he will be out of hospital in about two months' time. He has had two fairly bad wounds — one in each leg and a number of minor cuts on his chest and arms. He has also had a slight injury to his right eye which should be cured quite quickly (He is able to see with it but there is a certain amount of blood still in the eye). The specialist seems very confident that all the injuries will heal and that he will make a rapid recovery.

---

[13] Despite this permanent disability of partial vision due to the loss of his right eye, Tapu never let it come in the way of his professional training and duties.

[14] All this correspondence was addressed to Rai Sahib A.N. Raina, 47- J, Model Town, Lahore, Punjab, India.

We are all very sorry that this incident has occurred to your son and hope that he will soon be back with us in the Battalion. As a matter of fact, he is well on the road to recovery already, as yesterday he demanded — and got a bottle of beer![15]

I know that you will be very anxious about your son, so I will tell him that he is to write to you as soon as he is able to. Don't expect a letter from him just yet because any movement causes pain to his wounds and writing a letter would be very difficult for him until the wounds have stopped stinging.

Yours sincerely,
Roland Muirhead

Letter 2

Captain U.C. Pant

1/19 Hyderabad Regiment,
C/O PAI Force,
16th March 1944.

Dear Rai Bahadur Sahib,

I understand that you have already been informed about the accident which caused some injuries to Tapu on 12th instant (March 1944). I had a long talk with him in the evening yesterday and he asked me to write to you so that any undue alarm or anxiety which might have been caused by the information, may be eased.

It was indeed very fortunate that he did not sustain any injury which might have resulted in any form of physical disability. The admirable courage and will power shown by him to face the shock, made me proud of his friendship — he smiled when he saw me shortly after the accident.

His wounds are healing quickly and I am assured by the doctors that he will be on his work in two weeks' time. He is a bit weak, has pain now and then, otherwise he is perfectly all right.

---

[15] If only Tapu knew that his father was being informed about his desire for a bottle of beer! All his life he never drank or smoked in front of his father and as far as he knew, his father was not aware of the fact that he did both!

Tapu was very popular with the hospital staff before this thing happened. He is therefore receiving hearty attention from all quarters. He has every possible comfort and let me assure you that there is absolutely nothing to worry about.

Letters from home have a strange magical effect on all of us. The other day when Tapu received your post card he came to me and I could read the joy in his eyes which cannot be expressed. I hope you will please write to him as soon as possible and request other members of the family on my behalf to do the same.

Yours sincerely,
U.C. Pant.

Letter 3

Major R.R. Muirhead

1/19 Hyderabad Regiment,
C/O PAI Force,
20th March 1944.

Dear Mr. Raina,

I regret to inform you that your son has had to have his right eye removed. The eye specialist who had been called up to examine him, after a very careful examination of the eyes decided that unless the right eye is removed, it would probably cause near blindness in the left eye. In any case there was no hope, he said, of saving the right eye.

Your son is being amazingly brave and is quite cheerful. The other injuries on his body are not causing him so much pain, and we are all hoping for his full recovery.

Yours sincerely,
Roland Muirhead

Such correspondence from Tapu's brother officers, both seniors and peers, shows the close and affectionate bonds that existed between all officers of 1/19 Hyderabad Regiment, of which Tapu was a proud member. While he was undergoing treatment for his wounds, his battalion officers used to take turns to visit him and read out letters from his father and other members of the family. Similarly, Tapu's dictated his letters and replies to his fellow officers, who would mail these to his family.

On 23rd March 1944, a telegram was sent to Jagdish Narain Raina, Tapu's elder brother, informing them that Lieutenant Tapishwar Narain Raina had been removed from the "seriously ill" (SI) List.

On 25th March 1944, Tapu replied to his father (addressing him as "Bhai Sahib Ji", as per the custom in many Hindu families of Punjab in those days).

Letter 4

Lieutenant T.N. Raina

1/19 Hyderabad Regiment,
C/O PAI Force,
25th March 1944.

Dear Bhai Sahib Ji,[16]

Received your post card dated 17.3.44. It is true that I was severely wounded by a bomb which exploded about 3 yards in front of me. There is nothing to worry now as I am out of danger.

I am still in the hospital and it will take some time for the wounds to heal up.

I am afraid I can't write mail. Please don't worry about me.

Yours affly.
Tapu

---

[16] It was customary among Kashmiri joint families that the eldest Uncle was referred by all the children of the family as "Papaji" and their own father as "Bhai Sahibji".

Letter 5

Major R.R. Muirhead

1/19 Hyderabad Regiment,
C/O PAI Force,
1st April 1944

Dear Rai Bahadur,

I received your two post cards — one yesterday and one today. By the time that you receive this letter you will have had news from Tapu himself. He is very much better now and has been taken off the S.I. (seriously ill) list. He had another operation two or three days ago in which the surgical specialist cleaned up the wounds in his legs. He is now allowed out of bed and is able to sit up in a chair out in the sun. As you will realize, this cheers him up a lot.

The Battalion has moved during the last few days and I am no longer able to visit Tapu in the hospital where he is at present, but I have arranged that he shall be moved to a hospital near the Battalion as soon as he is fit enough to travel.

You can rest assured that he is getting the best medical treatment that is available. About losing his eye, there is the consoling fact the he should develop "double sight" in his left eye.

It is a very difficult thing to ask his parents, but — for his own good — when you write to him do not distress him by telling him of your own grief over his misfortune. You see, if he can be made to believe that there is nothing seriously wrong with him, he will recover from his injuries very much more quickly and completely, than, if he thinks that they are of a very serious nature.

You can be very proud of your son's conduct and strength of Will during the time since he had the accident. The hospital staff and all of us in the Battalion have been astonished at the bravery that he has shown and at his cheerfulness. The nursing sisters in the hospital have made a "pet" of him and he gets very special attention from them!

One of Tapu's friends — an officer named Owen — has gone up to visit him during the weekend and I have given him a message for Tapu that he is to write to you regularly. I understand that in his letter to you he did not mention the fact about his eye — that is typical of Tapu, as he didn't wish to distress you!

I am very sorry that you cannot be present with your son, but I can assure you that he does not require any consoling as he is very cheerful. Once again, in your letters, please do not depress him by telling him of your anxiety and grief — rather, cheer him up by telling him how pleased you are at his recovery and his cheerfulness.

Yours sincerely,
Roland Muirhead.

Tapu to his father:

Letter 6

1/19 Hyderabad Regiment,
C/O PAI Force,
5th April 1944.

My dear Bhai Sahib ji,

Received your all letters and snaps. You will be pleased to know that I am much better now. My wounds on the chest have all healed up (except one). The stitches from the thighs have been taken off. My right hand is working alright and my damaged eye has also healed up. I sat in the sun for two hours yesterday. I will be walking within few days. With this speed of recovery I will be able to leave hospital by the end of this month.

Even with the loss of one eye, I am still "A-5", which means that I can go back to my unit and be fit for active service. I will be taking on my duty in May.

You better cheer up. There is nothing to worry. We are supposed to fight against fate and not to accept defeat.

Yours,
Tapu.

As mentioned by Major Roland Muirhead in his letter to Rai Sahib A.N. Raina, Lieutenant Edward Owen, another young subaltern of 1/9 Hyderabad Regiment and a buddy of Tapu Raina, was detailed by the commanding officer, Lieutenant Colonel R.C. Mullar, to visit Tapu in the hospital and keep him updated of activities in the battalion. After visiting Tapu Raina in Beirut's military hospital in Lebanon, Lieutenant Owen wrote to Rai Sahib A.N. Raina, Tapu's father, on 7th April and 28th April 1944, respectively:

Letter 7

Lieutenant E. Owen, 1/19 Hyderabad Regiment,
C/O PAI Force,
7th April 1944.

Dear Mr. Raina,

I have just come back from spending four days leave with Tapu. As you no doubt learned from Ms. Raina (Tapu's sister) in my letter to her, I explained my relations with Tapu and my presence at the time of his misfortune. It was indeed a severe blow to me that one so dear to me should meet with harm in front of my own eyes.

I have some excellent news of his condition but first let me apologize for not writing to you before. I am rather a coward in bearing bad news and combined with this, I had a sincere belief that all would be well.

Tapu's recovery has been a miracle of speed. His condition is really wonderful. I wish that I could lend you my eyes to see for yourself! Believe me when I tell you that he is almost his normal self again. His wounds have healed beyond all recognition and with the exception of one sad deficiency; he is on the road to perfect health and strength again.

His terrific stamina, strength of heart, courage (of which no praise be too high) and good physical standing combined with the skill, care and attention of the hospital staff has rendered this accident almost without any effect on his future efficiency. This I say with confidence that when Tapu does come home to you on leave, then you will have difficulty in knowing that an accident ever befell him.

It is hoped to have him on his feet again next week and in two weeks fit to walk around at leisure. I can hardly believe this miracle myself and I have seen it, how can I then expect you to understand, but it is true.

I am yours very sincerely,
Edward Owen.

Letter 8

Lieutenant E. Owen

1/19 Hyderabad Regiment,
C/O PAI Force,
28th April 1944.

My dear Mr. Raina,

A few moments ago I received your air mail card telling of your receipt of my letter to you. I was pleased indeed to hear from you, and it pleases me even more to think that my letters are a help to you.

Now, for the news of Tapu! His wounds are almost completely healed and in many places where I thought perhaps a nasty scar may be left are now perfect and un-noticeable. You have heard no doubt of the skin grafting to his right thigh. The doctors and nurses pronounced it as an absolute success.

I have been present on some occasions of his dressings and the results each occasion have been wonderful. Tapu has been up and walking since two weeks back from this date, but a pain in his chest has confined his activities. This the doctors assured me would soon disappear as he regains his strength. You can be certain Tapu will be perfectly normal very soon.

Unfortunately, I being for the past two weeks very many miles away from the hospital have not been able to visit him, but I correspond and am in constant communication with him.

His spirits are very high and I believe he is quite happy and without worry or want.

Tomorrow, God permitting, I hope to take a few days leave to go and spend with him in hospital. Whilst there I shall again write to you and convey the latest news. For the while, rest assured that all is well and will continue to be so. The cheerful and energetic youth that is your son is still that same youth, full of cheer and energy. I will convey to him your love and wishes

Please forgive the shortness of this letter, however, I promise to write again soon.

May God bless and grant you peace and happiness and a joyous reunion with Tapu soon.

I am your very sincerely,
Edward Owen.

On the reverse of this letter is a brief note by Tapu.

My dear Bhai Sahib Ji, Thanks for your air card which I received a few days back. Owen is here on leave — while I am writing this letter he (Edward) is sitting by my side. He looked after me very well during my sickness. I am perfectly alright now and leaving this hospital in three days' time.

With best respects,
Yours affly,
Tapu.

Move to Burma

After full recovery from his injuries and on discharge from the hospital, Tapu Raina was promoted to the rank of captain and attached with Headquarters 80 Indian Infantry Brigade serving in Burma (now Myanmar) in South East Asia Command (SEAC). Thus, just as the momentum of war kept growing for the Allied Forces in the SEAC Theatre, so did Tapu's experience in a variety of operational situations in different countries of South East Asia. On re-joining his battalion, the 1/19 Hyderabad Regiment in North Burma, Tapu displayed exceptional bravery and leadership qualities.

This was his second experience in Burma. The first is described briefly by his wife Ninette Raina who recalled from memory the many discussions she had had with her husband during their married life together.

> On becoming a commissioned officer in 19 Hyderabad Regiment, Tapu joined the 2/19 Hyderabad Regiment and went to Burma first of all. There he took part in the retreat of the British XIV Army, as Japan pushed into South East Asia, including Burma. Tapu told me that as a junior subaltern (lieutenant) in Burma he was so exhausted all the time that he collapsed and cried every night from sheer physical fatigue. But his older brother officers cheered him up and helped him adjust to the new life. He was later transferred to 1/19 Hyderabad Regiment and saw action in the Iraq theatre, where war in Iran, Iraq, Syria and the Western Desert was raging.
>
> He told me of his experiences in Iraq and the Middle East, Syria, and Persia, while in PAI Force. Once I innocently asked him if he had fought against Field Marshal Rommel? He laughed and replied that Rommel had left Africa by then! But talking about German soldiers he added, "God bless them, what good soldiers". It is not every man who would respect and bless his former enemy!

The 1/19 Hyderabad Regiment returned to India from Iraq in July 1944. Six months later the battalion under Lieutenant Colonel R.C. Muller moved by rail from Shimoga (Mysore), to Ledo (Indo-Burma border). Thereafter, it went by air to form a part of 26 Indian Infantry Brigade to join in General Slim's famous campaign to push the Japanese out of Burma. So from Iraq, Tapu now moved to Burma. Tapu conveyed this news to his father in the following letter.

Letter 9

Captain T.N. Raina

HQ 80 Indian Infantry Brigade,
S.E.A.C.[17]
February 1945

Dear Bhai Sahib Ji,

Thanks for your letter received some time ago. I couldn't answer it earlier due to the present operations which are nearly over.

You will be pleased to know that I have been promoted to the rank of Captain from 26th June 44.

We are having terrible rainfall in Burma. The whole country is flooded and one has to fight in water which is neck deep. The paddy fields look like lakes and at some places the patrolling (by troops) is done in small boats.

I was pleased to learn that your skin trouble is nearly over.

How is Lahore these days?

Yours very affly,
Tapu.

What were the "present operations" in Burma that Tapu refers to in his letter above? To better appreciate this, a brief overview of the events in this part of the world would enable the reader to appreciate the role of the British Indian army in South East Asia.

Japan had been modernising since the start of the 20th century and had developed a vigorous economy and modern armed forces. The problem it faced, however, was that it had no natural resources of its own. It was dependent on external sources for oil, metals and other requirements of its industry. To expand its territory, Japan invaded Manchuria in 1931 and China in 1937. Despite having signed a pact with Germany in 1936, Japan did not join her ally in

[17] South East Asia Command.

the war in 1939. But by 1941, the Japanese campaign in China had got bogged down and Japan was resentful of the aid being sent to China by the United States and Britain.

On 21st July 1941, Japan occupied French Indo-China. This led the United States, Britain and the Netherlands to declare an economic embargo on Japan. Facing economic ruin, Japan decided to take offensive action to secure the Dutch East Indies with their oil, and to capture Burma, thus cutting off the route of supply to China. To protect these gains, Japan needed to spread its arc to cover much of the Pacific region. To achieve this, Japan attacked the US Naval Base at Pearl Harbour in the Hawaiian Islands on 7th December 1942, thus declaring war on the United States as well as on Great Britain. Simultaneous to the attack on Pearl Harbour, Japan also landed on the coast of Malaya and opened a new front. This narrative is not concerned with the fighting in the Pacific that was basically conducted by US forces but with the campaigns in Malaya and Burma where the Indian Army was deeply involved.

From the time of British evacuation of Rangoon on 7th March 1942 to its complete retreat from Burma in May 1942, Japan had overrun Burma and also Malaya. A massive effort now started in India both to raise new formations as also to train these and the older ones in jungle warfare at which the Japanese army was very adept. Throughout 1943 the army raised new formations which were trained in jungle warfare in the Ranchi Plateau (the present Jharkhand state). As the army's strength increased, new corps headquarters were raised and were grouped into the 14th Army, with General Slim as its army commander.

In August 1943, a new South East Asia Command (SEAC) with Admiral Lord Louis Mountbatten as Supreme Commander was established and became responsible for all operations in the SEAC Theatre. General Headquarters (GHQ) in India now became responsible for administration of the army in Burma.

General Slim was now ready to launch his operations to regain Burma. Operations commenced between 3rd and 4th December 1944. The 1st Battalion, the 19th Hyderabad Regiment fought, its first important action of the war, on 9th February 1945 at Myitson, a small village at the junction of the river Nammeik Chaung with the Shweli River. Here the Japanese were determined to hold on to their positions till their forces could withdraw from the area. When a frontal assault by a British battalion failed, the 1/19 Hyderabad Regiment was ordered to attack from the flank.

The success of the operation depended on whether the river Chaung was fordable, as it would have been foolhardy to attempt a crossing by boats in the face of the enemy. Between 2nd to 5th February, patrols from the battalion were sent out to ascertain Nammeik Chaung's depth. These patrols were led by Lieutenant (later Brigadier) R. Wood and Lieutenant Raina, respectively. They did not meet with success till the night of 5/6th February, when the patrol led by Tappy Raina[18] spotted an enemy party crossing the Chaung, confirming that it was fordable. This crossing place was then selected for the assault because of the ease of fording there. The assault by 1/19 Hyderabad Regiment was successful. Lieutenant Raina was "Mentioned-in-Despatches" for his part in this action of his Battalion.

After the action at Myiston, 1 /19 Hyderabad Regiment entered Mongmit on 9th March, and ten days later occupied the ruby-mining town of Mogok. By 8th April, the battalion had reached Maymyo. Soon thereafter, 26 Infantry Brigade was broken up and the 1/19 Hyderabad Regiment now joined the 80 Indian Infantry Brigade. By now Tappy had been promoted to the rank of captain and saw more action in the final battles that took the 14th Army to Rangoon.

Once while leading a patrol, Tappy came almost face to face with a Japanese patrol. Before the Japanese party could recover from surprise, Tappy immediately ordered his men to take tactical cover and succeeded in laying an ambush, killing most of the en emy soldiers. On searching the dead patrol leader, Tappy found a unique hand stitched cloth belt, soaked in blood, tied around his waist, which he brought back as a souvenir to his battalion, along with an all-weather silk map of the area. It is believed that as per

---

[18] Though he remained Tapu for his family, in his battalion his nick name became Tappy.

Japanese custom, each such "Thousand Stitches Belt"[19] was hand stitched by either the wife, mother or sister of a soldier as a good-luck charm, to protect their beloved kin in war. Such a belt used to have one thousand stitches in red thread on a white coarse cloth.

Gradually, other parts of Burma were reclaimed by the British Indian army. Meiktila was secured on 5th March and Mandalay on 20th March, and Rangoon was secured soon after.

Ninette Raina recalls what Tappy told her about his experience in Burma during his action at Mogok:

> In Mogok (Burma), while the fighting was going on, he stumbled upon some precious stones. He said the men were alternately firing and picking the stones. He gave me those stones when we were married! I never got them mounted for I did not care for jewellery. That never ceased to amaze him.

While mopping-up operations continued, the British Indian forces were reorganized to safeguard Burma and also to prepare for an amphibious assault to recapture Malaya and Singapore. However, with the dropping of the atom bombs by United States in August 1945 on Hiroshima on 6th August and on Nagasaki on 9th August, respectively, the Second World War came to a sudden end. Japan surrendered unconditionally on 14th August 1945, when Allied preparations for the Malayan landing were still in the final stage. The announcement of surrender by Japan brought great relief to a war-weary world. But the combat role for the troops of the 80 Infantry Brigade in general, and the 1/19 Hyderabad Regiment in particular, was not yet over.

Indian troops landed to take the surrender of the Japanese in Singapore and Malaya; troops were also sent to Thailand and Indo-China to disarm the Japanese in these countries.

---

[19] The two souvenirs, the Thousand Stitches Belt and the Silk Map of Burma captured by Tappy Raina during Second World War, were eventually presented by General Raina, MVC, COAS & Colonel of The Kumaon & Naga Regiments, for display at the newly inaugurated Kumaon Regimental Centre Museum at Ranikhet in 1976.

Tappy's destiny took him to Indo-China with the allied forces, who went there to take charge of Japanese prisoners after Japan's defeat in the Second World War. Saigon, in present day Vietnam, was also significant for Tappy at the personal level for it was there that he met his future wife, Marie-Antoinette Florence Kurtz (Ninette to family and friends).

Chapter 4

French Indo-China

Of all the many countries in which Tappy served as a young officer, French Indo-China is where his life was transformed in more ways than one. In order to appreciate the background of this region to which he was sent in the course of duty and of the young woman he met and eventually married, a background of the prevailing situation would be of interest to the reader.

Since the late 1880s, Vietnam, Laos and Cambodia were controlled by the French. Collectively they were referred to as French Indo-China and they were one of France's most lucrative colonial possessions.

When Germany occupied France during the Second World War, Japan which was an ally of Hitler's Germany, sought to fulfil its imperial ambition of ruling most of South East Asia. French Indo-China was invaded and occupied by Japan. All French personnel in Indo-China were detained by the Japanese as prisoners of war (POWs) in civil internee (CI) camps.

The following account of the situation in Indo-China is based on the narration of Marie Antoinette Florence Kurtz, affectionately called Ninette. Her father, Charles Kurtz, was a senior officer of the French Colonial Service. Ninette, eventually, became Tappy's wife, but that was much later.

> My father had wanted to take premature retirement in 1939 because he wanted to return to France and settle down there. He was concerned about our higher education for there was no

university for French education in Saigon where we were based. So he had the house packed and all the major stuff was sent back to Alsace, France, to a cousin's house that was large and spacious. Just then, however, the war in Europe broke out in September 1939 and we could not leave Saigon.

In 1940, because France was under attack by its ally Nazi Germany, Japan occupied Tonkin in northern Indo-China and effectively blockaded aid to China with which it was at war since 1937.

I was preparing for my exams in June 1940. One evening I came home elated with my success in school, only to find my father sitting before the radio, looking pale and alarmed. My mother was silently crying. Paris had fallen to the Germans who were now spreading all over France. This, naturally, had an effect on us in Indo-China. General Catroux, the Military Governor-General of Indo-China, sensing the hopelessness of the situation in a country threatened by the Japanese, and unable to stand on its own, declared his allegiance for the deposed government of General De Gaulle and fled to Noumea in New Caledonia.[20] He later joined General de Gaulle's Free France.

Overseas French colonies were now breaking into two camps: Free France, a government in exile led by Charles de Gaulle; and, Vichy France, the puppet government set up in Paris by the occupying German forces and headed by Marshal Philippe Petain.

My father knew that our family home in Alsace, near the tri-junction of the French, Swiss, and German borders, would be annexed by the Germans. And that is exactly what happened. My father, learnt to his horror, that all that he possessed in Alsace had been looted by the Germans! Before the outbreak of the War, he had shipped back furniture, silverware, a whole library (which to me was the most precious), and other household articles. All these were kept in a cousin's home, because my

[20] New Caledonia is a French territory comprising dozens of islands in the South Pacific. The capital is at Noumea, known for its palm-lined beaches and marine-life-rich lagoon, which, at 24,000 square kilometres, is among the world's largest.

father had planned to buy a house for us when we returned to France! During the war, the cousin died and the house was occupied by the Germans. They, other refugees, the French Army, people in the village — everyone helped themselves to our things. Thus we lost everything that we had in France.

My parents, therefore, decided to build a house in Saigon, because my father felt that it would be better to stay on in Indo-China than go back to a German occupied France. Little did my father know that our family house in Alsace would later be returned to us and that we would be compelled to give up our home in Saigon instead!

So we moved into our very own house in Saigon. We planted many fruit trees in the garden: guava, custard apple, mango, banana, lime, orange and papaya. Litchis were already growing on our land. In our kitchen garden we planted tomatoes and sweet potatoes. The latter were as tenacious as wild weeds. We also raised rabbits, poultry, some geese and turkeys. There was a kapok tree which bore pods and these were used to provide filling for pillows. The humid climate of Vietnam made plants grow very quickly. Our home garden was to prove very useful in the years ahead when we were placed under house arrest.

That period was one of intense unrest among the French community. French nationals whose loyalty to the puppet French government was doubtful were repatriated to France by the new Vichy regime. My father would have been one of the first to be packed off, but there arose a problem on his account. He had refused to swear allegiance to the new head of state, Marshal Petain, because he was against any "collaboration" with the enemy (Germany). Therefore, he had become stateless. He also refused to return to any place in France other than Alsace. This put the authorities in a predicament because they kept informing the community that the "friendly" Germans had not touched an inch of French territory whereas in fact they had overrun most of French territory. Therefore, my father could not be sent back to Alsace. So he was kept under house arrest and relieved of his job.

In July 1941, Japanese troops landed in Saigon to the general consternation of everyone. And for the next four years we lived as virtual prisoners. The Japanese were allies of the Germans and since France had signed an armistice with Germany, the two countries were not officially at war. That is why the Japanese did not harm us. They, however, installed themselves comfortably, occupied the best houses, took over the best hospitals and we, the French, could do nothing. We never protested because we did not want to be massacred.

When the Japanese arrived in Vietnam in July 1941 there was no war in the region at that time. However, in December 1941, they attacked British Malaya and Singapore for they had ambitions of becoming a great East Asia empire. On 8th December 1941, they bombarded the Americans in Pearl Harbour, and that was the start of war by Japan. They never declared war formally. They simply carried out a surprise attack. The Americans lost a whole fleet at Pearl Harbour. The British in Singapore were taken by surprise because all their canons were trained towards the sea but they were attacked, instead, over land from the rear. Having taken Vietnam, the Japanese crossed over to the British colony of Malaya and Singapore and then Dutch Indonesia. They perhaps had the same kind of dreams as Napoleon!

During this period I was at the Lycee[21] preparing my Baccalaureate. I must have been about seventeen years old. In some ways life continued as normal. We, the youngsters, continued going to school. The Japanese did not interfere with us and were generally courteous and polite. Some French citizens were nominated to assist them in civil matters that required their assistance. However, the Japanese did incite the Vietnamese against the French. They wanted the country to be taken away from the French. In fact, they wanted all Europeans to be

---

[21] The lycée is the second, and last, stage of secondary education in the French educational system. At the end of the final year of schooling, most students take the baccalaureate diploma.

thrown out of Asia. They dreamed of a Greater East Asian Empire. In this respect they behaved like Hitler!

After my Baccalaureate, the Education Department of the French Government appointed me as a part-time teacher and I began my training as a teacher of History and Geography. There was no college for higher education in the French system, but with the help of experienced professors and some other people, I began to teach at a local college i.e. one for only Vietnamese people where education was focussed on local needs. It was also run by the French but was distinct to the French Lycee which offered a completely French education, as in France. The local college was to train locals to take over governance of their country eventually. We all knew that someday we would leave this country. I taught French language, History of Annam and local Geography at this local college. However, this lasted only for six months.

De Gaulle and the Allies reclaimed France in August 1944. In April 1945 the Japanese overthrew the French Government in Indo-China and declared Indo-China to be independent. The French citizens were then imprisoned. We were all obliged to move into the same locality and stay at home — doing nothing! We had no right to work. We received meagre rations of rice and dowsan (lentils like whole moong daal) from the Japanese. Although they did not harass us in a daily manner, they did, sometimes, enter houses to search for arms and so on. Sometimes they were rude but on the whole it was okay.

What I do remember is that they never lifted a finger against children. They loved children. If they were walking on the street, they would often pick up children from their mothers and play with them. They even sometimes gave them toys. At such times we all appreciated their conduct. So we were all stuck at home. My father grumbled a lot privately, but could not do anything. The Japanese made us sweep the streets in order to humiliate us in front of the Annamites[22] (ethnic Vietnamese). But that did not bother us because in France, anyhow, we all had to do our own work. We the youngsters — my brother, sister and I — would sweep outside our own house barefoot, because we wanted to preserve our shoes. There was no money to buy new shoes or clothes. My father received no salary. Despite that my parents had some savings even though my father was not paid for four years.

During the years when we were under house arrest, my parents did not keep any domestic help even though the house was big. They did all the work and divided the responsibility amongst us all. That is how we survived for four years in Saigon from 1941-45. From time to time, my parents sold off certain household articles so that school fees for the three of us siblings could be paid and so that our education would not be interrupted. During those four years we did not have any radio and were not well informed about what was going on in the world. Whatever little information we received was from the local Chinese.

One day in August 1945, we suddenly noticed that there was no Japanese in sight. Later, we learnt from our Chinese friends about the dropping of atom bombs in Hiroshima and Nagasaki.

---

[22] The Vietnamese people were generally oppressed under the French rule, both prior to the outbreak of 2nd World War, and even after! In 1930, Ho Chi Minh drew up a charter for the Indo-chinese Communist Party. The objectives of the party were the overthrow of the French; establishment of Vietnamese independence; establishment of a workers', peasants', and soldiers' government; organization of a workers' militia; cancellation of public debts; confiscation of means of production and their transfer to the government; distribution of French-owned lands to the peasants; suppression of taxes; establishment of an eight-hour work day; development of crafts and agriculture; institution of freedom of organization; and establishment of education for all citizens. Ho Chi Minh' goal for his country was "equal rights for Vietnamese and French in Indochina, freedom of press and opinion, freedom of association and assembly, freedom to travel at home and abroad, and substitute rule of law for government by degree."

The Japanese had barricaded themselves in their camps and were nowhere to be seen.

Suddenly the streets of Saigon were full of people: French, Australians, Americans, British and Dutch. All these had been earlier detained as prisoners by the Japanese. The Annamites (as the Vietnamese people were referred to) who seemed to have disappeared during the Japanese occupation began to attack the French at night. They tried to burn the city. They understood that now that the Japanese were defeated, the French would try to re-establish their rule over Indo-China. They wanted the French to quit so that they could become an independent nation.

The French Army in Indo-China was not strong in manpower and equipment to combat the Soviet and China-backed Vietminh[23]. At this time, though my father was re-appointed to French Government service, he could not go back to France immediately. He was given one year to get his personal documents and records updated which had been destroyed by the Japanese. So although France was liberated in 1945 it was only on 31st December 1946 that the five of us (parents and three children) left Indo-China for good and went back to France. As we sailed away, I saw Saigon and the spires of its Cathedral disappear from view for the last time!

My father was well compensated, financially, by the new French Government for the loss of four years of service. That enabled him to make a fresh start in France.

The Indian Army in French Indo-China

The surrender of Japan at the end of war created many problems of law and order. There was hardly anyone to govern these colonies, which until recently had been ruled by the Japanese. Each of these freed former colonies by now had a section of local popula-

---

[23] It was in December 1946 that real violence erupted with the Vietminh, which finished in 1956 with the Battle of Dien Bien Phu, when the French abandoned the war and left Indo-China.

tion who aspired to independence from their earlier colonial masters. This was especially so since the South East Asia Command (SEAC) under the command of Admiral Lord Louis Mountbatten, handed back these countries to the colonial powers that had been ruling before the Japanese stepped in. The area of responsibility of SEAC now included Malaya, Singapore, Thailand, French Indo-China, the Dutch East Indies (now Indonesia), Hong Kong and Borneo. There were about five hundred thousand Japanese troops in this area who had to be disarmed. Thousands of Allied prisoners were to be brought back, and civil administration restored in these territories.

In some colonies, nationalist forces armed with captured Japanese arms and equipment had seized power in the wake of Japan's surrender. In Indo-China, fighting had already started between the Annamites and the French, who had just come out of Japanese internment. To control the situation and take over the Japanese Supreme Headquarters in Saigon, a part of 20 Indian Division was flown there under Major-General D.D. Gracey, C.B., C.B.E., M.C. Captain Tappy Raina and his Battalion (1/19 Hyderabad Regiment) also arrived in Saigon in September 1945 as a part of the 80th Indian Infantry Brigade of the 20th Indian Division.

Their task was to restore confidence among the local people, and guard the communication centre and vital installations. They also had to deal with the Annamite rebels as well as other anti-social elements. The rebel forces in Indo-China were fairly well armed. During clashes with them between 24th September and 4th November, the Battalion suffered ten casualties (three killed, including a V.C.O., and seven wounded). 1/19 Hyderabad Regiment carried out raids on suspected locations to look for caches of arms and ammunition; they also organised flag marches through the city to make their presence felt.

Japanese troops who were still doing guard duty at various places in the city were immediately disarmed and relieved. "19 Hyderabadis" took over the Tanson Nhut Aerodrome, and also the city's power-house, pumping-station and civil jail. The most interesting take-over, however, was that of Banque d'Indo-Chine by "D" Company, the 1/19 Hyderabad Regiment, on 23rd September.

In a surprise move, the Japanese manager was brought from his house to hand over the vaults. The object was to get hold of documents and securities not already destroyed by him. Except for British India Army officers, "D" Company had orders to not allow entry of anyone else into the bank, not even US or French Army officers.

According to Ninette Raina, soon after their arrival the Allied Forces started to exercise administrative control and begun the rehabilitation of French detainees. Young Indian Army officers and soldiers soon became popular with the locals because of their civilised and cultured behaviour. The French in Saigon were jubilant to see the Indian Army. Youngsters like Charles Kurtz, brother of Ninette Kurtz, went out of their way to meet and befriend the officers of the allied forces. Tappy Raina was invited home by Charles Jr, to meet the Kurtz family. Ninette recalled her first meeting with Tappy and their subsequent friendship:

> My brother, Charles, had made friends with some of the Allied troops. One of them was an Indian. One evening, with the permission of my parents, Charles took me with him to attend a party in the mess. There he introduced me to his new friends. One of them was Tappy Raina.
>
> Thus, I first met Tappy in Saigon in the euphoria of the aftermath of war! We met a few times and when some others in the group of friends were posted overseas, Tappy and I continued to meet, usually at home. He was then a young captain, rather shy. His sensitivity and good manners were striking. I found him very different from his colleagues. He was less brash, less noisy and very considerate. He became very fond of my mother and I later learnt that he had not known his own mother.
>
> Tappy Raina soon became a regular visitor to the Kurtz household. Every Sunday he would invite the Kurtz family to lunch at the officers' mess. Usually, only my mother, my brother and I would join him for lunch. My father rarely came because he did not understand English. My mother was always delighted to come because she invariably met someone or the

other who could speak German, which she spoke fluently. Besides, she enjoyed meeting new people. My brother Charles then joined the French Army as a conscript and, thereafter, was not seen. My sister Alberte, meanwhile, was going around with George Martin, a friend of Charles, so she was fully occupied with him. She married him eventually in Vietnam and then moved back to France.

Tappy got on very well with my mother and she became very fond of him, almost like a son. What also struck me was that he was very modest, honest and upright. Tappy offered to teach me to drive a jeep. The driver was very reluctant and I could see his point of view. The vehicle was spick and span, the driver obviously spent hours every day cleaning and polishing it. Anyway, within a week I picked up the skill and we went on the roads. We were merrily driving along a deserted lane one day, when a young British Military Police (MP) stopped me and took Tappy's particulars. I was petrified. I knew I had no licence. But nothing was asked from me. The young man was very correct. I was shaking and Tappy was laughing. Two days later he came home and told me "I have been on the mat. My Brigadier has given me the order to drive the jeep only to your house and back with you. He likes you". So the driving continued. After we were married, I remembered this episode and told Tappy "Now I understand why you have been 'Mentioned in Despatches'; you are a very brave man indeed to have taught me driving". He laughed and laughed!

Tappy was very shy and I felt much at ease with him because I too used to feel tongue-tied in parties. He told me later that I was liked in his mess because I did not smoke and I did not drink. In my own house, of course it was taboo! Only wine was permitted, but with water. My father smoked a pipe but there were no cigarettes in the house. My brother smoked them then and I had tried one with him. It made me so sick I never went near a cigarette again in my whole life. It was just as well for my father could not abide women who smoked. My parents were very conservative. And so it went on, and Tappy's jeep was stationed before our house most days.

He wanted to visit my college and we talked a lot about our different systems of education but we were happy together and had a lot of interests in common during that period of our friendship, which gradually grew into courtship. But he was not a flirt. He was serious and sincere.

My first impression of Tappy was that he was squinting, particularly when he turned his head. One day he told me shyly, "I have a glass eye". I felt very sorry, for he was so young! Hesitatingly I asked him what had happened and he told me that he had been wounded in the course of duty. It was an accident that occurred when he had been detailed to destroy some ammunition captured in an arms dump somewhere in Iraq. A grenade that he lobbed did not sail through, and exploded mid-air prematurely as a result of which he was severely injured, suffering twenty-nine injuries on different parts on his body. I believe that he was rushed to a Military Hospital where his one eye had to be removed, because of two splinters in it. When he was initially evacuated, he was almost given up for dead! He remained hanging between life and death for a long time. Finally he found himself transferred to a hospital in Beirut (Lebanon). The scars from that grenade alone were not to be the only ones; he was to collect some more in his career! His family had been informed officially that he was very badly hurt. But Tappy, though very young, proved very robust and mentally tough. He thus survived. His brother officers in the Battalion kept on cheering and encouraging him, as if nothing was lost. Another friend said, "Don't worry. One day a girl will love you just the same without bothering about an eye"! He told me much later that he remembered that friend when he and I first met.

Only when he was to leave Saigon, did he ask the ultimate question, adding that we had to think at length about it since it involved so much for both of us! Besides, on the material side he was not yet a permanent commissioned officer. So we left it at that and "thought" about it! This "thinking" was to last three years for various reasons, which I'II explain later. We met in November 1945 and he left Saigon at the end of January 1946!

That was a very short period, but it proved decisive for both of us!

After Tappy left, life for me in Saigon was quite drab. By then it became clear that my college would not re-open as the students had all run away. It suited me fine. I went to work with the French Army Medical Headquarters and did all sorts of work there, teaching myself a little typing on my father's typewriter, which the Japanese, organised as they were, had returned intact. All the others in the office were in uniform, most of them being girls but I was the only civilian there. I also worked with the French Red Cross for about eight months and loved it.

Then my father's repatriation orders were received and we left Saigon for France. My parents eventually bought a house in Alsace and settled down to a retired life. I remained in Paris with my aunt (my father's sister) and found a job in a travel and tourist agency, where I worked for about eight months and then I left for India to get married.

Towards the end of January 1946, sufficient French troops had arrived in Indo-China to take over the commitments of the 1/19 Hyderabad Regiment. But the thought of going home to India was still a distant dream for its men. On 28th January 1946, the battalion sailed for Makassar (capital of Celebes), by ship *K.P.M. Tegelberg*. Their new task consisted mostly of helping with the repatriation of Japanese prisoners, and detachments of the battalion were located at Malino, Balik Papen and Pare in South of Celebes, which is now referred to as Sulawesi. Finally, on 30th June 1946 the battalion left the Celebes on board the *H.T. Dunera* and after a sea voyage of ten days, reached Indian shores. They were ceremoniously received at Madras (now Chennai) harbour, and welcomed by Major General Wade, General Officer Commanding, Madras Area, as the band of the Dogra Regimental Centre, played at the quayside. After the usual formalities, the battalion moved to Pulgaon in Central India.

During the troubled period following the bombing of Hiroshima and Nagasaki by the US, serious problems relating to law and order, governance of liberated colonies and repatriation of Japanese prisoners of war in South East Asia demanded firm action. A glimpse of the situation can be seen through the letters Tappy wrote to his father.

Letter 10

Captain T.N. Raina

HQ 80 Indian Infantry Brigade
S.E.A.C.
Dated: 18.9.1945

Dear Bhai Sahib Ji,

I was in receipt of your letter on my arrival in Saigon (French Indo China). I left Rangoon on 3rd of October and arrived here on the 16th. The voyage was pretty rough when we entered South China Sea, after Singapore.

It is a lovely country except for the local trouble, which I understand will shortly be over. We are fairly busy in disarming the Japs these days.

I have not heard anything from Model Town (their home in Lahore) for over a month?

With best respect,
Yours affly
Tapu

N.B. You will be pleased to know that besides "Africa Star" I have been given "Burma Star", 1939-1945 Star and Defence medal.

Letter 11

Captain T.N. Raina

HQ 80 Indian Infantry Brigade
S.E.A.C.
Dated: 25.1.1946

Dear Bhai Sahib Ji,

I am writing this letter from Singapore on my way to Celebes Island[24]. We left French Indo China on the 20th of this month for the new country. The boat has stopped for about two days to collect fresh supplies of rations, water and fuel from here. I will write you about the new place when I reach the other end, but I think it will not be as good as French Indo China.

The boat in which we are travelling is ORDUNA (15000 Ton) named after one of the most beautiful towns in Spain. How I wish the boat itself was half as beautiful as the well reputed town! The first two days, the sea was bit rough and I felt miserable as . . . but thank God it is alright now. How is everybody at home?

With best respects,
Yours very affly,
Tapu.

For the major part of 1946, Tappy remained pre-occupied with his duties, but at the same time his courtship of Ninette continued to progress with the exchange of letters between the two. By now, the next location for Tappy's Battalion was known to be at Pulgaon in India's Central Provinces and he advised his father to correspond in future to his new address — 1st Battalion, the Kumaon Regiment, Pulgaon (CP). Since availability of ships was uncertain, Tappy did not have any definite date of his arrival in India from his duty station in South East Asia. Therefore, he suggested that his father send letters to the above address which would be received by him on his reaching Pulgaon.

---

[24] Celebes, Indonesian Sulawesi, is one of the four Greater Sunda Islands, Indonesia. It has four distinct peninsulas that form three major gulfs: Tomini (the largest) on the northeast, Tolo on the east and Bone on the south.

Tappy finally disembarked at Vizagapatam (now Visakhapatnam) on the morning of 4th September 1946. He wrote to his father to inform him of his arrival in India and that he would be proceeding to Pulgaon the next day. He shared with his father in a letter that the last two days of his journey at sea were very hectic and rough because of having hit a storm.

He finally joined his battalion at Pulgaon on 6th September 1946. Tappy shared the happy news of finding a pleasant surprise awaiting him. He informed his father that he had been decorated with the award of “Mention in Despatches” for his bravery in Burma in February 1945 in one of the battles. He also informed his father that due to a great rush of work, he had little hope of getting any leave till November.

Chapter 5

Partition of India and Marriage

The partition of India led to great upheaval both at the national and individual levels. There were many challenges that Tappy had to face on his return to India in September 1946. These were to affect both his professional and personal life.

One of the greatest challenges for the government of the Indian Dominion after partition was the integration of princely states, of which undivided India had over seven hundred. The only reasonable course for rulers of these states was to accede to either of the new dominions within whose territory their states fell. By 25th July 1947 most of these states had signified their willingness to do so. The two notable exceptions were Hyderabad and Kashmir; their rulers thought their states were large enough to exist as independent kingdoms.

The Kashmir State (Jammu and Ladakh included) had a predominantly Muslim population but the Maharaja of Kashmir, Sir Hari Singh was a Dogra ruler. Pakistani leaders expected that Kashmir would cast its lot with them. When that did not happen, they formed a plan to annex Kashmir by other means.

On 22nd October 1947, Pakistan launched some five thousand tribesmen from the North-West Frontier Province (NWFP) into Kashmir with the objective of capturing Srinagar, the capital of Kashmir State. It was then that Maharaja Hari Singh appealed to the Government of India on 24th October 1947, for help to stem the tide of invaders. On Lord Mountbatten's[25] advice, Pandit Nehru, Prime Minister of the Indian Dominion, deferred the decision to send troops until the Maharaja of Kashmir signed the letter of accession to the Indian Dominion. The Maharaja signed the instrument of accession on 26th October 1947, whereupon Indian troops were airlifted to Srinagar.

Among the troops that were moved to Kashmir and saw action there was 1st Sikh and 1 (Para) Kumaon Battalion, now 3 Para (Kumaon), and 4 Kumaon.

Karachi Agreement 1949

The armies of India and Pakistan remained engaged in fighting with each other from October 1947 to December 1948. Just when the Indian Army was in a position to push the Pakistani forces out of the state of Kashmir, Government of India chose to take the matter of Pakistani aggression to the United Nations Security Council (UNSC). As a result of this action by India, a UN sponsored cease fire between the two armies was agreed upon with effect from 1st January 1949.

In July 1949, a United Nations delegation convened an Indo-Pakistani meeting at Karachi (then capital of Pakistan), to delineate the cease fire line (CFL) in the Kashmir State. Lieutenant General (later General) S.M. Shrinagesh, General Officer Commanding-in-Chief, Western Command, led the Indian delegation. It took seven days of hectic discussions to delineate an agreed 740-kilometre Long cease fire line from Lalealli in Akhnoor Sector in the south to NJ 9842 in Siachen, Ladakh in the north. This cease fire agreement later came to be known as Karachi Agreement of 1949.

---

[25] Lord Louis Mountbatten, undivided India's last British Viceroy and Governor General, became the first Governor General of the Indian Dominion when India became independent on 15th August 1947.

This, however, did not settle the Kashmir dispute and the confrontation has continued till this day. The 1947 partition of British India thus created the first international conflict. In fact, partitions have only produced festering sores as is borne out by Palestine, Cyprus and Northern Ireland, to quote just a few examples.

Impact of Political Situation on Tappy Raina's Personal Life

The partition of India and the country's first confrontation with Pakistan in Kashmir had an impact on the course of Tappy and Ninette's lives as well. As Ninette recalled:

> In January 1946, Tappy left Saigon with his unit and sailed to the Celebes. They returned to India in September 1946. Meanwhile my parents and I left Saigon for France on 31st December 1946.
>
> When we finally landed in Marseille, a port city on the Mediterranean Sea in the south of France, a raging snowstorm welcomed us! It turned out to be a particularly severe winter. Most of us who got off the ship had no coats and were not equipped for the European winter. Wool was only given on ration cards to those who were under the age of eighteen. All shelves were empty in every store! This was, after all, the aftermath of the war!
>
> The train from Marseille to Paris was not centrally heated because there was not enough coal in the country. And when we reached Paris there was no heating in apartments or houses, either!
>
> The country had been swept bare of everything, and life in France in the winter of early 1947 was grim and difficult. If you were over eighteen, there was no milk, no eggs and no sugar to be had. Butter and cheese were doled out once in three months and the quantity was restricted only to 100 grams per head. Bread was restricted to 250 grams a day per person and, that too, black bread. Luckily, vegetables and potatoes were freely

available; a legacy from the Germans! Despite these hardships, people were optimistic and displayed the proverbial zest for life.

By the time India and Pakistan agreed on a cease fire in J&K on 31st December 1948, my parents, had given up the fight against the idea of my marrying Tapu. However, they were still very worried about my future! They had moved to Alsace and settled down in a newly bought house, but my father refused to help me leave France for India. So I stayed in Paris with one of his sisters, a war-widow, and I continued to work to support myself and prepare for my journey to India, all alone!

I began working in a travel agency and got to know the ropes! In those days jobs went a begging, as there were not enough people to do so much work of reorganisation and reconstruction. Work in the country went on at breakneck speed. I found it quite easy to fit in with the life of Paris on my own. I realised that having been uprooted so much in my life, I had been conditioned to live anywhere!

My life experiences at that time had taught me how important it was to be able to adjust and adapt to everything in life, and to accept what came my way and not resist and fight it. This enabled me to face my life better, even when I chose India as my home with Tapu as my beloved husband.

When I look back, there were lots of coincidences in our life together. He said good-bye to me on the eve of his birthday, 21st January 1946 and sailed away from Saigon for the Celebes the next day. I said good-bye to him at his funeral in 1980 on the eve of my birthday and his ashes sailed away down the River Ganga the very next day!

Marriage

Even as Tappy was settling down in his appointment as GSO-2 (Operations) at General Headquarters, New Delhi, he was doing his best to convince his family about his proposed marriage with Ninette. It was in this desperation that he wrote a letter to his uncle, Brij Narain Raina, where he cried his heart out explaining how his war time commitments prevented him from keeping up communications with his uncle and other members of the family.

Major T.N. Raina | 73 Queen Victoria Road Mess,
New Delhi
Dated: 26th September 1948

My dear Papa Ji,

When heart is full, tongue is still. Having torn three pages this is my fourth attempt of putting down in words my sentiments evoked by your letter received sometime back. So if my ideas are woolly and expression poor, I beg to be excused assuring you that there is no lack of affection behind them.

I am entirely to be blamed for the sheer negligence of not dropping you a line, now and then. For this, please accept my humblest apologies. But I most definitely, beg to differ that this humble son of yours, who owes so much to you for his success in his profession, has at all forgotten you. How can I ever, ever dream of forgetting a person who devoted his entire life for the good of others and sacrificed all his joys and comforts? Those who have are not only ungrateful but extremely mean.

Tears are rolling down my cheeks as I write these few lines, recollecting those happy days which I spent under your most benevolent guidance when living in "Mohala Sudaan" (the street in locality of persons of Suds (Soods) denomination) in Ludhiana. It is a pity that Amma ji is not with us today to see me in this dignified position but I am certain her blessings are. May the Almighty bless her noble Soul. Amen!

I gather from Bhai Sahib ji that you will be leaving for Simla in the near future. Jaggu ji intends visiting you in October. I will do my best to get leave when possible and come to see you. I had no news of Somoji for long. I am certain he must be doing well.

I took over my job on the 15th of this month and due to operations in Hyderabad had been extremely busy. The work here never seems to be finishing. I usually leave at 8 a.m. and come back not before 7 p.m. I feel Delhi is the worst station I ever had.

Please do drop a line of your welfare.

Remember me to Shammo ji and Somoji,

With best respects,
Your most affectionate son,
Tapu.

From the letter above, it is clear how commitment to duty in far flung lands resulted in infrequent communication with families led to misunderstandings and social distancing with family members.

Finally, a letter from Tappy in India brought much joy and hope to Ninette. Her feelings and that of her parents are described below:

> And then, one day, in July 1947, a letter from Tapu arrived, addressed to my parents, informing them that he had got his permanent commission in the Indian Army and was now promoted to the rank of a Major. He sought my hand in marriage, and wanted to come to France and take me with him to India, as his wife.
>
> My family were most concerned at this development. They were apprehensive about my future in India and expressed their doubts as to what I would do there, would I not be lost, feel alone, and worse, what if I was abandoned?
>
> In a way, I was following my mother, Marie Schmidt, who had met my father when he had returned to France from French Indo-China in 1919. My father first went to Saigon in 1913 while in service with the French Army. He served there until 1919. My parents were married in Paris in 1920. Shortly thereafter, my father was posted to Madagascar, an Island in the Indian Ocean and a French colony. After a short stint there, he returned to France and was then posted to Dakar, capital of Senegal (West Africa) another French Colony, where I and my brother Charles were born. In 1925, my father completed his

fifteen years of service in the Army and after having earned his pension, we returned to France from Senegal. Sometime later, my father joined the French Police, and after a few months, he received orders to proceed to Saigon, then capital of French Indo-China. And that is where I grew up.

So to come back to Tapu's marriage proposal, my parents had all along hoped that our attachment was only childish infatuation! This matter had by now become a running battle in my family. Before they had time to adjust to this new development, however, the British decided to divide the Indian sub-continent.

The newspapers were full of horror stories about the cruelties committed on the sub-continent. My parents were aghast. They absolutely refused to let me go in such conditions. I could understand their point of view, particularly after what our family had gone through in Vietnam. But one always hopes for better days.

My mother was adamant that nobody from her family should ever think of going back to the East. Even my father, darkly prophesised that I would be lost and would disappear in such a big sub-continent! The question of my future life in India with Tapu became a ding-dong battle. To crown it, after that letter of July '47, I remained without news from Tapu for a long time. My parents were furious at my stubbornness. Luckily for me, they had known Tapu and were fond of him; but they were certain that I was making the blunder of my life!

To further aggravate the situation and, to my horror, news of a war between Pakistan and India in Kashmir started to pour in. We had barely absorbed the shock of the war in Kashmir, when the news of assassination of the Father of the Indian Nation, Mahatma Gandhi[34] on 31st January 1948, was received.

My opponents became more and more numerous and vocal. And then I discovered something strange: I did not know whether Tapu was in India or Pakistan, whether he was Hindu or Muslim. I only knew that when we met in Saigon, his home was in Lahore. The question of religion had never even been broached. It was immaterial to us. We were believers but not particularly attached to a particular religion as such. My parents themselves were products of mixed marriages between Catholics and Protestants. That, in itself, was a very rare state of tolerance!

I understood later that the question of religion is a very delicate one in the kind of mixed marriage Tapu and I were contemplating. My parents were very tolerant and attended both the churches. We children were raised as Catholics because of an insistent grandmother, whom I never knew. But I experienced quite a lot of misery in my convent because of my "divided" parentage, and soon came to adopt my parent's worship of a God who they considered as being the same for the whole of humanity, irrespective of narrow dogmas. Moreover, growing up amongst Buddhists and Hindus in Vietnam increased this feeling of religious brotherhood. Adopting my husband's religion made no difference to my beliefs. At least I found tolerance in that new life of mine.

However, to satisfy my curiosity, I went to the Indian Embassy in Paris, to make enquiry about Tapu. In those days Sir Girija Shankar Bajpai was the Ambassador of India in France. The staff at the Indian Embassy though sympathetic, could only assure me that Tapu's family name was not Muslim, that in all likelihood he would be a Hindu. Soon thereafter, I received a flood of letters from Tapu.

There had been tremendous upheavals in his family on account of Partition. They had had to give up their house in Model Town, Lahore, leaving behind all household effects and had migrated to Ludhiana in East Punjab (India). Some of the Tapu's relatives came to Delhi. Most of them had lost everything they possessed! Fortunately Tapu's father had invested in some property in Ludhiana in the thirties.

Before India could come to terms with such large scale migration from Pakistan; Kashmir was attacked and the Indian Army had to be rushed to Srinagar to fight Pakistan's aggression. The Indian army also had to send forces to prevent the Nawab of Junagadh and Nizam of Hyderabad from breaking away from India. Tapu found himself heavily preoccupied with his staff work at GHQ, leaving him hardly any time to write letters. Besides, he also had a regular "family war" on his hands!

Tapu's family was greatly upset with his choice of partner for marriage, and refused to accept his proposal. There were serious apprehensions about letting him marry a "foreigner", who, perhaps, "would smoke, drink and flirt around", something which would clash with their culture and religion!

Tapu eventually won his "family battle", but most dramatically! He simply let his people know that it was either accepting me or losing him and, to underline his stand, decided that no member of his family would attend his wedding. He was very serious about it. That was the end of the fight; for they were a very united family with strong bonds of love between them. Just as there was a cease-fire in my own family, the cease-fire between the India and Pakistan armies also eventually took place, paving the way for my journey to India.

Originally, it was decided that Tapu would come to France for our marriage. But the changed circumstances due to the partition of India made Tapu virtually penniless, as his bank account was in a bank at Lahore. Finding funds for undertaking a journey to France was now impossible for him. Instead, I embarked on a French Navy troopship, which was proceeding to Saigon to double as a Hospital Ship on its voyage back from France. Before that, I gave up my job in Paris and went to Bartenheim in Alsace, to take the blessings of my parents and say goodbye to them. My father accompanied me to Paris and then to Marseille and helped me board the ship on 26th January 1949.

Once again I was sailing at sea, all alone this time, amidst the tumult of French servicemen and their families going to Vietnam. Once again the familiar ports of call came one after the other! At every port of call on the way, there was a thick packet of letters awaiting my arrival from my parents in France, and from Tapu in India.

Then one day a low coast with coconut trees loomed on the horizon. There was no jetty, no wharf in Pondicherry (now Puducherry). We anchored offshore and big rowboats came to the ship. They were filled with branches of coconut trees and passengers perched on top of that heap, the luggage carefully disposed on the highest level. I soon understood why. By the time we had been rowed ashore the boats were full of water and my feet were soaking wet! It was February 1949, quite a pleasant time of the year there, but it felt as hot as Saigon in May. It was the first time for me in Pondicherry, when I landed on 23rd February 1949, on this French enclave on Indian soil!

My first impressions were that Pondicherry was very much like Saigon, mainly because, the buildings were mostly in French architecture and the French language was spoken in addition to Tamil. In Saigon also, there were many people from Pondicherry, and therefore I was not out of sync! Even the climate of this coastal town was similar to that of Saigon.

When I came ashore, Tapu was there to receive and welcome me. What a joy it was to see him again after nearly three years. He was there along with his close friend and colleague, Major Kolanda Velu[26] and his bride, Vimla nick named "Baby". Major Velu was posted at New Delhi where Tapu also was GSO-2 in the Military Operations Directorate at GHQ.

In Pondicherry, I was shocked to find dry sanitation. Never before in my life had I seen dry sanitation. Ever since I could remember, we had wet sanitation and modern plumbing in Vietnam. So that my very first query in India was "Where, oh where, are the Western style toilets?" I thought Pondicherry was a poor and ancient town. But my stupefaction in Delhi was greater to see that the same type of toilets prevailed even there despite the fact that it was the capital of India! Luckily these things started improving almost immediately.

The Velus and Tapu escorted me all the way by Grand Trunk Express train from Madras (Chennai) to Delhi. The train journey in that winter of 1949 was simply delightful to me. The

---

[26] Initially, Ninette stayed with Major and Mrs Velu, who had a house at King Edward Road (KER Officers' Mess), while Tappy stayed in Queen Victoria Road Officer's Mess for Single Officers (QVR Officers' Mess). After marriage, Tappy was also allotted accommodation in the KER Officers' Mess, which became their first home.

first exotic thing was the railway compartment itself! In those days, compartments were totally independent as there was no inter-corridor connection. Then I was given a bottle of soda to rinse my mouth with, after brushing my teeth, because the water in the train was not considered safe! And after crossing Nagpur in Central India, the weather started getting colder, and our arrival at Delhi was a cold one, indeed!

Soon after reaching Delhi, Tapu took me to meet his father and other members of the family, who received me and made me feel welcome. I thought that they were very genuine about it.

After a couple of days, Tapu and I travelled by car to Dehra Dun, where our marriage was solemnised. Besides the Velus, who had accompanied us from Delhi, Major and Mrs U.C. Pant of Tapu's Battalion (1 Kumaon), were the witnesses to our wedding. Major Pant had very kindly made all the arrangements for the wedding and our stay at Dehra Dun.

Our marriage was solemnised by Arya Samaj (Hindu) rites in the Officers Mess of 3rd & 9th Gurkha Rifles Training Centre (39 GTC) Dehra Dun, on 25th February 1949. Tappy was 27 years old and I was 25. Neither anyone from his family nor mine, attended our wedding.

The wedding ceremony lasted for the better part of two hours. There, we were both sitting before a fire that persistently sent smoke into my eyes, ladling ghee and seeds (*samagri*) into the holy fire. I listened to the priest droning his prayers and invoking the blessings of various gods! I could have promised anything, even my head, for all I knew! For the wedding ceremony, Tapu wore a dhoti (a loose piece of clothing wrapped around the lower half of the body, worn by men in India on such occasions) with which he was unfamiliar! I too was feeling a bit off in my sari. I only remember the smoke in my eyes and repeating words I did not understand! "Don't worry", whispered Tapu, "I don't understand most of it, myself"!

But somehow after those first three years of separation after Saigon (there were to be many more in our life) we had picked up the threads as easily as if we had parted only the week before! Tapu and I had decided that since I was going to live in

India, it was better to constitute one unit in everything. First they proceeded to convert me to a Hindu, and only then the proper wedding ceremony could take place. It all left me tired, bruised and half asphyxiated by the smoke!

In this same faith, we made our children Hindus and gave them Indian names. In my case the idea was that should anything have happened to me, my children would not be strangers in their own family. Fifteen years later when both children were old enough to think for themselves, they decided that, yes, they would live in India and be true secular Indians. Later on, I also took Indian citizenship, so that we could all be one unit.

And then we started our married life in Delhi, in King Edward Road Officers Mess[27], where Tapu was allotted accommodation. Later, sometimes when I passed in front of our old home I marvelled at how we had managed with such meagre accommodation! I remember the tree, almost a sapling then, which was growing in front of our dining room window. By "Dining Room" I meant a four by four foot recess! Now this tree is very venerable and thick, so many years and so many events have taken place in between.

Our house actually was very bare. Tapu had lost everything he had in Pakistan and my parents had lost everything in France and Vietnam. We both had just a few accessory things. A few curtains, bedding for two, few thick white crockery items, some cutlery and a "prehistoric" radio that mostly just groaned!

Our outings were morning and evening walks on the Central Vista lawns along Kingsway (now Rajpath), or visiting friends and relatives. On week days I was sorely alone, not knowing the native language, and Tapu being away the whole day. It was soon summer, and never had I known such heat! We used to joke about it when entering our suffocating flat and calling it "Home, sweet Home". We were young and very much in love and, so, what did it matter if there wasn't any desert cooler or a

---

[27] Later renamed as M.A.R. (Maulana Abul Kalam Road) Officers' Hostel, which was demolished to make way for a prestigious Government of India Building.

frigidaire (refrigerator). Our "suraahi" or earthen pitcher always gave us fresh cold water to drink.

Like everybody else at that time, Tapu went to work on a bicycle. For myself, I often hired a bicycle and kept him company for going to friends' houses or visiting socially. There was very light traffic in the streets. Connaught Place was almost innocent of cars; only "tongas" or horse-driven carts were the order of the day. They used to clip-clop on what was then Connaught Place and Connaught Circus. I found those tongas more comfortable than the ones I had known in Saigon during my childhood.

Settling down to life in India had its challenges. What Ninette found quite amazing was the variety of servants that people generally had, each one doing only one specified job: one man to only sweep and wash the floor, another to do the dishes, make the beds and dust the house. The cook prepared the meals, the washerman washed and ironed the clothes, and then there was a gardener too. In Vietnam, Ninette had seen how just one servant did all the above chores. There were problems of social adjustment, too, such as the lack of privacy, which was the experience of most Europeans in India. In Vietnam solitude for a part of the day had been mandatory. No Vietnamese would disturb a Frenchman between lunch and about 4 p.m. unless it was something serious. In Delhi there was no fixed time for anything. There was always someone knocking at the door or ringing the doorbell in the middle of the afternoon. She remembers visitors arriving even late in the night.

During all this time of the initial settling down process, Tappy was her tower of strength. His presence enabled her to cope and deal with the complex problems of life in India in the initial years. At times she wondered, and asked Tappy, whether he felt strange having a wife different from the others. And he would always reassuringly answer, "No. I don't even think about it". There was another thing that Ninette had to learn. Once a fellow officer's wife, commented, "Your husband is a Kashmiri Pandit, isn't he"? Ninette was taken aback because she knew and thought little about the caste system in India. Then she understood that Tappy was a

Kashmiri Brahmin and that was why he was referred to as Panditji in his family circle. A few years later, she found how the servants started addressing even their son Jyoti as "Pandit ji". According to Ninette, while in the outside world class distinction could be very rigid, it was nothing compared to the system in India, in those days.

Contrary to what her family in France had predicted, Ninette found that there were still a few British officers in the Indian Army. They and their wives were very warm and friendly. However, she did find that some Indian families, outside Army circles, were not as welcoming and friendly. A friend of Tappy understood her plight and advised her that she should not worry too much, as some people were still worked up against Europeans after the long struggle for independence! It was quite silly to find shopkeepers hiking up their prices shamelessly, whenever she went shopping. To beat them at this cunning practice, Tappy would usually enter a shop alone, settle the price of what they wanted to buy while Ninette was left loitering outside, out of view; then he would call her in, to the chagrin of the shopkeeper!

Ninette endured the situation philosophically. She lived in a small circle of servicemen and their families, who showered so much affection and care that the conduct and behaviour of a minuscule number of ignorant people was no more than a pinprick. Despite these initial adjustments, fate had something pleasant in store for the Rainas. Little did Tappy and Ninette dream that before the year was out they would be in England and that Ninette would meet her family again!

Personality traits are equally reflected in the personal and professional life of an individual. To separate one from the other, as one often tends to do, does not present a holistic picture of a person. In Tappy Raina, certain traits stood out very clearly: independent thinking, fearlessness and decisiveness. In him, physical strength went hand in hand with emotional strength. He also had complete clarity about what was right and what was wrong.

The spartan childhood, lack of maternal love, and the fact of being the odd one out in the family, nurtured an independent mind set with strong emotional resilience. The decision to join the army was his alone. It was taken without any consultation with the family for he was clear about it in his mind. Likewise, his decision to marry a French woman, going against tradition and family concerns, also shows his self-confidence, and his resolute and fearless disposition.

His ability to withstand serious injury, pain and debilitation without giving in to despair was also remarkable. To have twenty-nine injuries and spend months in hospital in a foreign land, without the slightest depression or discouragement is no mean achievement. When he lost his eye in Iraq at the age of twenty-one years, he did not turn to the family for consolation and strength. On the other hand, he tried to give them strength. He tended to underplay his own trials and tribulations in his concern for the well being of those who were dear to him. His commanding officer described him as "amazingly brave" while his fellow officer Edward Owen writes of his "admirable courage and will power". He remained persistently cheerful in the face of all odds. While battle is a test of courage, facing setbacks and lifelong handicaps is perhaps an even greater test and Tappy emerged with flying colours.

In a letter to his father after the loss of his right eye he said "we are supposed to fight against fate and not accept defeat" — in other words; accept fate and the bitter pill it may offer yet continue doing what one has set out to do. Giving up was just not in him. Perhaps this strength came from the *Bhagavad Gita* that remained the bedrock of his inspiration and strength. This strength of spirit had enabled Tappy to withstand peer pressure even as a youth. While his friends would raid a mango orchard he refrained from doing so because he did not consider it right. A professor giving him a character certificate described him as "dependable". It is what inspired Ninette to leave her family and native France and to sail alone on a war ship with full trust to join him in Pondicherry.

Tappy's tough exterior hid a very gentle and sensitive interior. This was reflected in the emotional letter to his uncle wherein he lauded how the uncle had "devoted his entire life for the good of others and sacrificed all his joys and comforts". It was clear that Tappy looked up to him almost with reverence. For Tappy, duty towards the family always remained paramount, even though he took his major decisions alone. Ninette found him different from his colleagues — "less brash, (less) noisy and very considerate." He was also "shy, serious and sincere".

Tappy's robust physique and sustained interest in activities that he took up became evident in his life at college, and later as a young officer in the army. The first was evident in his readiness to cycle approximately 16 kilometres every day to college and back. While in college the award of "best recruit cup" for his first year in the UTC, the position of vice-president of the rifle club and as "assistant" in the UTC detachment office were just the beginning of the many accolades he was to earn along the way. His superiors described him as "keen on work and disciplined." A fellow officer writing on his behalf from hospital spoke of "his terrific stamina, strength of heart, courage (of which no praise can be too high) and good physical standing . . . ."

When Tappy Raina dedicated himself to something, he gave it his best. This was not because he was ambitious and sought to achieve "results"; rather it was a sign of his abhorrence for mediocrity and lacklustre effort. These very qualities were to continue to impress those senior and junior to him later in life.

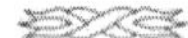

Part II

Indian Army After Partition

"Do not follow where the path may lead. Go instead where there is no path and leave a trail."

~ Ralph Waldo Emerson

Chapter 6

Life After Partition

This was a phase of tremendous professional growth where Tappy Raina's acumen, professional competence, prodigious foresight, creativity and capacity for work earned him a reputation that preceded him on each new appointment. It laid the foundation for his steady rise to positions of increasing responsibility and trust. It was also a phase of joyful family life and one of welcoming two children. Yet, it came with its challenges, particularly in the early years.

The partition of India on 15th August 1947 suddenly created a vacuum in the Indian Army due to the departure of Muslim officers who opted for Pakistan and of British officers who left India to return to Britain. As a result, promotions for officers and JCOs of the newly reorganised Indian Army came much faster than usual.

Tappy Raina had six years of army service by now which included participation in the war effort and, later, in the maintenance of law and order in the liberated countries of South East Asia. Back in India, he attended many professional courses, including the basic parachute course at Parachute Training School at Chaklala from 15th November 1946 to 30th April 1947, because 1st Battalion, the Kumaon Regiment had been selected for conversion into an air-borne battalion to form part of an Indian air-borne division. Due to the partition of India, however, 1 Kumaon (Para) became part of the Parachute Brigade of Indian Army.

In September 1947, Captain Raina was posted to the Infantry School, Mhow, as Instructor Class "C" from 29th September to 31st

December 1947. In January 1948 he was promoted to the rank of major and appointed Instructor Class-B. He was also selected for the first Defence Services Staff College course at DSSC Wellington (Nilgiri Hills) from 30th March to September 1948. Thereafter, he was appointed as GSO-2 (Ops) at the Military Operations Directorate, General Headquarters, New Delhi, an appointment which he held from 13th September 1948 to 19th July 1949. That was when Tappy and Ninette began their married life in Delhi in February 1949.

After just six months in Delhi, Tappy was selected to be the Indian Army Liaison Officer (IALO) [28] at Infantry School, Warminster[29], on the Salisbury Plains in Wiltshire (South England). Ninette just could not believe her luck! Geographically she would now be very near her parents' home in the northeast of France, just an overnight journey by ferry and train.

Tappy reported for duty at the Royal Infantry School, Warminster, on 24th August 1949. In addition, to better himself professionally, he enrolled in all the courses being run so that he could get more qualified and better prepared for his appointment as IALO. This schedule kept him busy from morning to night.

Meanwhile, Ninette was coping with her pregnancy and on 20th November 1949, she gave birth to a baby boy who was named Jyoti Narain. Ninette describes her experience of living in England thus:

> The summer went off easily, but I will always remember the winter of Warminster. Tappy used to come back at night from some training exercise or other, soaking wet and limping from chilblains. Taking off his boots was a problem and his feet were in a terrible state. He was in agony but never complained. He

---

[28] Since Independence, the Indian Army has been posting an infantry officer as IALO, who works under the Military Attaché at the Indian High Commission, London.

[29] Dating from Saxon times, Warminster is situated to the south west of Salisbury Plain, at the head of the enchantingly beautiful Wylye Valley with its attractive villages and impressive landscape.

used to look at our small son and say, "I want you and him to be proud of me".

After arriving in England, we initially spent three months in a hotel, where the Pakistani Army liaison officer was also living. One evening shortly after our arrival, both he and Tappy got talking in the lounge before a crackling fire while the two of us wives chatted. There entered a well-built elderly gentleman, who said, "How happy I am to see you both talking amicably". He was Field-Marshal William Slim! Both the officers were talking in Urdu. I remember Tappy telling me once that people who did not know him could not make out whether he was from Pakistan or India. And on top of it his mother tongue was Urdu, and not Kashmiri. He could also speak a fair Punjabi!

Tappy's tenure of duty at Warminster was for about a year and a half. Sometimes I used to get into sharp arguments concerning Vietnam. I was subjected to diatribes against colonialism of the French in Vietnam by people who had never been there but professed to know all about it. But soon I came to realise there was no point in arguing and trying to convince people who would not budge from their positions, right or wrong. It is much wiser to agree to disagree, smile and shrug, and keep one's own point of view, as it made no difference anyway. I shrugged off many things in life and found my peace of mind. I suppose that is what peaceful co-existence is about. Tappy told me once, on that account: "You are becoming a good Indian"!

Afterwards, we lived for a few months in a small flat in Warminster. It was here in Warminster that I took my first lessons in Indian cooking with Tappy as instructor!

Then we went on leave to my parental home in France and stayed with my parents. While my mother "baby-sat" our son, Jyoti (nick named Joe), Tappy and I would go and explore the surroundings. Tappy was indefatigable and wanted to see everything. His mind absorbed every information and activity like a sponge! Very soon, we had climbed all the surrounding fir-clad hills, and cycled far and wide. I had never before seen such boundless energy in Tappy, I would be left panting! After a memorable holiday with my parents, we returned to Westminster in Salisbury.

Soon, our sojourn in the Salisbury plains in Southern England came to an end on 5th January 1951. I had been very happy there and had made quite a few friends.

Back to Mhow

To utilise the knowledge acquired by Tappy at Westminster, General Headquarters (now Army HQ), New Delhi, posted him as Instructor Class "B" at Infantry School, Mhow, where he had served earlier as well.

Life in Mhow was enjoyable with plenty of cycling, swimming, reading and socialising. But there was heartbreak when the baggage arrived from the United Kingdom. The long journey had resulted in a lot of breakages. Most of the damage to breakable items had been due to hurried re-packing in the Customs shed in Bombay (now Mumbai). But with characteristic good humour and acceptance, Tappy and Ninette learnt to improvise and make do until those items could be replaced.

Ninette recalls how they were allotted an old bungalow where an old man, bent with age, occupied one of the many empty garages and stables in the huge rambling compound. Tappy had special regard for the old man for in his young years he had lost his wife and two sons, to cholera. He had told Tappy that since the death of his family members he, too, was as good as dead. Life meant nothing to him. Tappy was very touched by the old man's sentiments towards his dead wife and children. In fact, Tappy made it a point to meet and talk with all the people living in the "outhouses". He soon came to know the family history of each one of them. He showed concern for their problems and they did not hesitate to approach him in case of any difficulty. Tappy always believed that if he was in a position to help anyone he should do so. He once told Ninette how as a child he too had had lots of problems at home and knew exactly how these people felt.

There were many battles to be fought in Mhow, the first being against the stray cattle that would enter the compound at night and graze on the lawn grass. It was hard to keep a small patch of green in front of the house because water was scarce as Mhow is very hot and dry in the summer. In the 1950s it was common practice to sleep out in the garden and the Rainas initially did so. However, to wake up to a whole herd of cows around one was a little unnerving. Tappy used to refer to the herd as "Commando cows"! In addition, there were sometimes snakes at night. And so the idea of sleeping out was given up.

Sleeping indoors also had its share of alarms. One night they heard knocking at their door. Both Tappy and Ninette rushed to the door and opened it only to be met by a donkey. It appeared that the little fellow wanted company. He subsequently became a frequent visitor.

Those were happy years for Tappy and Ninette with their little son Jyoti. Life was simple and they had few needs. Tappy was happy professionally and both of them loved gardening and experimented with all sorts of plants and flowers. The gardener simply did the cleaning and watering.

It was here in Mhow that Tappy and Ninette welcomed their second child, a daughter named Anita, born on 16th October 1952, at Military Hospital, Mhow. Shortly, thereafter, Tappy received his posting orders to 4th Battalion, Gwalior Infantry Regiment: later 14 Kumaon (Gwalior), as Second-in-Command. Leaving Mhow in May 1953, he took over his new appointment on 11th May 1953. The battalion was then based in Govindgarh Fort, at the holy city of Amritsar. Ninette and the children stayed behind in Mhow for six months. In those days, separated army wives like Ninette, either went back to live with their own parents or with their parents-in-law. In Ninette's case, she was alone, for there were no women in her father-in-law's house which was really a bachelor's home.

This was the first real trial in Ninette's life as an army wife. Since there was no provision for separated family accommodation, she had to shift with her two little children from the bungalow with a huge compound to a privately hired single room. The room had no ceiling fan and was equipped with the bare minimum; one out-house for cooking, a covered veranda for the dining area and another covered recess for use as toilet with dry sanitation. The bedroom was furnished with just one single bed, one table and nothing else! Ninette bought a baby cot for Anita and a bigger bed for Jyoti who was then three-and-a-half years old. For entertainment and contact with the outside world, she had an old radio. Still she considered herself lucky for she had an ayah for the children and a good, faithful cook, Abdul. Ninette found it amusing that the cook now started addressing her as "Hazur", her son Joe was Baba Sahib and Anita was Baby Sahib!

Chapter 7

4th Gwalior Infantry

It was after a gap of over five years that Tappy Raina had reverted to regimental duty. The posting to 4 Gwalior was important both for him and also for this former state force battalion: for him, because he had to establish himself in a battalion which was not one of his "parent" regiment and, at that point, he was the first and only officer of the Kumaon Regiment in 4th Gwalior. This posting also saw the beginning of Tappy's long association with the Indo-Pakistan border in the western theatre where he was to distinguish himself at every level of command: from that of an infantry battalion to that of the Western Army command. As for all ranks of 4 Gwalior, they benefited from Tappy's immense acumen and energy in establishing themselves in the famous Kumaon Regiment in which they were soon to get integrated, as also in the Indian Army. At this point, a short background of 4 Gwalior will be useful to the reader.

4th Gwalior Infantry

The 4th Gwalior Infantry had its origins in the army raised by Mahadji Scindia. This army took part in the Third Battle of Panipat[30] in 1761 where the Marathas suffered defeat. The battalion was re-raised as Maharaja Bahadur ki Paltan[31] on 28th December 1852 by General Sir Dinkar Rao Rajwade, the then Prime Minister of Gwalior, at Lashkar (a locality near Gwalior Fort), and renamed as the 4th Infantry Gwalior in 1860. The battalion played a gallant part in assisting the Maharani of Jhansi in the Battle of Maharajpure during the Rebellion of 1857 which was crushed by British forces. When the British Crown assumed direct responsibility for ruling India, the raising and maintaining of troops by princely states was encouraged for they could be called upon in the service of the Crown, when needed. Most princely states maintained their own state forces until the partition of India in 1947. The strength of these forces depended on the size and importance of the respective state. The states of Kashmir and Gwalior had the largest and best trained armies. To assist in the training of these troops and advise the state governments on military matters, the Government of Brit-

---

[30] Site of an ancient town, approximately 85 kilometres north west of Delhi on river Yamuna, and close to Kurukshetra, where the mythological war described in the great epic *Mahabharata* took place. Its strategic importance can be noted by three historically decisive battles of Panipat in 1526, 1556 and 1761, respectively.

The 3rd Battle of Panipat on 6th January 1761 culminated two months of manoeuvres between the forces of Ahmad Shah Abdali supported by Mughal feudatories, the Rohillas and the Nawab of Awadh. Against them stood the Marathas Forces led by equally powerful chiefs; the Peshwa of Poona, Bhosle Raja of Berar, the Gaekwad of Baroda, Holkar of Indore and Scindia of Gwalior.

Though the initial tactical advantage lay with the Marathas, but a series of reverses forced the Marathas to retreat to their respective home bases. However, after plundering Delhi Ahmad Shah Abdali returned with a rich booty to Kabul, and the power vacuum in Delhi was filled by the British East India Company.

[31] In 1899, its name was changed again to 4th Gwalior Rifles and two years later to 4th Gwalior Imperial Service Infantry. In 1908 it became the 4th Gwalior Maharaja Bahadur Battalion; that name endured till 1940 when it was changed to 4th Gwalior Infantry.

ish India had an Inspector-General of Imperial Service Troops with a team of inspecting officers under him.

From 1903-1904, the Gwalior Infantry distinguished itself in the Sino-Japanese War and later was employed in the British colony of Hong Kong. The Scindias of Gwalior reorganised their state force with modern weapons and equipment at par with the British Army in India. Between the two world wars, reorganisation of the Gwalior state forces[32] took place to bring it at par with the British Indian Army.

During the First World War, 4 Gwalior Infantry was deployed in the Middle East for four years. During World War 2, the battalion once again fought alongside Indian Army in Eritrea and Ethiopia, both former colonies of Italy. The battalion also saw action in Palestine, Sicily, Haifa and Scarpanto fighting against German forces.

Post 1947 the government of newly independent India decided to integrate the armies of the princely states with the Indian Army in stages.[33] In the initial reorganisation, the state forces of central India were grouped together as Madhya Bharat Forces. These included the troops of Maharajas of Gwalior and Indore. In 1948, 4th Battalion, Gwalior Infantry, took part in Operation Polo for the liberation of Hyderabad (also known as Hyderabad Police Action). After the surrender of the Nizam of Hyderabad in September 1948, the battalion remained stationed in Hyderabad state for almost four years and operated against lawless elements that had been terrorising its Telengana region.

---

[32] After Independence and merger of princely states, it was no longer necessary for them to maintain their own state forces. It was decided in principle, to integrate their state forces with the Indian Army.

[33] Initially, such troops were grouped regionally. Then the officers and men were put through a process of screening for their suitability for service with Indian Army. The final stage was reached on 1st April 1951 when the transfer of selected units and personnel to the Indian Army took place.

Amritsar

The battalion moved from Hyderabad to Amritsar in June 1952 and was billeted in the historic Gobindgarh Fort. To integrate the 4th Gwalior Infantry with the Indian Army, it was decided, initially, to merge it with the Rajput Regiment. However, in February 1953, these orders were revised and 4 Gwalior and Indore infantry battalions were ordered to be merged with the Kumaon Regiment. In May 1953, their designations were changed to 14th Battalion, the Kumaon Regiment (Gwalior), and 15th Battalion, the Kumaon Regiment (Indore), respectively. The suffixes “Gwalior” and “Indore” enabled both battalions to maintain links with their past history.

The formal admission of these two battalions into the Kumaon Regiment took place on 27th October 1954 (Kumaon Day) when Lieutenant. General (later General and COAS) K.S. Thimayya, DSO, Colonel of the Kumaon Regiment, presented the two battalions with regimental flags at the Kumaon Regimental Centre in Ranikhet.

After a gap of five years Major Tappy Raina reverted to regimental duty, but not to 1 Kumaon (Para) as he had become a “Non-Para” volunteer. Instead, he was selected by Army Headquarters for posting as Second-in-Command of 4th Gwalior Infantry, and Tappy came with impressive credentials. He had seen active service in World War 2, in two separate theatres where he had been Mentioned-in-Despatches. He had held important instructional appointments, besides having qualified at Defence Services Staff College (DSSC), Wellington. In addition, he had held a Grade-2 appointment at Military Operations Directorate, GHQ, New Delhi, where he gained experience of operational planning at the highest level of the army during the Indo-Pak War of 1947-48. Tappy was now a married man with two young children.

When Major T.N. Raina reported for duty as second in command to 4 Gwalior in May 1953, the Officer Commanding was Lieutenant Colonel J.R. Mehra, who had been commanding the Battalion when it was affiliated to Rajput Regiment, prior to its merger with Kumaon Regiment. With the merger of the 4th Gwalior Infantry as 14th Battalion, the Kumaon Regiment, it now became the responsibility of Kumaon Regiment to provide regular officers for the complete integration and reorientation of all ranks to professional standards compatible with the rest of the regiment. Tappy Raina's posting to 4 Gwalior was important both for him personally and for the battalion. Not only did he have to establish himself in a battalion which was new to him, but he was also the first and only officer of the Kumaon Regiment posted to this battalion.

Tappy joined the battalion which was then barracked in Fort Gobindgarh, Amritsar, as part of 123 Infantry Brigade. This fort had been built in the 18th century by a Bhangi Misl chieftain. Later, Maharaja Ranjit Singh enhanced and fortified it, as it defended the invasion route from the west to the Harmandar Sahib, the Golden Temple at Amritsar. The Maharaja named it after the tenth Sikh Guru, Gobind Singh. In its Toshkhana (treasury), it is said, was kept the famed Kohinoor diamond. It is also believed that a tunnel connected Gobindgarh to the capital, Lahore.

After the Second Anglo-Sikh War in 1849, the fort was captured by the British and later garrisoned by the British Indian Army. After the partition, Indian Army units were stationed in Gobindgarh Fort[34] for the next fifty years.

The fort has an impressive gate, an outer wall with numerous gun emplacements, surrounded by a moat and an inner wall. On the ramparts were barracks which housed the troops. There was a circular inner courtyard with a road along its perimeter. Almost in the middle was a mound on top of which the Officers' Mess and six single officers' suites were located. Tappy Raina moved into one of these suites.

Tappy's focus in his new post was to integrate this newly inducted state force battalion, the 4th Gwalior Infantry into the fold

---

[34] Finally, this fort was taken over by the civil authorities of Punjab, and is now open to the public as a major tourist attraction.

of Kumaon Regiment, blending its rich history with that of their new regiment. Because of its prolonged overseas deployment from 1940-45, the upheaval of Partition, and the reorganisation consequent to integration, the cohesion and administration in the battalion had suffered. Even so, the men and junior commissioned officers (JCOs) had great pride in their ancestry and traditions. The biggest void, felt sorely by the officers, was the absence in the Officers' Mess of all those things which make it respectable: old records, photo albums, war trophies, exotic artefacts and memorabilia of service and battles in distant lands, mahogany and redwood furniture, leather sofas, billiard tables, paintings, and so on. The ex-Gwalior state force officers, who were still serving with the battalion had explained, though not very convincingly, that the need of an officers' mess was never felt because in peacetime the battalion had always been located at Morar, the Military Cantonment of Gwalior State. All the entertaining and regimental functions were held at the Maharaja of Gwalior's palace.

Tappy had the difficult and challenging task of helping the new battalion adopt the customs and traditions of Kumaon Regiment. In addition, he had to introduce the prevailing system of administration, accounting, interior-economy, standards of individual and collective training as prevalent in Indian Army.

The 123 Infantry Brigade located at Amritsar had two infantry battalions under its command. In addition to 4th Gwalior, there was 1st Sikh Light Infantry, which was located at Khasa, close to Attari on the international border with Pakistan. The brigade headquarters and ancillary units like independent artillery battery, supply depot and the EME workshop were based in Amritsar Cantonment, off the Grand Trunk Road, about five kilometres from Fort Gobindgarh. Here, in the fort, were located the Flag Staff House for the brigade commander, and a few bungalows for married officers. The brigade commander was Brigadier G.I.S. Khullar, Punjab Regiment. His brigade major (BM) was Major (later Lieutenant General) Zorawar Chand Bakshi, VrC. Major Bakshi was known as "Zoru" to friends and he later became the most decorated General officer of the Indian Army.[35] "Zoru" Bakshi's career ran almost parallel to, and just one step behind, that of Tappy Raina's. Both were thorough professionals and had mutual personal and professional respect, so it is no surprise that they became lifelong friends.

The tenure for 4 Gwalior at Amritsar was typical of the peacetime routine followed in the Indian Army of that period. About such tenures of an infantry battalion, it was commonly believed that though it was peacetime, there was hardly any peace. Besides high pitched individual specialist and collective training, there were promotion cadrės, battalion training events and sports competitions. There were also brigade events like sand model discussions and tactical exercises without troops (TEWT). In addition, the more senior officers of the battalion proceeded to other stations on temporary duty, to participate in divisional level events, thus making it an extremely packed training calendar.

---

[35] Lieutenant General Z. C. Bakshi, PVSM, MVC, Vr C, VSM, had commanded a Battalion of 5 Gorkha Rifles, as Brigade Commander captured Haji Pir Pass, later, he was GOC 26 Infantry Division and GOC 2 Corps. He was also Military Secretary at Army HQ.

Chapter 8

Life in the Battalion

Life in the Battalion with Tappy Raina as Second-in-Command is best understood through the experiences of those that served under him. Ravi Mahajan was one such officer who was commissioned as Second Lieutenant in 4th Gwalior Infantry, after passing out from the Indian Military Academy in June 1953. His first predicament at having been posted to this Battalion was that no one at IMA knew of its antecedents. So Mahajan surmised that it must be a battalion from one of the ex-princely states. His fellow Gentlemen cadets at the academy pulled his leg telling him that he would have to forget the "salute" that had been taught at the Academy's Drill Square and instead learn the royal courtesy of the Maharaja's Court — *"farshi sallam"* or bowing to the superior! To add to his consternation was the fact that even the tailor shop at the academy could not produce the Gwalior Infantry cap badge and shoulder titles. He searched other shops in town and ultimately one shop near Ghanta Ghar (Clock Tower) in Dehra Dun town yielded the priceless item. When Second Lieutenant Mahajan arrived at Amritsar Railway Station, he was utterly mortified when Captain Kazi Sapru, the officer who had come to receive him at the station, pointed out that the battalion's cap badge was silver and not the brass that Mahajan was wearing!

It was only on joining duty that Mahajan learnt that the 4 Gwalior was 101 years old and had taken part in both world wars. Post-independence, it had also been employed in the Hyderabad police action. Second Lieutenant Mahajan was the first regular

Tappy Raina as a student of FC College, Lahore.

Champion Platoon at OTA Mhow: Cdt L/Cpl J.F.R. Jacob is carrying the Banner; Cdt "Tapu" Raina is to his right (4th from left).

Saigon 1945: The jeep in which Tappy used to visit Ninette and her family.

Pulgoan 1947: 1 Kumaon (Para) returns to India after World War 2.
Tappy Raina is seated in the middle.

Tappy and Ninette's marriage by Arya Samaj rites on 25th February 1949 at Clement Town, Dehradun.

Major T.N. Raina as Instructor Class "B", Sniper Wing, Infantry School Mhow, 1953.

Three generations: Mr A.N. Raina visiting Tappy, Ninette and grand children, Jyoti (Joe) and Anita Raina at Mhow, 1953.

On the occasion of the Centenary Celebration of 4th Gwalior Infantry at Amritsar on 28th December 1953. Major Tappy Raina (2nd from right) with fellow serving and retired of cers and JCOs.

Visit by General T.N. Raina, MVC, COAS to his alma mater, DSSC Wellington. Maj Gen A.M. Sethna, Commandant DSSC is on his left, while Maj Yogesh Prasad, Dy MA to COAS and Capt Dara J. Govadia, ADC to COAS are walking behind.

Addressing the student of cers and staff of DSSC Wellington.

Another view of the audience listening to the lecture by COAS.

Ninette with Joe and Anita in Nainital before Tappy's departure for Ladakh in August 1962.

IAF Dakotas were the lifeline of Ladakh Sector from 1949 to 1962 (Photo courtesy: Wg Cdr S.S. Randhawa IAF Retd).

Tappy Raina on a frozen Pangong Tso in the Chushul Sector in Ladakh.

Kumaon Memorial erected in memory of the valorous Ahirs of "C" Coy, 13 Kumaon, who fought most bravely at Rezang La at Chushul in 1962.

officer to be directly posted from IMA Dehra Dun on the grant of Permanent Commission, to 4th Gwalior Infantry after it became a part of Indian Army.

After a formal interview with his Commanding Officer, Lieutenant Colonel J.R. Mehra, Mahajan was attached to one of the rifle companies. His first meeting with Major Raina took place the following day at breakfast in the Officers' Mess. As he entered the dining hall, Mahajan saw a person already seated at the dining table, reading a newspaper. Mahajan described it thus:

> "Good Morning, Sir", I said as nonchalantly as I could and without coming to attention, to the person seated on the dining table, hidden behind *The Statesman* newspaper. The person looked at me over the newspaper and I instantly knew, from Kazi's briefing, that he was Major Tappy Raina, because his one eye looked artificial. But the gaze of his other eye seemed to pierce through me. Tappy had a broad forehead, a characteristically Kashmiri Pandit (hook) nose, a square face, straight and neatly brushed jet-black hair and a (firm) jutting jaw.
>
> "Humph", was the response to my greeting before he disappeared behind the newspaper again. Seated opposite him, I tried to concentrate on my porridge and, later, eggs. In due course, the major neatly folded the paper, poured himself a coffee, placed his serviette on the table and, fixing his left eye on me, asked, "Why did you join the Army"?
>
> I had been asked this question before. The first time, it was from the psychologist at the Services Selection Board, more than four years ago. My answer then and now to Major Raina was: "To earn a living"!
>
> The major pushed back his chair and stood up. He was short, broad and robust. He walked out of the room. His stride was that of a man who had planned to accomplish important things during the day.

After Major Raina's departure, Second Lieutenant Mahajan breathed more easily and finished his breakfast at leisure. Like any young officer, he wondered what kind of impression he had made on Major Raina.[36]

As he settled down to his new life in the battalion, Mahajan felt that he had been given multifarious duties: running of the officers' mess, doing boards, courts of inquiry, drafting unit standing orders. All these were, of course, in addition to his main function as a rifle platoon commander for which he received orders from his company commander. For each task, he received guidance from the battalion second-in-command, Major Raina. Of the correspondence received from Brigade Headquarters by the Battalion, at least one letter everyday sought "comments" or "views" on some military subject. Major Raina would task Mahajan to draft replies to such letters. He would give him the relevant references and reading material and then say, "There is no particular hurry; you can let me have the draft reply tomorrow morning!"

On a particularly hot afternoon one day, Mahajan heard the sound of rifle fire. On inquiry, he was told that Major Raina was practicing firing on the short range, so that despite being partially visually handicapped, his military skills would not be diluted. In the same way he trained himself to play golf; and continuous, persistent practice at the game enabled him to focus on the ball with only one eye, a difficult task. He never hid his infirmity behind dark glasses.

In early 1954, Second Lieutenant Mahajan was detailed to do a pre-course training for the Platoon Weapons Officers' (PWO) course at Infantry School, Mhow. It was normally the first army course a young infantry officer of the battalion attended. During the pre-course training, however, seven NCOs were also selected to train with him. The pre-course training was hard and having been grouped with sub-ordinate ranks, Mahajan tried, perhaps for

---

[36] Little did Mahajan know at the time that Major Raina would become his mentor, friend and confidant and would, in due course, attain the top rung of the professional ladder. Also, that he would suffer irreparable personal loss and that Mahajan would weep with him and, later, for him when he became incurably ill in a foreign land, twenty-seven years later.

the first time in his life, to outperform the rest. Tappy kept a close watch on his progress.

At Indian Military Academy, Mahajan had secured 82nd position in order of merit, from among 181 gentlemen cadets (GC). Thus, he was considered "average" at the Academy. Neither was he proficient in sports, or at least not up to the standard that was then required. But Tappy Raina had high expectations of him. The evening before Mahajan left for Mhow, Tappy called for him and said, "You have prepared well. We would like you to stand first in the course."

"I will try my best," said Mahajan, "but, Sir, how does one stand first?"

Tappy's reply was typical of him: "The course consists of a number of parts: lessons in handling weapons, bayonet training, instructional practices and firing. Be the first in each part and you will be the first in the Course." Tappy did not believe in shortcuts!

The way Second Lieutenant Mahajan was introduced to the regimental culture, its training and, above all, being accepted in the battalion, became, in due course, a tradition. Future young officers and junior leaders were similarly trained, and became worthy officers, JCOs and NCOs, not only of the battalion but of the entire Kumaon Regiment. Although Second Lieutenant Mahajan did not pass out of IMA high in the order of merit, he went on, nevertheless, to excel in all army training courses and obtained a "D" (Distinguished) grading on the Junior Commander (JC) Course at Infantry School (now War College) at Mhow, Madhya Pradesh. This highest grading was rarely awarded then, and even subsequently.[37]

Mahajan attributed these distinctions to the mentoring he received from Major Raina after joining 4th Gwalior. It is typical of the kind of support Tappy gave to numerous others who served with him at various levels. At the same time, Tappy had little time

---

[37] Mahajan was later selected to undergo the Associated Officer's Career Course at the US Army Infantry School at Fort Benning, Georgia, United States. At this course he was adjudged Distinguished Honours Graduate from amongst 191 officers drawn from US Army and many other armies of the world.

for shirkers and slackers. He set a high example and was an inspiration to many who were later to be his colleagues, sub-ordinate commanders and staff officers.

The commanding officer of the Battalion, Lieutenant Colonel Mehra, formerly of Mahar Regiment, was known amongst the officers as the "old man" although he couldn't have been more than thirty-two years old at that time. According to Mahajan, Colonel Mehra was short, broad, fair and handsome. He appeared genial but was a strict disciplinarian. The harshest possible punishment within his power was meted out to the defaulters in his orderly room. He was very stingy about granting casual leave, even of the shortest duration but he was hot on administration. Thus, activities like kit, line and stores inspection, condemnation, stock-taking and audit boards, framing and updating standing orders found him in his element.

Besides Tappy Raina, other officers in the battalion included Sayyad, Patrick and Naqvi, all of whom were Majors. Those of the rank of Captain, included Katju, Ramadhar, Phogat, Sapru, Hanspal and Ranvir. Their backgrounds were varied: Katju and Sapru were scions of famous Kashmiri families. Ramadhar and Phaggy (as Phogat was called) had their forebears in the army. Others came from a variety of different backgrounds. Mahajan's father was a university professor.

Ramadhar, a Rajpput from Balia in UP, commanded "D" Company. He had risen from the ranks to become a JCO as Jemadar (present Naib Subedar) Quartermaster of 4 Rajput during World War 2. Later he was granted commission as an officer. Habitually, he went into every detail of training and administration, minutely. Such thoroughness kept his company at a high professional standard. So it was "D" Company that had the best stick orderly, the best quarter guard, the best Kote and the best documentation in the battalion. If an NCO of his company was due for promotion, he was made highly visible in the battalion and Ramadhar lobbied for him most cleverly and ensured that he got promoted.

The Katjus, that is Gyani Bhai and his graceful wife Malti, were the most likeable couple in the Gwaliors. Mahajan's company commander, Major Khulque Hussain Naqvi, was addressed by everyone as "Nawab Sahib". He was short, stocky and bald. An inveterate pipe-smoker, Nawab Sahib was easy going, always cool, calm and imperturbable. He accepted life as it came and was never petty. He allowed his senior "sirdar" (JCO) Subedar Satnam Singh to run the company pretty much as the latter pleased.

Major Patrick who commanded "A" Company was referred to as "Shikari" though no one knew why he had earned that name. Shikari was indolent and not always a good example. Major Sayyad was the senior-most company commander. Though in service he was even senior to Major Raina; but he was not found fit enough by Military Secretary, Army HQ, to be appointed as the Battalion's Second-in-Command.[38] The fact that he should rank next to an officer junior to him in service was not to Major Sayyad's liking, and he made no effort to hide his feelings. He frequently resented instructions emanating from Major Raina. Tappy, however, had to be very firm and he made sure that his writ was implemented

Kazi Sapru and Ranvir were originally commissioned in the Garhwal Rifles. It was said that to "serve with Garhwalis was to love them." Thus, it took Kazi and Ranvir many years to forget Garhwal Rifles and become real Kumaonis, but when they did, they were among the staunchest Kumaonis. Hanspal had a lot of go in him. With numerous initials before his surname — D.S.M.S. — he came to be referred to as "Dismiss". Phogat (Phaggy) came from the Grenadiers, in which regiment his father had also served. An archetypical Adjutant, he was never to be found without a notebook in which he recorded the point given to him by the Commanding Officer during his rounds and at conferences.

[38] In those days, the Second in Command was posted by name, after selection by the Military Secretary at Army Headquarters. Normally an officer who was likely to be selected for promotion to the rank of Lieutenant Colonel and command the battalion, was appointed as Second in Command of Infantry Battalion.

Although transferred to 4th Gwalior Infantry, most of these officers were still emotionally attached to their parent regiments. They fervently hoped that some favourable tide would take them back. And it fell upon the shoulders of the only officer hailing from Kumaon Regiment, Major Raina, to build and generate that special love and pride for their new Regiment amongst all officers of the 4th Gwalior, which would make them lead their men through the thick and thin of professional challenges.

Tappy introduced "*chancharis*" or Kumaoni dance tunes into the band repertoire. Soon, officers and their wives were dancing to the lusty singing of *Nainitalo*, *Chhaina-bilori* and *Bheru-Pako*. The process thus initiated had to be continued and, in Mahajan's reckoning, it was not until 1960 that the Gwaliors became true Kumaonis.

The senior among the officers wore a number of war ribbons. However, except for Tappy and Ramadhar, none, including the Commanding Officer, had been bloodied in battle. Some had never gone beyond the shores of India, despite the fact that they were in service during Second World War. Differences of opinions often arose among the officers, especially where procedures, methods and norms were involved. Clearly the officers had to do a lot of living together and achieve much more collectively before they would attain the amity, confidence and pride of a winning team.

In the next few years, the older officers moved out to softer appointments which their age and years of service demanded. Younger officers joined from other Kumaon battalions or from the Indian Military Academy to form a strong core of officers. The team got honed and all Ranks of the Battalion began to swagger as they realised that they had the competitive edge in numerous areas over other battalions.

Family and Social Life in the Battalion

The married officers lived in hired houses or in bungalows in the cantonment. They all lived very simply and were sticklers as far as "form" were concerned. Only the Commanding Officer had a car. All other officers cycled to work. When ladies and children had to attend an organised function in the battalion, a truck with chairs or benches placed inside, brought them, and the officers were charged in their respective mess bills for this "amenity". Ice and soda for the evening peg generally came out of an icebox and not from a refrigerator. Despite the low pay and allowances, officers invested their meagre savings in educating their children in public schools where they not only received good education but also developed all round personalities. Many officers did so at great personal sacrifice.

When Tappy was finally allotted married accommodation at Amritsar, he went to Mhow to bring his family and the household baggage by train. On their way north to Punjab, the family travelled across central India and broke journey in Ludhiana to visit Tappy's father and uncle.

Upon reaching Amritsar, Ninette and the children settled down in a house which Ninette described as follows:

> Our two bedrooms were on one side of a big house and the living room was on the opposite side of the house. It was winter and very cold in Amritsar and I just could not keep warm. Moreover, it appeared to me as if all the flies of India had made our bedroom their headquarters! But the garden was nice, green and open and well-manicured. There we had many happy cups of coffee in the sun with the young officers of the unit.

Ninette adapted to regimental life at grass root level for the first time. Here, she involved herself in family welfare activities with missionary zeal.

On 28th December 1953, 4 Gwalior celebrated their centenary, one year later than due. All ranks of the Battalion lent a hand in organising the event and participated whole heartedly. It was decided to hold a centenary commemoration parade, a battalion durbar (now referred to as sainik sammelan), a *Pagal-Gymkhana* (a fun fare) along with a *Meena Bazar* and a *Bara Khana*.

One of the senior officers of the battalion had volunteered to make the fruit cocktail and agreed to reach the Officers' Mess half an hour before the arrival of guests. Second Lieutenant Mahajan was there well before the appointed time of the function to check all the arrangements regarding seating, illumination, food and drinks. Noticing that the senior officer was nowhere to be found, Mahajan got worried for he had no idea how a cocktail was prepared. So he sought the advice of the Mess Waiter, Amar Bahadur, who seemed to know something about everything. Amar Bahadur rattled off what he thought were the ingredients: rum, gin, vodka, lime-juice, mint and Worcester sauce. Mahajan asked him to have all these ready in the pantry.

When only a few minutes remained for the guests to arrive, Mahajan decided to act without waiting any further for the wayward major. Into a bucket he poured bottle after bottle from the stock Amar Bahadur had lined up. Some crushed ice was also thrown in and the concoction vigorously stirred. Mahajan sipped it and found it not too distasteful! The spirit was then poured into a large cocktail bowl and placed near the entrance to the Mess. It was indeed a powerful potion. Anyone who had a glass of it shot straight into orbit and had very little urge left to imbibe other drinks. The wine bill of the party thereby was much reduced.

The celebration was a great success and the *Meena Bazar* organized by Ninette Raina and ladies of the battalion as the first of its kind was a particular success.

This happy family life for the Rainas lasted just three months. The battalion was then ordered to move north to a field area and families had, once again, to fend for themselves.

Chapter 9

The "Hell Division" and Dalhousie

Tappy moved with 4 Gwalior to the field area in Jammu and Kashmir, to be operationally deployed in the 25 Infantry Division Sector. Major General U.C. Dubey was the General Officer Commanding of 25 Infantry Division (he lived to complete a hundred years!).

After the Indo-Pakistan War of 1947-48, this sector remained highly under-developed with a long Cease Fire Line (CFL) running through it. It came to be known as the "Hell Division" perhaps because of the long tortuous journey along unmetalled winding roads that ran from Akhnoor through Sunderbani, Naushehra and Rajauri to Poonch. During the rainy season, the road became slushy and slippery and was prone to landslides. In dry weather, dust covered everyone travelling as they were in World War 2 vintage 3-ton trucks. The halt at the transit camp at Narian[39], almost midway to Poonch, was most welcome for refreshments and overnight stay for those heading onward.

4 Gwalior was part of 120 Infantry Brigade with headquarters at Galuthi on the road from Rajauri[40] to Poonch. The Brigade was

[39] As per local folk lore, it was here that after the death of Mughal Emperor Jahangir on his return journey from Srinagar to Lahore, his intestines were removed by the Royal Hakim and secretly buried, and the death of Jahangir was kept secret till after reaching Lahore.

[40] Tradition has it that the Kingdom of the Panchals was located here. Draupadi, the daughter of the Panchal king married the five Pandava princes (story from the epic *Mahabharata)*

commanded by Brigadier Sher Jung Thapa, MVC, popularly known as the Lion of Skardu.[41] The Battalion was based at Sarol, a scenic place in the broad valley leading up to the hills, while two rifle companies were located at posts on a high ridge: one at Pir Badeshar, which was the most dominating feature in this sector and from where, on most clear nights, one could see the lights of Marala Headworks near Sialkot in Pakistan. The other rifle company was located at Lisrian and Ramgarh Fort. These were observation posts which sent out small patrols and were also listening posts at night for watch and ward against any intruders. The civilian population was sparse, mainly graziers who grazed sheep and cattle, commonly called *Bakarwals*.

It was a period of relative peace on this border. Minor incidents did occur mainly due to disputes relating to the Cease Fire Line. Then the United Nations observers, with an insatiable thirst for beer, would descend from their headquarters at Srinagar to adjudicate.

At the Battalion Headquarters at Sarol, Major Tappy Raina oversaw training, promotion cadres and field firing at the nearby ranges. He was instrumental in improving the living environment, setting up a new information room and constructing messes, both for officers and for the junior commissioned officers. After taking over the operational responsibility of the posts, Tappy Raina, Battalion 2IC, visited these routinely and made it a point to spend at least one night at each post. He, thereby, ensured that troops were familiar with their operational tasks. He checked and corrected the arcs of fire of the automatic weapons, the siting of platoon Mortars (defensive fire i.e. DF tasks) of 2-inch, 3-inch and 4.2-inch. He also guided the commanders of the rifle company regarding the observation and listening posts and night patrolling tasks and planned ambush areas. To accompany Tappy on such a visit was a

---

[41] Skardu was the summer capital of Ladakh where, despite having been surrounded by Pakistan Army, Lt. Col. Sher Jung Thapa inspired his troops to resolutely defend Skardu. After an epic fight, Thapa became short of men, ammunition and rations and thus surrendered on 14th August 1948.

learning experience for any young officer. While walking in the hills, he always set a brisk pace for everyone.

Before leaving Fort Gobindgarh (Amritsar) for his Battalion's employment in Field Area, Tappy had made arrangements for his family to stay at Dalhousie (now in Himachal Pradesh), a nearby hill station close to Pathankot. So while Tappy settled in the "Hell Division" Ninette found settling down in Dalhousie a challenge of a different sort. She described her experience thus:

> So at the beginning of 1954, a wife, two children and two servants migrated to the Himalayan Hill Station called Dalhousie, under rain and snow. Our family specialised in moving to the hills in winter and to the plains in the middle of the summer! We found ourselves in a deserted place; most people had gone to spend the winter in the sunny plains!
>
> Soon after our arrival, it snowed and snowed and then it rained and rained and we could barely keep warm. My children saw snow for the first time. Regular electricity supply was a problem; only a few hours a day, early morning and evenings. At 9 p.m., it was lights out. And if it rained in the day we were in the dark. Supplies were a problem, too. One lived mostly on lentils (dal) and potatoes. We had meat only once a week. Eggs were almost non-existent in the winter. But it, too, passed; suddenly it was spring and life improved and became glorious.
>
> Mail was a God-sent event. Our only visitors were "langoors" and monkeys, rumbling on our metal roof and sliding down the rain water drains and pipes. There were some wild animals also, bears and hyenas. But as there was no dog with us, they left us alone. The only beauty was our location, situated on the flank of a hill, overlooking a deep valley closed at its end by the Bakloh Cantonment. It was a beautiful view. For away in the distance, the yellow and brown patches of the plains could be seen.

There was only one civilian doctor in Dalhousie, and in winter, he wasn't there at all. So if there was any problem with the children, I was forced to walk down to the Military Hospital, down in Balloon, as the Cantonment was called. If it was raining it became an expedition indeed, and often the cook had to come with me to carry a sick child. It was only towards the end of our stay that the Army came back in force to Dalhousie at the closing of 1954.

Joe and Anita were growing up and I was very involved with them. By now they were old enough to enjoy Dalhousie. As I said they had never seen snow before. Joe had, in England, where he was born. But he could obviously not remember the mornings I let him sleep in the snow, warmly tucked in his pram with blankets and a hot water bottle to keep his little limbs warm, as was the custom with all British children. At Dalhousie, he thought snow was some kind of stone and kept filling his pockets with it only to have it melt down his clothes. Joe spoke only Hindi, and a little French. So to familiarise him with English, he was sent to the local convent when he was four years old; instead, he learnt fluent Punjabi, which other children spoke, and hardly any English, in spite of all the efforts of teachers.

Tappy came to see us a few times till, the unit left for the North. And, then, in October 1954 he arrived quite suddenly, now a Lieutenant Colonel posted as an instructor to the Defence Services Staff College, Wellington, in the Nilgiris.

After working very hard to integrate 4th Gwalior Infantry as a valuable member of the elite Kumaon Regiment, Major Raina received his promotion-cum-posting order. He was to be GSO-1/Instructor Class "A" in the rank of Lieutenant Colonel at the Defence Services Staff College, Wellington (Nilgiris). As he left the region of "Hell Division", little did he know that destiny would bring him back there several years later as its General Officer Commanding (GOC).

After collecting Ninette and the two children from Dalhousie, the family drove down to Pathankot, from where they boarded the train to the Nigiris. Thus, commenced another of the many long train journeys that the Raina family was to undertake. The journey from Pathankot to Mettupalaiyam near Coimbatore entailed spending over four days and three nights in the train. From Mettupalaiyam the family travelled by road to Wellington although there was the option of a narrow-gauge train. The day after reaching Wellington, Lieutenant Colonel Raina reported for duty on 19th October 1954.

Chapter 10

Defence Services Staff College, Wellington (Nilgiris)

The Defence Services Staff College (DSSC), where Lieutenant Colonel Raina had been posted to, is an inter-service training institution. It trains officers of all the three services of the Indian armed forces for command and staff appointments, and also those from friendly foreign countries. Founded in 1905 it is one of the oldest military training establishments in India.

Background of the DSSC

In 1856 the British Indian Army felt the need for specially trained officers to improve their military efficiency. The Staff College to train British officers in organisational skills and intellect was thus set up at Sandhurst. In 1862, the college shifted to Camberley. When Lord Kitchener became the Commander-in-Chief of Indian Army in 1905, an Indian Staff College, similar to the one at Camberley, was established temporarily in Deolali (Maharashtra). It was finally shifted to Quetta in Baluchistan (now in Pakistan). Officers who graduated from the Staff College came to be regarded as the "brains-trust" of the British Indian Army. Their role was to advise on strategically important matters, supervise training of officers and men, study military plans, collect and collate military intelligence and direct the general policy in army matters. The first King's Commissioned Indian Officer (KCIO) to attend the 1933-34 Staff Course was Captain K.M. Cariappa (later the first Indian

Commander in Chief and Field Marshal). Several future army and air force chiefs, heads of state and future commandants of Defence Services Staff College, Wellington had attended the short war courses at Quetta during the Second World War.

After partition, the Staff College was shifted to Wellington situated in the picturesque surroundings of the Nilgiri Hills (the Blue Mountains). Wellington was a suitable location because the hills were ideal for mountain warfare exercises, the nearby Coimbatore plains for mobile warfare, and the Mysore jungles were reasonably easy to reach. The college was designated as Defence Services Staff College (DSSC) and its opening ceremony took place on 5th April 1948. It was set up by Col. S.D. Verma who was also appointed as the first officiating Commandant.

The first interim course of twenty weeks' duration commenced on Monday, 5th April 1948. It had fifty student officers, selected by the respective service headquarters on the basis of their reports from the units and qualification (not less than B grading) at the Tactics and Administration School. Another pre-requisite for selection to the course was a recommendation by the Infantry School commandant. Officers who completed the interim course were to be awarded the symbol "isc". This distinguished them from others.

The interim course was designed to train officers for grade three staff appointments at various military formations; and to select some outstanding student officers for grade two staff appointments. This policy was to continue with these courses till it was possible to resume full courses, with the object of training officers for command and Grade-2 employment. Major Tapishwar Narain Raina and Squadron Leader H. Moolgaonker were students of this first interim course and went on to become the chiefs of their respective services.

By 1950, the institution was transformed into a fully integrated Defence Services Staff College, imparting training to officers of the three services of the armed forces in the company of some selected officers from the Indian civil services, central police organisations and from friendly foreign countries.

Life in Wellington

In recognition of his outstanding performance on staff, instructional and regimental duties, Army Headquarters selected Major Raina for promotion and appointment as GSO-1/Instructor Class "A" in the rank of Lieutenant Colonel at DSSC, Wellington. Colonel Raina reported for duty and assumed his new appointment as Instructor at DSSC on 19th October 1954. Colonel (later Lieutenant General) Prem Bhagat, VC, was the Chief Instructor.

Ninette described the process of settling down at Wellington and the life there as under:

> Compared to the kind of married quarters that we had lived in so far, accommodation at Wellington was palatial! Even the wooden floors were polished and not painted. The children also had good schools. Keeping house was a thrilling affair. The climate was nice if rather mild and humid, people polite and gentle and for us, it was a lovely stay, which lasted three years. There were flowers everywhere, rounded hills so easy to climb and explore, little lanes and paths all over the area. Life included horse riding in the morning, club meetings and socials, weekly shopping expeditions to the town with a "brunch" of coffee and snacks before returning to home, loaded to the gills with supplies.
>
> Although we had enough vegetables growing in our kitchen garden, normally, three of us friends used to hire a car and go shopping for a week's supplies of house hold needs. Husbands did not like these shopping days for it meant lonely lunches for them!
>
> Pets were very much loved in our house. In Wellington we acquired an Irish setter dog. That was a great joy in the house. Tappy was so gentle with the pup that it wanted all the time to sit on his lap. That posed some problems when the dog was full grown. And one day I introduced a cat in the house. Tappy nearly blew a fuse! He did not like cats. "Because you are not used to them," I said. Tappy declared vehemently that the "dratted thing" would not be allowed in his room. One day I caught

the cat stretched out on his bed and Tappy was petting it! He admitted grudgingly that my "Siamese" was a well-behaved cat and when she had kittens he changed his tune. "Never would I have believed", he said," that cats can be such good mothers, even better than humans"!

We had a birthday party for both our children. Tappy was the biggest child of them all, running all over the garden with a shrieking mob of children behind him. He was just like a six year old boy and I am sure he enjoyed himself, certainly more than his children! And when on Sundays I did not have enough partners to play mah-jong, there was Tappy crossed-legged on the carpet, playing with us very seriously and enthusiastically. He was a great hit with my friends.

Our children, Jyoti (Joe) and Anita, were then five and two, respectively. For the first few months of our arrival, both children were admitted in the Staff College Nursery School. Later, our son, Joe, started going to school in Lower Conoor.[42] It was a long way on foot for a boy who by then was hardly six, two miles each way, carrying his bag and a lunchbox. In the beginning the other boys used to bully him. When we got tired of seeing Joe returning home every day with torn clothes and scratches all over him, I made him understand that nobody could fight his battles for him when we were not there. He had to fight back even if he lost; going down fighting was the honourable thing to do. He was not to accept any beating. He did listen and started fighting back. Within a year, complaints started coming that he was thrashing other boys. But Tappy and I maintained that children ought to sort out their own problems themselves without interference from parents, except in the serious cases.

[42] Conoor, a nearby hill station, known for its tea estates in the surrounding Nilgiri hills. Sim's Park is a sprawling public garden with plants like rhododendrons, roses and eucalyptus trees. The steam Nilgiri Mountain Railway travels between the towns of Mettupalayam and Ooty via Coonoor. Dolphin's Nose is a vantage point with views of the cascading Catherine Falls.

> At Wellington, an Inspector of Police used to visit the Staff College regularly to keep an eye on the many foreigners there. I was also one of them in those days. The first time he came to my house he took all my particulars; when did I come to India first; when and why did I leave France? When did I go to London and when did I return? We parted as good friends.
>
> The week after that he (Police Inspector) was back, stiff-looking and severe. He blurted out: "You did not tell me the whole truth". Aghast I let him have his say. The first question was: "You left India on 25th July 1949 and reached London on 15th August. Madam, where were you in between those dates?" I just laughed at him and replied "but I was at sea, on a ship"! Never have I seen a man looking so silly. He had no more questions to ask me and made a hurried departure.

After very happy and satisfying three-year tenure at Wellington, it was time for the Rainas to leave the Nilgiris and move to the north-west of India. This time the destination was Ferozepur Cantonment in Punjab. Tappy had received his posting orders to take over as Commanding Officer, 14th Battalion, the Kumaon Regiment (Gwalior), with which he had already had a close association.

Ninette remembers leaving Wellington in pouring rain with two small children, a dog, servants, luggage, all the while looking longingly one last time at the tall blue hills where the family had been so happy for three years. They piled into the toy train that crawled down to Mettupalayam in the hot plains of Coimbatore where a big broad gauge train swallowed them all.

After a long gap, Tappy and Ninette could spend some time with Tappy's father and the rest of the family. Rai Sahib Anand Narain Raina was naturally delighted to see his grandchildren, Jyoti and Anita. After this vacation, Tappy Raina and family resumed their journey to Ferozepur in mid-September 1957. Lieutenant Colonel M.M.S. Mathur, Tappy's predecessor in the battalion, had already proceeded on posting. On arrival, no sooner did the Rainas alight from the train on the platform, than they were welcomed by noises, smells, dust, coolies dressed in red shirts and a cheerful "reception party" from 14 Kumaon (Gwaliors) with broad smiles on their faces. Lieutenant Colonel Raina was welcomed by Major P.H. Honawar the battalion 2IC along with a few other officers and JCOs of the battalion.

Chapter 11

Commanding 14 Kumaon (Gwalior)

Lieutenant Colonel Raina returned as commanding officer to his old battalion the 4th Gwalior Infantry, which, since October 1954, had been officially re-designated as 14th Battalion the Kumaon Regiment (Gwalior). It was now based in Ferozepur Cantonment as part of 167 Infantry Brigade.

There were another two battalions that formed part of 167 Infantry Brigade under the command of Brigadier Apji Randhir Singh, formerly of Kumaon Regiment. A second infantry brigade was also located in Ferozepur with its own three infantry battalions. Hence Ferozepur had a large army population with six infantry battalions in addition to other major units from the armoured corps, artillery and engineers.

The appointment as the Commanding Officer of an infantry battalion is a coveted one. Such a tenure of command is a stepping stone to higher command and staff appointments; as the officer transits also in age from his 30s to his 40s! Thus it takes place about midway in his career and is vital if he is to climb high on the professional ladder of success.

Much was expected of Tappy Raina, the new commanding officer, by all ranks. While he had been gone, the overall standards in the battalion had somewhat deteriorated. Later, in the Officers' Mess, over a cup of tea, some of the younger officers told their new CO, "Sir, we are sick of marching past last in all competitions in the formation. We could easily be first!" They were, of course, not to be disappointed for much longer.

It is said that a good leader's reputation travels ahead of him. Lieutenant General G.L. Bakshi, PVSM (Retd.) known as "Guru Bakshi" who was then a young officer in 14 Kumaon (Gwalior) recalls how he received the news of the posting of the new commanding officer to his battalion:

> Barely nine months after having been commissioned into 14 Kumaon (Gwalior), here I was attending an Officers Physical Training Course at Army Physical Training School, Pune. Shortly before completing the course, I received a letter from the then Battalion Adjutant, Captain Ravi Mahajan, informing me that the battalion had reached its new location at Ferozepur Cantonment. He further informed me that Lieutenant Colonel T.N. Raina had been posted as the new commanding officer of our battalion. Ravi Mahajan also added for my benefit that all officers of the battalion should now get ready to work hard and experience a phase of immense professional activity and growth under their new CO, who was reputed to be a dynamic man and a "hard core" professional.
>
> Few days prior to the arrival of the new CO, I reported back to my battalion at Ferozepur Cantt. Captain (later Lieutenant Colonel) S.L. Sharma, who was Adjutant, informed me that I would be taking over the duties of Battalion Intelligence Officer (IO). As the IO of Lieutenant Colonel Raina, began what I consider as the most eventful and educative phase of my career.
>
> During late 1950s, the Indian Army had become a peacetime army! The hard professionalism that characterises it today was just not there. However, Lieutenant Colonel Tappy Raina transformed the battalion into a first- rate professional outfit, which distinctly stood apart as a result of major qualitative improvement in professional, administrative, and welfare activities. All ranks were exposed to the vision of a highly competent, motivated, dynamic, committed and energetic leader as the commanding officer. During his tenure as CO, a great deal happened in the battalion.

Raising the battalion's all-round standards was an uphill task. The senior lot of field officers[43], for one, were mere passengers. They let things take their own course, happy to swim with the tide. Their standard can be gauged from the fact that six of them remained, till retirement, in the same ranks they then held. On the plus side, however, were the younger officers all of whom were eager and keen. They genuinely loved their battalion and aspired to see its flag fly high. As did most of the men, who had received their basic military training at Kumaon Regiment Training Centre (KRC), Ranikhet, and who had enlisted after the merger of 4 Gwalior with Kumaon Regiment. They were found to be very fit and fine soldiers in every way. Their standard of discipline was very high.

Tappy Raina gave top priority to the training of men, junior leaders and sub-unit commanders. Training and promotion cadres were conducted to train young soldiers and junior leaders. Thus all rifle companies were trained for individual and collective training by rotation. Concurrently, they also did their classification range firing and field firing. Ferozepur, being an old cantonment, had ample facilities for this training. Each rifle company's training cycle culminated in a camp, when a tactical exercise was set for the company. To put it simply, all ranks were kept on their toes. "The more you sweat in peace, the less you bleed in war", became the motto of their training!

Regimental life with its norms was also addressed. Regimental Dinner Nights for officers at the Officers' Mess were regularly held, culminating in games of prowess while the Pipes and Drums played martial music. Regimental folk songs were sung to which all officers danced.

At the same time, Tappy also turned his attention to the unit's administration, including logistics and interior economy. He minutely went through the battalion's stores, kotes (armoury) and the armourer's shop. He instructed the Battalion Quarter Master, Ravi

---

[43] Traditionally, officers of the rank of Major were designated as field officers. They were authorized to wear trousers made of corduroy cloth as part of their uniform. Officers below the rank of Captain were addressed as "Mister".

Mahajan, in the areas of record keeping where much improvement was required. As Tappy had himself once been a mechanical transport officer (MTO),[44] he was able to expertly guide its platoon commander, Captain Nair, where improvement was required.

In order to give an impetus to sports, Tappy obtained the services of Otto Peltzer[45] as coach for training the battalion's sports teams. He realized that standing first in such competitions with other battalions would be a tonic for the morale of the battalion and would spur the efforts of officers and men in other fields as well.

Otto Peltzer was given a free hand in selecting his team of sportsmen. Lieutenants "Guru" Bakshi and "Fattu" Thopte were to assist Otto Peltzer. At all times of the day for many months, this lot was seen in sports dress running, skipping, and frog-jumping. The enthusiasm of the men to be a part of this endeavour was infectious.

Tappy set a high premium on physical fitness. The morning "Road, Walk and Run" was led by him. Most of his company commanders were either overage or in low medical category. Tappy did not allow this to become an impediment as he himself led the PT parade and set an example. He was also at the head of all "route marches". Competitions in such events were routinely held, and all companies vied with one another for the Battalion Championship Banner.

There was one particular event that Guru Bakshi recalled vividly even many years after it happened. The event was intended to achieve maximum participation from each company, including officers.

---

[44] The mechanical transport officer is responsible for upkeep, maintenance and meeting the unit's requirement of vehicles.

[45] Otto, a German, was then 57 years old and was an athletics coach with the National Sports Club, New Delhi. Although, few knew it, and Otto did not make it known, he had been once been the national record holder in eight events and captain of the German Olympics Team in 1928 and 1932.

Soon after assuming command in September 1957, Lieutenant Colonel Raina set two important key result areas (KRAs): 1) physical fitness and mental toughness of all ranks, and 2) battle worthiness of the battalion.

In pursuance of the first KRA, it was decided to hold an inter-company cross country competition, which became my responsibility since, in addition to being Battalion IO, I was also the Battalion Sports Officer.

I organised the Inter-Company Cross-Country, keeping it almost identical to that of the Gentlemen Cadets at the IMA Dehra Dun, ensuring maximum participation of all ranks. A fairly tough and long route was laid, with full "bandobast" (administrative preparation) including Check Posts (CPs), Medical Aid Posts (MAP) with Ambulance and Signal communications. There was tremendous enthusiasm, and it generated healthy inter-company spirit and the "boys" practiced feverishly for nearly two months, before the competition.

Finally, when the weather was considered acceptable for such an event, the competition was conducted in September 1958. As I recall, approximately eight young officers, including myself, took part.

It so happened that on the actual day of the event, weather turned out to be particularly hot and humid. Somehow, none of us gave much thought to it. The race was run with the kind of "josh" and frenzy never witnessed in the Battalion earlier! As the competitors started trickling in the "Finish Enclosures", we started receiving reports of some men dropping out and fainting en-route, mostly in the last kilometre or so of the route. Of course, they were promptly attended to by the medical personnel and the ambulance was used to evacuate those who were serious and delirious to the local Military Hospital. By the time the event was over, out of approximately 400 participants who had run the race, 20 were admitted in MH, 4 of them were placed on "DI list". Unfortunately, on the following day, two of the jawans expired due to heat exhaustion.

This cast a shadow on an otherwise very well conducted activity of our battalion! Naturally it evoked reaction all the way up the chain of command, and a Court of Inquiry was ordered by the Division HQ. The Court of Inquiry, as usually happens when things go wrong, went about posing some very awkward and even somewhat unfair questions such as, "Was the temperature taken before the start of the race?" "Was the medical opinion taken before holding the events" and so on?

At that stage, I was called by my CO, Lieutenant Colonel Raina, who briefed me to tell the Court of Inquiry, honestly and truthfully, about what we did and how we organised the event. "If they ask, as to why something was not done, tell them that it was not done because the CO did not feel it was necessary and called for. I, as your CO, am fully convinced that whatever was humanly possible, by way of good and prudent organisation of the event, was done. What has happened is most unfortunate and no outsider, whatever his rank and status, can be sorrier, more concerned or more aggrieved than us the officers of the *paltan* (Platoon), who have lost our two fine boys".

The essence is that, sometimes, things do go wrong in spite of best intentions and efforts. In such situations, it is the leader whose leadership qualities are put to test; he has to lead the outfit out of trouble without loss of morale and we had such a leader in our CO. He made sure that the unit did not sink into a pall of grief. Normal activity of training and sports carried on, uninterrupted.

Officers were encouraged to participate with along with other ranks and jawans in most sports and games. All this cultivated a healthy and friendly bond and promoted team spirit. The unit officers also made their presence felt at Ferozepur Club, the garrison's social hub. They were on friendly terms with other officers of the garrison, including a few civil and police officers of Ferozepur.

In the field of sports and games, some of the battalion's teams came out as champions, and some of its athletes stood on the victory stand at last. This brought great cheer to all ranks. Meanwhile, the battalions' swimmers were making waves in higher level competitions. One day, the welcome news was received that two of the swimmers, Ram Dev Singh and Shyam Lal Singh, had won in the

National Swimming meet. Ram Dev Singh had made a new national record in breast-stroke. The two heroes were received at the railway station by the Subedar Major and the Pipes and Drums. They were brought in a noisy procession to Tappy's office, where he received both of them with a warm embrace and gave them instant promotion. What greater tonic could there have been for 14 Kumaon; it was a golden moment!

As Commanding Officer, Tappy encouraged healthy discussion amongst his officers. He guided them well then, and even later throughout their careers. He took pains in getting to know them, their professional aspirations and family problems. The officers too became more confident. At brigade level discussions, they expressed their views with full confidence and conviction. At such conclaves, Tappy was always heard with respect.

A few months into his command, an inspection team descended on the battalion. Arms and weapons were inspected by the AIA, ammunition by MARS, stores by the CAOC, and vehicles by CEME; all these were experts from divisional headquarters. Tappy had prepared the battalion well; in all these fields it got excellent reports. This was followed by the annual inspection by the brigade commander, a yearly ritual that was followed in the whole army. The brigade commander that year was Brigadier M.G. Dewan. He was an officer with an impressive personality, an engaging manner and the most charming social graces. His report on the training, equipment management and administration of the battalion was excellent.

About a year into the command, while in his office, Tappy, one day felt pain in his chest. The regimental medical officer (RMO) examined him and suggested a private consultation with a good cardiologist in Amritsar. Tappy rejected this suggestion outright. If required, he stated, he would go to the Military Hospital[46]. It was to become a chronic problem, surfacing every now and then. The pain was caused by the injuries he suffered during World War 2 as

---

[46] Later during his cancer, too, Tappy was prompt in getting formal medical advice. He was regular in getting himself medically examined as the regulations required. So, too, he obtained medical advice for Mrs. Raina when required.

a result of which some splinters remained lodged in his body and would, from time to time, cause discomfort.

Guru Bakshi, recalls another event, when one Sunday morning at about 1000 hours, information was received at the Battalion Headquarters that a fire had broken out in the company defended locality at Ghatti Kamalewala. Thick dark smoke was also seen rising from the area. Ghatti Kamalewala was a fairly large island in the Sutlej, full of thick sarkanda grass. The far bank of the island constituted the border with Pakistan. The *sarkanda* (reed) grass was highly inflammable and such fires usually tended to go out of control. The company defended locality had ammunition stocked at many places in makeshift bunkers and, if the fire reached there, it could have been a catastrophe, leading to many explosions and casualties. According to Guru Bakshi:

> As soon as news about outbreak of the fire reached Battalion Headquarter, the commanding officer rushed out of his office, taking me along to the Sutlej River bank, where we got into a waiting motorboat and headed straight for Ghati Kamalewala, as fast we could go.
>
> On reaching the island, the CO moved from one post to the other, walking very briskly (he used to walk extremely fast), organising fire-fighting at one place, getting the sarkanda grass cut at another place to prevent the fire from spreading into areas where the ammunition was stored and, at the same time, evacuating ammunition boxes to safe areas. A careless disposal of a cigarette, in all probability, had started the fire. Both, Indian and Pakistani troops were labouring equally hard to put out the fire!
>
> I kept marvelling at my CO's immense anticipatory and quick thinking, reactive capabilities, together with his unbounded energy and abilities to harness and motivate all ranks to give their best in any crisis situation. Throughout, Lt. Col. Raina remained totally poised, calm and collected, unmindful of his personal safely. We were at the scene for over six hours, rushing on foot from place to place, without a thought of hunger and thirst.

After the fire was controlled, and damage to weapons, ammunition, telephone line, the telephone exchange and other equipment assessed, Lieutenant Colonel Raina returned to the unit at about 1700 hours.

Of course, there was a staff Court of Inquiry held, and everything was openly and truthfully stated. There was no attempt for any "cover ups" during Colonel Raina's tenure in command.

While returning to the Battalion Headquarter, Colonel Raina explained to me, "While wars are the real test of a leader's soldierly attributes and leadership qualities, emergencies and crisis situations like the one that happened today are somewhat akin to war situations. They present opportunities to test and observe all ranks closely, to get to know how they would respond and conduct themselves in a real war"!

Even after almost six decades, Guru Bakshi could still recall a few anecdotes of lighter moments that contrast with the professionally serious nature of Colonel Raina.

The battalion had moved out of its permanent location for intensive collective training for two months. There used to be frequent "briefing" and "debriefing" sessions of the Commanding Officer, which all officers had to attend. At one such session, prior to the commencement of an exercise the following day, doubts were raised by some company commanders on our ability to commence the "Advance to Contact" exercise early next day, due to threatening weather conditions. The CO immediately laid all doubts at rest by loudly stating that "Rain, Hail or Storm — we go". This, thereafter, became the motto for all of us, particularly the young subalterns, which included myself, Sucha Singh Rana, late Fatu Thopte and late Gautam Mittra (an attached AOC officer).

On the days when the Battalion was not out on a Tactical Exercise and remained in the camp, Company Commanders used to take their respective Companies, early morning for a long and robust "Road Walk and Run" and "Physical Work Out". If ever any of us expressed the view that the weather appeared to be too inclement for a "work out" the following day, the rest of us would pip our motto, "Rain, Hail or Storm, We go", and put all doubts at rest.

Two officers who served under Tappy Raina, and thereafter continued to receive his guidance rose to become Lieutenant Generals. They remember Tappy's dedication and the precepts he lived by:

- Ask questions, that is the only way to learn.
- Make as many mistakes as you can as a young officer; you will be forgiven;
- Don't be afraid of making mistakes.
- No short cuts.
- Study widely and regularly.
- Be honest with your men; they deserve the best; treat them with consideration.
- No cover up. It is not required if your intention is good and your effort genuine.
- Follow a good example; reject what is bad.
- Try your best to resolve a problem. If you can't, seek help.
- Don't show off in professional or personal life.
- If you do something, you may be right; if you do nothing, you are always wrong.

Chapter 12

Family Life in 14 Kumaon

The practice of unmarried officers of the battalion "calling-on" married officers was encouraged. Whenever young officers visited their commanding officer's house, they were received warmly by Lieutenant Colonel and Mrs Raina. Their children were usually found to be very pre-occupied: while their daughter, Anita (nick name Annu) would be seen patting rabbits and other pets, their son, Jyoti (Joe) would be digging up the garden. "He has learnt in school that there is water below the ground and if you dig deep enough water will gush out. So we let him dig to find out for himself," explained the father.

The Rainas' life style was simple, dignified and befitting their status. Guests were always welcome in their home and were received with genuine warmth. At home, Tappy never talked shop in front of his wife or other ladies of the battalion. While Tappy was busy in honing the professional skills of all ranks of 14 Kumaon (Gwalior), Ninette Raina applied herself with tremendous zeal and dedication to the welfare of families. It was a new experience for her to be referred as the "First Lady" or "CO Memsahib" of the Battalion!

After their three-year stay in the salubrious climate of Nilgiri Hills, the Raina family found summer in Ferozepur unbearably hot and dusty. Ninette narrates her experience of regimental life in Ferozepur Cantonment, as under:

> Our home was a long building (barrack) of five rooms in a row, with a cemented veranda in the front, a garage and three or four

servants' quarters at the back, a desiccated garden and clouds of dust everywhere.

Within a short period we met everybody in our 14 Kumaon family; eager young officers as well as the more experienced senior ones and smiling wives. They gave us information on life in Ferozepur: school, canteen, club, and market; everyone was very nice and friendly. We quickly became a big family. The Battalion Lines were quite far and officers were veteran cyclists by force! None of us had a car or other luxuries; we had no desert cooler or refrigerator. But we had deep camaraderie and bonding. There was time for the ladies to talk and share and organise their chores.

The daily life was routine and regulated enough: up in the morning, open the curtains (and get a shower of sand on the head for one's pains), organise tea and breakfast, send the kids to the local Army School, then the husband to work, women to shop, getting out as early as possible so as to avoid the midday heat. There were days to visit the lines, check on the lives of the young soldiers' wives, their children, and their little illnesses, the cleanliness of the dwellings, the classes where they were taught, etc. They came from various backgrounds: Kumaonis, Gurkhas, Marathas, Rajputs, and Brahmins. They were taught haphazardly; some learning knitting, others stitching, some of them advanced and wise, others young and timid, almost as innocent as small children. (One girl even thought that having children was like trees giving fruits every year!).

The men were busy, often on route marches, exercises and training, regularly posted at the border on the River Sutlej so that very often, we families were left alone. Our husbands' orderlies (*sahayaks*) became very useful, and I remember some amusing incidents that took place.

One day, a telephone call from the office informed me that Tappy would require the Summer Mess Dress (white monkey jacket, white shirt, white trousers and Regimental Cummarbund[47]), as CO Sahib had to attend a stag dinner; so everything

---

[47] Regimental Waist Band

was to be got ready for him to change after office hours. His very enthusiastic orderly hung the clean clothes complete with decorations etc. and, to my amazement discarded with contempt the Wellington boots I had taken out, replacing them with tennis shoes. He patiently explained to me that Sahib had to be all in white. I kept quiet, because I looked forward to watching Tappy's face when he came home. Of course there were roars of laughter and a sheepish grin from the soldier!

I used to go shopping on my bicycle to the market in the morning but when I was occupied with other things I used to send the orderly. He always forgot what I wanted and brought back all sorts of things telling me that what he had bought was anyway better tasting than what I had ordered. That way I became familiar with a few vegetables I had never known and had to learn how to cook them.

The summer was so hot that we used to cycle furiously at 3.00 p.m. in the blazing sun to the swimming pool and immerse ourselves there till sundown. In winter, we froze! During that period Tappy was usually out on the border. It is then that I used to receive phone calls at 2.00 or 3.00 a.m. in the freezing night, usually to hear "checking the lines." And all that time babies were born to the jawans' wives — some girls would never tell us when the children were to be expected, so they happened to arrive in the wee hours of the morning, usually when their husbands were away. So I and the other officers wives would have to ensure that the mothers were transported to hospital for there was only a skeleton staff left in the lines. During my stay in this unit, I saw at least a dozen little ones growing up; some of them were a great joy, plump and placid. Others were weaker and required a lot of care. One of our officer's wives was a lady doctor and her help was much appreciated.

There were times when I had quite some spare time on my hands at home. The children spent the afternoon either sleeping or playing with water in the bathroom. Only then could they enjoy that gruelling heat. I spent the worst afternoons sitting in a galvanised iron bath-tub in my bath-room, reading a book, when not going out to the swimming pool.

To amuse the kids I started keeping a small poultry yard. I sat some hens on eggs and within a short time there was a small tumult in the outhouses, and the poultry population grew and grew. Accidents then happened. A clumsy boot broke a few legs, or a few wings, or in winter pneumonia attacked the young pullets. Some wild bird attacked some chicken and hurt them (one of them lost an eye), so one of the out houses became a hospital! Limbs were put in splints (and they mended), colds and fever were treated with aspirin and small draughts of brandy or whisky! Unfortunately Tappy did not agree with such a treatment. "My whisky for the chicken!" he would lament!

So the hospital was closed. Little by little the flock dwindled and thus ended our poultry project.

Another image remains in my mind. It was an evening when our Battalion had arranged a Sports Meet on the Maidan (playground). The sun was setting, a beautiful twilight as we see often in semi-desert lands, was spreading all over the sky. While, the Pipes and Drums of the Battalion were playing and officers, Junior Commissioned Officers and Other Ranks and their families were dancing, our son, Jyoti (Joe), smart in his light blue top and grey pants, after a mad dance, excitedly announced, "When I grow up, I will join this (14 Kumaon) *Paltan* (hindi for battalion)."[48]

During the second year of our stay at Ferozepur, there arose a rumour that the unit was to go "up the hills" to a non-family station in Field Area. It was at this time that I began losing weight steadily, without any visible reason. So Tappy arranged to send me and our little girl, Anita, to Ranikhet, where the Kumaon Regimental Centre is located. Our son, Joe, was by then already a boarder in Sherwood College at Nainital. Ranikhet is a lovely cantonment situated at an altitude, varying from 6,000 to 9,000 feet, with thick pine forests.

---

[48] Joe joined NDA and later passed out as Commissioned Officer when he was barely nineteen years old. He was commissioned in his father's Battalion (14 Kumaon).

With our move from Ferozepur to Ranikhet, my stint as the wife of an Infantry Battalion Commander came to an end!

Should life be lived again, I would choose to go through the same experiences again and live once more, that life of simplicity, companionship and camaraderie, which the Indian Army always provided.

Tappy's two years of command of 14 Kumaon (Gwalior) came to an end on 15th September 1959. He was again selected to return to the corridors of power in South Block, Military Secretary's Branch at Army Headquarters, New Delhi. His tenure with 14 Kumaon had been fulfilling and he had converted the battalion into a team of achievers. Their upward graph continued in the years ahead.[49]

---

[49] In the next decade, the battalion undertook the successful and acclaimed attack on "OP Hill" in the 1965 War. Before the decade ended, in 1970, it was declared the Best Battalion among 36 battalions of 8 Mountain Division in Nagaland. It was a performance that the battalion repeated in the following year. It also fought valiantly in the Bangladesh War. In 1979, it was selected to be converted into a Mechanised Infantry Battalion, and re-designated as the 5 Mechanised Battalion (14 Kumaon). Currently, it is the best unit in overall performance in an Armoured Division.

Chapter 13

Army Headquarters, New Delhi

This was Tappy's second posting to Army HQ, the first having been as General Staff Officer-2 (GSO-2 Ops) in the Military Operation Directorate in 1948-49. The nature of work in the Military Secretary (MS) Branch was new for him but with hard work and his characteristic perseverance and vision, Tappy quickly settled down in his new appointment.

When Tappy arrived at Army HQ to report for duty as Assistant Military Secretary (AMS) in the MS Branch, Major General Banerjee was the Military Secretary. He was succeeded by Major General Amreek Singh. Brigadier Tahal Ramani was the Deputy Military Secretary. Tappy Raina took over the charge as AMS-2, dealing with the careers of armoured corps and infantry officers. His other colleagues were Lieutenant Colonel Ved Batra as AMS-1 dealing with posting of officers on staff and extra-regimental employment (ERE), and Lieutenant Colonel Eric Sen as AMS-4 dealing with confidential reports of officers.

Shri D.C. Aggarwal[50] was a civilian staff officer (CSO) who was already working in MS-2 Section when Tappy joined his new appointment. Aggarwal, along with two majors, was holding the appointment of Deputy Assistant Military Secretary (DAMS) and

[50] The author met Shri D.C. Aggrawal at his post-retirement and modest residence in a DDA Flat in New Delhi. Despite his failing eyesight, he displayed a sharp memory, and could narrate the years of his association with Tappy from September 1959 until Tappy's tenure as Chief of Army Staff, when the Shri D.C. Aggrawal was Deputy MS (X), MS Branch, AHQ.

Tappy came as their immediate superior. Aggarwal came to have a very long association with Lieutenant Colonel Raina, whom he saw steadily rise up the ladder and, finally, attain the highest rank in the Indian Army.

D.C. Aggarwal was to later recall the experience of working in the team led by Tappy Raina:

> I still vividly recall the trepidation with which we, in Section (MS-2), awaited his arrival! Since his personal record, like that of the other infantry officers, was maintained by us in the Military Secretary's Branch, we knew all about his career in the army: he ranked very high amongst infantry officers of his seniority. It is said that reputation travels faster than the man. Tappy Raina, as he was popularly known, had several aspects to his personality which made us careful in dealing with him. He was a Kashmiri Pandit, reputed as a class for their keen intellect and generally for an equally sharp tongue! He had been an instructor at the Defence Services Staff College, Wellington; no mean achievement even today. He had a European wife, and, like Nelson, he had just one eye, with all the characteristics that nature produces as compensation for such a handicap. We had therefore to maintain a formal distance with him at least for some time, and to forget the informality that we were used to and had enjoyed with his predecessor.
>
> His predecessor had been nicknamed the Great Paper Writer (GPW) by us since he was always planning to write lengthy papers for which he made us compile interminable statistics. These papers, if I may add, did not always contain much substance! Perhaps the GPW believed in keeping his staff always busy. In addition he often bellowed at his juniors out of anger and frustration and kept them on a tight leash. He was a chain smoker, always tense, and an endless tea drinker — eleven trays of tea, was his normal daily intake! Towards the end, however, he relaxed and we were able to exchange many a joke with him.
>
> It was thus natural for us to be apprehensive of the change that was going to take place. We soon discovered, however, that our new boss was a totally different person: very concise in his

writing and one who hardly ever prepared lengthy papers or got unnecessary statistical data compiled. But he was quite stern, both in appearance and in his dealings. He once rebuked a Superintendent in the office, merely because he had not spoken to him formally in English! He believed in being friendly but at the same time formal in his official duties.

Lieutenant Colonel Raina set about his assignment in a very systematic and business-like manner. First and foremost, he made it a point to study everything available about the officers whose careers he was going to deal with. Patiently, he would go through the confidential and career record of all officers, until he had studied almost 8,000 dossiers! Gifted as he was with a formidable memory for faces, names and such other details, he could now readily select the best man for any appointment or to post any officer to the appointment for which he was most suited.

Quick witted and confident of himself, Tappy Raina never hesitated to take a decision. He could get his point of view across to his seniors and colleagues alike, since he always mastered his facts and arguments before any meeting or discussion. This habit stayed with him throughout his career. Aggarwal and other subordinate officers in MS-2 Section marvelled at the great pains that Tappy would take to prepare his brief before going to any conference or delivering a talk. At that time, however, they never imagined that Lieutenant Colonel Raina belonged to that rare class of individuals from whom the highest leadership emerges.

Very slowly, a bond of mutual understanding and even affection grew between Tappy and his subordinate officers and staff. The process was slow because as Tappy told Aggarwal much later, that it was for the first time that he was working with a team comprising mostly of civilians. Therefore, he was somewhat apprehensive. Once the ice was broken, and he had formed his opinion about the civilian staff, they could be at ease with him. They felt they could go to him directly, disagree or even argue with him. Once in a while they would even exchange gossip and pleasantries. It had now become a real team. All the juniors warmed to their new boss.

D.C. Aggarwal further recalled:

At that time we had in our clerical staff, one Mr Maudgill, who belonged to a family of astrologers attached to a princely state in Punjab. He himself was also an amateur astrologer. Being the only civilian officer and hence slightly less disciplined than army officers, I was much more informal and asked Colonel Raina if he had a horoscope. Like most Hindus, he did. Mr. Maudgill studied the horoscope and elaborated on it. I can remember very few details now. But what I do remember quite clearly is one prediction which years later proved correct, unbelievably. Maudgill's prediction was that the native of this horoscope (astrological language) would rise to the highest position in his profession; and that reaching nearest to the highest position was an absolute given.

How could we then have believed that this Lieutenant Colonel, our boss, would one day become Chief of the Army Staff, or at least an army commander? It was uncanny how the horoscope had revealed this fifteen years in advance!

Once the mutual trust had been established, Lieutenant Colonel Raina started depending on his team and could confidently leave many matters to their judgement and also share his personal problems with them. He had then started the construction of his house in South Delhi and had to visit the site quite frequently, mostly before or after office hours and, sometimes, during lunch break as well. By now, it had become quite a pleasure working for him.

Tappy Raina believed in meticulous planning well in advance. I remember that he delivered a talk to all officers of the MS Branch about the threat to the country in the north and the logistics advantages which the Chinese enjoyed, having the Tibetan plateau under their control. That was more than a year before the Chinese aggression, when there was hardly a pre-shadow of the events to come. But it seems that either he had his eye on the command of a brigade opposite the Chinese or that he was just getting ready for any eventuality.

But the opportunity came to him in 1962. In the meantime, he carried out a detailed study of Tibet going through old books of travel, current literature and intelligence reports alike. And, thus when the occasion arose, it did not find him unprepared for it.

Tappy Raina loved work and never tired of extolling the virtues of a hardworking person, who, according to him, was far more worthy than a flamboyant one, who did not steadily work hard. He always ensured that the top-notches from the Indian Military Academy were not posted to his own Kumaon Regiment because he believed that they were too sure of themselves and would not be inclined to work that hard. A man of strong likes and dislikes, Tappy abhorred laziness and made no secret of it. Rather guarded, he would not disclose his hand until the time was opportune.

In August 1962, Lieutenant Colonel Raina was promoted to the rank of brigadier and appointed to command 114 Infantry Brigade, operationally deployed in Ladakh, just in time to meet the Chinese threat!

A small circle of family members, close friends and colleagues assembled at New Delhi Railway Station in September 1962 to bid him farewell and wish him Godspeed in his new assignment.

Little did D.C. Aggarwal and his colleagues realise at that time that within two months, Tappy Raina would become a national hero and earn the country's second highest gallantry award, Maha Vir Chakra (MVC), in recognition of his courage and exceptional leadership in facing the Chinese in the Battle of Chushul (Ladakh)[51].

Perhaps the greatest tribute paid to Tappy was that by those who worked under him. They saw him as a man of few words, always highly motivated, dynamic and competent, with a determined and

---

[51] A detailed account of the Battle of Chushul can be found in Chapter 19.

robust air about him. He was able to bring out the best in his juniors inspiring some to transform from "average" performers to outstanding ones. An excellent mentor, he set high standards by personal example in all aspects of battalion life — physical fitness, dealing with crises, ensuring that his juniors went on a variety of professional courses and developed into all-round personalities. While building confidence in his men and encouraging healthy competition, he was generous in celebrating and rewarding their successes.

His interests covered multiple spheres of life — reading, sports, music, dance, special celebrations, in addition to the professional aspects of army life. All spare time was spent in improving himself. For example, despite his handicap be continued to practice rifle shooting to ensure that he did not fall back on any military skill. In the same way he trained himself to play golf. Tenacity and perseverance characterized him and he carried no chip on his shoulder about having just one eye. That same resilience both he and his wife sought to pass on to their son encouraging him to stand up for himself and deal with bullies the way they understood best.

Integrity was the hall mark of Tappy's character. When things went wrong, despite all preparation and forethought, Tappy made no efforts to cover up. As he told his juniors, it was necessary to come clean and speak the truth in the face of any inquiry. As the leader, he took full responsibility on himself. Qualities such as a formidable memory for faces and names, a systematic approach to work and detailed preparation of facts and figures before any briefing or meeting were carefully cultivated. The motivating factor was not so much an eye to future promotions but an overall dedication to the army to which he had total commitment.

He had the ability to become carefree as a child when playing with his children and had the greatest fun with them. Above all, he was a man of simple tastes with minimum personal needs. Fortunately, he had a supportive wife who demanded little and readily made do with whatever was available; thereby giving him the mental space he needed to focus on his career.

Part III

Invasion by the Dragon

"No one is so foolish as to choose war over peace. In peace, sons bury fathers. In war, fathers bury their sons."
~ Herodotus, 484 BC

Chapter 14

India-China Border Dispute on the Himalayan Frontier

In order to understand the Sino-Indian War of 1962 and the role of the soldiers and officers of 114 Infantry Brigade under the command of Brigadier T.N. Raina, some background information of this region and all that led to the war is vital. Without it, the reader cannot fully appreciate the valour and indomitable spirit of the Indian soldier in the face of all odds and the exceptional leadership under adverse conditions displayed by Brigadier Raina, his subordinate commanders and staff officers at this crucial juncture of Indian history.

The Himalayan Frontier

From time immemorial, the mighty Himalayas have formed a natural frontier against invaders. Extending for nearly 4,000 kilometres (2,500 miles), they separate the Indian subcontinent from the Tibetan Plateau in the north. The seasonal routes and passes of this great mountain wall helped establish constant trade and cultural links with Tibet and China. Through these routes Buddhism spread from India to the countries of south east Asia. Pilgrims, students, teachers and philosophers from both sides trekked across, seeking and spreading knowledge and wisdom.

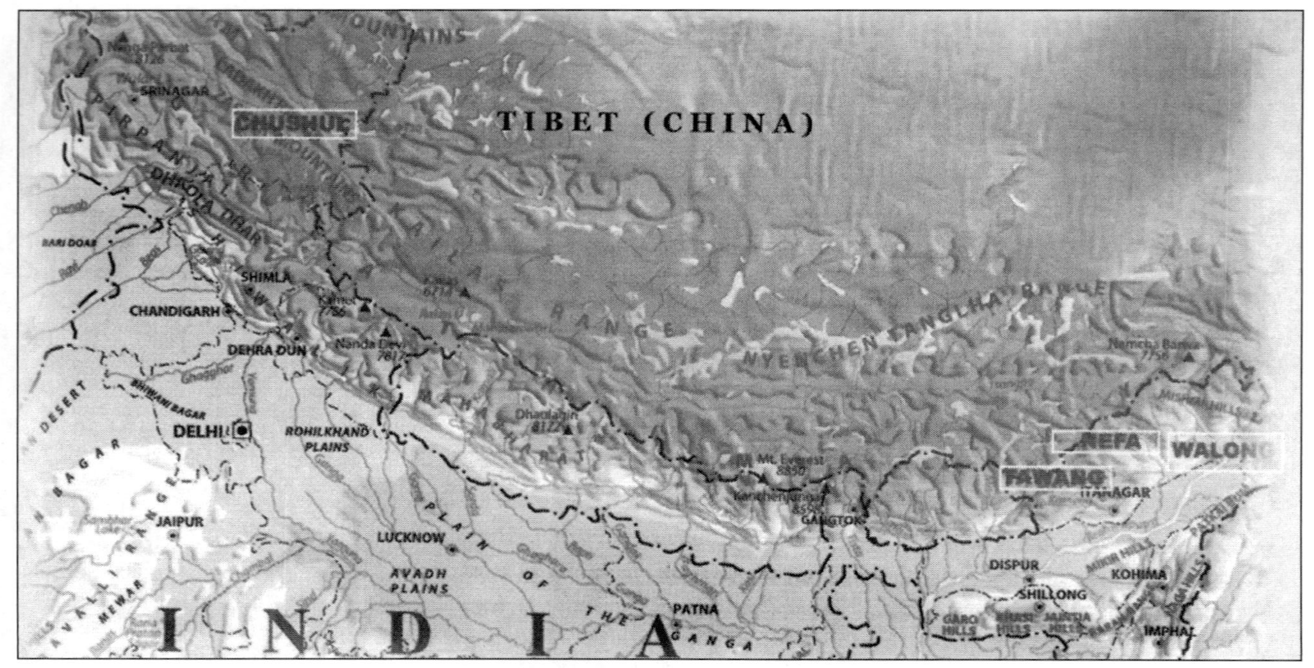

Map 1: Himalayan Frontier.

Historically, India was successfully invaded from the northwest, and not from the north. And, therefore, the northern frontier with the Tibetan Plateau beyond was never the focus of military presence and defence. This was so until, by virtue of an agreement between Tibet and the British government in India, the British Indian Army established garrisons at the capital, Lhasa, Shighatse and Yatung.

The erstwhile kingdoms of Kashmir and Assam lie at the two extremities of the northern frontier, and the Muslim rulers did not find it as easy to subdue these two regions, the way they did the rest of northern India. In 1586, Akbar annexed Kashmir but Ladakh remained independent. Although Ladakh fluctuated between war and peace with Tibet for much of the 17th century, from about 1690 the Gyalpo or Chief of Ladakh became a tributary of the rulers of Kashmir. In the 19th century, Ladakh was conquered and annexed by Raja Gulab Singh of Kashmir. Raja Gulab Singh was himself a feudatory of Maharaja Ranjit Singh of Punjab. In 1841, General Zorawar Singh, one of Raja Gulab Singh's top military commanders invaded Western Tibet. He was defeated and expelled, but when the Tibetans, with the aid of the Chinese, advanced to Leh they were, in turn, driven back and a peace treaty was signed in 1842. Four years later, Kashmir came under the suzerainty of the British and Gulab Singh was recognised as the Maharaja of the whole of Kashmir, including Ladakh.

In the northeast, the kingdom of Kamarupa (now Assam) was ruled by the Ahoms who resisted Muslim efforts to subdue them. The Ahom raja briefly surrendered to Aurangzeb in 1662 but regained his territory four years later. Later, the British annexed Assam in 1838. But there were numerous tribes in the north, east and south of Assam and it took nearly seventy-five years for the British to establish some kind of administrative control over the highland regions inhabited by them. By 1912-13, administration of this northern region of Assam had been established to a considerable extent. The various tribes in the north of Assam that occupied the area between Assam and Tibet, such as the Monpas, Akas, Daflas, Miris, Abors and Mishmis were ethnically different from the Tibetans. Tawang, inhabited by the Monpas, had been a part of India for centuries and Tibetan spiritual influence had grown there only since the early years of the 19th century. By the second decade of the 20th century, sufficient information about the frontier had also been acquired by the British to enable the definite delineation of the Assam-Tibet boundary. From the east of Bhutan, the McMahon line[52] extended to the tri-junction with Tibet and Burma.

In the early years of the 19th century, the British also wrested from the Gorkhas of Nepal the control of Garhwal, Kumaon and the neighbouring hill states of undivided Punjab, which then also included the present Himachal Pradesh. By the Treaty of Sagauli in 1816, the Raja of Nepal recognised British sovereignty over these areas along the border with Nepal and Tibet.

Thus India's present northern boundary is along the whole stretch of the Himalayas. The countries along this border include China, Tibet, Nepal, Bhutan and the erstwhile Protectorate of Sikkim.

Sino-Indian Border

After India became an independent sovereign republic, the Indian government initially tried to follow the British policy towards its northern borders. While China sought to establish its authority over Tibet from 1950 onward, the Tibetan government asked India to hand over certain parts of the Tibetan territory that the British had taken from them adjoining Ladakh, Assam, and some other areas. Thus, as China tightened its grip over Tibet, Ladakh and the North East Frontier Agency (NEFA), later renamed as Arunachal

---

[52] After 1947, particularly in the early 1950s, the Government of India established better control over this area by locating some posts manned by the Assam Rifles. While India kept on maintaining the McMahon Line, a watershed, as the real boundary between India and Tibet; a close study of the map, however, would indicate that a line passing through SELA (Pass) was a more appropriate watershed. In all probability the Chinese might have accepted the McMahon Line with some modifications as the International Boundary if the Government of India had accepted part of Aksai Chin as Tibetan territory, which China needed for its strategic highway to connect Xingjiang (Sinkiang) and Lhasa, the Capital of Tibet.

Pradesh, an integrated state of India naturally became contested areas in Sino-Indian relations.

Ladakh, which means the "land of high passes" is historically and culturally closely related to Western Tibet. Even the language, Ladakhi, is a western Tibetan dialect. Until 1947, Ladakh included the Baltistan (Baltiyul) valleys (now mostly in Pakistan occupied Kashmir), the entire upper Indus Valley, the remote Zanskar Valley, the Nubra Valley to the north, and Aksai Chin in the north east. Aksai Chin had become a problematic spot by the end of the 19th century.

Contemporary Ladakh borders Tibet to the east, the Lahaul and Spiti regions of Himachal Pradesh to the south, the Valley of Kashmir, Jammu and the Baltiyul regions to the west, and Sinkiang (China) across the Karakoram Pass in the far north.

In the next sub-sector of the northern border, which covered Punjab (now Himachal Pradesh) and part of UP (now Uttrakhand), the British accepted and the Chinese by and large regarded the line of main "passes" as the boundary features. In the middle sector, with Nepal, Sikkim[53] and Bhutan as a chain of protectorates in varying degrees, the British were content to rest the boundary at the foothills and ensured that Chinese or Tibetan influence did not penetrate into these kingdoms and buffer states.

Hindi-Chini Bhai-Bhai — India's Pro-China Stance at Occupation of Tibet

When China invaded Tibet in October 1950, Tibet appealed to the United Nations. However the then Government of India defended China's annexation of Tibet in the UN General Assembly, and justified it by quoting historical facts. As a result, Chinese assertions that they would respect Tibet's autonomy and would stop all violence were accepted and the matter was dropped.

The Tibetan question created considerable resentment and severe criticism in India and abroad. Unlike the United States and

---

[53] Sikkim joined the Indian Union as a state in 1976, thus becoming an integral part of India.

many Western countries which were against the communist government of the People's Republic of China, which was relatively weak at that moment of Chinese history, India displayed complete solidarity with China. The Government of India supported China's admission to the UN, even when China was engaged in the Korean War at that juncture. The Government of India, however, failed to assert its influence or authority vis-à-vis the Chinese at such an opportune time for the permanent delineation of India's boundary with Tibet. The Indian Government mistakenly believed in China's repeated statements of eternal friendship.

The Panch Sheel Agreement

While making peaceful statements that lulled India into a false sense of security on her northern borders, China consolidated its occupation of Tibet. The Chinese built two strategic roads, one through East Tibet and the other from Sinkiang through Aksai Chin to Lhasa. In this period, China never raised the border problem. Instead, numerous cultural missions and other delegations were exchanged between the two countries. In such a congenial and friendly atmosphere, India and China signed the famous (which actually proved infamous later) Panch Sheel Agreement, the main provisions of which were:

- Mutual respect for each other's territorial integrity and sovereignty.
- Mutual non-aggression.
- Mutual non-interference in each other's internal affairs.
- Equal and mutual benefit.
- Peaceful co-existence.

This ensured China's complete control over Tibet while India failed to get any reciprocal benefit of a border agreement, which might have been possible at that time. The Panch Sheel Agreement turned into a slogan of brotherhood, *Hindi-Chini Bhai-Bhai*, which acted as a policy guideline for the Government of India, particularly for the ministries of Finance and Defence, who believed that there would be no war with China in the foreseeable future!

Military Build up

Shortly after independence, when Pakistan launched an aggression to seize Kashmir, it had succeeded in temporarily cutting off Ladakh by occupying Zojila, the only entry point to Ladakh from Srinagar, the capital of Kashmir. Zojila was retaken by the Indian forces but it became clear that a strategy had to be in place to deny the enemy approaches into the region from the north and north-west. The army raised an irregular unit of Nubra Guards, primarily for dislodging the Pakistani raiders who had infiltrated into Ladakh. Later, these volunteers were integrated into the Jammu and Kashmir (J&K) Militia[54] under the Ministry of Home Affairs. The Government of India made the Home Ministry responsible for the border with China and maintained a section of Indo-Tibet Border Police which occasionally patrolled Aksai Chin, but maintained no fixed posts.

In 1958, General K.S. Thimayya, the then Chief of the Army Staff, during a visit to the troops deployed in Jammu and Kashmir suggested to the local formation commanders that they should start paying more attention to the Ladakh frontier. An improvised airfield at Leh had already been constructed in 1948, mainly for light transport aircraft like the Dakotas. It was decided to make the airfield fit for heavier transport aircraft which were proposed to be inducted for service in support of Ladakh. The Ministry of Defence decided to acquire and induct a Soviet heavy load carrying transport aircraft, AN-12. India Air Force pilots from transport squadrons had already been sent to Soviet Union for conversion

---

[54] In response to the Pakistani invasion of Kashmir in 1947, local militias were raised for specific sectors, such as Jammu, Leh, Nubra, etc. The militias were a paramilitary force under the Ministry of Home Affairs, Government of India, and operated on the Cease Fire Line (CFL) in J&K. Following the Sino-Indian War of 1962, in 1963 the 7th and 14th battalions of the J&K Militia were spun off to form Ladakh Scouts, responsible for the Indus and Nubra sectors, respectively. Troops of these battalions were semi-trained, and comprised mostly of locals from the state of J&K.

training on these 12 aircraft. Work for improving the airfield at Leh was set into motion on a war footing.

The Army, under General Thimayya, recognized the Chinese threat on the northern border and strongly recommended to the government that serious thought be given to raising the strength of Indian Army, to the procurement of weapons and equipment, and the construction of strategic roads. But Thimayya's appreciation of the situation only met with a political veto, that no military preparation against China was necessary. Similarly, a suggested change in manuals for training based on war experience in Korea was also rejected.

The General Officer Commanding (GOC) 15 Corps with his headquarter at Udhampur (J&K) under Western Command was responsible for the international border with Pakistan as per the Karachi Agreement of 1949. It also had the responsibility of the Sino-Indian border. When this frontier started gaining importance from 1958 onwards, no official records were available about the historical aspects of this part of the border. As a first step, Headquarters 15 Corps felt that Ladakh should be garrisoned by an infantry brigade group along with some stock holding logistic units, better medical and staging facilities on the road from Pathankot, the rail head, to Srinagar, and then onward to Leh. It was decided that logistic units for the despatch and receipt of stocks, both at the rear and forward airfields be located and, most important of all, signal communications be provided to them.

It is believed that some time in the 1950s, information of a Chinese highway passing through the Aksai Chin plains was reported by the Indo-Tibetan Border Police to the Ministry of Home Affairs, at New Delhi. The report, however, remained secret from HQ 15 Corps. The latter, on their own, sent out a small patrol led by Major Iyyengar of the Corps of Engineers. This patrol was ambushed and captured by the Chinese, for "intruding" into their territory. Subsequently, during a flight in a C-119 Fairchild Packet aircraft over Aksai Chin area Air Vice Marshal Pinto and Brigadier (later Major General) Joginder Singh, BGS, HQ 15 Corps saw the Chinese road, built in two parallel strips, each about a metre wide, with some crossing place in the form of parking platforms.

After a few days, information was received at HQ 15 Corps from Army HQ that the missing patrol[55] was in Chinese custody. Members of the patrol had been arrested while moving on the Chinese Sinkiang-Tibet Highway, which ran through Chinese territory, as per their claim[56]. From that day onward, Chinese intentions about their claim and right to vast areas in Ladakh became obvious. Despite that, the Government of India continued to believe in the Chinese facade of "reasonableness" in discussing the border problems.

This was a period of prodigal neglect. Nehru and Krishna Menon chose to hear from their advisers only what pleased them, and they lost their composure whenever contradicted. By 1959, perhaps Prime Minister Nehru began to realise the gravity of the situation, but his Minister of Defence, Krishna Menon, kept him in an insulated glass case.

In 1959, the Dalai Lama fled to India via Tawang (NEFA, now Arunachal Pradesh) as conditions in Tibet continued to deteriorate due to excesses committed by the PLA of China. This development attracted worldwide attention, and naturally, had its impact in damaging Sino-Indian relations. A collision course appeared on the horizon.

How the Balloon Burst

In August 1959, the first shooting incident took place in the Northeast on the McMahon Line between the Chinese and Indian patrols near Longju, in NEFA. Thereafter the Government of India announced that the NEFA (now Arunachal Pradesh) border was being made the responsibility of the Army. The same yardstick was applied to the Ladakh sector, too. Both regions until then had been the responsibility of J&K Militia in Ladakh and Assam Ri-

---

[55] The patrol led by Major Iyyengar, was eventually released and pushed back over the Karakoram Pass on Diwali day in 1959.

[56] In 1958, some Chinese maps were published showing large tracts of land in Ladakh as Chinese territory and the Aksai Chin area, which was part of the old Kashmir Riyasat, as part of China.

fles in the Northeast which included NEFA. The responsibility of these borders remained under the Ministry of Home Affairs. In the NEFA area it was Assam Rifles that were the only paramilitary force.

Handing over responsibility to the Army was one thing, but, thereafter, the army's assessment of the ground reality needed to be heard by the government. However, the Prime Minister, advised by his Defence Minister Krishna Menon, incorrectly briefed by B.N. Malik, the Director of Intelligence Bureau (IB) and his backdoor adviser Lieutenant General B.M. Kaul, did not give full weightage to the shooting incident by the Chinese at Longiu. Those in the General Staff, at every level, more so at HQ 15 Corps in J&K, on the other hand, appreciated the consequences more realistically, as they were at the receiving end.

By September 1959 China's attitude had hardened. It now laid claim to much larger areas in the North East, almost down to the foothills, as also the entire Aksai Chin area in Ladakh. In reply to a protest by the Government of India on China's occupying a large chunk of Indian Territory in the Ladakh sector, China laid claim to a much larger area in the east, south of the McMahon line in NEFA. Thus the Chinese linked the two areas, leaving no doubt that if India insisted on the right to patrol in Aksai Chin, the Chinese could claim a right to patrol south of the McMahon Line. India's military weakness and the neglect by the government to expand the strength of the army to meet the growing Chinese threat, created a situation in which, in addition to control over Aksai Chin, the Chinese could claim NEFA as well.

In October 1959, Chinese troops ambushed a small Indian police patrol in Chang Chenmo Valley, in the Hot Springs area. Nine Indian policemen were killed and ten were taken prisoner and, thereafter, subjected to the most inhuman treatment. The Chinese also established a post in the Indian territory at Spanggur, near Chushul. By the end of the year, they had spread west and south of the Aksai Chin road and established new posts, disregarding Indian protests. About 2,240 square kilometres of Indian territory in Ladakh had been occupied by the Chinese by then.

Map 2: Area of India claimed by China, 1962.

Despite these developments, the gist of the instructions of Government to HQ 15 Corps in the early winter of 1959-60, were:

- While patrolling Aksai Chin, an armed conflict with the Chinese forces should be avoided;
- If the Chinese forces intruded into Indian Territory, they should be asked to go back. Fire should be opened only if Indian troops were fired upon (the limit or boundary of Indian territory was not defined);
- This instruction applied to Chushul and Aksai Chin areas. No provocative action was to be taken but patrols or new posts should remain firmly on our side of the line (this line was not clearly defined).

As all attempts at negotiation between the two governments failed and the Chinese approach hardened, HQ 15 Corps recognised that fighting was inevitable. Their demand was that Army Headquarters should provide the means for fighting a war. The government, however, continued with its "Forward Policy" which required the establishment of Indian presence in Aksai Chin by the setting up of Indian posts between the Chinese posts. The aim was to interfere with the Chinese supply system and force them to withdraw. It was also believed to be a means of blocking further Chinese advance. Many posts were established almost within visual range of the Chinese. This was ordered without any due consideration on the part of government regarding the terrain and all that implied: acclimatisation of troops, logistics, availability of additional manpower, communications, snow clothing and the like.

As Maj. Gen. Joginder Singh in his book *Behind the Scene* describes it:

> Ultimately our deployment became a "chequer board" of posts, all of which had to be supplied by air. The supply system was most unsatisfactory as quite often the air drops landed near the Chinese posts . . . . Our posts were in precarious and tactically unsound positions at the mercy of Chinese encirclement, particularly in the Chip Chap Valley and the Spanggur gap.

Meanwhile, HQ 15 Corps completed most of the work required for the construction of the Leh airfield and also obtained information, mostly through air reconnaissance, that the Chinese had established posts in Kongka La, Khurnak Fort and the Chip Chap Valley in Ladakh. They were about 96 kilometres from Chushul. HQ 15 Corps had recommended a progressive build-up of forces in Ladakh ultimately leading up to an infantry division of four brigades with supporting arms, including a medium machine gun battalion (MMG Bn) and one regiment of medium artillery; but it took five years before this build up was completed.

Chapter 15

Battle Preparedness in the Ladakh Sector

HQ 114 Infantry Brigade was inducted into Ladakh only in 1960 after the Government of India ordered that responsibility of the defence of the Northern border be handed over to the Army by the Home ministry. When Brigadier Rawind Singh Grewal took over as its commander in 1960, he had under his command only two battalions of J&K Militia. Considering the extent of the international border in the Ladakh Sector, this force was grossly inadequate to keep a watchful eye on the Chinese, leave aside to protect it. A year later, in April 1961, an additional infantry battalion (1/8 GR) and some ancillary troops were inducted into the sector. However, there were still large gaps to be covered in the Brigade sector, requiring additional infantry. The frontage of 114 Infantry Brigade's sector extended over an area of approximately 480 kilometres, stretching from the Karakoram Pass (DBO) in the northwest, to Demchok in the east. Troops deployed on these posts braved great physical hardships due to the extreme climate and rugged terrain.

The Forward Policy

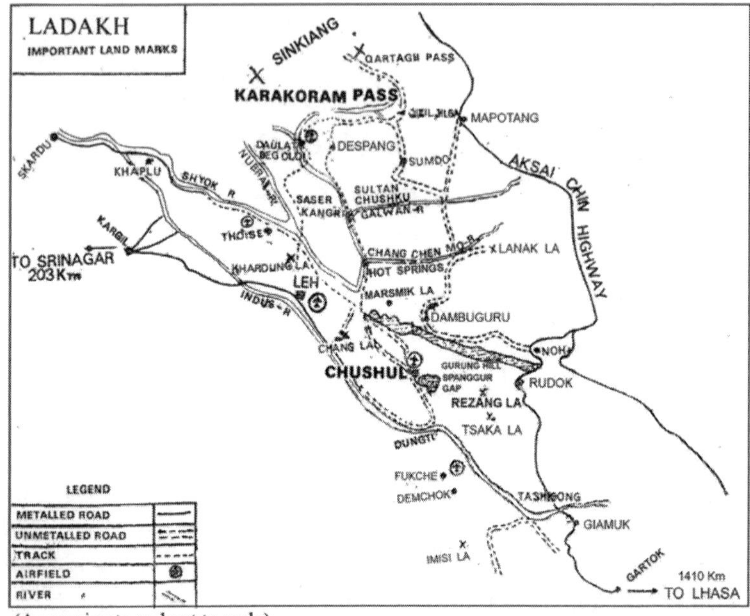

(Approximate and not to scale)

Map 3: Ladakh Sector – Important Places.

To carry out the forward policy of the Indian government, an additional infantry battalion, the 5th Battalion, the Jat Regiment, was inducted into Ladakh in April 1962. The headquarters of 114 Infantry Brigade now had two infantry battalions and two J&K Militia battalions in Ladakh. Nonetheless, this force was still grossly inadequate for the operational task entrusted to the brigade. To set up new posts, troops were moved as far forward into unoccupied Indian Territory as was logistically possible. Perforce, troops had to be dispersed into small, isolated posts, each held by a weak Section or Platoon. Obviously, these posts were to have limited defence potential; at best, they could act as flag posts, merely to show the physical presence of Indian troops in those areas.

Whenever and wherever the Indian Army established a new post, the Chinese promptly set up one opposite it. For them, the exercise was much simpler than it was for Indian Army. The PLA had already built a network of roads connecting their territory with the disputed area. These had been easy to make in most cases, because the terrain under Chinese occupation was generally flat and open plateau. Through this network, they brought in their troops on fast mechanical transport and used the same fast means to service them.

On the other hand, the 114 Infantry Brigade had to use yaks and ponies on difficult mountainous tracks for carriage of ammunition, rations and baggage, with troops alongside on foot. There were no road communications in Ladakh at that time. And, whenever there was a shortage of animal transport, troops also had to give a helping hand in load carrying. And, so, where Indian Army moved twenty personnel with so much difficulty, the Chinese were able to press in two hundred with ease. Rarely had so few been pitched against so many!

The state of communications and logistic support being what it was, the establishment of each new post meant a test of human endurance, operational efficiency and administrative planning! Yet in a period of sixteen months, from April 1961 to August 1962, 114 Brigade was able to raise the number of defended posts from thirteen to sixty-five.

In addition to establishing new posts, whenever possible, a helipad was made in the vicinity of each post. It was also during this period that the world's highest landing strip was prepared at an altitude of 4,997 metres (16,395 feet), in the area of Daulat Beg Oldi (DBO) situated approximately 16 kilometres southeast of the Karakoram Pass.

It is well known that soldiers of the Indian Army are expert at improvisation. They developed this skill on account of an acute shortage of material resources, particularly during the early years of India's independence. But the marking of the landing airstrip at DBO, perhaps, took the cake. The only means available at this post to indicate the limits of improvised landing strip to the pilot of the Packet aircraft carrying out the test landing, were human and animal skeletons[57] of old Ladakhi and Yarkandi caravans. These were laid in clusters to mark the landing strip: a reminder of the traders and their animals of long ago who had frozen to death wherever they had huddled to escape the snow blizzards!

This period of immense activity, with the entire burden of command and control resting on a single Brigade HQ, was quite nerve-wracking for the Commander and his staff. The deployment of troops in the extreme high altitude area (HAA) began to affect the health of the troops, animals and equipment. In addition, the troops had to face the Chinese psychological warfare. In May 1962, approximately one hundred Chinese soldiers advanced on Post "Alfa" in the DBO/Depsang in assault formation. They approached within 300 metres of Indian troops. As Major Jagjit Singh describes it, this was "followed by playing of loud Indian music and propaganda announcements on loudspeakers, asking our troops to vacate Chinese territory, as Hindi-Chini were brothers (Hindi-Chini-Bhai Bhai). Troops therefore were confused as they had been instructed not to open fire unless they were actually attacked by the Chinese."

In setting up tiny, isolated posts with little ability of own troops to defend themselves, India had fought a "political battle" so far. The task had been quite hazardous and had been completed under the most trying conditions. But from the defence point of view, it had not helped 114 Infantry Brigade. Rather, as the Brigade HQ saw things at Leh, the military situation in Ladakh was definitely deteriorating. The "Alfa" incident, in the assessment of Brigade Staff, signified Peking's intention to use force eventually. It was a sample of things to come. The writing was there on the wall, but

---

[57] Depsang Plateau, at an altitude of approximately 17,000 feet, was a dreaded death trap for caravans passing through due to snow blizzards which would last from three to five days, forcing the caravan travellers to take shelter amidst a few rocks, along with their animals. Often they froze to death! Over the years, innumerable human and animal skeletons littered the track passing through the Depsang plateau, when the trade route between Yarkand (in Xingang) and Leh in Ladakh was closed after occupation of Tibet by China in 1950.

were the Army HQ and the Government of India at New Delhi reading it?

Soon there after, 114 Infantry Brigade was ordered to set up a Platoon post at a specific area in Galwan Valley. The Commanding Officer of 1/8 Gorkha Rifles was ordered to establish it. No sooner was the post established on 10th July 1962, than it was surrounded by approximately 350 soldiers of the PLA of China, keeping about 50 metres away from the post. The next day, the Chinese vacated the area to the south and southeast of the post and fell back to about 200 metres on their other side, suggesting to the 1/8 Gorkha Rifles Platoon manning the Indian post, the option to withdraw.

For the Commander of 114 Infantry Brigade, however, the option of withdrawing the post in Galwan Valley was just out of question, because such a withdrawal would have invited similar pressure on all other posts in the brigade sector. The stalemate in Galwan continued for the next few days, during which the Chinese started applying the pressure of psychological warfare by setting up a microphone and amplifier aimed at our post. These threats on loudspeakers were punctuated by Indian music, to soften the minds of Indian troops.

In June 1962, Lieutenant General Daulet Singh, GOC-in-C Western Command, after assessing the operational situation in Ladakh, conveyed to Army Headquarters that the Prime Minister and his cabinet were being led astray by Krishna Menon, B.M. Malik and Lieutenant General Kaul, as they were ignorant of the ground situation and were, thus, putting the troops to grave risk. In fact, the entire defence of Ladakh in general, and Leh in particular, was at the mercy of the Chinese. In August 1962, the GOC-in-C further emphasized that there was no short cut to military preparedness, that there was danger of losing the territory India claimed as its own, certainty of unnecessary casualties and the consequent loss of morale and faith in the high command. In short, the GOC-in-C Western Command alerted the Army HQ of an impending self-created disaster. He also emphasized that unless they could induct a division of four brigades, the forward policy should be suspended and diplomatic means used to prolong the stalemate.

Map 4: Area of Ladakh under Chinese occupation.

Brigadier Raina as Commander 114 Infantry Brigade

Brigadier Tappy Raina arrived in Ladakh to take over the command of 114 Infantry Brigade from Brigadier Rawind Singh Grewal on 31st August 1962 at Leh. Brigadier Grewal left on promotion to the rank of major general and was awarded PVSM for his meritorious services in Ladakh.

Tappy Raina was keen to see the relief of 1/8 Gorkha Rifles by troops from 5 Jat. Accompanied by Major Jagjit Singh, his Brigade Major (BM), he went to supervise the relief programme personally.

Major Jagjit Singh recalled the morning of September 1962, when the first flight of IAF MI-4 helicopters took off with troops of 5 Jat, from Hot Springs to relieve the troops of 1/8 Gorkha Rifles at Galwan. Major Jagjit vividly remembered how enthusiastically the Jats displayed their eagerness to take on the Chinese:

> The Jats were all dressed in their winter kit, with their personal weapons and ammunition slung across their shoulders. All of them had fully anticipated the situation that they were soon to face. One would think that men about to leave for such a hazardous mission would betray some fear, tension or suspense; but this was not so with the gallant Jats! On the contrary, they were full of enthusiasm and self-confidence, thus displaying the inherent stoicism and simplicity of the Indian soldier. It was really heartening to see their enthusiasm!
>
> The first helicopter took off at the appointed time. But on the return flight, its engine started to lose power and the pilot decided to force land. He, however, landed very close to a so far unknown Chinese post. We at HQ 114 Infantry Brigade were not aware of the existence of this post between Hot Springs and Galwan, which perhaps was set up very recently and so the pilot had not been briefed to avoid flying over it.
>
> Within minutes of the force-landing of the helicopter, a hundred odd Chinese troops rolled down-hill and surrounded it. Fortunately, the helicopter had landed facing Post Galwan. Shortly, a strong tail wind started blowing, taking advantage of this, and showing a great presence of mind, Squadron Leader Badhwar, the pilot and Squadron Leader Narayanan as the co-pilot, immediately started the engine and took off without spending any time even on the normal instrument check! This left the Chinese completely stupefied by this sudden action. Squadron Leaders Badhwar and Narayanan were later decorated for their pluck and presence of mind.

The relief programme was completed without any further mishap. But Post Galwan continued to be under siege by Chinese PLA.

Tappy used to visit his Brigade sector to familiarize himself with the deployment and welfare of the troops. On such visits he used to camp at Chushul with his TAC HQ. It was during one of his stops at Chushul that Major General Joginder Singh made a dash to Chushul airfield to meet Tappy Raina and discuss the brigade's plan and deployment. This is what Major General Joginder Singh had to say of his visit to Ladakh as Chief of Staff (COS), HQ Western Command, Simla (Shimla) to assess the ground situation there:

> I flew to Chushul and met the Brigade Commander, Brigadier T.N. Raina, a good soldier, whom I knew very well.
>
> I asked him if he had made any contingency plans for the withdrawal of the posts, should the situation deteriorate. We discussed the situation and came to the conclusion that two regular battalions should defend the eastern boundary of the airfield, with one battalion in depth. He would use the remnants of forward troops as they withdrew from forward posts, to reinforce the depth position around Brigade HQ, and light tanks could cover the gap in the hill feature between the two forward battalions.
>
> He asked for some other equipment and to make up the shortages in the Field Regiment, some mortars, LMGs, additional clothing, ammunition and rations. He particularly asked for a spare high powered radio set and a generator.
>
> I had to leave Chushul within two hours as the weather was deteriorating.

The supply and movement of all these items were arranged by HQ Western Command. AMX-13 tanks were dismantled at Chandigarh into suitable loads for airlift to Chushul airfield where they were reassembled. The two forward battalions were 1/8 Gorkha Rifles and 13th Battalion of the Kumaon Regiment. Both these battalions prepared their defensive positions as best permitted by the terrain and limited available defence stores. The tanks were also suitably deployed.

Meanwhile, according to General Joginder Singh, the Ministry of Defence received a very stiff warning note from the Chinese because of the army's movements in Ladakh and NEFA, particularly as a result of Indian Army's penetration at Khinzemane on Thagla Ridge in the extreme northwest of the McMahon Line. Many Assam Rifles posts had apparently been established by Mr. Malik, IPS, Director IB, although the positions were supposed to be under army control! General Daulet Singh summed up the situation thus:

> Our civilian and military junta's game of bluff had perhaps reached its climax! The joint civil and military set up in New Delhi was living in a fool's paradise and the Indian and foreign press were still being briefed that there was no likelihood of a war with China!
>
> Thus Indian politicians were still being made to believe that China was being defied with a posture of political make believe, without pausing to think that the "lamb was being fattened for the slaughter"!
>
> The GOC-in-C Western Command further added that during September 1962, Prime Minister Nehru had gone abroad and in his absence, Defence Minister Krishna Menon gave orders to shoot if necessary. When the COAS had asked for orders in writing, Krishna Menon evaded. Instead, he too pushed off to the United States to attend a UN session. So, all orders for "shooting if necessary" were issued verbally. When Chief of the Army Staff insisted upon the Defence Secretary for issue of written orders, these were given after obtaining Menon's approval from the United States.

The spark for the fighting on the border was lit when Defence Minister Krishna Menon sent a written order to General P.N. Thapar, Chief of the Army Staff, which became known as the "Eviction Order" in army circles. It ordered the eviction of the

Chinese from the Kameng Frontier Division and Thagla area in NEFA.

Western Command now anticipated that the eviction order in the Eastern Sector might result in a retaliatory attack on posts in Aksai Chin in the Ladakh Sector. Accordingly, a warning order by HQ Western Command was issued that troops should be prepared for an attack by the Chinese, and be ready for a fight.

Reasons for the Sino-Indian War

There have been speculations on the motive of the Chinese for their sudden aggression on India's northern frontier and also their equally sudden subsequent halt and cease fire. The reasons put forth are that hitting out at India's economy had been the basic objective of the Chinese military operations. In addition, the purpose was to snub India's attempt to gain leadership of the Non-Aligned Movement (NAM).

At the end of the World War 2, India and China were in the same position: a vast population in a huge area of land, where despite a number of rather highly developed industrial centres, the majority of the population lived in rural areas engaged in agriculture of a traditional nature. By 1960, there was a contrast. While China suffered natural calamities such as famine combined with miscalculation in industrial planning, India had made slow but steady progress. The Communist Chinese aggression in 1962 not only affected India's military and political position, but also her economy. The uncertainty following the ceasefire was not limited to the military and political field either, but it encroached upon India's economic life as well.

The consequences of a military build-up on the economic life of a country are equally strong, because modern armament cannot be produced overnight. Still, a beginning had already been made by India. Under pressure of politico-military necessities, the reconstruction of heavy industry was accelerated. Steel capacity, above all, was speedily raised. All this required a higher measure of readiness for sacrifice and stronger efforts on the part of the people of India.

That the politico-military humiliation inflicted by China on India not only jolted Prime Minister Jawaharlal Nehru and his cabinet, but also invoked a spirit of sacrifice and firm resolution for stronger efforts, was beyond doubt. This, in the long run, was to be an advantage because India thus received an impetus which was to prove extremely valuable for her economic development.

Chapter 16

The Dragon Strikes in Ladakh

Within a month of having taken over command of 114 Infantry Brigade, Tappy Raina had finalised the deployment of troops in his brigade sector covering a frontage of approximately 480 kilometres. By early October 1962, 114 Infantry Brigade was deployed as under:

(a) Northern Sector (Daulat Beg Oldi-Sultan Chusku)	14 J&K Militia[58]
(b) Central Sector (Galwan River-Lukung)	5 Jat
(c) Chushul Sector (Sirjap Spanggur)	1/8 Gorkha Rifles
(d) Southern sector (Dungti-Demchok)	7 J&K Militia[111]
(e) Leh	13 Kumaon [59]

[58] The 7 and 14 J&K Militia battalions comprised mostly of soldiers from the Ladakh District of Jammu and Kashmir. After the unilateral cease fire declared by China with effect from midnight 21/22nd November 1962, Indian government approved the re-organisation of these two militia battalions into a new regular infantry regiment, The Ladakh Scouts, to be trained in the special role of "scouts", i.e. to act as the "eyes and ears" of 3 Himalayan Division, deployed for the defence of Ladakh Sector. Lieutenant Colonel R.M. Bannon, Dogra Regiment, Commanding Officer of 7 J&K Militia became the first commandant of The Ladakh Scouts.

At this stage, there was no armour or artillery in support of the brigade.

Operations in the Northern Sector

By this time 114 Infantry Brigade had re-occupied about 6,475 sq. kilometres of territory in Ladakh through acting on the forward policy. Hereafter, it was not possible to set up any more posts in the forward areas as the Chinese were becoming more aggressive every day. They could afford such arrogance and bellicosity for theirs was the mightier force.

The bellicose intentions of China were established on the night of 19/20th October when Chinese troops advanced on the Indian Army's forward posts in Depsang Plateau which was under the immediate command of Major Sardul Singh Randhawa, Second-in-Command 14 J&K Militia stationed at the command post at Daulat Beg Oldi.

The concentration of Chinese troops was first noticed opposite posts Parmodak and Bishan. This was at about 10 p.m. Havildar Tulsi Ram, post commander at Parmodak, informed Major Randhawa about this development. The seventeen men who were "standing to" at these two posts, with bayonets fixed and eyes focussed on the approaching Chinese, wondered what this was all about. Were the Chinese indulging in yet another display of force to scare them away at this time of the night? Would their posts be surrounded like Post Galwan leading to living under continuous siege thereafter? These posts were to be the first victims of Chinese aggression in Ladakh.

At about 11 p.m., the Chinese started shelling the two posts. The post commanders immediately passed this information to Major Randhawa at DBO and sought further orders. "You will hold your posts and fight to the last man and the last round", was the order from Major Randhawa. This was in keeping with the orders, earlier issued to the Brigade HQ by the higher authorities.

---

[59] This battalion was inducted into Ladakh in September 1962 and was temporarily at Leh. (13th Kumaon)

The shelling stopped after some time but under its cover the Chinese had already closed in on the posts. Arrayed in assault formation, they were now barely 180 metres away. Frenzied, indoctrinated and well equipped, the determined soldiers of the People's Liberation Army of China were pressing their first attack against India in Ladakh. It required raw courage for the grossly outnumbered and ill-equipped Indian troops of 14 J&K Militia to face such an attack. But Parmodak and Bishan were occupied and led by dedicated men of great courage. They began hitting back hard.

What the Chinese had started on the night of 19/20th October 1962 in DBO Sector, was not an isolated attack on a few Indian posts. It was a full scale undeclared war against India. They were now using the Aksai Chin road for the real purpose for which they had built it.

Post Parmodak

Post Parmodak was the smallest post in Ladakh and was held by five men in all, Havildar Tulsi Ram and four others. However, it enjoyed a great tactical advantage over the attacker. Located at a height of about 5,485 metres (approximately 18,280 fee), it dominated the surrounding area tactically and by observation. It was, therefore, not easy to assault this position. The Chinese shelling however killed the soldier manning LMG No 1 at this post, so Havildar Tulsi Ram himself took over the weapon. Before long, the remaining three men had also fallen, leaving Tulsi Ram as the only survivor. A man of lesser courage would have tried to run away for safety, but Tulsi Ram held on. Firing his machine-gun at the advancing enemy he was taking a heavy toll from it for killing his brethren-in-arms. But as his ammunition started diminishing and the Chinese approached dangerously close, he found an opportunity to leap out of his trench, carrying his machine-gun with him, and slip downhill towards DBO. For his dauntless courage, Havildar Tulsi Ram was later decorated with Vir Chakra.

Post Bishan

Set up at 5,650 metres (approximately 18,830 feet), Post Bishan was the highest post in the 114 Infantry Brigade sector. It was held by a weak platoon with a strength of just twelve men. This post also had the same tactical advantage as Parmodak. The Chinese shelled this post for about 45 minutes, killing four of the men and destroying all the bunkers of the post. But that did not deter the rest who continued to fight gallantly under the inspiring leadership of Company Havildar, Major Anant Ram. Two Chinese assaults were beaten back, inflicting heavy casualties. The Chinese retaliated by surrounding the post and laying a siege, which forced Anant Ram to withdraw. Finding a small opening, which the Chinese had somehow left uncovered, he extricated his men one by one along a precipice. For his resolute leadership and courage, Company Havildar Major Anant Ram was decorated with Vir Chakra.

Post Chandni

This was yet another post in DBO Sector which gave a hard fight to the attacking Chinese. It was held as a platoon defended locality by twenty five other ranks (ORs), commanded by Subedar Sonam Stopdan.

The Chinese attacked this post early on the morning of 20th October. They first subjected it to intense artillery and mortar shelling for about an hour, which was followed by an infantry assault. Under the inspiring leadership of Subedar Sonam Stopdan, the Ladakhis put up a heroic defence. But the momentum of the Chinese attack kept increasing. Chinese soldiers kept advancing in waves. Finally, one by one, the brave Indian jawans laid down their lives and the post fell into Chinese hands. An emotional Randhawa[60], with choked voice, spoke to Major Jagjit Singh, the Brigade Major, on wireless — *Chandni Khatam ho gai, Chandni jal gai!* (Chandni is finished; Chandni has been reduced to ashes.)

---

[60] Major Randhawa had served with 14 Jammu and Kashmir Militia for many years and knew the men well. He had led a couple of difficult patrols during the early phase of the setting up of new Indian Army posts in the Depsang Plains for which he was decorated. The death of his former colleagues naturally made him emotional at the time of reporting. After re-organisation of 7 & 14 J&K Militia into Ladakh Scouts, Major (later Lieutenant Colonel) Randhawa became the Deputy Commandant and was the third Commandant of the Ladakh Scouts.

The Chinese, however, suffered heavy casualties. Subedar Stopdan was awarded the Maha Vir Chakra and sepoys Chiring, Wangchuk and Phunchok, each a Vir Chakra, for their brave deeds[61].

Post Bhujan

After the fall of Chandni, the Chinese attacked Post Bhujan. Naib Subedar Rigzin Phunchok and his fifteen men fought heroically but again they were also crushed by the heavy numbers of the assaulting Chinese. The few who survived fell back and made a tortuous journey to Sultan Chushku. Naib Subedar Rigzin was awarded the Vir Chakra for leadership and bravery.

From 20-21st October 1962, a number of other Indian posts were similarly attacked by the Chinese. By the afternoon of 22nd October, of the total of eighteen posts in this sector, only two remained intact — Daulat Beg Oldi and Talwari. The rest had fallen fighting, adding a few more gallantry awards to 14 J&K Militia. In his book *The Saga of Ladakh*: *Heroic Battles of Rezangla & Gurung Hill — 1961-62*, Major Jagjit Singh has described the deterioration in the relations between India and China during this period, as follows:

> By the autumn of 1962, China had unleashed an undeclared war against India; an expected "finale" to her incessant propaganda of hatred. Sino-Indian relations had now taken a new bitter turn. The age-old ties of goodwill between the two countries had snapped, opening a new and bitter chapter in Sino-India relations.
>
> The icy Depsang Plateau, now thundered with Chinese shells and bullets. So did the neighbouring hills: obviously, taken aback they stood bewildered.
>
> The Depsang Plateau and DBO, on the ancient trade route of caravans, were used to the soft jingle of the bells of double-

---

[61] During the President's investiture ceremony a year later, however, only Phunchok was present to receive his award. The others were posthumously decorated for bravery, having laid down their lives defending Chandni Post.

hump camels, ponies, yaks and dogs of peaceful caravans of old, who went their way to and from Yarkand in Sinkiang (Xiangang) to Leh in Ladakh, but never before had they ever witnessed this ghastly spectacle; this brutal killing of men and the flow of human blood! Never before had these snowy mountains heard the deafening sound of gun-fire and the groans of the wounded! The Himalayas had been rudely woken up from their long, deep slumber. Thus, the hitherto impenetrable barrier had been pierced by the lustful designs of man for power and supremacy.

Was this an attack in the normal sense of the word, by a state engaged in a border dispute with another? No, it was something far more sinister; a betrayal of one whom the attacker had proclaimed a "Bhai" (brother). It was a stab in the back! Chinese cloak-and-dagger diplomacy had shed the cloak; only the dagger was now brandished. An expansionist China had put back the clock of history to the era of the Celestial Empire; the only difference being that a neighbour friendly through the ages had become her target number one.

A journey's end it was for those who laid their lives on the bloody battle field of Depsang plateau. Little did they know during their early struggles against the winds and freezing cold that this was not all: the worst was still to come! That it was not weather which was to act treacherous, as in the case of Daulat Beg, the caravan leader of old, but man himself, in the garb of the People's Liberation Army of China.

DBO and Talwari

The DBO defended area had strength of 125 all ranks, whereas Talwari Post was about 10-strong. At about 4 a.m. on 22nd October, a patrol led by an officer reported a concentration of over 1,000 Chinese troops, not far from DBO; about 300-400 troops to the south, and over 700 to the south-east. Their intentions were obvious. They were planning to annihilate the post.

In the face of such enemy strength, DBO could not be expected to hold out for long. Lieutenant Colonel Nihal Singh, CO 14 J&K Militia, who had flown from his headquarters at Thoise to DBO at the outbreak of hostilities to take over personal command of troops in the Depsang Plateau, saw this helpless situation and requested the brigade commander, Brigadier Tappy Raina for permission to withdraw.[62] As there was no logic in sticking to the posts and sacrificing troops, by 3.30 a.m. on 23rd October, DBO was abandoned[63].

Operations in the Central Sector

The Central Sector where 5 Jat was deployed also became a simultaneous target of Chinese attack.

Post Galwan

This post was the first target in this sector. Commanded by Major S.S. Hasabnis, it had a total strength of sixty all ranks. It may be recalled that this post manned by 5 Jat, was encircled by the Chinese ever since its establishment in July 1962.

Early on the morning of 20th October 1962, the Chinese opened up with heavy small arms, machine gun, rocket launcher and mortar fire on the post from all directions. The firing lasted for about an hour and then followed the assault by approximately 500 to 600 Chinese soldiers. Major Jagjit Singh, the Brigade Major of HQ 114 Infantry Brigade, has narrated the actions fought by troops of 5 Jat, deployed at Galwan Post as under:

> Hasabnis and his men fought back as best as they could, but the outcome was inevitable. Thirty all ranks, including two JCOs and Captain Paul, who was the medical officer attached to the

---

[62] The order "to fight to the last man and last round" had by now been cancelled by the higher authorities.

[63] Naib Subedar Bhimu Kamble of the Mahar Regiment was in command of a platoon of medium machines-guns at Daulat Beg Oldi. According to orders, all heavy equipment was to be destroyed. But Kamble decided not to part with his medium machine-guns and ordered the platoon to carry these with them.

post, were killed. Eighteen others, including Hasabnis,[64] were wounded.

So ended the Galwan episode and with it the constant suspense and vigil of a brave body of men who had faced this unusual and unfair military situation courageously, cheerfully and with good discipline, in the highest traditions of the Indian Army. And when the attack came, they presented the enemy with a rain of bullets, rather than a display of white flags.

Subedar Amar Singh with a platoon was holding a patrol base, south of Galwan valley. This gallant JCO would inspire his men by saying, “We have come here to fight the Chinese. Remember we are not going to leave this sacred soil, whatever be the odds”!

On 21st October, Subedar Amar Singh received order from the CO 5 Jat to leave one section at this patrol base and to withdraw the remaining men of his platoon to an alternative position in the rear. The section was to watch Chinese movement in the area and to provide early information to the post at Hot Springs. It was not to get involved in the fighting but to withdraw at an opportune moment. True to his words, however, Subedar Amar Singh decided to stay back with his Section.

At about 11.30 a.m. on 22nd October, the Chinese started shelling the section observation post. Subedar Amar Singh moved forward from the section post to the observation post, presumably to make a personal assessment of the situation. Soon this observation post came under attack by the enemy. After some time, the rest of the section also came under attack. Amar Singh and his men held their ground till physically overrun by the Chinese. Subedar Amar Singh was killed in action, along with most of his section.

---

[64] A few years later, recalling the Chinese assault on his post at Galwan, Hasabnis wrote to Maj Jagjit Singh that even his jawans felt agitated at the tactically unsound location of the post. “I could give no answer, except to say that there may be political reasons or some one’s error in ordering the post to be sited there. The only thing we could do was to fight as best we could and leave this question for others to answer . . . .” said Hasabnis.

Similar reports about Chinese assaults on other posts scattered in penny packets, were also being received at HQ 114 Infantry Brigade. Posts like Kongma and Nulla Junction fell to the Chinese.

Post Kongma

At about 2 p.m. on 22nd October, Major Jagjit Singh, BM 114 Infantry Brigade received a message at the brigade headquarters from Post Kongma, since the post was not in wireless communication at the time with their Battalion HQ: "About 300 Chinese are advancing towards us. They are approximately a thousand yards away at present".

Within minutes of sending the message, this post came under shelling by the Chinese. The soldiers at the post kept fighting till late evening, by when all their ammunition was exhausted. Kongma's indomitable post commander, Subedar Surjit Singh, who despite his wounds had been directing the fire of his post, also laid down his life in the line of duty. Further fighting was now futile and the last six soldiers of this gallant platoon of 5 Jat were then compelled to withdraw; the post fell to the Chinese.

Post Nulla Junction

The next night, on 23rd October, the platoon post at Nulla Junction also pulled out after a brief engagement. The forward section, out of three, had come under Chinese shelling at about 2230 hours and, an hour later, the battle was over. The Chinese had overrun this section post. It had been a brief but bloody fight for Naik Maya Ram's section. For the last few minutes, before receiving orders to withdraw, Maya Ram fought single-handedly. Four of his comrades had been killed and two wounded. At this stage, Company Commander Major Ajit Singh ordered the entire post to withdraw and build up at Hot Springs. The wounded were told to pull out first, while Naik Maya Ram kept covering their movement. And, finally, he abandoned the post himself.

Post Hot Springs

With the above developments, the post at Hot Springs was left out on a limb. Brigadier Raina recognized that troops from Post Hot Springs should withdraw and build up at Lukung, a strong defensive position, where 5 Jat were busy preparing the defences.

Operations in Chushul Sector

Posts Sirijap I and II

Posts Sirijap I and II were held by a Company of 1/8 Gorkha Rifles commanded by Major Dhan Singh Thapa. On 21st October 1962, at about 6 am, the Chinese aimed a heavy barrage of artillery fire on Sirijap I. Some shells fell on the command post and damaged the wireless set, thus putting the post out of communication. Under the resolute leadership of Major Thapa, Sirijap I put up a gallant fight. With hardly 40 all-ranks, two successive enemy attacks were beaten back. The Chinese, who had attacked with about 10 to 1 superiority, suffered about 100 casualties.

An eye-witness account of this heroic battle was given by Naik Rabi Lal Thapa, who saw the grim spectacle from barely 1,000 metres away. Naik Thapa had volunteered from Thakung, a small post on the eastern shores of Pangong Tso, to take a storm boat to Sirijap I and report the latest situation. He saw the Chinese closing in on the post and entering its perimeter. The Gorkhas manning Sirijap I had also leapt out of their trenches and with their war cry *Ayo Gurkhali* ("Here come the Gorkhas") engaged the enemy in mortal hand-to-hand combat. Rabi Lal then knew that Major Dhan Singh Thapa and his men were, perhaps, fighting their last battle. By about 8.30 a.m. most of the Gorkhas had fallen and the post reduced to smoke and rubble. The Chinese then turned to Sirijap-II, which also fell but only after severe fighting. By 22nd October, all the forward posts in the Chushul Sector had been either withdrawn or overrun by the Chinese.

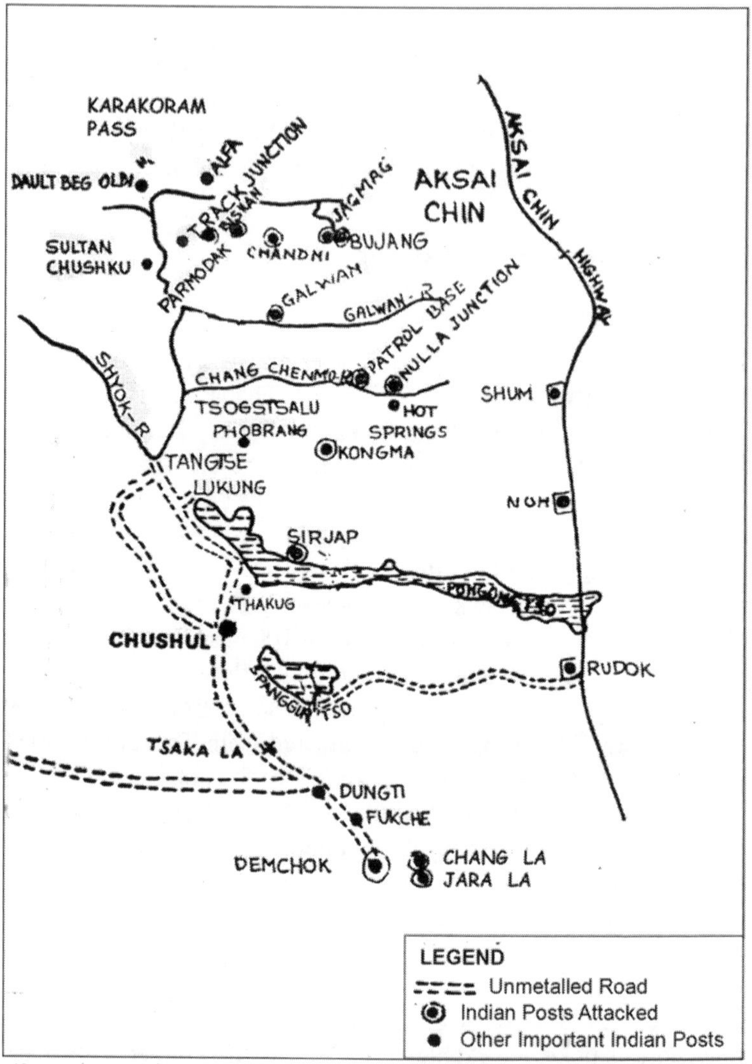

KARAKORAM PASS
DAULT BEG OLDI
ALFA
TRACK JUNCTION
BISKAN
JAGMAG
AKSAI CHIN
AKSAI CHIN HIGHWAY
SULTAN CHUSHKU
PARMODAK
CHANDNI
BUJANG
GALWAN
GALWAN-R
PATROL BASE
NULLA JUNCTION
SHYOK-R
CHANG CHENMO-R
TSOGSTSALU
HOT SPRINGS
SHUM
PHOBRANG
KONGMA
TANGTSE
LUKUNG
NOH
SIRJAP
PONGONG TSO
THAKUG
CHUSHUL
RUDOK
SPANGGUR TSO
TSAKA LA
DUNGTI
FUKCHE
DEMCHOK
CHANG LA
JARA LA

LEGEND
Unmetalled Road
Indian Posts Attacked
Other Important Indian Posts

(Approximate and not to scale)

Map 5: Indian posts attacked by the Chinese PLA in October 1962.

Southern Sector

The operational responsibility of Southern Sector was that of 7 J&K Militia, commanded by Lieutenant Colonel Banon[65] of the Dogra Regiment. Here the posts Chang La and Jara La both fell on 27th October 1962. The Chinese aim appeared to be to force the post into submission by a sheer show of numerical superiority of almost 20:1.

By 28th October 1962, the Chinese aggression came to a temporary halt. Presumably they now wanted some respite to lick their wounds after the severe fighting and to regroup for further offensive operations. They now held the line Daulat Beg Oldi-Sirijap-Demchok.

These had been a devastating eight days for troops deployed in the 114 Infantry Brigade Sector. The Chinese had thrown in masses of infantry, heavily supported by artillery, against small isolated posts which were equipped with only personal small arms and 2-inch mortars. Only in some cases a section each of 3-inch mortars and medium machine guns were deployed to strengthen the defended locality. And, yet, it had not been an easy walkover for the Chinese. They had faced stout opposition and suffered considerable casualties; their blue uniformed porters were seen carrying truckloads of their killed and wounded casualties during each single day of fighting.

In the Ladakh Sector, the Indian troops fought the enemy with courage and displayed extreme devotion to duty. Thus, over 50 per cent of the Chinese troops who came to actual grips with the enemy were killed, wounded or captured. The ratio of killed to wounded and captured was about 4:5, a very high ratio of killed for any battle!

---

[65] Post the merger of 7 &14 J&K Militia battalions into The Ladakh Scouts, Lt. Col R.M. Banon became the first Commandant of The Ladakh Scouts.

The first reaction to this naked, unabashed aggression by China was one of profound shock when India woke up on the morning of 21st October 1962. Next day, on 22nd October, Prime Minister Pandit Jawaharlal Nehru in his broadcast to the nation asked his country-men, to gird up their loins to meet the threat posed by China:

> Perhaps there are not many instances in history where one country, that is India, has gone out of her way to be friendly and co-operative with the Chinese Government and its people, and even, to plead their cause in the Councils of the world, and then for the Chinese Government to return evil for good and even go to the extent of committing aggression and invade our sacred soil. No self-respecting country, and certainly not India, with her love of freedom, can submit to this, whatever the consequences may be!

The prime minister had aptly summed up the nation's feelings. On 26th October, Dr S. Radhakrishnan[66], the President of India, under Article 352 of the Constitution, declared a state of Emergency in the country. The Defence of India Ordinance was also promulgated. Morarji Desai, the Finance Minister, announced the setting up of a National Defence Fund for voluntary contributions towards the nation's defence. To ensure wider participation of the people in the defence effort, two important committees were formed; the National Defence Council and the Citizens' Central Committee.

In 1962, Deepawali, the Indian festival of lights, passed without any traditional celebration in the country; no lamps were lit as there was little joy in the hearts of people because of the Sino-

---

[66] Accomplished academic and scholar, erudite philosopher and teacher, Sarvepalli Radhakrishnan was elected the second President of India. Radhakrishnan had been knighted in 1931 and had received the Bharat Ratna in 1954. His election to the office brought a great emphasis on the education system and academic development of the country. Before his election to the President's office, Radhakrishnan had remained free of any political involvement.

India War. But for the front-line soldier came hundreds of packets of the choicest sweets as a token of the nation's appreciation.

Parades and public meetings were held throughout the land, condemning China's aggression and expressing the people's will to fight the invader. Opposition parties set aside their political differences and declared full support to the Indian government.

In Leh, the district headquarter of Ladakh, able-bodied Ladakhis offered their services to HQ 114 Infantry Brigade to help in the preparation of defences, improvement of roads and tracks, to serve as porters, or to fight alongside the army to defend their hearth and home.

Elsewhere in India, huge crowds thronged the recruiting offices for an opportunity to serve the country. There were long queues at the hospitals for donating blood. Housewives started to knit garments for the soldiers when they were told of the shortage of woollens at the front. Trade union workers pledged not to resort to strikes or undertake any agitation which might hamper production. Canteens were set up on railway stations to serve free refreshments and meals to the troops, passing through on their way to battlefields. Women volunteered their services to attend to the wounded at various military hospitals.

Contributions poured in from all corners of India for the National Defence Fund; from the rich and poor, young and old. A new tide of emotion swept the motherland. From the shores of Kanya Kumari in the south, to the northern most tip of the country, from arid Rajasthan in the west to Bengal and Assam in the east, India's 500 million stood as one man behind Prime Minister Nehru and the Government of India. For the soldier in the field, it was immensely encouraging to note this resurgence in the nation.

Chapter 17

The Himalayan Division

As the defended posts along the vast frontage of 114 Infantry Brigade defended sector kept falling back in the face of the Chinese onslaught it became obvious to Army HQ and the government that there was an urgent requirement of re-enforcing the Ladakh sector with additional troops. All that 114 Infantry Brigade could now be expected to do was to concentrate its force on the outskirts of Leh, to give a "last man, last round" battle for the defence of Ladakh's capital. If Leh fell, the whole of Ladakh would be lost to the Chinese.

Brigadier Raina was directed by HQ 15 Corps in a signal message, "to take over personal command of the Chushul Sector, which was vital to defend Ladakh in general, and Leh, in particular." The reaction to this signal at HQ 114 Infantry Brigade is narrated by Major Jagjit Singh, the Brigade Major:

> The signal was quite perplexing to us at Brigade Headquarters. 1/8 Gorkha Rifle was already deployed in the Chushul Sector with some medium machine-guns; facing them, on the other side, the Chinese had approximately one regiment (equivalent of our brigade) in area Spanggur-Rudok. A Chinese attack on Chushul, at this juncture, would have meant a virtual walk-over for them. What then was the logic in the Brigade Commander moving to Chushul for personal command of one infantry battalion defended sector?

This signal was, however, soon clarified. A new Himalayan Divisional Headquarters[67] was to be raised at Leh with additional forces, comprising two infantry brigades, an armoured squadron less one tank troop, one field artillery regiment, and one heavy mortar battery, engineers and medium machine guns. These were already on the move and would be inducted in the Ladakh Sector.

Construction of the Srinagar-Leh highway had by now been completed. A few Soviet built AN 12 transport aircraft were based at Chandigarh airfield. Induction of additional troops had, thus, become an operational necessity for defence of the Ladakh Sector.

The new command set up, and areas of responsibility, were fixed as under:

(a) Northern Sector (Nubra Valley-DBO Sultan Chusku)	14 J&K Militia, (under the direct control of HQ 3 Himalayan Division).
(b) Central Sector (Lukung-Chushul-Tsaka La)	114 Infantry Brigade Group, comprising of 1 Jat 5 Jat 13 Kumaon 1/8 Gorkha Rifles Sqn less 2 tps ex 20 Lancer 38 Field Battery ex 13 Field Regiment Troop heavy mortars MMG Company ex 1 Mahar Company field engineers
(c) Southern Sector (Dungti-Fukche- Demchok)	70 Infantry Brigade, comprising of three regular infantry battalions and 7 J&K Militia, with one

[67] Raising of HQ 3 Himalayan Division commenced w.e.f 26th October 1962 at Leh, followed by induction of 70 & 163 Infantry Brigades.

	battery of field artillery, one heavy mortar troop, one company of field engineers and one company of MMG.
(d) Leh Sector	163 Infantry Brigade, with one battery ex 13 field regiment, one heavy mortar troop and one company of field engineers.
(e) Leh	HQ 3 Himalayan Division[68] and Div troops.

114 Infantry Brigade Moves to Chushul

On receiving the fresh deployment plan, Brigadier Tappy Raina, accordingly briefed his Brigade Major, Major Jagjit Singh:

> If we are to fight now at Lukung-Chushul-Tsaka La, we must move the Brigade HQ to Chushul, at once . . . . Please fix up with the helicopter boys for a flight tomorrow morning. I would like you and the GSO 3[69] to accompany me. The DAA & QMG[70] can bring the Brigade Headquarters personnel, essential stores and equipment by road.

By about 5 a.m. the next day, the mobilisation of 114 Infantry Brigade had commenced and the road convoy was on the move from Leh to Chushul. A couple of hours later, Tappy Raina and his Tac HQ also set course for Chushul in an Indian Air Force helicopter.

---

[68] Later redesignated as 3 Mountain Division

[69] GSO 3 (General Staff Officer 3) assists the Brigade Major in his duties.

[70] DAA & QMG (Deputy Assistant Adjutant and Quartermaster General) the counterpart of the Brigade Major deals with administration and coordination of logistics.

Deployment of 114 Infantry Brigade

As stated earlier, the Sector of 114 Infantry Brigade's operational responsibility now extended from Tsaka La in the South to Lukung in the North, a distance of approximately 80 kilometres as the brigade frontage. This sector was subdivided into two sub-sectors, Lukung Sector and Chushul Sector. Between the two sub-sectors there was a gap of about 40 kilometres which was linked by an unmetalled Class-9 road, fit only for up to 3-ton vehicles[71]. While the Lukung sub-sector was the operational responsibility of 5 Jat commanded by Lieutenant Colonel Bakhtawar Singh, the Chushul Sub-Sector was the responsibility of the rest of the brigade with the following troops:

- 1 Jat commanded by Lieutenant Colonel C.S. Tanwar.
- 13 Kumaon commanded by Lieutenant Colonel H.S. Dhingra.
- 1/8 Gorkha Rifles Commanded by Lieutenant Colonel Hari Chand, MVC.
- Squadron 20 Lancers less troop, commanded by Captain A.K. Dewan.
- 38 Field Battery ex 13 Field Regiment, commanded by Major S.P. Joshi.
- MMG Company ex 1 Mahar (commanded by Major Reddy) — Company Field Engineers
- 114 Brigade Signal Company commanded by Captain Percy Route.

Chushul was an egg-shaped sub-sector, centred on the Chushul Valley, with an unmetalled road linking it to Lukung in the north and Dungti in the neighbouring brigade in the south. Chushul Valley itself is 7- to 10-kilometre wide and almost 40 kilometres long. It is both barren and sandy, at an average altitude of 4,115 metres (approximate 13,720 feet), above sea level.

---

[71] From Lukung this road went up to Darbuk. The portion between Darbuk and Leh, across the Chang La was still under construction. The going from Lukung to Darbuk was very rugged.

Thakung, a ground of tactical importance, dominated the northern approach from Lukung to the Chushul Valley and onwards to Tsaka La on the inter-brigade boundary in the south. In contrast, the dominating features on the east and west, respectively, of nearly 2 kilometres wide gap and 6 kilometres deep, through the eastern range of mountains (presently known as Kailash Range), near Spanggur Tso, referred as the Spanggur Gap, was appreciated as the major approach to Chushul Sub Sector.

Main Chinese Approaches to Chushul

Brigadier Raina appreciated that the Chinese could attack Chushul from three directions (*see* Map 6):

1. **Tsaka La Approach.** By rolling down the mountain east of Dungti-Tsaka La. In the absence of any road communications from this direction, they could, however, attack mainly with infantry. Alternatively, they could advance along the Road Demchok-Dungti. In such an event their attack could be supported both by armour and artillery. This approach, however, would have meant fighting a major battle at Fukche and Dungti, in the sector commanded by Indian Army's 70 Infantry Brigade and where the bulk of this brigade was deployed. Moreover, the River Indus was an obstacle on this side, adding to the defence potential of this sector.
2. **Thakung Approach.** Where the enemy could arrive in three possible ways:
   (i) By advancing along the land route from the direction of Marsmik La to Lukung and, thereafter, along the road Lukung-Thakung-Chushul.
   (ii) By an amphibious assault across Pangong Lake.
   (iii) By an attack along both the above routes.

   In all these three cases, the Chinese could attack mainly with infantry, as there were no road communications to the east. Further, the column coming by the land route would have to eliminate Indian troops at Lukung, a strong defensive position, before being able to hit Chushul.

3. **Spanggur Gap Approach.** A road capable of carrying heavy vehicles was available to the Chinese up to their most forward post located at the eastern extremity of the Spanggur Gap. By attacking from this direction, the Chinese could make maximum use of their resources, including armour and artillery.

It followed from the above that an attack on Chushul via Rudok along Spanggur was the most likely approach for the Chinese offensive aiming to capture Chushul Valley. Opening the Spanggur Gap would be their obvious aim and for that the ground dominating the Gap would also have to be captured. The two features that dominated the Gap were Gurung Hill to the north and Magar Hill[72] in the south. Thus, the Spanggur Gap, the Gurung and the Magar Hills were considered to be the main Chinese objectives in Chushul Sub-Sector.

Subsidiary thrusts were, however, possible along the entire eastern range of mountains. The most important of them was *via* Rezang La, located between Magar Hill and Tsaka La. If this was captured by the Chinese, they could roll down Magar Hill and cut off the road from Leh-Dungti-Tsaka La to Chushul, in conjunction with their main thrust astride the Spanggur Gap axis.

In view of all the above considerations, Brigadier Raina deployed his Brigade as under: (*See* Map 6)

1. *1/8 Gorkha Rifles:* One rifle company each in areas, Spanggur Gap, Chushul Airfield, and Gurung Hill.[73]
2. *13 Kumaon:* Two rifle companies to be deployed in Area Magar Hill, and one Rifle Company to be deployed at Rezang La. The Battalion, less three rifle companies deployed in the area south of Chushul airfield.

---

[72] 1/8 Gorkha Rifles, who had been in token occupation of these heights till now, had given them these nicknames, after the Gurung and the Magars — the two main sub-castes of this unit.

[73] The fourth company of 1/8 Gorkha had been badly mauled in the fighting at Sirijap and Yula posts earlier in October 1962 and was not available for the battle of Chushul.

3. *1 Jat:* Approximately two companies to be deployed between Thakung and heights north of Gurung Hill. The Battalion less two rifle companies, deployed at brigade depth position, in the area of Chushul village.
4. *5 Jat:* Battalion less one Rifle Company in general area Lukung and Phobrang, with a troop ex 114 Lt Bty (4.2 Hy Mor). One Rifle Company at Tsaka La.
5. *Armour:* Sqn (less one Tp) ex 20 Lancers (AMX-13 tanks), deployed below Gurung Hill.
6. *Artillery:* A troop each ex 38 Fd Bty[74] (ex 13 Field Regt) at the foot of Magar Hill and Gurung Hill, respectively.
7. *Brigade Headquarters* in the area High Ground, behind Chushul village.

Preparing for the Challenge

Effective defence requires detailed planning and preparation. At first, it needs proper ground reconnaissance of the area. Based on that, a deployment pattern is worked out. Then troops have to dig down in order to withstand the inevitable bombing and shelling by the enemy. Defences are camouflaged to prevent the enemy's observation, and then ringed with mines, booby traps and barbed wire fences. Ammunition and supplies are stocked up and a network of signal communications organised. And finally, time permitting, suitable measures to deceive the enemy regarding the layout of defences have to be taken. It is a fact that defensive preparations can never really be considered complete.

Within a few days of the arrival of HQ 114 Infantry Brigade, the reconnaissance phase of the commanders was over and the troops moved to their allotted defended localities, where they got down to digging trenches, laying weapon pits, linking posts with crawl trenches, laying mines ahead of barbed wire obstacle and telephone lines, netting-in radio sets, dumping of ammunition, collection and storage of rations and a host of other activities con-

[74] 38 Field Battery ex 13 Field Regiment and 114 Lt Bty were flown into Chushul between on 21st and 23rd October 1962.

nected with the operational task of the brigade that lay ahead. But there were problems galore. Often while digging the defences, rocks had to be blasted. Animal transport was usually in short supply and, therefore, troop labour had to be employed to carry the bulk of the requirement of defence stores, rations and ammunitions. It was a mad rush for the troops manning the posts, as they could see the Chinese building up equally fast on the opposite side. It was a race against time, and so every hour mattered. Everyone was hoping for enough time to prepare defensive positions and not get caught in the open against enemy artillery shelling.

Major Jagjit Singh described the situation in his book, *The Saga of Ladakh (Heroic Battles of Rezang La and Gurung Hill: 1961-1962)*:

> It takes much longer to prepare defences in the high altitude mountains than in the plains; the ground is hard due to permafrost soil and therefore physical exertion is much more taxing. In view of this, as well as of a potential threat of an imminent Chinese attack, the Brigade had to make the defence preparations at top speed.
>
> The bitter cold mornings would start with a conference by the Brigade Commander, which were known as the "Morning Prayers"! These were attended by all Commanding Officers, accompanied by their Adjutant and Quartermaster, and Brigade Staff.
>
> Brigadier Raina would generally start by reminding all present that, "God has granted us yet another day. For Heaven's sake, gentlemen, let's prepare fast. Tomorrow, we may be at battle!"

Tappy Raina was a hard taskmaster. A perfectionist himself, he expected nothing less from others, juniors as well as seniors. He was a man of few words and always gave a straight answer. Major Jagjit Singh recalled an incident when Tappy Raina was briefing a senior formation commander and explaining a point with a pointer staff on a sand model. The visiting senior officer made an off-the-cuff and out of context comment on Tappy's operational planning for his brigade. Brigadier Raina, who had fully prepared his brief, was so upset that he threw the staff on the sand model and said, "This is what I feel about the problem, sir"! The visiting senior not only understood his point but also realised his error, and gracefully ignored the incident. Normally, of course, Tappy Raina was very polite and respectful to those above, and never harmed his juniors, if he could help it. But he did not like shirkers at all. Another facet of his personality was that he did not easily place faith in any one, but once he did, it was life long.

Having given the battalion commanders their areas of operational responsibility, the Brigade Commander laid down priorities for detailed reconnaissance and siting of each forward defended locality (FDL). The battalion commanders, therefore, planned their daily routine accordingly.

Every morning Brigadier Raina would review the progress made on the previous day and tie up activities for the day. Then he would set out to check the detailed siting of some particular locality. And after he had approved, the troops would be moved up for occupation and preparation of field defences.

Major Jagjit Singh often accompanied the Brigade Commander on those reconnaissance-cum-siting missions. The massifs of Gurung and Magar Hills, and Rezang La looked fairly easy to climb, but one soon got out of this illusion by learning the hard way. Major Jagjit Singh recalled one such experience:

> The Brigadier and I had gone to Rezang La for confirming the siting of the company locality there. On the return trip we dropped in for a cup of tea at the headquarters of 1/8 Gorkha Rifles. While having tea, the Brigadier suddenly decided to visit Gurung Hill on that very day. Although he had already confirmed the layout of defences at this feature the previous day, he wanted to re-examine certain aspects. It was 3 p.m. when, along with Commanding Officer 1/8 Gorkha Rifles, we started up the Gurung Hill.
>
> A Subedar from this unit, who knew the area well, accompanied us. By the time we reached our destination, there were only 40 minutes of daylight left for reconnaissance. Anyhow, we had barely managed to complete our task, when it started to

get dark. To make it worse, we neither had a torch nor a compass, which was a serious slip on my part. As a Brigade Major, I should have remembered to carry these items before setting out for reconnaissance.

By then a strong wind had set in, bringing with it the biting cold of the Ladakh winter. Our limbs soon began to ache. We were at the eastern extremity of the Gurung Hill. To go back via the long route from the west, by which we had come up was now out of question. The answer lay in rolling down into the Spanggur Gap; that being the shortest way down. We could thereby reach the Section Post located in the Gap and from there call for a jeep back to Brigade HQ.

There was only one snag: a Chinese post was also located in the neighbourhood. If we got lost on our way down, we would be in the hands of the Chinese. But since we had no other option, we let the Subedar of 1/8 Gorkha Rifles lead us to the Gap. The JCO forewarned us that movement along this route would be tough going.

Indeed the route was tough and very difficult. We literally had to crawl down at places. It was at about 8 p.m. when we finally managed to reach the 1/8 Gorkha Rifles Section Post, having descended only a few hundred metres in two long hours!

Employment of Armour

At noon on 26th October 1962, a squadron less two troops ex 20 Lancers[75] (AMX-13 tanks[76]) rolled out of an AN-12 aircraft at

---

[75] The airlifting of tanks to an altitude of approximately 4,570 metres (15,233 feet) not only surpassed the Zoji La performance of 1948, but also set a world record of sorts.

[76] The loading of tanks in the AN 12 aircraft at Chandigarh airfield had not been easy; the initial attempts being unsuccessful. Considerable improvisation had to be done and finally after trial and error, the AMX-13 tanks were loaded on the nights of 24/25th and 25/26th October. The Air Force Squadron went all out to help, cutting down fuel, removing certain fitments and so on, to reduce the all-out weight of each transporting aircraft!

Chushul airfield. This was a very welcome arrival. With the anti-tank recoilless guns (RCL) held by infantry battalions and the anti-tank mines laid by the brigade in the Spanggur Gap, it was now possible to confidently face a Chinese tank attack through Spanggur. Wisely, the Chinese kept their armour back during the battle that ensued.

In 114 Infantry Brigade Sector, the general area west of Chushul airfield was best suited to deploy tanks. From here, our tanks could meet any Chinese tank assault through the Gap more effectively than from any other area. Being central to the brigade sector, tanks could also be moved fast in any counter-attack in conjunction with infantry, and wherever required. The only snag was that any deployment of tanks in this area could be effectively observed by Chinese artillery observation posts! The much stronger Chinese artillery would thus accurately engage our tanks and curtail their effectiveness. The armoured squadron was, therefore, located in a hidden position below Gurung Hill, with an alternative position prepared for occupation in the area west of the airfield.

In the event of a Chinese attack using tanks, or to support a counter-attack if one was to be launched by 114 Infantry Brigade, the tank squadron was to move from its concealed location to the prepared position in the airfield area. The squadron was also to provide limited fire support to Gurung Hill, if it were otherwise uncommitted.

Employment of Artillery

Just as in the case of tanks, the area west of the airfield was considered ideally suited for the deployment of field battery guns of 13 Field Regiment. But this deployment also suffered from the same drawback as that of the tanks, i.e. the Chinese could spot it and their gunners could open counter-bombardment fire and silence Indian guns. Therefore, the only available Field Battery was split up with one troop deployed behind Gurung Hill, and the other behind Magar Hill, in such a manner that gun positions were hidden from Chinese observation. With this deployment, both troops could shoot into the Spanggur Gap, but the troop in support of Gurung Hill, could not support the Magar Hill defences, and *vice versa*. Though such splitting of artillery violated the principle of providing the maximum number of guns to engage the maximum number of targets, yet in the prevailing situation, there was no alternative. Such deployment, however, provided one major advantage; gun positions were concealed from the direct observation of the Chinese and Indian guns would be free to shoot.

Deception Plan

To deceive the enemy about these deployments, Brigadier Raina planned to prepare dummy artillery and armour positions in the area west of the airfield, and orders were issued accordingly.

Gun pits were dug and dummy gun structures were placed accordingly and camouflaged. To make it appear absolutely real, movement of gunners was simulated there during the day and a couple of hurricane lamps lit at the site during the night.

For the armour deception, unserviceable bulldozers, once employed for the construction of Chushul airfield and which were lying there since then, were used. A wooden log was fixed on each of the bulldozers to simulate a tank gun barrel. Then these dummy tanks were properly camouflaged. The tank crew also employed tactics similar to those of the gunners to create an appearance of normal activity there round the clock. This deception plan paid rich dividends during the Chinese attack on Chushul defences. During actual battle, not a shell was fired by the enemy at either of Indian gun positions; instead, the dummy gun and tank positions were heavily shelled by Chinese gunners!

Brigade Administrative Base

Tactically, the administrative base should have been located further west of Chushul airfield, well away from the line of forward defences, but due to transportation problems and shortage of pony and porters, it remained at the airfield. The administrative base for Chushul garrison was established when stores started arriving by

IAF's AN-12 transport aircraft from Chandigarh. The Brigade Administrative Base remained located in the same area where these were unloaded, due to a paucity of transport. It was so located because of convenience of unloading the aircraft and collection of stores by units. Some stocks of POL rations, ammunition and other military hardware that arrived by air, were held at this ad-hoc administrative base.

After the Chinese attacks in the Northern Sector (DBO-Galwan) during October 1962, the Chinese threat to the Central Sector, defended by 114 Infantry Brigade under the command of Tappy Raina, now loomed large. The administrative base at Chushul airfield was vulnerable, being under enemy observation. It had become imperative to shift it to the rear area of the brigade sector. Though the transport situation had eased somewhat, the Brigade Commander decided to shift the containers which were full with POL, and let the empty containers and packing material remain at the existing unloading point near Chushul airfield. Thereafter, all empty packing material including empty containers were added on to this dummy administrative base[77], thus giving the impression to the Chinese that the POL dump continued to be there.

In nearly a month or so, the brigade made satisfactory progress in occupation of various battalion defended areas and localities, with minimum basic preparations. Under normal circumstances, the brigade would have aggressively patrolled the No Man's Land and liaised with the flanking sectors. But the orders from higher headquarters restrained the brigade from any action that could escalate the situation. The Superior Headquarters believed that the Chinese build up against the 114 Infantry Brigade defended sector was mere simulation of a large scale attack. It was only meant to intimidate Indian troops psychologically with the purpose of get-

---

[77] During the actual attack by the Chinese on this sector, they heavily shelled all the dummy positions. 114 Infantry Brigade thus successfully deceived the enemy by forcing him to waste artillery resources, which otherwise would have been employed against the Brigade's defences during the main battle of Chushul Sector.

ting them to vacate the area falling within what the Chinese claimed as their territory. The Brigade Commander, however, was mentally prepared for the worst, but he was under orders not to induce or give any excuse for the Chinese to launch an attack. This logic was one that neither Tappy Raina, the brigade commander, nor his subordinate commanders could appreciate.

Another aspect of the "no-escalation" order was that the meagre artillery in support of 114 Infantry Brigade could not even register the important targets by actually firing a few rounds! Normally this was not essential because with an accurate survey of targets and taking care to make necessary adjustments to offset local meteorological effects, guns are expected to fire accurately. In the present situation, however, it was important to do so because the brigade had never tested the fire of supporting guns at such high altitudes as in Chushul and in temperatures which could go down to minus 20-30 degrees Celsius.

Major Jagjit Singh was an officer of the Regiment of Artillery. He could, thus, advise his Brigade Commander that the fire of guns should be adjusted on some possible targets within the Brigade Sector. Tappy Raina readily agreed with his brigade major and limited registration was done under the supervision of Major Joshi, the Battery Commander, who was also a competent former gunnery instructor.

Bunkers and trenches had by now been prepared at all forward defended localities and adequate rations and ammunitions had been stocked at the posts. The most threatened approaches of the enemy were mined and barbed-wire was laid ahead of each locality. Some bunkers on each locality were provided overhead protection.

Communications[78] in the brigade sector had been provided, telephone lines laid and wireless sets tuned and netted. Great care

---

[78] The importance of good signal communications need hardly be emphasised in any battle. Their failure leads to confusion and chaos, at times to defeat. This is particularly so in a defensive battle where, commanders at all levels can exercise command and control best from their respective command posts. Duplication of communications was the normal teaching.

and attention had been given to this aspect of the brigade's operational preparations. Sure enough, Major Jagjit Singh was asked by Brigadier Raina:

> "I hope you have thoroughly buttoned up the network of signal communications in the Brigade Sector"?
>
> To which the Major replied, "Yes Sir, we have ensured the duplication of communications, both wireless and telephone." The Brigade Commander immediately quipped, "But, that is not enough, my boy: Beg, borrow or steal but ensure that, at least, some more telephone lines are laid".

At first Major Jagjit Singh wondered where would he "beg, borrow or steal" in this wilderness! But then it struck him that most units usually kept some reserve stock of cable, undisclosed! So, the worthy brigade major appealed to them for their reserve stock and, sure enough, it was produced.

The brigade commander was correct in taking this precaution. During the battle, most telephone lines were cut by enemy shelling. But for the extra lines, it would not have been possible to ensure uninterrupted telephonic communications during the battle.

The tanks stood ready for the call to action, hidden from Chinese observation at the base of Gurung Hill. And so also the artillery guns, their barrels laid on the most dangerous targets to ensure immediate response. Major Jagjit Singh appreciated the importance of infantry-artillery cooperation as being vital for success in the battle. It is said that the artillery has the highest respect for the "Queen of the Battlefield – the Infantry". As a proud gunner, Major Jagjit Singh did not hesitate to add, "The Queen also", I may say, "feels lost without the King of the Battlefield-the Artillery, or the 'God of War', as Russian gunners would say"!

King and Queen apart, it is the infantry which bears the major brunt of any battle. Gunners, who have to work in close cooperation with the infantry, know it only too well and hence their high regard for the infantryman is, mutual. For them, therefore, provision of fire support to the infantry is not merely compliance of military manuals; it is something far more: an unwritten pledge. And so a great deal of mutual respect and admiration has grown between the two. This is so particularly in battle even though during peace the King sometimes feels ignored by the Queen.

Brigade vehicles operated during the day in the airfield area for the transportation of supplies, ammunition, and so on as these arrived by IAF aircrafts and at night these were moved to the rear. The only transport allowed to stay the night in the airfield area was the minimum essential requirement of armour, artillery and infantry units deployed in front. In the rear, vehicles were parked under the centralised control of brigade headquarters, well away from Chinese gun range, till the next morning. This was a regular routine, and it proved beneficial during the battle.

The Chinese build-up, meanwhile, continued unabated. Indians, too, had by now achieved some measure of preparedness. Above all, the spirit of all ranks of 114 Infantry Brigade was high and a fine atmosphere prevailed.

The two Battalions facing the Chinese were commanded by two veteran soldiers, Lieutenant Colonel Hari Chand, MVC, Commanding Officer of 1/8 Gorkha Rifles and Lieutenant Colonel Hari Singh Dhingra, Commanding Officer 13 Kumaon. Between these two commanding officers, they set the pace for the rest of the officers of the brigade for strict compliance of orders without questioning.[79] Both these Commanding Officers had, in turn, inculcated the same spirit in their worthy adjutants, Captains P. Kher and D.D. (Dhiru) Saklani. Both were meticulous and mature and understood the nuances of the battle situation to assist not only their CO and battalion officers in battle, but also the brigade staff.

Operational Task of Brigade 114

In the event of an attack by China, the order given to the commander of 114 Infantry Brigade by HQ 15 Corps, was:

> To inflict maximum casualties on the Chinese at our forward line of defences (Rezang La — Magar Hill — Gurung Hill),

---

[79] In war, an argumentative or "belly-aching" subordinate is a serious liability during the hour of trial in battle.

and then to withdraw to prepared depth positions, along the range of hills, west of the Chushul valley.

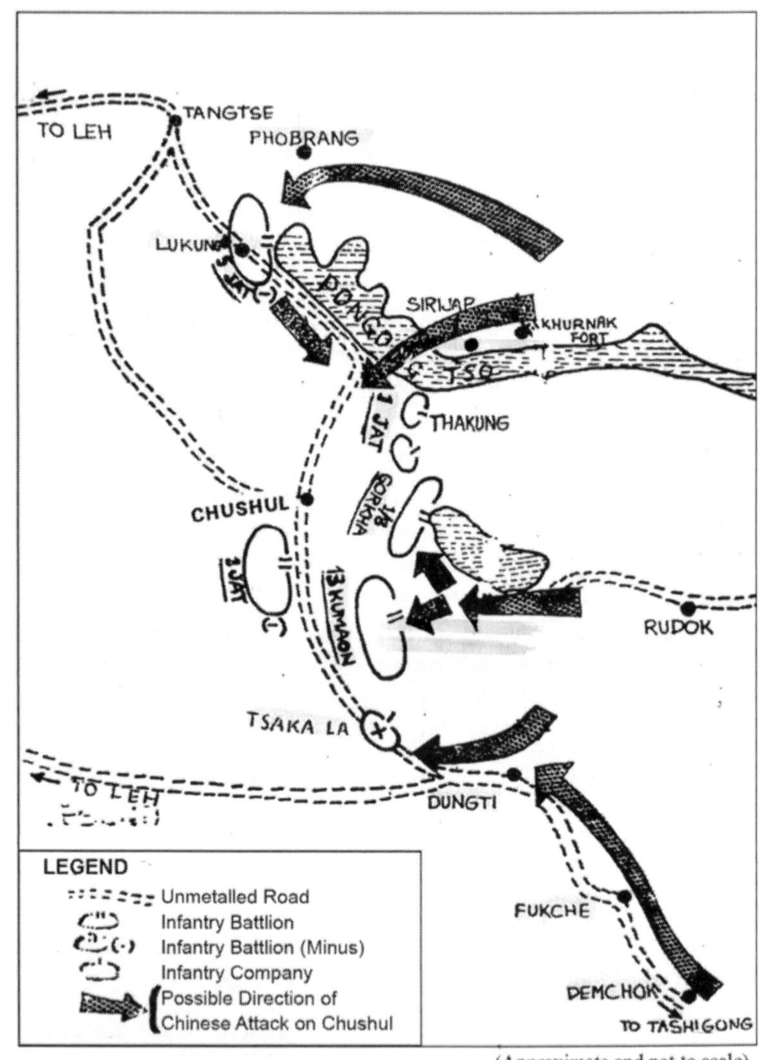

(Approximate and not to scale)

Map 6: Deployment of 114 Infantry Brigade.

Investiture Ceremony at Rashtrapati Bhavan: President of India Dr. S. Radhakrishnan presenting the second highest gallantry award of Maha Vir Chakra to Brigadier Tappy Raina in 1963.

Maj Gen Tappy Raina, MVC met Maj Gen Atiqur Rehman, GOC 12 Division of Pakistan Army at a Flag Meeting at Chakkan ka Bagh on 20th March 1966.

Maj Gens Raina and Rehman signing the minutes of the Flag Meeting of 20th March 1966.

Visit by Defence Minister Y.B. Chavan along with Gen P.P. Kumaramanglam, DSO, COAS, Lt Gen Harbaksh Singh, VrC, GOC-in-C, Gen K.P. Candeth, GOC 15 Corps, and Maj Gen T.N. Raina, MVC, GOC 25 Inf Div (extreme right) for review of the Tashkent Agreement.

Lt Gen T.N. Raina, MVC, with GOC 9 Inf Div Maj Gen Dalbir Singh and of cers after the capture of Jessore Air eld in 1971.

Left to right: General T.N. Raina, MVC, Admiral S.N. Kohli, PVSM and Air Chief Marshal O.P. Mehra, PVSM, Chiefs of the Indian Army, the Indian Navy and the Indian Air Force, respectively, at the Republic Day Parade, 26th January 1976.

Two ef cient ADCs to COAS in action at COAS Secretariat in 1975; from left to right Capt D.J. Govadia and Capt S.K. Sapru.

Courtesy call by Gen T.N. Raina, MVC, COAS on Fakhruddin Ali Ahmed, President of India and Supreme Commander of Armed Forces, in June 1975.

Defence Minister Jagjivan Ram addressing the Army Commanders Conference in 1977; Gen Tappy Raina, Lt Gen Vir Vohra, Lt Gen I.S. Gill, Lt Gen Harish Rai, Lt Gen E.A. Vas.

Defence Minister Jagjivan Ram addressing the Army Commanders Conference, 1977. Clockwise from left: Lt Gen O.P. Malhotra, Lt Gen Jacob, Lt Gen J.S. Nakkai, Lt Gen Jaswant Singh (DCOAS), Lt Gen S.P. Malhotra (QMG), Lt Gen Kundan Singh (MS), Lt Gen J.S. Bawa, (E-in-C).

Prime Minister Indira Gandhi at the Army Day Reception at DSOI, New Delhi, 15th January 1976.

This order appeared to be both contradictory and contrary to military teaching. It created a doubt as to whether the Indian forward line was the main position or a delaying one. If it were the former, there could not be any reason for the troops to withdraw to depth positions. On the other hand, if the defences along this line were meant only to be delaying positions, these should have been held thinly, expected to inflict limited casualties on the enemy, and having imposed an element of delay, withdraw to the main defences in depth.

Needless to say, the higher formation HQs were aware of this contradiction and deviation from the normal concepts of Defence. But the situation in Chushul Sector was peculiar; whereas tactical requirement was to dominate Chinese Line of Actual Control (LAC), by deploying own troops on tactically important ground so as to pre-empt the Chinese from capturing these positions in pursuit of his aim of capturing Chushul Valley. Yet, 114 Infantry Brigade had been ordered to prepare main Brigade Defended Sector on heights west of Chushul Airfield, so as to deny the enemy access towards Leh!

Chapter 18

The Battle of Chushul

Dawn was breaking on Sunday, 18th November 1962, when the Chinese People's Liberation Army (PLA) launched its well-planned attack on Indian forward positions in the Chushul sector. Perhaps the choice of Sunday was deliberate, for in the past as well the Chinese had chosen Sundays[80] to catch Indian Army troops off guard, knowing that this usually was their day of "mend and make" parade and personal administration.

This time, however, the Indian troops on the forward defended localities (FDLs) were well aware of enemy movements which were under careful observation of their observation posts round the clock. For November, it was an unusually cold morning. There was a blanket of mist all around and visibility was restricted to about 200 metres. Just then, it also started snowing heavily.

Major Jagjit Singh, BM, narrated how on the previous night he had gone to bed early and had therefore woken up earlier than usual on that fateful morning of 18th November 1962. He lit the *bukhari* (oil stove heating) to warm up his bunker, and then switched on his battery-operated reading lamp to read for a while. He had barely started reading his book when he heard loud explosions in the distance. Jagjit's first reaction was, "How come the engineers had started their 'rock blasting' (they were preparing

[80] 6th May 1962 was the day that the Chinese tactic of intimidation was tried for the first time opposite our posts in the northern sector of Ladakh, with a show of overwhelming force, and it was a Sunday! Likewise some other incidents of similar tactics also were launched on a Sunday!

living bunkers for troops) so early in the morning?" But this illusion was soon dispelled and it suddenly dawned on him that the long awaited Chinese attack had begun.

Immediately, the entire Brigade sector had come to "stand to" in response to the imminent Chineses attack. The Brigade Ops Room also got activated. For a while it was all quiet in the command post of HQ 114 Infantry Brigade at Chushul. No one spoke. Then Brigadier Raina broke the spell and asked Major Jagjit Singh to send for his jeep. He emphasised that the jeep should have the flag and star plate. The Major wondered if his commander wasn't taking an obvious risk in driving out with his flag flying, exposing himself to Chinese observation and artillery fire.

But to the Brigade Commander, it was more important to drive around the brigade sector, in full view of his command so as to boost the morale of the troops. The battle having just begun, it was unlikely that any serious developments would take place just yet. Brigadier Raina could, therefore, afford to be away from his command post for some time, leaving his brigade major and the rest of the brigade staff to collate information and handle any minor situations that might arise.

The Battle of Chushul was fought on the snowy heights of Rezang La and Gurung Hill. Both were attacked simultaneously. It is believed that the Chinese attacked these positions with an overwhelming numerical superiority of over 10 to 1, arriving in human waves, one after another, unmindful of their casualties. Their attacks were well planned and were pressed home with vigour and determination. The Chinese mortars and guns shelled the FDLs in the brigade sector for almost an hour before their actual assault. Enemy shelling was intense and aimed not only at inflicting casualties, but also at breaking the will of the troops to stay and fight.

Though vastly outnumbered and outgunned, Indian troops did not lose their nerve. In keeping with the order, which was "to inflict maximum casualties on the enemy and withdraw to depth positions", the defenders of Rezang La and Gurung Hill fought, both bravely and with skill.

Battle of Rezang La

Rezang La is a pass dominated by a massive feature that is approximately 5,180 metres (17,266 feet) high. It was part of the 13 Kumaon Defended Area. On 24th October 1962, "C" Company, 13 Kumaon, commanded by Major Shaitan Singh occupied this feature. Platoons 7, 8 and 9 of "C" Company, were deployed in a linear fashion (*see* Map 7. Though it was advisable to place some troops in depth as reserve, the important ground required to be covered at Rezang La was much larger than what could be covered by the available troops. A linear deployment was, thus, unavoidable. Some depth was, however, arranged within each platoon, with the company HQ in depth between Platoons 8 and 9. The section of 3-inch mortars was behind the company HQs. The company administrative base, with its cook house, reserve rations and clothing was located at the base of Rezang La in the valley below.

The "C" Company defended locality, although well prepared within the limits of time and resources available, was, nevertheless, isolated from the main Battalion defended area. No mines could be laid ahead of FDLs due to the paucity of these in the brigade sector. Priority of laying mines in the brigade defended sector had been given to important positions like Spanggur Gap and Magar Hill. Due to a shortage of artillery guns, Major Shaitan Singh's company was without any artillery support. It, thus, had to rely on its own section of mortars for fire support.

Inspired by the leadership of their Officer Commanding, Major Shaitan Singh, and Brigade Commander Tappy Raina, the soldiers at Rezang La, however, possessed one vital asset; they had stout hearts and the will to fight. With this essential pre-requisite, Major Shaitan Singh and his men waited for the enemy. The broad pattern and sequence of attack by the Chinese on Rezang La on Sunday, 18th November 1962, was as follows:

- A silent approach march by the Chinese troops to Rezang La;
- Frontal assaults on Platoons 7 and 8;

- Intense Chinese artillery and mortar fire to cover the movement of their troops, for subsequent attacks from the flanks and rear;
- Attack on Platoon 7 and 8 from the flanks;
- Attack on remaining defences from the rear.

Major Jagjit Singh in his book, *The Saga of Ladakh*, offers an account of the Battle of Rezang La fought by Major Shaitan Singh and his company atone of the highest battle grounds in the world.

> The battle started hours before the shelling that was seen by troops deployed in depth around Chushul High Ground. In fact, the first Chinese assault was silent. Their intention was to surprise the defenders of Rezang La. In this, they failed.
>
> The enemy had brought up its troops to forward assembly areas during the night of 18/19th November. At about 4 a.m. a patrol from No. 8 Platoon under Naik Hukam Chand discovered a large body of enemy troops scrambling up through the gullies towards the Platoon Post. He immediately raised the alarm by firing a red Very light and a burst from an LMG. No 7 Platoon had a LP on the north-west toe of Rezang La. Those manning it had also seen the enemy forming up and, within moments, all men in the Company were at their action stations. Between No. 7 and No. 9 Platoons were a couple of gullies that also led down, like the others, to the sandy Rezang Lungpa. To ascertain whether these were clear of the enemy, Major Shaitan Singh ordered No. 9 Platoon to send out a patrol. It soon returned; these gullies too were swarming with enemy troops.
>
> It was still pretty dark. All ranks of the "C" Company were now sure that it was going to be a big attack. With bated breath they waited, their fingers on their triggers. Around 5 o'clock, when dawn was just beginning to break, the first wave of Chinese became visible through their gun-sights. Unfortunately for the enemy, the gullies through which they had decided to assault had been ranged and all of "C" Company's LMGs and mortars were now trained on them. As soon as the attacking Chinese troops came within range, Major Shaitan Singh's Company let them have it. Many of the enemy fell; others continued to advance. But with every weapon in "C" Company fir-

ing, the gullies in front of the three platoons were soon full of dead and wounded Chinese[81].

Their frontal attack having failed, the Chinese quickly modified their plan, and began shelling Rezang La. The intensity of the shelling and the diversity of the weapons used were an indication of their determination to take the position at any cost. From the blinds recovered, it was evident that they employed three types of mortars: 120-mm, 81-mm and 60-mm. To destroy bunkers, they used 75-mm and 57-mm recoilless guns; they brought those on wheelbarrows to the flanks of "C" Company FDL and fired these en masse[82]. The four feet deep craters found in solid rock around Company HQ and No. 9 Platoon were clear indication that they used a certain number of 132-mm rockets also.

Under the cover of the shelling, the Chinese had managed to come on the flanks of the forward platoons. At No. 8 Platoon locality, they succeeded in blowing a gap through the wire obstacle on the southern side, using Bangalore torpedoes. But when some of them tried to push through the gap, they were repulsed with hand-grenades that were lobbed, forcing the Chinese to make a long detour and attack from the west.

Getting wind of the enemy's move, Jemadar (re-designated as Nb Sub) Hari Ram took his platoon back to an alternative position that had already been prepared. The Chinese must have been surprised; as soon as they formed up for the attack, they were greeted with well-aimed small-arms fire. But the odds against the defenders were heavy; superior numbers and fire-

---

[81] Evidence of the large number of enemy casualties came when Rezang La was visited three months later, in February 1963.

[82] No bunker on Rezang La could survive such an onslaught. When the place was re-visited in February 1963, corrugated iron sheets were found in bits; the *ballies* (wooden logs) had been reduced to matchwood and the sandbags were just shreds of gunny. But there was no sign of panic or a withdrawal. The bodies of some men were found in their trenches, still holding their weapons, broken LMG bipods, and men holding the butts of their rifles while the rest of the gun blown off, bore witness to the intensity of enemy fire!

power were bound to tell and, section by section, the position fell.

The attack on No. 7 Platoon had also come at the same time, from the platoon's northern flank, where a large enemy force had collected. While the first wave of the assault troops was forming up, the Platoon Commander, Jemadar Surja, had asked the 3-inch mortar section to provide defensive fire. The first three bombs landed right in the middle of the Chinese front-line. Despite their many casualties, they continued their assault towards the top Section. Instead of waiting to engage the enemy from their trenches, about a dozen soldiers jumped out and charged the oncoming Chinese, who were thrice their number. And they fell upon the enemy like tigers, in the true spirit of the "Man Eaters of Kumaon"!

The battalion's 3-inch mortar section, deployed on the reverse slope of Rezang La, had also been playing havoc with the enemy. As the enveloping attack on No. 7 and 8 platoons developed, the Chinese had come nearer the mortar section[83] on both flanks. The Section Commander, Naik Ram Kumar Yadav, had to keep on reducing the range till he was firing mortar bombs without any secondary, from 40 to 50 meters. The only survivor was Ram Kumar. With his nose blown off by a hand grenade and eight other wounds from bullets and splinter, he managed to reach his Battalion HQ, on 19th November, after escaping from Chinese custody.

Having finished the two forward Platoons and the Mortar Section, the Chinese turned their attention to Company Headquarters and No. 9 Platoon. Major Shaitan Singh knew he was surrounded on three sides; after the initial shelling by the Chinese, he reorganized the position and re-sited the light machine-guns to take on the attack.

---

[83] When Rezang La was revisited in early 1963, tail-fins of Indian bombs were picked up as close as 30 yards from the mortar position. Every man was in his trench; one of them was actually clutching a live bomb, ready to fire. Of the stockpile of 1,000 bombs, all had been fired, except seven; these too were kept prepared for firing when the section was overrun.

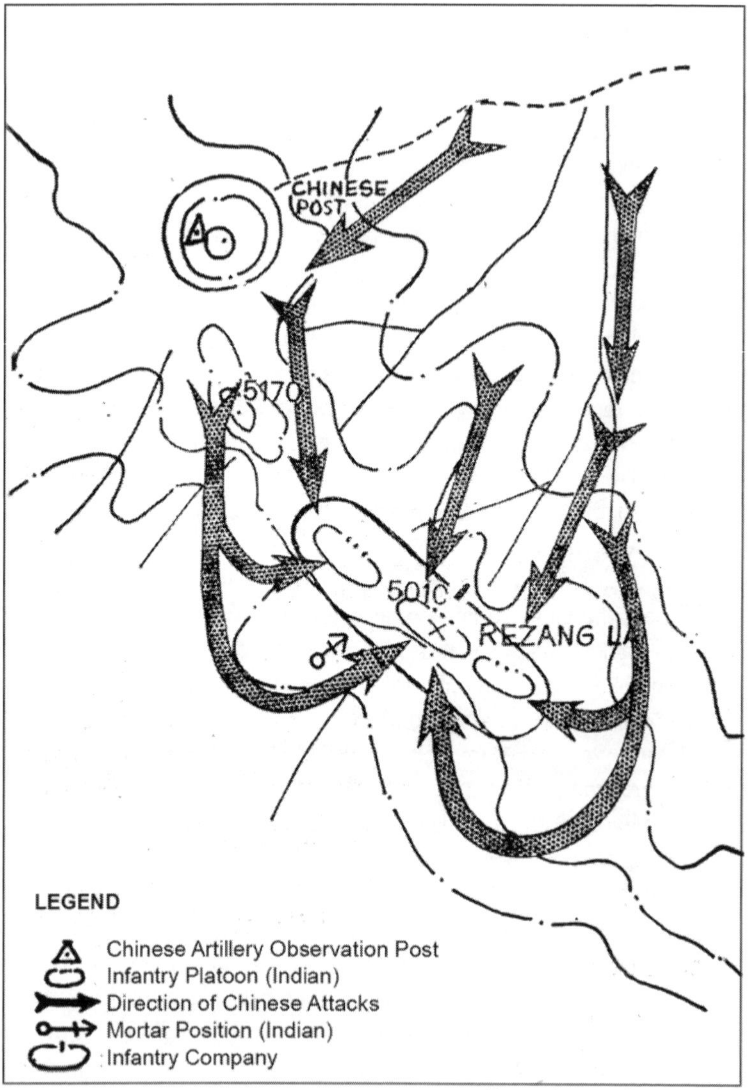

CHINESE POST

5170

5010

REZANG LA

LEGEND

Chinese Artillery Observation Post
Infantry Platoon (Indian)
Direction of Chinese Attacks
Mortar Position (Indian)
Infantry Company

(Approximate and not to scale)

Map 7: Battle of Rezang La.

The guns kept firing till they were knocked out from the hands of the firers. By now, most of the men of No. 9 Platoon had become casualties. While reorganising his Company defences, Major Shaitan Singh received a burst of fire in one arm. His Company Havildar Major Harphul Singh had been with him all the time. He persuaded Shaitan Singh to move out with those who could walk down to "C" Company base.

This Group was, however, soon discovered by the enemy, and CHM Harphul Singh fell mortally wounded. Major Shaitan Singh also received a machine-gun burst in the abdomen. The remaining two men of the party bandaged his wound and, picking him up, descended into one of the ravines that led to "C" Company's Base. But they had not gone very far, when they were caught in the cross fire of enemy machine-guns. Bullets were flying all round. Major Shaitan Singh realised that there would be no chance of escape even for these two men if they had to carry him. Therefore he ordered them to leave him where he was and save themselves. Reluctantly, they left. Three months later, Major Shaitan Singh's body was found at that very spot!

Battle of Magar Hill

The defences at Magar Hill, located south of Gurung Hill (occupied by 1/8 Gorkha Rifles), were held by B & D Companies of 13 Kumaon, under the overall command of Major R.V. Jatar. The Chinese did not assault Magar Hill on 18th November, but they shelled it heavily. Indian artillery and MMGs effectively engaged the enemy, and a fire-fight went on throughout the morning. "B" Company had good observation over the Spanggur Gap and directed artillery fire on the enemy guns which were shelling 13 Kumaon Battalion HQ and Gurung Hill. Major Jatar ordered the Artillery OP with his Company to engage the enemy armoured cars which were forming up in the Spanggur gap. The timely and effective artillery fire forced the Chinese to withdraw their armoured cars from the Spanggur Gap.

At an early stage of the ongoing battle at Rezang La FDLs, "D" Company had sent out a patrol to Rezang La under Naik Rup Ram. By then the Chinese had occupied Point 18300. A medium machine-gun on that hill engaged the patrol, killing two men on the spot and wounding another two. The survivors managed to make their way back to Battalion HQ.

Approximately six hundred shells fell upon 13 Kumaon's Battalion HQ at High Ground on the morning of 18th November. But thanks to the sturdiness of their bunkers, not a single casualty occurred due to Chinese shelling. "A" Company, deployed near Battalion HQ, had been earmarked as Brigade Reserve. It was kept in readiness for a counter-attack in conjunction with tanks. But the swift course of events precluded such a move. When news of the happenings at Rezang La reached Battalion HQ, Lieutenant Colonel Hari Singh Dhingra immediately ordered a patrol to be sent to locate and evacuate Major Shaitan Singh's party. But this patrol could not go beyond "C" Company's Administrative Base, where CQMH Havildar Jai Narain held on to his stores dumped there, till he was ordered to destroy these and withdraw to Battalion HQ.

The Chinese attack on Rezang La and its stout defence by "C" Company 13 Kumaon, was a battle that would be remembered by future generations of both countries, China and India. The Chinese will remember it for the incredible heroism they saw. Indians, undoubtedly, have every reason to be proud of the brave Ahir soldiers of the gallant Kumaon Regiment who laid down their lives fighting, rather than surrender, even when they were outnumbered and faced a preponderance of artillery and mortar fire. They fought and fought in the true spirit of the motto of The Kumaon Regiment, *Parakramo Vijayate* (Valour Triumphs).

By any yardstick, every soldier of "C" Company of the 13th Battalion, The Kumaon Regiment, who fought against the Chinese and laid down his life at Rezang La was a hero. A grateful nation still remembers each one of them as such. The name of Major Shaitan Singh, who inspired these men under his command, with the spirit that "death" was better than "surrender", will live forever in the pages of the history of Indian Army.

In recognition of such exceptional leadership, courage and sacrifice, Major Shaitan Singh,[84] was posthumously conferred the nation's highest gallantry award, the Param Vir Chakra. He thus became Kumaon Regiment's second recipient of the highest gallantry award, after late Major Somnath Sharma, PVC, who was the first to be conferred this highest honour in the Battle of Badgam during operations in Jammu and Kashmir against Pakistan in 1947-48.

Of the others who fought at Rezang La, Jamadars Hari Ram (posthumous), Surja (posthumous) and Ram Chander and Naiks Hukam Chand (posthumous), Gulab Singh (posthumous), Ram Kumar Yadav, Lance Naik Singh Ram (posthumous) and Sepoy Dharam Pal Dahaiya (posthumous), were each decorated for their conspicuous gallantry with Vir Chakra (VrC). CHM Harphul Singh (posthumous), Havildar Jai Narain, Havildar Phul Singh and Sepoy Nihal Singh were awarded Sena Medal (SM).

For his inspiring leadership and devotion to duty, Lieutenant Colonel Hari Singh Dhingra, Commanding Officer 13 Kumaon was awarded VSM Class II, (now Ati Vishisht Seva Medal — AVSM).

It was to the High Ground, the place where the Battalion HQ of 13 Kumaon was located during the Battle of Chushul, that the remains of the brave heroes of Rezang La were brought in February 1963 and cremated with full military honours. Later, a memorial was raised in their honour at the cremation spot, and named Rezangla Memorial. Inscribed on it is the following verse by Macaulay:

How can man die better
Than facing fearful odds
For the ashes of his fathers,
And the temples of his gods.

---

[84] The mortal remains of Major Shaitan Singh, PVC, were recovered from Rezang La in February 1963 and flown to his home town, Jodhpur, where he was cremated with full military honours, befitting a national hero.

13th Battalion of The Kumaon Regiment was later the proud recipient of the Battle Honour, *Rezang La* and the Theatre Honour, *Ladakh 1962*. Emblazoned on its regimental colours, these names remind successive generations of the brave soldiers who died fighting for the nation's honour on 18th November 1962.

Battle of Gurung Hill

Gurung Hill, like Rezang La, was a massive feature, which extended over approximately 3,000 metres in length and 2,000 metres in width. The average height of Gurung Hill was about 5,030 metres (16,766 feet), and it overlooked both Spanggur Gap and Chushul airfield. It was a position of vital tactical importance.

Its neighbouring feature, Black Hill, a name derived from its black rocks, dominated Gurung Hill and was held by the Chinese. Their troops were deployed on its reverse slopes. The artillery observation post of the Chinese Army, located on the highest point of Black Hill, could observe all movement on Gurung Hill. At one stage, Black Hill was held very thinly by the Chinese. But for the orders from HQ 15 Corps that there would be "no escalation", 114 Infantry Brigade would have certainly captured Black Hill during the early stages of the Chinese build-up, thus making our defensive position far stronger.

Gurung Hill was divided into two distinct parts. The portion joining Black Hill was flat. The rest of Gurung Hill looked like a camel's back. To facilitate description, these two parts will be referred to as "Plateau" and "Camel's Back", respectively (*see* Map 8).

Unlike Company Defended Locality in area Rezang La, which was totally isolated, Gurung Hill occupied a central location in the network of the Brigade Defended Sector. Despite that, Gurung Hill could not be supported by any type of fire from troops deployed on its flanks, because of wide gaps between Battalion Defended Areas and its localities. (*See* Map 5) The shortage of troops including inadequate Artillery Support on the one hand, and the tactical necessity of occupying ground dominating the Chinese LAC, by own troops, on the other! Thus the Commander 114 Infantry Brigade was compelled to adopt such a defensive posture.

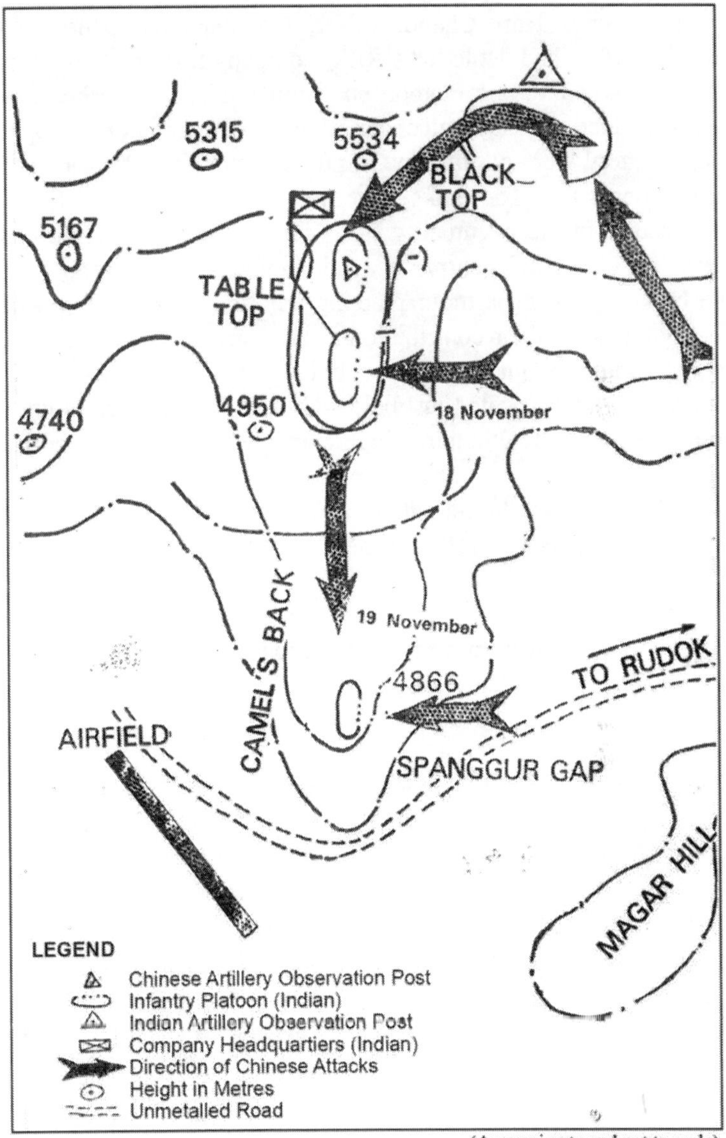

5315
5534
BLACK TOP
5167
TABLE TOP
(-)
4740
4950
18 November
CAMEL'S BACK
19 November
4866
TO RUDOK
AIRFIELD
SPANGGUR GAP
MAGAR HILL

LEGEND
Chinese Artillery Observation Post
Infantry Platoon (Indian)
Indian Artillery Observation Post
Company Headquarters (Indian)
Direction of Chinese Attacks
Height in Metres
Unmetalled Road

(Approximate and not to scale)

Map 8: Battle of Gurung Hill.

Lt. Colonel Hari Chand, MVC, Commanding Officer 1/8 Gorkha Rifles, had deployed a Rifle Company less one Platoon on the "Plateau" and, one Platoon on "Camel's Back". Furthermore, due to its tactical importance, a section of MMG and one troop of Field Battery were allotted to Gurung Hill and, as a bonus, some tank support too. The tanks were, however, primarily to fight a tank battle, in the eventuality of a Chinese tank assault through Spanggur Gap. Tanks carry very little high explosive ammunition, the bulk of it being armour piercing ammunition for use against enemy tanks, so their contribution in breaking up any Chinese infantry assault on Gurung Hill was going to be very limited. Nonetheless, the tanks located just below Gurung Hill, if uncommitted, could well fire a few hundred high explosive rounds in support of Gurung Hill.

In the event, the broad pattern and sequence of Chinese attack on Gurung Hill was as follows: (*See* Map 8)

18th November:

(a) Heavy artillery and mortar firing on Gurung Hill, in general, and the Plateau, in particular.

(b) Initial assault on the Plateau from the direction of Black Hill.

(c) A subsequent two-pronged attack on the Plateau from Black Hill and nullahs (gullies) leading to the Plateau from Spanggur Gap.

19th November:

(a) Heavy artillery and mortar shelling on Camel's Back.

(b) A two-pronged attack on Camel's Back from the direction of the Plateau and the nullahs leading to Camel's Back from Spanggur Gap.

The Chinese commenced the assault on Gurung Hill at 0630 hours on 18th November 1962 with a heavy volume of artillery and mortar fire. The entire network of defences in the Gurung Hill-Spanggur Gap, Magar Hill complex, the Dummy Brigade Administrative Area (dump of empty petrol and kerosene containers), artillery gun and tank positions, Battalion HQ 13 Kumaon, and the Chushul Airfield itself in the Brigade Sector were the targets engaged by enemy artillery. The main Chinese thrust was, however, chiefly directed against the "Plateau", which became the actual objective of the Chinese PLA attack.

Within minutes, Indian guns and mortars boomed back in reply. The guns of the artillery troop in support of Gurung Hill had rightly picked on the Chinese Artillery Observation Post as the top priority target. Its destruction, or even partial neutralisation, would have denied the Chinese proper direction and control of fire on the Plateau.

The duration of fire on Gurung Hill was much less than that on Rezang La. The reason was simple. The enemy had to carry out long outflanking moves for their attacks on Rezang La, and the whole move was required to be covered by artillery fire. On the other hand, in the case of attack on Gurung Hill, the reverse slopes of Black Hill provided a covered Forming Up Place (FUP) for the Chinese infantry, obscured from Indian observation.

Assault on the Plateau

While still engaging our troops with guns and mortars, the Chinese infantry rushed down Black Hill to assault the Plateau. Their strength was estimated to be about 300 to 400.

The Gorkha soldier has been known as the finest fighting man in the world. His simplicity and obedience of orders, his physical toughness and mental robustness have earned him this reputation over many a past war. The soldiers of 1/8 Gorkha Rifles holding the Plateau had the same warrior blood in them, but the battle that they were about to fight was between two unequal forces, and with vast disparity in strength.

Indian artillery fire, supplemented by the fire of the infantry's own mortars at Gurung Hill had, meanwhile, started engaging the assaulting Chinese. Artillery fire was accurate and Indian gunners were paying back their Chinese counterparts for the massacre of Company HQ and No. 9 Platoon at Rezang La. To compensate for the lack of guns, the Artillery OP officer at the Plateau, 2nd Lieutenant Goswami, had ordered "Intense Fire."[85] Young Goswami had, however, correctly appreciated this requirement in the present context, as also the capability of his men with a high standard of training and physical fitness, to fire accurately.

Indian artillery fire appeared to have blunted the initial onslaught of the Chinese who suffered considerable casualties. The survivors had gone down to ground to save their lives. Indian medium and light machine-gunners also contributed in halting the Chinese assault. The Gorkha riflemen, however, still held their fire. They were to start shooting when the assaulting troops approached nearer their Forward Defended Localities (FDLs).

At about 1030 hours on 19th November, the Chinese PLA commander threw a second echelon into the attack. Wave after wave of Chinese soldiers was seen rolling down from Black Hill. Chinese troops were also seen advancing to the Plateau along the nullahs (gullies), from the Spanggur Gap area. There appeared to be no shortage of manpower for the Chinese attacks.

The initial waves of the second echelon also suffered heavy casualties. By now the Gorkha riflemen too were getting their share of shooting, loading 5 rounds in the magazine at a time, in their outmoded 303 bolt-action rifles! To thicken up the fire for the Company FDLs at Plateau, Indian tank troops had also been ordered to move out of concealment at the base of Gurung Hill. In a matter of minutes, the tank troop of 20 Lancer had also joined the battle and carried out some direct shooting with high explosive shells. Despite the stiff resistance put up by 1/8 Gorkha Rifles for nearly 30 hours, however, further assaults by the Chinese, gave them possession of the feature by 1500 hours on 19th November.

---

[85] It is not usual to fire guns at "intense" rate because the barrels get heated and wear out faster, the men are soon exhausted and the ammunition expenditure is unduly heavy. Further, since it involves fastest possible loading and laying of guns, firing could be somewhat inaccurate.

Withdrawal to Main Brigade Defended Sector

With the capture of Gurung Hill and Rezang La, the Chinese had successfully breached the 114 Infantry Brigade Defended Sector and were now in a position to cut off the remaining troops deployed in front.

As per plan, 114 Infantry Brigade, therefore, withdrew to its previously prepared positions in depth. The withdrawal was carried out in pitch darkness during the night of 19/20th November, without any chaos or confusion. By the time it was daylight on 20th November, Indian troops were now holding defences, ready to face the Chinese once again. However, the Chinese did not follow up and Chushul and its airfield remained in Indian hands. 114 Infantry Brigade came out successful, undefeated and denied the Chinese PLA the capture of Chushul Sector and the Airfield.

On 20th November 1962, China announced a unilateral cease fire, to come into effect from midnight of 21/22nd November 1962.

1/8 GR had fought a gallant battle for two days before making a tactical withdrawal to their main Defences on the night of Nov 19/20. The Artillery OP Party comprising of 2nd Lieutenant SD Goswami, His Technical Assistant and two Signalers played a sterling role in disrupting the Chinese Assault by inflicting very heavy bombardment on the enemy. The Battalion earned the following Honurs and Awards while facing Chinese PLA assaults, first at Sri Jap Posts 1 & 2 and later on the Gurung Hill Defences, during Battle of Chushul – 1962:

1. Major Dhan Singh Thappa – PVC.
   2nd Lieutenant S.D. Goswami, Arty. – MVC.
2. Nk Rabi Lal Thappa – MVC.
3. Sub Maj Jung Bahadur Gurung – VSM – II (Present AVSM)
4. Capt P.C. Kher – Vr C.
5. Hav Tulsi Ram – Vr C.
6. Nk Amar Bahadur Thappa – Vr C. (Posthumous)
7. Nk/Tech Assistant Gurdip Singh, Arty – Vr C.
8. Nk Pritam Singh, Signals – Sena Medal.
9. L/Nk Sarwan Singh, Signals – Sena Medal.

The contrast between how the operations were conducted in Ladakh as compared to North East Frontier Agency (NEFA now Arunachal Pradesh) was a reflection on the leadership quality displayed in the respective Sectors. While the situation in Ladakh in the Western Sector was under control, there was discouraging news from the Eastern Sector in NEFA (*See* Map 9). There, due to wide dispersions, lack of adequate fire support and communication, the command and control collapsed. The fall of Sela, Walong and, finally, Bomdilla, and a general disorderly retreat everywhere led to heavy casualties among Indian troops; many were also taken prisoners of war. General P.N. Thapar, COAS, resigned and Lieutenant General B.M. Kaul was replaced by Lieutenant General (later Field Marshal) Sam Manekshaw, MC, as GOC 4 Corps.

Brigadier Tappy Raina and all ranks of 114 Infantry Brigade were full of appreciation for the role played by the Indian Air Force, for their selfless and untiring efforts to keep the Brigade well supplied despite the hazards of flying in the Ladakh Sector. However, for some unexplained reasons, the IAF failed to utilise the inbuilt facility of photo cover from AN-12 aircraft,[86] which according to Maj. General Jagjit Singh (the then BM 114 Infantry Brigade) could have helped the Commander 114 Infantry Brigade gain information about the enemy's build up for the attack on Chushul Sector.

The Air Force kept the Army provided with a wide range of essentials: fuel, oil and lubricants, rations, clothing, military hardware, including tanks, construction material for defences, air transportation of troops, and evacuation of casualties. The daily schedule of the pilots was a gruelling one! It meant reporting at the Base Airfield at 5 a.m., or earlier, for the Met briefing about the weather, and then carrying out a landing sortie in the morning

---

[86] Because of the barrier of terrain, it was difficult to make accurate visual observations of the Chinese build up. Had these aircraft been equipped with cameras, every sortie would have provided valuable information, which would have made it so much simpler for the Commander 114 Infantry Brigade and his General Staff to assess the Chinese intentions.

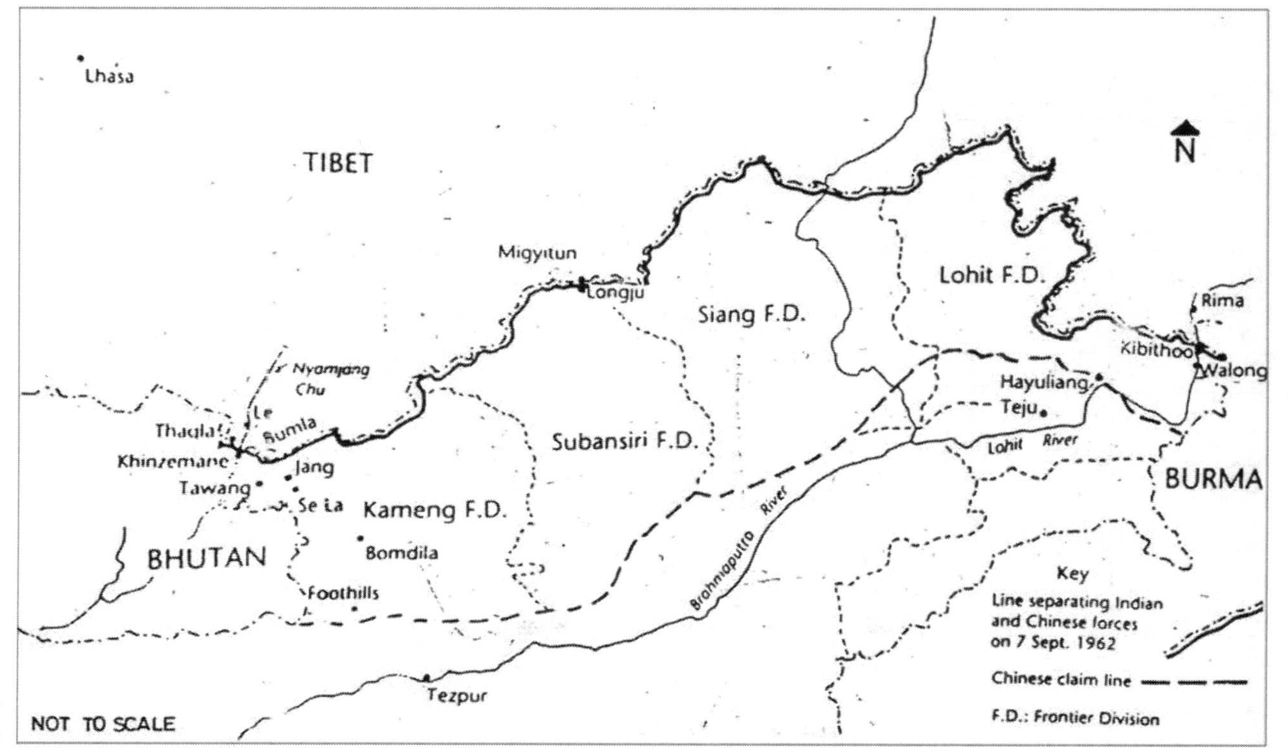

Map 9: The North East Frontier Agency (NEFA).

and air-drop missions later in the day. The strain on the pilot and crew was immense. But there appeared to be no alternative if troops in Ladakh were to be maintained to requisite strength.

The aircraft available were the American Fairchild C-114 Packet,[87] also nick-named "flying box car". They were operated by 12 and 19 squadrons based at Pathankot. The Dakota aircraft were flown by 43 Squadron, augmented by a detachment of the Soviet built IL 14,[88] operated from Srinagar airfield. The AN-12 aircraft, also of Soviet origin and based at Chandigarh, operated by 25 and 44 squadrons, were extensively employed for air support to the troops deployed in Ladakh.

A flight of Soviet built MI 4 helicopters was located at Leh airfield for communication and transportation of small bodies of troops and casualty evacuation. In addition, the newly acquired French-made Alouette helicopters (later named Chetak by IAF), were versatile flying machines operating at extremely high altitudes in Ladakh. The Fairchild Packets could land at all airfields in Ladakh, including DBO[89], Thoise in Nubra Valley, and Fukche in Dungti Sector whereas the AN 12 aircraft could operate at

---

[87] The twin-engine Fairchild C-114 Packets were old machines used during the 2nd World War. To fly them at the high altitudes of Ladakh, where the mechanical efficiency (engine performance) was much reduced and the terrain provided few places for forced landing, was indeed hazardous. Yet IAF pilots kept flying them day in and day out, thus displaying doggedness of purpose and sustained courage of a high order. The Packet pilots, in fact, created world records by landing at Daulat Beg Oldi and Chushul. Fairchild Packet's landing at the improvised airstrip at Daulat Beg Oldi, two years later, on 23rd July 1962, was another feat in airmanship. Squadron Leader C.S. Raje (later Air Marshal) who carried out the landing at DBO was decorated with Vir Chakra.

[88] 42 Squadron (Illyushin-14) was based at Air Force Station, Chandigarh, and one detachment operated alongwith 43 Squadron (Dakotas) from Srinagar.

[89] For operational safety from Chinese guns, the landing of this aircraft was discontinued, but it was extensively used for air drop of supplies, FOL, vehicles, essential equipment and ammunition. When this author visited Depsang plateau in September to December 1963, the area of DBO landing ground and Track Junction, it was littered with air drops, perhaps just before the withdrawal from DBO was carried out!

Chushul and Leh airfields. The MI 4 helicopters made use of every conceivable helipad.

In 1960, when it was decided to try landing a Packet aircraft at Chushul, the American manufacturers who were consulted prior to the attempt, wrote back to say that the height of the landing strip, i.e. 13,000 feet (3,965 metres) mentioned by Indian Air Force, was obviously an error in typing. According to them, to land at such a high altitude was full of risk. But Air Vice Marshal Pinto[90] and Wing Commander L.S. Grewal,[91] two renowned pilots of Indian Air Force carried out a successful landing, defying the manufacturers' warning. The IAF engineers devised a "jet pack" engine, which was mounted on top of the cockpit that gave additional boost to the Packet aircraft's engine power. The AN-12 aircraft, too, achieved the incredible feat of transporting AMX-13 tanks to Chushul, just before the battle. AN-12 aircraft were not originally equipped to transport these tanks. In fact, it took considerable improvisation to load the tanks while keeping in view the aircraft's centre of gravity. Even the Russians must have been surprised to learn of the AMX-13 tanks landing at Chushul in their AN-12 aircraft.

Major General Jagjit Singh had narrated to this author that "Helicopter pilots who were flying in Ladakh in early 1960s, were both skilful and courageous, but they tended to be rather independent minded, since Headquarters 114 Infantry Brigade had no authority to exercise any control over their functioning! Only personal relations and charm of the Brigade Commander and his Brigade Major worked!"

Special mention must be made of two infantry Battalions, namely 13 Kumaon and 1/8 Gorkha Rifles whose gallant troops defeated the Chinese plan of capturing Chushul. There were many acts of gallantry by officers and brave soldiers, some of whom earned gallantry awards, notably, Major Dhan Bahadur Thapa, 1/8

---

[90] It is unfortunate that he did not live long. He died in a helicopter crash three years later, depriving the country of an outstanding military leader.

[91] Grewal rose to the rank of Air Marshal. This highly decorated airman (PVSM, AVSM, VrC) retired after 38 years of distinguished service.

Gorkha Rifles, and late Major Shaitan Singh, 13 Kumaon, who were both awarded the highest gallantry award, Param Vir Chakra (PVC).

How Brigadier T.N. Raina, Commander 114 Infantry Brigade, met the Chinese assault in his sector is now a part of history. He demonstrated what a determined commander could do against an enemy superior in numbers and equipment. His planning for the battle highlighted the importance of creativity in devising strategy. The deception plan of "dummy" artillery and armour Positions that were set up to delude the enemy was a stroke of genius. The Chinese wasted considerable effort and ammunition on shelling that dummy base and, as a result, Indian hidden gun positions were saved. Tappy Raina's meticulous planning included being prepared for the very worst regardless of what government or others thought. When the Chinese attack began, he drove in his jeep among his troops with his star plate and flag to boost the morale of his men. His fearlessness inspired his soldiers and officers.

The fortunes of war in that particular sector did not go against India and Indian Army. The Chinese PLA attack on Chushul Sector was blunted by the resolute courage of the troops of 114 Infantry Brigade under Brigadier Tappy Raina's command. It was his personal inspiring leadership that enabled the airfield at Chushul and the villages in 114 Infantry Brigade sector to be saved and the cohesion and fighting capacity of the troops under his command retained after the fierce battles of 18th and 19th of November 1962. In recognition of such exemplary leadership, a grateful Government of India conferred on him the award of Maha Vir Chakra (MVC), the nation's second highest gallantry award.

Part IV

Higher Command, Staff Appointments and Birth of A New Nation

"Having made pleasure and pain, gain and loss, victory and defeat the same, engage in battle for the sake of battle; thus you shall not incur sin."
~ Bhagavad Gita 2.38

Chapter 19

Staff and Higher Command

The making of a combat General in any army of the world is a complex process. The situation in Indian Army is no exception. Much goes into this process: the right type of family background and upbringing as a youth, grounding in the art and science of soldiering, grooming under a good commanding officer, actual combat experience of commanding troops, a flair for man-management and dedication to a cause. Brigadier Tappy Raina had all of this. But the real test of any general officer comes on the battlefield, when he pitches his skill against that of the enemy.

Having experienced battlefield environments as a young officer during Second World War, and as a major in the Cease Fire Line combat environment; however, Tappy Raina's first real test came as Commander of 114 Infantry Brigade in Ladakh in 1962. The second time Tappy was tested, when on promotion to the rank of Major General, he was appointed the General Officer Commanding of 25 Infantry Division deployed south of Pir Panjal Range opposite Pakistan Occupied Kashmir. This was followed by his promotion to the rank of Lieutenant General, and appointment as General Officer Commanding of the newly-raised, 2 Corps, earmarked for war in East Pakistan.

After the successful command of an infantry brigade in the high altitude area in Ladakh during the war with China in 1962, Brigadier Raina's further rise in the army ran along a well-recognised pattern. He successfully completed a course at National Defence College (NDC) in 1964, was appointed BGS of a Corps in the Eastern Sector, and followed by promotion and appointment as

GOC of a Division in the state of Jammu and Kashmir (J&K). He then went on to become Chief of Staff of a Corps in J&K, followed by his appointment as Deputy Adjutant General at Army Headquarters.

National Defence College (NDC)

Brigadier Raina's selection for attending the 4th NDC Course in 1964, based on his career profile thus far, was well merited. Completion of this course carried potential for higher appointments and responsibilities in the army. A brief introduction to the NDC will enable the reader to appreciate the importance of a course of study undertaken here.

NDC was set up in 1960 under the administrative control of the Ministry of Defense to offer broad-based training to senior decision makers on matters related to national security. It was intended to provide joint training and instruction to both, senior defence and civil officers, and would cover the strategic, economic, scientific, political and industrial aspects of the national security in India. The members of the course would also analyse the formulation of national strategy for various contingencies up to and including the outbreak of war.

NDC was conceived on the pattern of similar institutions in other countries. Lieutenant General K. Bahadur Singh MBE, formerly of the Kumaon Regiment and an alumnus of the Imperial Defence College (IDC), UK, was appointed the first Commandant of the newly established National Defence College. The College is located in the former office of the High Commission of the United Kingdom in India, after it shifted to its new premises in Chanakyapuri, New Delhi.

The first NDC Course commenced on 27th April 1960. The curriculum covered the economic, social and political aspects of internal threats. External threats were analysed on the basis of the economic and defence policies of the world powers namely, the United States, the former Soviet Union and China along with that of the adjacent countries that could pose a threat to national security due to their own or world power dynamics. With this overall background, students of the NDC were required to recommend strategic policies in diplomacy, economy and defence. It was believed that this method proved to be very sound as the studies in the first two courses correctly forecast the war with China in the winter of 1962 and with Pakistan in 1965!

Right from the start, the emphasis in the NDC was on minimal faculty. The designation, of "Senior Directing Staff" (Sr DS) was coined to make it clear that the staff merely directed the institution's daily affairs while the lecturers were always guests. Participants of the Course were exposed to some two hundred lectures on a wide range of political, economic and strategic issues. The speakers included politicians, statesmen, administrators, journalists, scientists, historians, economists, philosophers and diplomats. The speakers spoke freely since the lectures were not to be reported and the students were asked not to discuss anything outside the College. The lecturers were probingly questioned, issues were discussed threadbare and students sharpened their ability of synthesizing thoughts and ideas. There was no attempt to brainwash but rather to catalyse the process of absorption, analysis and synthesis. The mental attitude of students at the NDC was outward and forward looking.

A pioneering institute of its type in Asia, the role of NDC had remained largely unchanged since its establishment[92], till Gen Tappy Raina was the COAS & Chairman COSC. It has continued to provide future decision makers of the Government of India with the necessary skills and background for filling senior positions in national security and associated fields.

BGS HQ 33 Corps

After successful completion of the 4th NDC course in 1964, Brigadier Raina was appointed BGS at HQ 33 Corps. He took up this

---

[92] As per the Cantonment Gazette, this building was an evacuee property under occupation by UK High Commission and maintained by CPWD In March 1960, the building was acquired by MES from CPWD (Ministry of Rehabilitation). Area of the compound, including building, is 7.30 acres i.e., 35350 square yards.

new appointment on 4th January 1965 when Lieutenant General Gopal Gurunath Bewoor[93] was the General Officer Commanding 33 Corps.

With Tappy's previous battle experience against the Chinese army while in command of an infantry brigade in Ladakh, he could now contribute in a most meaningful way in refining the plans of the Corps which was operationally responsible not only for Sikkim and Bhutan, but also for the North Bengal Corridor against threat from East Pakistan. Moreover, Tappy was able to enrich his knowledge of East Pakistan which proved useful to him when he later became GOC 2 Corps during the Indo-Pakistan War of 1971.

[93] Nine years later, Brigadier Raina took over as COAS, Indian Army from General G.G. Bewoor, PVSM, in June 1975.

Chapter 20

GOC 25 Infantry Division

On the successful completion of his appointment as BGS 33 Corps, Brigadier Raina was promoted to the rank of Major General and appointed GOC 25 Infantry Division on 10th January 1966. He succeeded Major General Amreek Singh who proceeded to HQ 15 Corps as COS. 25 Infantry Division was part of 15 Corps Sector in Jammu & Kashmir.

The news of Brigadier Raina's promotion and appointment as GOC 25 Infantry Division was received with great joy and pride by all ranks of the Kumaon Regiment in general and the 14th Battalion, the Kumaon Regiment (Gwalior), in particular. General Raina was equally pleased to learn that the Battalion which he had the privilege to command earlier was now deployed in 93 Infantry Brigade Sector of, under the operational command of 25 Infantry Division that he was going to command.

It is customary that when an officer rises to become a General Officer Commanding a formation, he usually selects an officer from his regiment, preferably from the battalion in which he has served and later commanded, for appointment as his Aide-de-Camp (ADC). The top-brass of 14th Battalion (Gwalior) selected Captain Yogesh Prasad[94] (nick named Yogi), a decision that was, naturally, subject to the approval of the GOC designate.

[94] In 1976, Major Yogesh Prasad initially proceeded on deputation to Cabinet Secretariat where he was later absorbed permanently and where he rose to be a Joint Secretary, Cabinet Secretariat, Government of India.

After consultation with the staff at Divisional Headquarters, Yogi was deputed to receive the GOC (Designate) at Pathankot Railway Station, the then railhead for Jammu and Kashmir, at 06:00 hrs on 10th January 1966. Yogi accompanied Lieutenant Colonel Harish K. Bakshi, 5 GR, who was GSO-1, HQ 25 Infantry Division. Kashmir Mail from Delhi arrived on time and Tappy Raina emerged dressed in winter uniform with the badges of rank of Major General on his shoulders. Suddenly there was commotion in the reception party! The jeep in which the GOC (Designate) was to travel from Pathankot to Jammu had only one star displayed as per the instruction of GSO-1. He was under the impression that the GOC (Designate) would wear the badges of rank of a Major General, only when he would reach Division Headquarters and actually assume command of the Division.[95]

During the two-hour road journey from Pathankot to Jammu, General Raina asked the GSO-1 to brief him on the current operational situation prevailing in the Divisional Sector. On reaching Jammu Airfield, the General and his GSO-1 boarded the waiting Indian Air Force helicopter to fly to HQ 25 Infantry Division located at Rajauri, whereas Yogi travelled from Jammu to Rajauri by road, along with the baggage.

Operational Familiarisation

General Raina soon settled down in his new appointment. He asked to be briefed on the operations carried out in the 25 Infantry Division Sector during the recent Indo-Pakistan War in 1965 and the post-war operational situation. During the first operational briefing, the Division staff explained how the Pakistan Army had launched "Operation Gibraltar", during the summer of 1965, for large scale infiltration into Jammu and Kashmir, from bases across

---

[95] At a later date, when Captain Yogesh Prasad, ADC to GOC had become better acquainted with the General, he mentioned in a casual conversation the apprehension of the GSO-1 about the stars on the stars plate to be displayed on the vehicle, to which the General retorted, "The command of the Division is to be assumed in the rank of Major General and not Brigadier"!

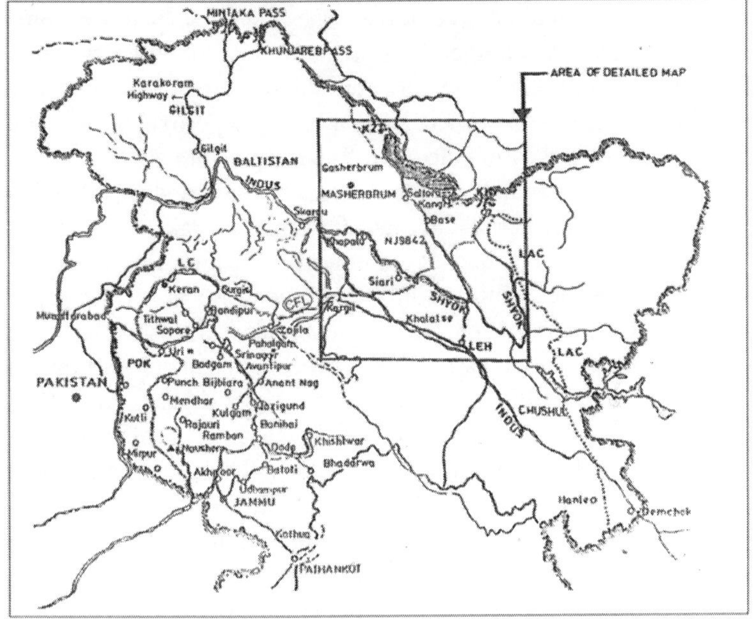

Map 10: Cease Fire Line in J&K, 1st January 1949.

the Cease Fire Line (CFL) in Pakistan Occupied Kashmir (POK). Amongst various routes of infiltration into the 15 Corps Sector, the Pakistani Infiltration Force also used huge gaps in the defences of 25 Infantry Division Sector whose frontage extended over 160 kilometres (100 miles), from Munawar Wali Tavi, East of Nowshera, to Poonch, in the North, along the CFL[96]. (*See* Map 10)

Operation Gibraltar

Operation Gibraltar by Pakistan Army envisaged guerrilla operations inside Jammu and Kashmir by a number of guerrilla groups

---

[96] After the Simla Agreement of 3rd July 1972 between Indian and Pakistani military delegations, the CFL as per the Karachi agreement of 1949 was replaced by Line of Control (LOC).

of roughly a battalion size force. These groups included some Kashmiri volunteers trained by Pakistan Army, the Pakistan Army Special Services Group (SSG) commando personnel and some regular infantry troops. There were a total of approximately 5,000 to 7,000 personnel subdivided into five main columns.

Operation Gibraltar proved to be too ambitious and was found to be beyond the means of Pakistan. Contrary to Pakistani expectations, the local population of Jammu and Kashmir, by and large, neither co-operated with the infiltrators nor rose in revolt against India. By 18th August 1965, Operation Gibraltar lost its momentum.

In response, 15 Corps launched two major counter-infiltration operations inside POK, to destroy the logistic bases in Hajipir Bulge situated on the boundaries of the 19 and 25 Infantry Divisions, and in Neelam Valley in 19 Infantry Division Sector. Both these operations succeeded and Pakistan Army's Operation Gibraltar ended in a failure. The capture of Hajipir Pass on 28th August 1965, which was a principal logistic base for the infiltrators, and the Indian successes in 19 Infantry Division Sector opposite Uri on 29-31st August 1965, unnerved the Pakistani GHQ. They now feared that Muzaffarabad (in POK) was about to be attacked.

Some infiltration groups, which were commanded by officers of Pakistan's elite Special Services Group (SSG), succeeded in penetrating some of the forward defences of 25 Infantry Division Sector. They secured control of villages in depth areas of the Division Sector, falling between the CFL and the Pir Panjal Range: this was the boundary between 19 Infantry Division (North of Pir Panjal) and 25 Infantry Division, (South of Pir Panjal Range). The infiltrators, with a fair degree of success, had disrupted the line of communications within the 25 Infantry Division Sector, especially between Rajauri and Poonch. The villagers of Darhal, Thanamandi, Bafliaz, Surankot, Sauji and Gali villages, and some of the local Bakarwals in the Pir Panjal ranges had provided logistical support to the Pakistani infiltrators, which left 25 Infantry Division somewhat off balance, during the War in 1965.

It was highlighted to Tappy Raina, the incoming GOC by the Staff officers of General Staff (Operation) Branch at HQ 25 Infantry Division that in the aftermath of Operation Gibraltar, counter-infiltration operations were undertaken in the Divisional Sector, to flush out the infiltrators and re-capture the strategic areas and heights. This was done well before the imposition of the ceasefire accepted during the Tashkent Agreement of 1965[97], where it was agreed by Lal Bahadur Shastri, Prime Minister of India and Field Marshal Ayub Khan, President of Pakistan that both nations would return the areas captured by either side in their respective territory during the Indo-Pak war 1965.

Having understood the operational plans, Major General Raina accorded top priority to visiting these locations to get acquainted with the terrain and troop deployment on the ground. Within days of assuming command, the General tasked his staff to draw out plans for his tour of the Divisional Sector. He was determined to do this well before the actual return of troops of both countries to the pre-September 1965 positions as per the following tour plan:

- Visit all the captured Pakistani posts which would be handed back to Pakistan, as stipulated in the Tashkent Agreement. These included the strategic posts of Raja and Rani in the Poonch Sector, OP Hill in Mendhar Sector, the Haji Pir Pass[98] which fell in the neighbouring 19 Infantry Division.
- Haji Pir Pass was captured by 68 Infantry Brigade, then commanded by Brigadier (later Lieutenant General) Zorawar Chand

---

[97] Tashkent Agreement: This accord of 10th January 1966, was signed between Indian Prime Minister Lal Bahadur Shastri and Pakistan's President Ayub Khan, in the wake of the Indo-Pakistan War of September 1965, which had ended in a cease fire. Soviet Premier Alexei Kosygin lent his good offices and invited both sub-continental leaders to the Central Asia city of Tashkent, to discuss an easing of tensions. India and Pakistan agreed to restore diplomatic relations, withdraw their forces to pre-war positions, and settle their disputes peacefully. Shastri's sudden death at Tashkent within hours of his diplomatic success and the return of his body to New Delhi for funeral rites lent greater drama and importance to the agreement than its modest provisions perhaps deserved.

[98] This pass, 2,637 metres above sea level, had been given to Pakistan in accordance with Karachi Agreement of 1949, which denied access to Uri-Poonch road, as it dominates this road, though it was 8 kilometres from CFL.

Bakhshi, known to his friends as "Zoru" Bakshi[99]. Instead of travelling by helicopter to Haji Pir Pass, Major General Raina chose to travel by road as he believed that visiting the neighbouring sector by road would provide an opportunity to familiarise himself with the area of Poonch Bulge and Kahuta.

- The Commander of 68 Infantry Brigade, one of whose Battalions, 1 Para, had captured the Haji Pir Pass, personally organised the visit of Major General Raina, to his Brigade Sector, including a visit to the Haji Pir Pass defended area.
- Visit all posts and pickets along the CFL in the Division, extending from Nowshera to Poonch.
- Visit areas in the interior of the Division Sector which were used by the infiltrators for setting up bases.
- Construct an alternate road link with Poonch *via* Rajauri – Dera Ki Gali – Bafliaz – Surankot – Poonch.
- Impress on the civil administration the need for improved interaction with the villages in the interiors. This included fraternisation, visits by medical teams, improving connectivity within villages in the interior; in short, not to neglect the welfare of the population in the rear areas. The General felt the need to win the loyalty of the local population who showed visible sympathy with the infiltrators, causing havoc in the 25 Division Sector

---

[99] One of India's highly decorated General Officers, Lieutenant General Zoru Bakshi was recipient of gallantry awards MVC, VrC and Mention-in-Despatches, besides the award of PVSM for his distinguished service.

After graduation from Gordon College, Rawalpindi, in 1942, Zoru Bakshi joined the Army and was commissioned in 1943 into the Baloch Regiment (now in Pakistan Army). A veteran of the War in Burma, he was transferred to 5 Gorkha Rifles of Indian Army after partition in 1947. He took part in Indo-Pak War of 1947-48 and was awarded VrC. He was awarded MVC (Maha Vir Chakra) for his bold plan to capture the strategic Haji Pir Pass during the 1965 War with Pakistan.

During his long 36-year service, Zoru Bakshi commanded 2/5 Gorkha Rifles, 68 Infantry Brigade, 8 Mountain and 26 Infantry Divisions and 2 Corps. He retired in 1979 after serving at Army HQ as Military Secretary (MS). He passed away in New Delhi at age of 97 years in May 2018.

during the Pakistani misadventure of launching Operation Gibraltar in 1965.

- Lay emphasis on training in his Division, with focus on "Attack by Infiltration and Counter-Infiltration".
- Trek to Tosha Maidan-Baramulla in the 19 Infantry Division Sector through the Pir Panjal Pass to study the route of infiltration via Sauji and Gali villages in the Poonch area. Subsequently, regular patrols were sent on this link route with the Valley to ensure that Pakistan was denied this route of infiltration in future.

In compliance with the Tashkent Agreement of 1966, the Indian Army had to return the following posts in the 25 Infantry Division Sector, captured during Indo-Pakistan War of 1965:

- **120 Infantry Brigade Sector:** OP Hill in the Mendhar area and the Raja and Rani Posts.
- **93 Infantry Brigade Sector:** Poonch Bulge including Langoor Post, just below the famous Pritam feature, which dominated Poonch, both by fire and observation.

Major General Raina's assumption of the command of 25 Infantry Division coincided with the signing of the Tashkent Agreement. He had to quickly understand the nuances of the proposed troop withdrawal from areas in POK captured by Indian Army during the Indo-Pakistan war of 1965. Not only did he visit all the captured posts in the Divisional Sector, he also decided to motor down to the Haji Pir Pass. This was a very emotional visit for the General as the unit which had captured this important pass was 1 Para (Punjab), commanded by Lieutenant Colonel (later Lieutenant General) Tirath Singh Oberoi, a former officer of 1 Kumaon (Para)[100], the Battalion in which General Raina had served soon after becoming a commissioned officer in the 19 Hyderabad Regiment (now The Kumaon Regiment). The General

---

[100] "Tappy" saw action in PAI Force in Iraq and FM "Bill" Slim's 14th Army in Burma as part of 1/19, Hyderabad Regiment, later re-designated as 1 Kumaon (Para), before becoming 3rd Battalion, Parachute Regiment in 1952.

was received at the Haji Pir Pass by Lieutenant Colonel Oberoi, and Major (later Lieutenant General) Ranjit Singh Dayal, who had led the attack on Pakistan Army, deployed on Haji Pir Pass, and captured it after a fierce fire-fight. Ranjit Singh Dayal was awarded the MVC for gallant action.

Flag Meetings

In accordance with the Tashkent Agreement, Flag Meetings were scheduled in February 1966, between the local Formation Commander of the Indian Army and his Pakistani counterpart. The first meeting was held at the check post on the Rawalakot-Poonch Road, under the mediation of the Military Observers of the United Nations Military Observer Group in India and Pakistan (UNMOGIP) who were stationed on both sides of the CFL, as stipulated in the Karachi Agreement, 1949.

Major General (later Lieutenant General) Mohammed Attiqur Rahman[101], Pakistan Army, General Officer Commanding 12 Infantry Division with its HQ at Murree[102], was nominated by Government of Pakistan for the meeting with his Indian counterpart,

---

[101] Lieutenant General (retd) Mohammed Attiqur Rahman MC (24th June 1918 – 1st June 1996) was a distinguished General Officer in the Pakistan Army, a noted military historian, as well as a senior government official. After schooling at St Paul's in London, he joined the Royal Indian Military College, and later the Indian Military Academy, Dehra Dun, where he was awarded the Sword of Honour as the best all-round Gentleman Cadet. Commissioned in 4/12 Frontier Force Battalion, where his best friend in the Battalion was Major (Later on Field Marshal) Sam Manekshaw, MC. Theirs was a deep and special friendship that lasted a lifetime. He is the author of the book, *Our Defence Cause: An Analysis of Pakistan's Past and Future Military Role*, and many other books on Leadership.

[102] 12th Infantry Division was Pakistan Army's largest Infantry Division, which was based at Murree Cantonment, Punjab, close to POK. The Division's formation sign was "Chinar". Six Infantry Brigades of Pakistan 12 Infantry Division, were deployed all across Pakistan Occupied Jammu and Kashmir and the Line of Control (LOC). With one divisional Artillery Brigade and a number of supporting units of Air Defence, Supply and Remount Veterinary Corps under its command, Pakistan 12th Infantry division was the largest division of Pakistan Army.

Major General Raina. While there were some stipulations on the composition of each delegation, General Raina decided to include his ADC, Captain Yogesh Prasad in the Indian delegation, as "Yogi" was also performing the duties of GSO-3 (OPS) at HQ 25 Infantry Division.

Major Prasad recalls that there was visible bonhomie at the flag meeting but it surprised the Indian side that the staff of Major General Rahman had not made comprehensive preparations, resulting in some embarrassment to the Pakistani Division Commander. Because of that, the talks between the two delegations remained inconclusive. The two Generals, therefore, decided to meet again at the earliest, since the deadline for the withdrawal by both armies from the captured areas had to be adhered to as per the Tashkent Agreement.

The deferred flag meeting between Major General Rahman and Major General Raina, along with their delegations, was later held in a cordial atmosphere in the spirit of the Tashkent Agreement. It was, however, to the detriment of Indian Army's operational task since it implied the return by the Indian Army of captured areas in POK to the Pakistan Army.

In his book, *Our Defence Cause: An Analysis of Pakistan's Past and Future Military Role*, Lieutenant General Mohammed Attiqur Rahman analysed that the cause of Pakistan's defeat by India in the Indo-Pak war of 1971 was "Pakistan's 1965 misadventure".

During the Indo-Pakistan War of 1965, the Pakistani army's plan, "Operation Gibraltar", to infiltrate well trained commando units through large gaps in the Indian defences along CFL, to cut off logistic support to the vastly extended troops of 25 Infantry Division had nearly paid off. This had been coordinated with their operational plan, Operation Grand Slam for a major offensive in the Chhamb-Jaurian area in Akhnoor Sector, with a view to crippling the defensibility of the 25 Division sector. The Pakistani offensive was blunted successfully by Indian Army. Unfortunately, Indian Army lost Brigadier Jal Master, commander of 191 Infantry Brigade Group, who was killed in action. To deal with the grim situation in the initial stages of the operations, and to flush out infiltrators from the interiors of 25 Infantry Division's sector,

52 Mountain Brigade, commanded by Brigadier (later Lieutenant General) R.D. Hira was inducted into the 25 Infantry Division sector.

All the brigades under the command of HQ 25 Infantry Division were committed to holding the posts along the CFL, leaving hardly any reserves for dealing with the menace by Pakistani infiltrators in the depth areas. This scenario is recalled to highlight the complete inadequacy of the role of the United Nations Military Observers Group in India and Pakistan (UNMOGIP) to monitor the CFL and its gross violation in 1965. In the 25 Infantry Division Sector, there was only one UNMOGIP Observers' Station in Poonch, which had the responsibility to monitor violations along the CFL. In the POK Sector opposite 25 Infantry Division, there were UNMOGIP stations at Kotli, Muzafrabad and Rawalakot. For effective monitoring and liaison it was appreciated that a Senior Observer Group of the UNMOGIP should be positioned at the HQ 25 Infantry Division, Rajauri. Thus in the middle of 1966, a UNMOGIP station was opened at Rajauri with Colonel Owen Browne of the Canadian Artillery as Station Chief.

In 1965, Pakistan had, to a degree, been successful in winning over the loyalty of the UNMOGIP which did nothing to expose Pakistan for its wilful violation of the Karachi Agreement, 1949. Had the UN Observers been impartial and faithful in fulfilling their role, the vicious designs of Pakistani aggression in 1965 could have been exposed to the world. Maybe, Indian diplomacy, too, was weak and was unable to draw support from the international community in exposing Pakistan for being the aggressor in the conflict. It was because of this background that a UN station was also set up at Rajauri, alongside the Division HQ.

Major General Raina assumed command of 25 Infantry Division immediately after the announcement of the Cease Fire in January 1966 which marked an end of hostilities following the Indo-Pak war of 1965. Tappy's predecessor Major General Amreek Singh, a thorough gentleman, had been somewhat let down by his staff and the commanders, resulting in massive infiltration by the enemy and control of the areas in the depth of the 25 Division sector. Despite this, however, in the closing stages of the war the Division salvaged its image following the capture of some strategic Pakistani posts and by driving out the infiltrators. Though Pakistani infiltrators had achieved some initial success and caused embarrassment to the Division, they had not been able to sustain themselves in the face of action taken by 25 Infantry Division to drive them out.

HQ 25 Infantry Division

Two Principal Staff Officers at HQ 25 Infantry Division were Lieutenant Colonel Harish Kumar Bakshi, 5 Gorkha Rifles, who was GSO-1, while Lieutenant Colonel Gyan K. Katju, Kumaon Rregiment was the AQMG. They were assisted by Major Jujjhar Singh Bains, Artillery, GSO-2 (OPS), later succeeded by Major S.K. Pasricha, Artillery. Major G.P.S. Bindra, ASC was DAQMG and was later succeeded by Major (later colonel) Ajai Mushran, AOC. (Maj Ajai Mushran came from a landed family of Narsinghpur in Madhya Pradesh. A promising officer from Army Ordinance Corps, who rose to the rank of Colonel, but his career in the Army had to be cut short, due to his health. Instead, politics of Madhya Pradesh drew him to become an MP in Lok Sabha and later a long stint as Finance Minister of MP Government.)

The mainstay of the Operations branch was Major Bains who enjoyed full confidence of his GOC. Lieutenant Colonel Katju was always addressed by the GOC as "Gyani Bhai", since the GOC and AQMG were from the Kumaon Regiment and well known to each other. "Gyani Bhai" (Wise Brother) had his own limitations. Every time Tappy sent for Lt Col Katju for discussion in his office on some administrative matter, he was always seen going to the GOC with his office orderly trailing behind with a large number of files and papers. He would first park himself in the office of the ADC for a breather and check with him what the GOC had in mind to discuss! So the ADC on one such call enquired from him the reason for lugging so many files, to which Gyani Bhai replied, "God knows what he is going to ask; I do not wish to take any chances. Therefore I carry files relating to all possible queries that the GOC may have in mind"! General Raina, in a lighter mood, sometime would quip, the combination of two Kashmiris, both, AQ and DQ was "frightening"!

General Raina was a keen golfer. All senior staff officers at Rajauri would show up at the golf course in the afternoon for the game. Initially, the GOC played golf only with his ADC, Captain Yogesh Prasad. Soon the commander of the Artillery Brigade, the GSO-1, and heads of some other arms and services also sought to join the GOC's "Four Ball"! It soon led to some friction and heartburn, as the ADMS was not a part of this elite "Four Ball"! This led to an ugly turn one day, in a pre-lunch altercation between the C-Arty and the ADMS. The two red tab officers nearly came to blows and the GSO-1 (Lieutenant Colonel Wajinder Singh Bakshi) had to intervene and separate the two. The ADC alerted the GOC about the ugly incident but advised him to stay away from the "messy" situation in the Mess, which he did.

The General was very particular about the "time and space" factor and expected his ADC to keep an upto date Time and Move Table on the driving time to destinations or walking time to all posts, names of the COs, company commanders, staff officers at Brigade HQ, and to record minutes of all discussions and tour notes. The ADC and accompanying SO from Division Headquarters were thus constantly kept on their toes.

At that time, the families of all ranks were not permitted in Rajauri as it was a field area. As a special dispensation, however, adult sons of officers could visit their fathers during vacation. In the summer of 1967, Tappy's son, Cadet Jyoti Narain Raina, fondly called "Joe", then undergoing training at National Defence Academy, Khadakvasla, visited his father at Rajauri. Joe was fond of outdoor activity. He loved riding and reading, but only what he liked to read and not what his father wanted him to! To gain experience of life at a Forward Post, Joe was sent to visit some important posts, the highest of which was Doda (approximately 10,000 feet), in the Disional sector under operational control of 93 Infantry Brigade. Being young and physically fit, Joe politely declined the offer to go up to the Post on a pony, and instead chose to trek all the way up. Joe was also fond of handling weapons and lessons in firing were arranged for him and he had good practice sessions at the short and long ranges.

General Raina was obsessed with high standards in professional training, perfection of skills, discipline, and turnout; those found wanting in these attributes were not spared. He was a stickler for military etiquette and expected all ranks to follow these in letter and spirit. Sloppy movements and casual attitude in dress and general conduct were also unacceptable to him. A "second position" was not in his dictionary as he strived to achieve perfection.

One fine morning, GOC sent for the GSO 1 and in all seriousness told him that his ADC was uneducated and that he must be made to attend some useful courses at army training schools. The GSO 1 replied, "Wilco, Sir" and back he walked to his office to return in minutes with all the vacancies in courses available with the Division. The GSO 1 recommended the Commando course as being the most appropriate for the ADC and that he could leave for Mhow in three days' time. The GSO 1 was taken aback by the reaction of the General, who asked him how anyone could be sent to attend an Army course without adequate pre-course training. He went on to add, "I am surprised to know what your concept of "Education" is. Can you think of something better"? The GSO 1 then proposed the General Intelligence Course (GICO) at the Intelligence School, Pune. During his two-year tenure as ADC, Captain Prasad attended three courses; but there was one stipulation — that he forego half his entitlement of annual leave. During his absence, no substitute ADC was appointed. The General had his own reason for not taking any one temporarily because of the confidential nature of this appointment. Before proceeding for each course, the ADC was made to attend, in a nearby Infantry unit, the pre-course cadre. The GOC even sent his orderlies (*sahayaks*) to attend courses. Even his golden Labrador, Mischief, had to undergo training! Every morning when the GOC walked to his office, Mischief was seen walking by his side with the newspaper firmly held in her mouth.

In the aftermath of the Indo-Pakistan War of 1965 and the Tashkent Agreement concluded in 1966, there were several dignitaries and officials who visited Rajauri to be briefed on the prevailing ground situation. Moreover, some intrusions had taken place in the 120 Infantry Brigade Sector. Although minor in nature, these engaged the attention of New Delhi and resulted in the visit of a high-powered government delegation, comprising the following senior bureaucrats:

- Mr V. Shankar Indian Civil Service, Defence Secretary.
- Mr L.P. Singh, Indian Civil Service, Home Secretary.
- Mr D.R. Kohli, Indian Civil Service, Joint Secretary (G)[103], Ministry of Defence.

They were all escorted to the Bhimber Gali View Point to acquaint them with the prevailing ground situation along the CFL in 25 Infantry Division Sector.

One of the recurring problems affecting the local civilian population was the way in which the villages had got divided because of the CFL. Whereas villagers inhabiting the POK side of the CFL, were not disturbed by Indian troops while cultivating their land, on the other hand Pakistani troops invariably opened fire on villagers on the Indian side of the CFL, whenever they tried to cultivated their land. Village huts were also used as cover to inch forward with a view to grabbing land. Mr B.K. Nehru, Sheikh Abdullah, the Governor and Chief Minister of Jammu and Kashmir, respectively, and Yuvraj Karan Singh, former "Raj Pramukh" of Jammu and Kashmir then a Member of Parliament, were among the civilian hierarchy, who also visited Rajauri. It was thus decided that villagers would be compensated for their inability to cultivate their land adjacent to the CFL

In the spring of 1968, Major General Raina received his posting order from Army Headquarters to report to Headquarters 15 Corps, Udhampur, as Chief of Staff (COS) to succeed Major General Amreek Singh yet again. Some thought that this "lukewarm" appointment marked an end to Tappy Raina's military career!

---

[103] Mr. D.R. Kohli, Indian Civil Service, was later appointed Secretary, Ministry of Defense, Government of India, when General Raina, MVC, became the Chief of Army Staff of the Indian Army.

Chapter 21

Chief of Staff, HQ 15 Corps

After the completion of a very challenging tenure of two years and two months as GOC 25 Infantry Division, General Raina assumed his new appointment as Chief Of Staff, HQ 15 Corps at Udhampur on 17th March 1968.

The area of responsibility for 15 Corps extended in the north from the Karakoram Pass in Ladakh to Pathankot in the south. It had the following formations on its Order of Battle (ORBAT), with their areas of responsibility as under:

(a) 3 Infantry Division — Ladakh.
(b) 121 Infantry Brigade Group — Kargil and Drass Sectors.
(c) 19 Infantry Division — CFL from Zojila to North Pir Panjal.
(d) V Sector — Kashmir Valley and South Kashmir.
(e) 25 Infantry Division — South of Pir Panjal to Sunderbani.
(f) 10 Infantry Division — Akhnoor Sector.
(g) 26 Infantry Division — Jammu Sector.

Lt. General K.P. Candeth, PVSM, who was GOC 15 Corps[104] could not have wished for a more competent Chief of Staff at the Corps Headquarters to assist him in his operational responsibility of such a vast Corps Sector. Major General Tappy Raina was no stranger to the Corps Sector, having served with his Battalion, 4th Gwalior Infantry, in 25 Infantry Division Sector, having commanded 114 Infantry Brigade in Ladakh (3 Infantry Division Sector) and having been GOC 25 Infantry Division, prior to his present appointment. Therefore, he took hardly any time to settle down in his new appointment.

General Raina took particular interest in improving the logistic problems, especially of units and sub units located in remote high altitude areas, like the Kargil, Dras, Gurez and Tithwal Sectors. He did so by personally visiting these places even at the height of winter and falling snow. Such visits were greatly appreciated by all ranks and helped maintain the morale of the troops.

Mrs. Ninette Raina and the children, Jyoti (Joe) and Anita remained in Sangli Officers' Hostel, New Delhi, as a "separated family". This had already become their home since 1959, when Tappy came on posting to Army Headquarters in the MS Branch. Later, when he proceeded to command 114 Infantry Brigade in Ladakh, his family remained separated in the same house. Even during the NDC Course in 1964, they continued to reside at Sangli Mess. On completion of the NDC Course he had two successive postings to field areas; first to HQ 33 Corps and later as GOC 25 Infantry Division. Joe was a boarder at Sherwood College,

---

[104] After the Indo-Pakistan War of 1971, the Government of India decided to raise a separate Command Headquarters to oversee operations along the northern borders with Pakistan and China. Lieutenant General Premindra Singh Bhagat, VC, PVSM, was appointed as the first GOC-in-C Northern Command in June 1972. Lieutenant General Bhagat's main responsibilities as GOC-in-C Northern Command were the improvement of defences, the living and working condition of his troops. With HQ 15 Corps having been moved to Srinagar, HQ Northern Command was now established at Udhampur (J&K). HQ 16 Corps, a new Corps HQ was also raised at Nagrota, near Jammu on the National Highway to Srinagar, operationally responsible for Area south of Pir Panjal.

Nainital, while Anita was shifted from St. Mary's Convent in Nainital to Convent of Jesus and Mary in New Delhi. Tappy Raina's posting to HQ 15 Corps at Udhampur, permitted the families of officers to visit and stay for short durations. This enabled the General to enjoy some semblance of family life.

At this stage of his career, General Raina had to face a great deal of anxiety in his personal life. His wife, Ninette, was detected with cancer and required urgent treatment. He took leave and had her treated at the Tata Memorial Cancer Hospital at Bombay (now Mumbai). On return from leave, General Raina once again applied himself to his duties. After completion of one year and six months as COS at HQ 15 Corps, he was posted to Adjutant General Branch at Army Headquarters New Delhi, as Deputy Adjutant General (DAG) on 18th September 1970.

Deputy Adjutant General, Army Headquarters

General (later Field Marshal) Sam Hormusji Framji Jamshedji Manekshaw, MC, popularly known as "Sam" to his peers and "Sam Bahadur" to his soldiers, was Chief of the Army Staff, whereas Lieutenant General H.K. Sibal, MVC,[105] was the Adjutant General, under whom General Raina was to work as Deputy AG.

The Adjutant General Branch at AHQ is responsible for discipline, manpower planning, including recruitment of officers and other ranks, condition of service of all ranks, welfare of serving and retired army personnel, including their families, honour and awards, including honorary commission to JCOs, and ceremonial duties.

A second tenure for Tappy at Army Headquarters now helped him to understand the major and minor issues which Army Headquarters had to deal with the Ministry of Defence. Many of the unresolved and pending cases which came to his knowledge as Deputy Adjutant General were brought to their logical conclusion a few years later when Tappy Raina became the COAS. This ap-

---

[105] Lt Gen H.K. Sibal, MVC, formerly of 5 Gorkha Rifles (FF) was GOC-in-C Central Command, Lucknow from June 1972 to November 1973.

pointment as Deputy Adjutant General gave him the opportunity to work in close coordination with other important branches at Army Headquarters.

Colonel of the Regiment

In May 1970, during the Biennial Conference of the Battalion Commanders of the Kumaon Regiment held at the Kumaon Regimental Centre (KRC), Ranikhet, General Raina was selected to be the Colonel of The Kumaon Regiment (COR), in succession to Lieutenant General Kanwar Bahadur Singh, MBE (retd.) who had held the appointment for ten years.

With General Raina's appointment as COR, the COAS delegated the responsibility of raising a new Infantry Regiment in our Army — the Naga Regiment,[106] to the Kumaon Regimental Centre, Ranikhet. The raising of this unique new Regiment in the Indian Army commenced on 1st November 1970. As per Army HQ orders the class composition of The Naga Regiment would be 50 percent Naga (including erstwhile surrendered insurgents) and 50 percent other hill tribes (OHT) comprising of Kumaonis, Garhwalis and Gorkhas. The new Regiment was affiliated to The Kumaon Regimental Centre for Training, Records, Manpower, and Pay and Accounts. Lieutenant Colonel R.N. Mahajan, VSM, formerly Commanding Officer of 14 Kumaon (Gwalior) was selected to raise the Naga Regiment as its First Commanding Officer.

---

[106] The 16-point draft agreement between Naga People's Convention, which was submitted to Prime Minister Nehru, contained a proposal for a separate state of Nagaland and clause 14 of the Agreement was the demand for a separate Naga Regiment in the Indian Army. Though the state of Nagaland was created in 1960, it was only in early 1970 that the Government of Nagaland revived the idea of a Naga Regiment. This proposal was accepted by the Government of India to raise the Naga Regiment, initially with one battalion. The nucleus of manpower for the proposed Naga Regiment was to be drawn mostly from erstwhile hostile Naga insurgents, who had surrendered and were kept in rehabilitation camps in Nagaland. In early September 1970, the government conveyed its approval to Army HQ for raising this new Regiment.

Once the Naga Regiment had completed the initial period of its raising, Lieutenant Colonel Mahajan approached Major General Raina, Colonel of The Kumaon Regiment, to accept the unanimous request of all ranks of the Naga Regiment to become The Colonel of the Naga Regiment as well. The proposal of the Commanding Officer of the Naga Regiment was conveyed to Army Headquarters by Colonel (later Brigadier) Dhanraj Thamboo, Commandant Kumaon Regimental Centre, Ranikhet. Army Headquarters approved the appointment of General Raina as the first Colonel of The Naga Regiment on 8th June 1971. It was a rare distinction for any General Officer of the Indian Army to be the Colonel of two Regiments!

On completion of its raising at Ranikhet, carefully nurtured by Tappy as its first COR during its raising period, the Battalion received orders to join 7 Infantry Brigade at Gaya (Bihar). This Brigade was part of 4 Infantry Division, which in turn was under the command of the newly raised HQ 2 Corps.

Chapter 22

Prelude to the Break-up of Pakistan

In the spring of 1969, General Yahya Khan took over as President of Pakistan. Soon thereafter, he announced the special framework within which the 1970 elections were to be held. In doing so he failed to realise the possible consequences of this electoral reform. The Pakistan National Assembly election of 17th December 1970 resulted in Sheikh Mujibur Rehman and his Awami League Party of East Pakistan winning an overwhelming victory. The Awami League thus emerged as the party with a large majority, winning twice the number of seats as Zulfikar Ali Bhutto's[107] Pakistan People's Party (PPP).

[107] Born on 5th January 1928, Zulfiqar Ali Bhutto served as Prime Minister of Pakistan from 1973 to 1977, and prior to that as the fourth President of Pakistan from 1971 to 1973. In 1963, when he was barely 35 years old, he was appointed Foreign Minister of Pakistan. He was a proponent of "Operation Gibraltar" in Jammu and Kashmir, leading to war with India in 1965. After the Tashkent Agreement, hostilities ended but Bhutto fell out with Field Marshal Ayub Khan and was sacked from government.

He founded the Pakistan Peoples' Party (PPP) in 1967 and contested general elections in 1970. While the Awami League won a majority of seats overall, the PPP won a majority of seats in West Pakistan. The two parties were unable to agree on a new constitution. Subsequent uprisings led to the secession of East Pakistan and the birth of Bangladesh, after Pakistan lost the war with India in 1971. Bhutto was handed over the presidency of a bifurcated Pakistan in December 1971.

Bhutto set about rebuilding confidence and hopes for Pakistanis for the future! By signing the Simla Agreement on 3rd July 1972, Bhutto brought back 93,000

This landslide victory was a reflection of the simmering discontent that prevailed in the eastern wing of Pakistan against the political and economic domination perpetuated by successive military dictatorships in West Pakistan. Besides religion, there was nothing common between the two wings of Pakistan. West Pakistan had continuously bled the eastern half of its economic resources for its own benefit without paying any attention to improving the living conditions in disaster prone East Pakistan, or of giving a fair proportional representation to her people in the Armed Forces and in government jobs.

Mandate for the Awami League

The clear mandate won by Mujib-ur-Rehman in the 1970 general elections in East Pakistan brought Bengali aspirations to a boiling point. Mujib's Six-Point Programme promised to remove the political and economic disparities between East and West Pakistan. The acceptance of these results meant the conceding of greater autonomy to East Pakistan as well as the "end of Military Rule". Zulfikar Ali Bhutto, however, had no intention of letting political power slip from his hands and threatened to plunge Pakistan into a civil war if Mujib was allowed to form the government. General Yahya Khan, the President, also did not relish the prospect of power shifting to East Pakistan, or of relinquishing military rule in East Pakistan.

POW and 5,000 square miles of Indian-held territory, and recognised the sovereignty of Bangladesh. Domestically, the Pakistani parliament, unanimously approved a new constitution in 1973, and Bhutto assumed office as Prime Minister. He also played an integral role in initiating the Pakistani nuclear programme.

Though PPP won the 1977 parliamentary elections, the Pakistani COAS General Zia-ul-Haq deposed Bhutto in a bloodless coup and had the former Prime Minister controversially tried and executed by the Supreme Court in 1979 for authorising the murder of a political opponent, Ahmad Raza Khan Kasuri. Bhutto was hanged on 5th April 1979.

Martial Law in Pakistan

On 21st February 1971, Yahya Khan dissolved his cabinet, imposed Martial Law on the country and within one week announced an indefinite postponement of the promised National Assembly Session. When this happened, the Bengali population felt cheated and outraged. Violent agitations broke out in East Pakistan and people began agitating for independence. Mujib called for a non-violent, non-cooperation movement, but even he could not control the mobs. The Pakistan Army was deployed to suppress the agitation. This resulted in the killing of a large number of Bengalis. Mujib demanded the withdrawal of troops to the barracks, failing which he threatened to intensify the agitation.

Lieutenant General Sahibzada Yakub Khan, Governor and Martial Law Administrator of East Pakistan, agreed to Mujib's demand and the troops were pulled back. However, General Yahya Khan removed Lieutenant General Yakub Khan and replaced him with Lieutenant General Tikka Khan[108] as the new Governor and Martial Law Administrator of East Pakistan.

On arrival at Dhaka, Tikka Khan found the Eastern Province of Pakistan in total paralysis. The build-up of troops meanwhile continued unabated. General Yahya Khan and Bhutto visited Dacca during this period and a plan was hatched to break the movement by force. Yahya Khan, issued orders to Tikka Khan to "sort out" the Bengalis before returning to West Pakistan.

Operation Blitz, East Pakistan

On 25th March 1971, instead of the meeting of the Pakistan National Assembly, the Pakistani leadership unleashed the full might of the Pakistan Army to ruthlessly suppress the Bengalis. Sheikh Mujib was detained. Before his arrest, however, Mujib declared the independence of "Bangladesh" and called upon the people to throw out the occupation forces. On the same night, mass slaugh-

---

[108] Lt Gen Tikka Khan, who had already earned the title, "Butcher of Baluchistan", was now appointed to suppress the revolt in East Pakistan.

ter, rape, and destruction were unleashed on the unarmed people of East Pakistan. Operation Blitz, as this infamous operation came to be called, horrified the world but Bhutto was said to have exclaimed, "Thank God, Pakistan has been saved." He was to realise not very much later that this was actually only the beginning of the end!

Mukti Bahini (Bangladesh Liberation Force)

At this stage, Bengali officers and men of the Pakistan Armed Forces united with college students to resist this genocide. It was this resistance that gave birth to the Bangladesh Liberation Force that ultimately came to be called the Mukti Bahini. The Pakistani Army's strength in East Pakistan had now grown to more than four Infantry Divisions, besides another 25,000 paramilitary troops.

Effects of Pakistani Operation Blitz on India

Operation Blitz resulted in a mass exodus of terrified civilians from East Pakistan. By the middle of April 1971, more refugees began to pour across the East Pakistan border into India. First they came in their hundreds, then thousands, and then in millions, and still the Pakistani rampage continued. By May 1971, the refugees in India numbered more than ten million. The influx of so many refugees with the attendant problems of housing, food, water, medical care, hygiene and sanitation, imposed an unsustainable burden on India. Dangerous law and order as well as security implications were also implicit in the alteration of the demographic pattern. The presence of these refugees, apart from imposing an unacceptable economic burden, created intolerable tensions in the Indian border states of Tripura and West Bengal. Besides social disparities which caused a near breakdown of law and order and administration there was, in addition, the omnipresent potential for communal disharmony. The refugee issue therefore was unacceptable to India politically, economically and militarily.

By 10th April 1971, Tikka Khan was able to restore some semblance of law and order in East Pakistan after pushing out rebellious troops and disgruntled elements. Having accomplished this, he handed over military control to Lieutenant General A.A.K. Niazi as the General Officer Commanding-in-Chief, Pakistan Eastern Command. Tikka Khan then reverted to his role as Governor and Martial Law Administrator of East Pakistan. By the end of May, except for a few pockets of resistance in inaccessible peripheral areas, the rebellion appeared to have been suppressed.

The Terrain

East Pakistan had an approximately 4,000-kilometre long border with India. It was surrounded by the Indian states of West Bengal to the west, Meghalaya to the north, the Cachar district of Assam and the state of Tripura to the east, and the Bay of Bengal to the south. To the southeast lay the Chittagong Hills area, which shared a common border with Myanmar (Burma).

Three major rivers flow through the country, the Padma, the Jamuna and the Meghna, which, before emptying into the Bay of Bengal, form vast deltas. With the exception of the Chittagong Hill Tracts and Sylhet, the countryside is low-lying and water logged, consisting mostly of paddy and jute fields, intersected by numerous tributaries. The rivers flow from north to south and are very wide becoming tidal in the lower reaches. Hills, lakes and marshland cover the southern region. The monsoon breaks with full force by the middle of May and lasts until the middle of October. The heavy rains in the catchment areas of the rivers in the north, cause floods and widen the rivers by several miles southwards.

The low-lying countryside, heavy monsoon rains, paucity of communications and mighty rivers made East Pakistan a military planner's nightmare. The Indian Army's advance in this terrain, especially in the context of a swift and short campaign would have required vast resources of bridging equipment, assault and rivercraft, the entire needs of which could not be mustered even after pooling the entire country's resources.

Those who had fought in Burma during the Second World War knew the problems of fighting in such a terrain and the advantage it gave the defender. A military offensive in such a terrain was a formidable task, as not only troops but also ammunition, stores and supplies had to be transported across one river after another. Many doubted the possibility of a quick success in the quagmire that was East Pakistan. There were only a few arterial roads, and rail communications were undeveloped. The main ports were Chittagong and Chalna. Other important ports were Cox's Bazar, Chandpur and Khulna. The main airport was at Dhaka. Airfields also existed at Jessore, Sylhet, Shamshernagar, Comila and Chittagong. The rivers of East Pakistan divided the country into four distinct sectors or regions for military operations-the North-Western Sector, the South-Western Sector, the Northern / Central Sector and the Eastern Sector.

By the end of October 1971, the border clashes became more violent and were now accompanied by artillery and mortar fire. The Mukti Bahini, meanwhile, had established a major base in East Pakistan, adjacent to the Indian village of Bogra. On 21-22nd November 1971, Pakistan troops supported by tanks, artillery and the Pakistan Air Force (PAF) launched an offensive against the "liberated" territory around Bogra, which came under intense shelling, resulting in heavy casualties to Indian troops.

The Indian Army launched a local counter-attack destroying thirteen Pakistani Chaffee tanks and threw the Pakistanis back. The Indian Air Force employed Gnat fighter aircraft that brought down three Pakistani Sabre jets that had intruded into Indian air space. Two of the Pakistani pilots who had parachuted down into Indian territory were captured. The Indian Government now took the decision to permit Indian troops to cross the international border (IB) in self-defence, that is, to counter-attack in case of Pakistani aggression against posts in Indian territory.

Similar incidents took place in other areas along the India-East Pakistan border, particularly near Hilli, where Pakistan launched two attacks on Indian positions with armour and infantry, losing nine tanks and suffering heavy casualties. Indian forces also suffered fairly heavy casualties in these attacks and retaliated by advancing 5 to 7 kilometres into East Pakistan.

From all indications it appeared that Pakistan was escalating the scale of operations for an all-out war. Pakistani President General Yahya Khan also made provocative statements, like, "In ten days I will be off fighting a war" and "War with India is very near", and "in case of war, Pakistan will not be alone". That, too, after the visit by Bhutto to China in November in 1971. It was also evident that Yahya Khan was banking on the support of the United State of America, China and Muslim Middle Eastern countries.

Indo-Soviet Treaty of August 1971

In order to ensure that India was not politically isolated, a "Treaty of Peace, Friendship and Cooperation" was signed by India with the Soviet Union in August 1971. Meanwhile, internal pressure by Indian Opposition parties, the public and the press continued to blame Prime Minister Indira Gandhi and her government, for failure to take military action against Pakistan.

The Indian government commenced action as soon as the enormity of the refugee problem from East Pakistan became public. Immediate military action against Pakistan was sought, so that more than ten million refugees could return to their homes in East Pakistan. The Prime Minister had her own political compulsions against precipitating any action against this problem created by Pakistan, for which there were no easy solutions. Some of these were:

- The need for justifiable reasons for convincing international community for the invasion of a neighbouring country. Would the world accept the enormity of the refugee problem being faced by India as reason enough to warrant military action in East Pakistan, by India?
- If the independence of East Pakistan was achieved, would the world and the United Nations accept it as an independent nation?

General Sam Manekshaw, the Chief of Army Staff and Chairman, Chiefs of Staff Committee, was asked by Prime Minister Indira Gandhi asked to brief her on the implications of military intervention. War clouds over East Pakistan had spread and the clash between the two armies was imminent. By April 1971, the situation in East Pakistan made war with Pakistan a distinct possibility. Indian Army commanders were therefore directed to review and revise their plans in view of the changed circumstances.

Military Considerations

The first major consideration was choosing the timing of the Indian offensive, should such a choice be available. One option was to launch an offensive straight away and relieve the agony of millions of East Pakistanis. The problem lay in assembling such a large force for an offensive. Moreover, providing for its basic infrastructure of administration, logistics and communications, takes time and the Indian Army would have inevitably got caught by the monsoon before being able to achieve its objectives in the riverine delta of East Pakistan. Moreover, that time of the year would not only permit easy infiltration from Pakistan into the higher reaches of J&K but would also permit Chinese intervention.

General Manekshaw appreciated that the Indian Army would have better chances of success if the Army waited till December 1971. He conveyed his reservations against any early intervention and advised the Prime Minister against any inconclusive involvement! Manekshaw had the moral courage to stick to his convictions and was able to withstand the pressures that had built up against him. His reasons were many. Existing plans against East Pakistan catered only to specific areas. Now that the area of operations was wider, and since the relative strength of Pakistan's army in East Pakistan had more than doubled, revised operational plans were needed.

Finding additional troops for an offensive from existing resources was a near impossibility, considering the counter-insurgency operations in the North-East, the threat from China, and the aid to civilian authorities in West Bengal. These had already tied up the better part of two Infantry Divisions. Further, there were endemic shortages in units and formations, not only of manpower but also of arms, ammunition, and equipment, including heavy equipment, artillery guns, bridging equipment and armour. And even if all these shortages were resolved, time would still be required for intensive training to handle such equipment.

The climate of the intended area of operations dictated its own timetable. It was very likely that any offensive launched in May 1971 would bog down the Indian Army in a riverine terrain by the monsoon. Last, but not the least, was the factor of foreign intervention. Would China intervene across the passes in the Himalayas to take the heat off Pakistan? Would the United States also intervene to help its ally, Pakistan?

Considering all these factors, General Manekshaw felt that the time was not opportune for any intervention. He was of the opinion that end November or early December would be the most suitable time for the launch of military operations because of the following reasons:

- The terrain after the monsoon would have hardened, thereby permitting the movement of armour, guns and vehicles.
- The Chinese intervention would be difficult due to closure of snow-bound Himalayan passes.
- The intervening time could be used for making up shortages of manpower, equipment, training units and formations, and for building roads and tracks, communications and support bases for the offensive.

The Prime Minister appreciated the above reasoning and General Manekshaw's recommendation for the postponement of military operation from the summer to winter of 1971. In the interim, she chose to resume diplomatic initiatives for finding a peaceful solution to the problem with East Pakistan.

Military Options

The Chiefs of Staff Committee (COSC) comprising Chief of the Army Staff, Chief of the Naval Staff and Chief of the Air Staff, headed by General Manekshaw, (de facto Chief of Defence Staff)[109] considered various operational options, which were placed for consideration to the government. They were:

- To attack Pakistan, both in the east and the west, simultaneously.
- To carry out a holding attack in West Pakistan and to attack in East Pakistan.
- To hold in East Pakistan and to carry out the main offensive in West Pakistan.

The Government of India and Chairman COSC opted for the second option, that is, "to hold in West Pakistan and to attack in East Pakistan." It was appreciated that this would yield quicker result and had better chances of success, thereby permitting the return of the ten million Bengali refugees.

By the beginning of November 1971, the relative strength of the Indian Army for operations against East Pakistan had increased to about seven infantry divisions, including the raising of the HQ 2 Corps. The build-up of infrastructure on the Eastern Front in Silchar and Tripura had also been done, including the widening and paving of roads which were now ready.

Whether General Yahya Khan was to declare war in the west, or General Niazi, GOC-in-C East Pakistan Command were to carry out his threat to invade Indian territory, Indian Eastern Command was now ready for any threat of war.

---

[109] The need for creating the appointment of Chief of Defence Staff (CDS) had been recommended to successive Indian governments since the appointment of C-in-C, Indian Army was abolished in February 1955, when General S.M. Shrinagesh was informed by Mr M.K. Vellodi, Indian Civil Services. The Defence Secretary, that Government had decided to do away the appointment of C-in-C. Vellodi further informed Shrinagesh that, on promotion to the rank of General, he would be appointed as the first Chief of the Army Staff (COAS) in succession to General Maharaj Rajendrasinhji, on his retirement on 15th May 1955.

Chapter 23

The Birth of Bangladesh

By the time the monsoon rains ended, Lieutenant General Jagjit Singh Aurora, General Officer Commanding-in-Chief, Eastern Command had assessed the military implications of the worsening situation in East Pakistan. After approval by Army Headquarters of his operational plan to meet the likely threat from Pakistan, It was decided to make up the shortfall of additional troops and a controlling HQ. Army HQ approved the raising of a new corps HQ[110] on top priority.

Raising of HQ 2 Corps

The new corps HQ was raised at Krishnanagar (West Bengal), the administrative headquarters of Nadia District, located 110 kilometres north of Kolkata. Krishnanagar is situated on the southern banks of river Jalangi and has been a centre for art and culture. It is believed that the city was named after Lord Krishna during the reign of Zamindar Krishna Chandra Ray and it is also a tourist attraction. Major General Tapishwar Narain Raina, MVC, Deputy AG, AHQ, was promoted to the rank of Lieutenant General and appointed GOC of the new 2 Corps, that was to be raised.

General Raina arrived at Krishnanagar on 7th October 1971, which coincided with Durga Puja, an important festival for the people of West Bengal. Brigadier (later Major General) B.K.

[110] In similar circumstances, HQ 1 Corps was raised to plan and execute the thrust into Sialkot Sector during the Indo-Pakistan war of 1965.

Bhattacharya, Madras Regiment and Lieutenant Colonel (later General and COAS) S.F. Rodrigues, Artillery, were the newly posted BGS and GSO-1 (Ops) respectively. Lieutenant Colonel Lamba, 4 Kumaon, was GSO-2 (Intelligence), Brigadier (later Major General) Rajeshwar Singh, Artillery, was Brig i/c Adm, while Lieutenant Colonel Krishnamurthy, ASC was the AQ on the staff of the truncated HQ of 2 Corps[111] which was in the process of being raised. Other heads of arms and services were, Colonel (later Major General) H.K. Kapur and Colonel (later Major General) "Bir" Paintal who were CE and C Sig, respectively. Captain (later Brigadier) Swatantra Kumar Sapru, popularly called "Sherry", 14 Kumaon (Gwalior) was selected as ADC to GOC 2 Corps.

Captain Sapru received his posting with mixed feelings. as his Battalion, 14 Kumaon (Gwalior), was entrenched in the 23 Mountain Division Concentration Area, in the East, as part of 4 Corps Sector at Taliamura Forest (Tripura), preparing for impending operations in East Pakistan.

The scene in the Battalion was a flurry of hectic activity, involving digging down, improvement of perimeter defences, ensuring track discipline, briefing by company commanders and training of troops and the collection of stores and ammunition. Amidst all of this was the possibility of patrolling into enemy territory with Mukti Bahini. It was an opportunity for any young officer to be bloodied in battle. It all seemed very exciting as all ranks of the Battalion were told that they were on the verge of going to war.

Sapru accepted his posting with mixed emotions, as these were the orders from Army Headquarters. Senior officers in the battalion explained to Sapru that his selection as ADC to Lieutenant General Raina would be an honour for the battalion, as the general was not only Colonel of The Kumaon and Naga Regiments but was also a former CO of this very battalion.

Captain Sapru's journey began the next day in a 1-ton truck from his unit location to Agartala (Tripura), on the way to his new duty station, which happened to be diametrically on the other side

---

[111] The Corps HQ was authorized only 18 officers, including the GOC.

of East Pakistan. He narrates his experience of his move to the new Corps HQ at Krishnanagar, under raising:

> I arrived at Agartala, somewhat apprehensive. There was an air of uncertainty. Trains were taking over four days around the Eastern Corridor to Calcutta, the move by road was unthinkable and flights in and out of Agartala Airport had become a rarity. Each time an Indian Airline or Kalinga Airline aircraft took off from Agartala Airport, the flight path overflew the local Pakistani Army on the other side of the border with East Pakistan, and it attracted flak. Just when I decided on the rail journey the following day, I learnt that an aircraft was expected the next day, so my hopes soared.
>
> The next day a Kalinga Airline Dakota aircraft landed in the afternoon. With ticket in hand, I walked up the gangway to be greeted by an Anglo-Indian purser, but was taken aback by the aircraft's occupants — sheep and goats stuffed from nose to tail of the aircraft; I was the odd one out. This "meat on hoof" (MOH) was originally meant for some destination in the North East, but for some reason their mission got aborted. Thus the aircraft got diverted and landed at Agartala, en route to Calcutta (Kolkata). The smelly journey ended at Dum Dum Airport, Calcutta (now Kolkata), from where one of the local trains finally took me to Krishnanagar on the following day.
>
> HQ 2 Corps was still in the process of raising. An abandoned poultry farm was the location of its Main HQ! Here neither were there any chicken nor eggs. The Corps Commander's residence was on the first floor of the main building, whilst the Ops Room, Signal Centre and other offices were on the ground floor. The heads of services had their offices in the chicken coops and it was amusing to see the ADST and ADOS hop in and out of their coops each day!

It is learnt that the billets for living of officers were in a nearby school building, where initiative was the order of the day, be it in bathing, eating or drinking. Bathing was done in open cubicles with camp buckets. On one occasion having lathered himself, Captain Sapru turned around to find his bucket missing. With lather as Sapru's only camouflage and protection, the ADOS had quietly picked up his bucket of water for his own royal bath. Sapru promptly repaid the ADOS in the same coin the next day!

On the second day of his arrival, Sapru was ushered into the office of General Raina, who welcomed him with warmth and genuine affection. Soon after the preliminary pleasantries were over, the GOC told his newly arrived ADC:

> Sherry, you as my ADC, will hear some good and a lot of bad about me. There will be kudos and bricks; keep these to yourself, and, finally, think like a General, but don't act like one! That is all!

Captain Sapru always followed this advice in letter and spirit. Life was busy but full of excitement as he also doubled up as additional GSO-3 (Ops) in the truncated Corps HQ which was still under raising. Sapru recalls how all heads of services and the Brig I/C Adm were keen that the Corps Commander visits the newly laid corps maintenance area (CMA), to approve the deployment and the local air defence arrangements.

The visit was carried out on one of those afternoons when the Corps Commander decided to go around the Corps Troops Workshop. Whilst driving past, he noted an L-60 Air Defence (AD) gun sticking out of its camouflage net. The Corps Commander decided to stop to make his way to the gun detachment lounging nearby! On seeing the Corps Commander, the NCO I/C Gun Detachment reported that his crew were ready! The Corps Commander ordered the NCO to demonstrate their gun drill. Promptly, all the men were in action, simulating enemy aircraft attacking from all conceivable directions. However, one man seemed out of sync in their great symphony! "Stand down-Stand at ease" — the Corps Commander ordered. Tappy Raina then spoke to each member of this gun crew of AD Regiment (Territorial Army): how much embodied service they had, when did each man fire, what target was used, were any hits recorded, and so on. On confronting the individual with the odd movements, General Raina repeated the same questions. The man said he had 10 years' service and that he had neither fired of late nor in the past. Perplexed the General queried,

"*Jawan, kyon nahin fire kiya* (Jawan, why did you not fire so far)"? The individual, while looking at his Detachment Commander from the corner of his eyes, replied, "*Sahib, main Dhobi hoon"* (Sir, I am a washerman)! The innovative detachment commander had rounded up the *dhobi* (washerman) to compensate for his manpower deficiency at short notice. The "Old Man" did a quick turn around and left smiling to himself, without admonishing the NCO.

At the crack of dawn every day, a visit to one of the two divisional sectors or other units under command of HQ 2 Corps, was a predictable ritual. As the operations commenced, sometimes the Corps Commander would drive up to the scout of the Point Section of the advancing rifle company of the battalion. Having conversed with and patted the soldiers of the vanguard platoon, he would turn back. General Raina had learnt from one of the GOCs while he was a young officer operating in Burma (now Myanmar) during Second World War, to visit forward most troops, as that raised the morale of fighting units. The sight of general officers with star plates and flag upfront, he stated, instilled a sense of belonging and confidence in the soldiers. That was true indeed, but Sapru remained anxious whenever his boss did that because there was obviously some risk to his safety. At the same time, Sapru felt proud when he saw his GOC walking those few steps with a different motivated soldier of a different unit each day.

On one of those visits by the Corps Commander to Divisional Sectors, early morning, while proceeding from Darsana to Jhenida on those excellent roads; the local Division Commander, while driving the GOC 2 Corps, indicated a location and said, "Sir, last night we captured that enemy locality — you can see those Pakistani soldiers who were killed there". In his enthusiasm, the Divisional Commander forgot to slow down, whereas, the leading pilot vehicle had stopped, and consequently, he was catapulted forward and thankfully was saved by the windscreen of the vehicle and his turban which protected his head but was now in total disarray! The other occupants of the vehicle, however, were battered and bruised, to say the least.

"I am sorry, Sir," said the Division Commander, placing his turban back and getting his bearing straight, in that order.

"Sorry! We are lucky to be alive!!" retorted General Raina. "Now look here, in future you better improve your driving skills, or else we will be lying alongside those dead Pakistanis ourselves!"

Sapru did not know whether to wince or laugh, but, Tappy Raina got back ramrod straight into the battered vehicle and they drove on. The word got around, and, thereafter, all vehicles moved at a safe distance from each other, whenever all Formation Commanders visited the Corps HQ.

The *Khadga*: Formation Sign of 2 Corps

Army Headquarters had asked HQ 2 Corps to choose a suitable formation sign for the newly raised 2 Corps. General Raina consulted his principal staff officers (PSOs) and other heads of arms and services posted at his headquarter on this matter.

Brigadier B.K. Bhattacharya, being a Bengali himself, suggested that it was a good omen for the raising of 2 Corps to coincide with Durga Puja. Everywhere, the people of Krishnanagar were seeking the blessings of Goddess Durga in various *pandals*. Therefore, he suggested, that it would be most appropriate to adopt the *Khadga*, the weapon of the Goddess, a symbol of the destruction of evil, as the formation sign of 2 Corps. This suggestion appealed to General Raina. The approval of Army Headquarters was sought and was accorded immediately. Thus, the Khadga of Goddess Durga became the formation sign of 2 Corps.

Krishnanagar had been a princely state in the erstwhile province of Bengal since the time of the Mughals. Some descendants of the erstwhile royal family still lived in the city, and when they learnt of 2 Corps adopting the Khadga as their formation sign, they presented the family's silver Khadga to GOC 2 Corps. It was an offering of tribute, for good luck and the blessings of Goddess Durga for success in their impending operational tasks.

Operational Preparedness

By 3rd December 1971, the original question, "Will there be war?" had become "When will war break out"?[112]

By now, the Indian Army, including 2 Corps, and the other two services, were as balanced, ready and poised for war, as it was humanly possible to be, at that time. As far as the Indian armed forces were concerned, Pakistan could not possibly have selected a more appropriate time to start the war. The meticulous and detailed preparations made by India, in response to the Pakistani crackdown in East Pakistan, implied the enormous cost of mobilising the Army and the other two services from their peace-time locations to their battle positions, as well as importing equipment and increasing indigenous production to make up deficiencies. India was now well poised to meet the impending threat of war with Pakistan.

The Naga Regiment Joins 2 Corps

The Naga Regiment, which was under raising at Ranikhet, received orders to cut short their training and move to join 7 Mountain Brigade at Gaya in Bihar, to form part of 4 Mountain Division. The other battalions on the Brigade ORBAT were 5 Jat and 22 Rajput. Within 17 days of their arrival, the Nagas were ordered to proceed to the concentration area of 2 Corps. About the same time, Lieutenant General Tappy Raina arrived on promotion to take over as GOC 2 Corps, with 4 Mountain Division under his command. By this time, the Nagas had been moved to Berhampur where General Raina visited them as Corps Commander and Colonel of the Regiment.

The Naga Regiment was not even one year old, but their enthusiasm for tasting the blood of war was admirable. All ranks of The

---

[112] Note had, of course, been taken of Pakistan President's statement which he made, perhaps in a fit of drunken rage, that ten days hence he would be fighting a war. The significance of 3rd December 1971 being the first Friday after the Muslim festival of Eid-ul-Fitr and, therefore, an auspicious day as far as Pakistan was concerned to start whatever mischief it wished, had not been forgotten either.

Naga Regiment were jubilant that their Colonel of the Regiment, who was also their Corps Commander, would be visiting them. On arrival, General Raina was received by the commanding officer, Lieutenant Colonel R.N. Mahajan. He met all the officers and JCOs. Later, he had some refreshments with all ranks of the Battalion, where he met them informally. The General familiarised himself with the state of training and morale of all ranks of this newly raised Battalion. It is vital for a higher commander to be familiar with the combat fitness of troops, before he tasks a unit in operations during combat.

Sometime later Lieutenant General Raina asked Lieutenant Colonel Mahajan, his former Adjutant in 14 Kumaon (Gwalior), to meet him at his headquarters. During his visit to Tac HQ 2 Corps, Mahajan observed that while the Corps HQ was spartan, there was an air of expectancy and efficiency. It was every bit an operational headquarters, ready for imminent operations.

A few days later, the Nagas were bloodied in a spirited action at Dharamdah.[113]. It was also the first action against the Pakistani Army in the 2 Corps Sector. On completion of the task, as the Naga troops were pulling back across Matabhanga River, General Raina arrived. The mission was accomplished as planned after inflicting heavy casualties on the enemy, as it was later confirmed.

Lieutenant Colonel Mahajan recalled one of General Raina's visits to his Battalion. For briefing the GOC 2 Corps, Mahajan chose a vantage point on the home bank of River Matabhanga. He recalled that just as General Raina arrived, desultory enemy mortar bombs started landing near the site where Major General M.S. Brar, GOC 4 Mountain Division and Brigadier Zail Singh, Commander 7 Mountain Brigade were also present. The Divisional Commander anxiously informed General Raina of the enemy mortar fire and urged him to take cover, as some others at the scene had already done. Unmindful of enemy fire, Tappy Raina continued his interaction with the returning troops after completion of

[113] The task of the Nagas was to occupy and liberate the village of Dharamdaha, situated in a loop of the Matabhanga River opposite Shikarpur and due south of the Pakistani post of Pragpur.

their mission. This bold gesture had a salutary effect and was recounted amongst the troops with awe.[114]

Operation Cactus Lilly

By 30th November 1971, the operational preparedness of all the three Armed Forces of India was complete. Army Headquarters adopted the code word Operation Cactus Lilly for operations against Pakistan. It is believed that this fact was reported by General Manekshaw to Prime Minister Indira Gandhi and her approval obtained to commence operations on 4th December 1971[115].

On 3rd December 1971, an officer courier was despatched to Defence Minister Jagjivan Ram at Bangalore with a letter from General Manekshaw, informing him that the Prime Minister had approved the launch of operations and that since the Defence minister himself was out of town, he (General Manekshaw), in his capacity as Chairman, Chiefs of Staff Committee had issued the necessary directives. Later, the Defence Ministry was also apprised.

Pre-Emptive Strike by Pakistan

On 3rd December 1971, at about 1745 hours, Pakistan launched simultaneous pre-emptive air strikes at a number of Indian airfields: Srinagar, Avantipur, Pathankot, Uttarlai, Jodhpur, Ambala and Agra. This was the prelude to the planned Pakistani land offensive against Jammu and Kashmir, Punjab and Rajasthan. Unlike the earlier two wars of 1947-48 and 1965, Pakistan found, to its detriment, that this time the Indian armed forces were well prepared and ready.

---

[114] Lieutenant General Raina, GOC 2 Corps, visited the Nagas again when the Naga Regiment was well inside East Pakistan, on their way to their final destination — Khulna. He thanked all ranks of the battalion for their contribution to the success of 2 Corps in liberation of East Pakistan. He waved to them from his jeep and headed to the eastern border to battle the main Pakistan Army.

[115] After considerable debate in the Chiefs of Staff Committee, the three service chiefs decided the H-Hour and D-Day. It was decided to launch operations at first light so that the rest of the day was available for continuous air attacks.

Map 11: East Pakistan

The Indo-Pakistan war of 1971 was not of India's making. It was a war thrust upon her by an arrogant and aggressive neighbour. The origins of this war lay within Pakistan itself.

According to Lieutenant Colonel (later Lieutenant General) Depinder Singh, 8 GR, MA to COAS, that evening on 3rd December 1971, General Manekshaw, MC accompanied by his MA, was being briefed by the Director of Military Operations (DMO) and his staff in the Army Headquarters Operations Room. They were blissfully unaware of what was unravelling outside, but secure in the knowledge that everything was ready and all arrangements completed.

Immediately after the briefing, when the Army Chief was planning to leave the Operation Room for his residence, Defence Secretary K.B. Lal suddenly rushed in looking flabbergasted and broke the news that the Western Army Commander, Lieutenant General K.P. Candeth, had telephoned him a short while ago to say that three of our airfields in the Western Sector were under attack by aircraft of Pakistan Air Force.[116]

Lieutenant General Depinder Singh in his book, *Field Marshal Sam Manekshaw: Soldiering with Dignity* describes how the news of the Pakistani attack was received by General Manekshaw:

> I had imagined that when the news did come, the occasion would be marked by furious activity with people running around, wild gesticulations and everyone wanting to be heard. What actually happened was exactly the opposite there was a sudden hush and all eyes turned towards the Chief as if to reiterate that no one else could take the responsibility for the decision now required. This did not take long to be articulated and although I can't recall exactly what he said, it was something to the effect that, "the day for which we have all worked so hard has come; now let's get them"!
>
> Since Pakistan had taken the initiative, my first job was to contact the officer who had carried the letter to Bangalore for delivery to the Defence Minister, and instruct him to burn the letter and return home.

---

[116] The presence of COAS and other important staff officers of AHQ in the Operations Room, which for some obscure reason it did not have a telephone, and that was why Lieutenant General K.P. Candeth GOC-in-C Western Command, was unable to contact COAS, DMO or MA to COAS; instead, he rang up the Defence Secretary. Those were the days much before the advent of mobile and satelite phones!

Immediately after news of the war's outbreak was received, the Chief walked back to his office; the pace no brisker than usual, to give the staff at COAS Secretariat the cheery news that the COAS Office wasn't to be closed just yet. From his office, General Manekshaw rang up each of the Army Commanders and the Chiefs of the other two Services and shared the news of air space violation by the Pakistani Air Force and, at the same time gave the Army Commanders permission to put their operational plans into effect.

Neither Prime Minister Indira Gandhi, who was addressing a mammoth gathering in Calcutta (Kolkata), nor Defence Minister Jagjivan Ram, who was in Bangalore at the time, could be contacted by General Manekshaw. Consequently, the permission to the Army Commanders and other Service Chiefs had to be given by the Army Chief in his capacity as Chairman, Chiefs of Staff Committee (COS Committee)[117], and it is a measure of the confidence that existed between him and the Prime Minister that there was no hesitation or vacillation: orders were out within ten minutes of the Army Chief getting the news.

The progress of operations in each sector was reviewed daily at 9.30 am in the War Room where the Chiefs of Staff Committee met. The Defence Minister was briefed after the Chiefs of Staff Committee meeting, either in his office or, as happened sometime, in the Army Chief's office. It is believed that ego hassles were conspicuous by their absence.

After the daily Chiefs of Staff Committee meetings, General Manekshaw would telephone the three Army Commanders involved — Eastern (Lieutenant General Jagjit Singh Aurora), Western (Lieutenant General Kunhiraman Palat Candeth) and Southern (Lieutenant General Gopal Gurunath Bewoor). On some occasions, he would speak to the concerned Corps Commanders directly to obtain first-hand information.

It was obvious from the commencement of hostilities that everything hinged on how rapidly the operations in the Eastern Front could be brought to a successful conclusion. All eyes, therefore,

---

[117] Once again, the need of Chief of Defense Staff (CDS) became critically obvious.

were focused there and the progress of each one of the many "thrust lines" converging on Dhaka, was the subject of immense interest.

By daybreak on 4th December 1971, the war for liberation of East Pakistan and alleviation of the sufferings of Bengalis was launched by the GOC-in-C Eastern Command, General Aurora. He now had the sole operational responsibility of destroying Pakistani Forces in East Pakistan. General Aurora had already appreciated that the entire East Pakistan would have to be considered for operations in four geographical sectors, as dictated by the terrain, i.e, the eastern, central, north-west and south-west sectors. The Operational Plan of the Eastern Army Commander required 2, 4 and 33 Corps, besides 101 Communication Zone Area, to invade East Pakistan, with the following broad task:

North-Western Sector (33 Corps)

- **Task:** To cut the line Hilli-Gaibanda and to capture Bogra-Rangpur.
- **Troops:** 20 Mountain Division and 71 Mountain Brigade.

Central Sector (101 Communication Zone)

- **Task:** To capture Jamalpur and Mymensingh and, subsequently, Tangail.
- **Troops:** 95 and 167 Mountain Brigades. A Para Battalion to be dropped at Tangail.

Eastern Sector (4 Corps)

- **Task:** To capture Maulvi Bazar, Sylhet, Daudkandi-Mynamati and Lalmai Hills (South) Laksham and subsequently Chandpur respectively. 311 Brigade with Kilo Force to capture Chittagong.
- **Troops:** 8, 57 and 23 Mountain Divisions.

South-Western Sector (2 Corps)

- Task: To capture Jessore and Jhenida and subsequently secure Hardinge Bridge, Goalundo Ghat and Faridpur Ferries and Khulna.

➢ Troops: 4 Mountain Division, 9 Mountain Division, 50 Para Brigade, less a Battalion, a Regiment of Armour (PT-76 Tanks) and a Squadron of T-55 tanks.

Map 12: Force levels of Pakistan and Indian Army in East Pakistan (December 1971).

Operations in 2 Corps Sector

General Raina sent in two Divisional thrusts towards the Madhumati River to liberate territory west of River Padma. 2 Corps planned to accomplish this task by containing Pakistani strongholds near the International Border with East Pakistan while fast-moving columns bypassed these and raced for Madhumati River, to prevent the bulk of the enemy from withdrawing across the river and making for the Meghna Ferries to Dhaka.

The plan of GOC 2 Corps was to spread the two Divisional thrusts into several columns making for the important communication centres at Jessore, Jhenida, Khulna and Barisal, and, to cut the Khulna-Jessore-Kushitia Railway to prevent the lateral movement of the enemy. Subsequently, Khulna, Faridpur, Goalundo Ghat and Hardinge Bridge were also to be secured. General Raina considered Jessore to be the key to this sector, and he deployed 9 Mountain Division for this sector and 4 Mountain Division for the Jhenida Sector.

The Brigades in all sectors moved on foot without pause, across paddy fields, ponds, rivers, and marshland, carrying all their equipment with them. Every form of local transport was used, including cycles, cycle-rickshaws, bullock-carts, village boats, and rafts. The locals were very cooperative; in fact, they were only too eager to help the Indian Army go cross-country into battle!

Having cut the Jessore-Kushtia Railway Line on 5th December, the columns pushed on without rest. By 7th December, they had advanced another 30 kilometres to capture Jhenida, one of the important Pakistani strongholds and a vital communication centre, thus cutting the road link. On the same day, Jessore, considered to be a very strong fortress, was vacated by the enemy who pulled out without a fight. Kushtia was captured on 11th December after fairly heavy fighting and Hardinge Bridge was captured on 12th December. The Pakistanis had blown up the bridge on 11th December 1971.

The hasty evacuation of Jessore reflected the low morale of the Pakistan Army in East Pakistan. Like Hilli in the North-West Sector, Jessore was one of the strongest fortifications of the Pakistani

9 Infantry Division Sector held by an Infantry Brigade Group, supported by tanks and artillery; all together some 5,000 all ranks of the Pakistani Army. Yet when the time came to fight, the garrison just melted away.[118] For weeks Indian Army sources and other expert observers had been predicting a stern siege, involving heavy Indian casualties before Jessore Cantonment could be taken. The latter was a vast military complex covering an area of several square miles just outside Jessore town. Instead, in the stinging words of a senior Staff Officer of HQ 9 Infantry Division, "They (Pakistani Army) just ran away". In less than 24 hours, Indian tanks and infantry achieved an objective they had estimated might require up to a week's bitter fighting.

While 2 Corps was engaged in operations in the South-Western Sector, in the neighbouring North-Western Sector 33 Corps was busy clearing Rangpur and Bogra, which were theatre fortresses, and Hilli, Dinajpur, Nawabganj which were important communication centres. It is believed that Major General Nazar Hussain Shah, GOC 16 Pakistani Infantry Division had deployed his forces well ahead of his main defences to impose delay and then fall back to the main defences.

Lieutenant General Mohan Lal Thapan, GOC 33 Corps, was given the tasks of cutting the Hilli-Gaibanda line and capturing Bogra or Rangpur, depending on the situation. Defences opposite 33 Corps were strongly held and those put up stiff resistance, inflicting heavy casualties on Indian troops.

Psychological War

As the operations for liberation of East Pakistan progressed, the psychological propaganda war against the Pakistani Army by the Indian Army HQ, New Delhi, also started. Thanks to the foresight of General Maneckshaw, preparations for war had been made well in advance. Printed leaflets in Urdu, Pushto and English, showing

---

[118] Philip Jacobson of *The Sunday Times* (London) said, "The total collapse of the Pakistani Army's resistance at Jessore is one of the most intriguing puzzles of the war in the East"!

these emanating as from the Indian Army Chief, were airdropped over almost the entire area, even where the Pakistani Army was deployed. These leaflets suggested "Surrender" to save senseless waste of life. By then, the situation had arisen where any further resistance by the Pakistan Army was pointless. The text of this leaflet was also broadcast repeatedly by All India Radio (now Akashvani).

Exhortations from West Pakistan to their army in East Pakistan was, "to continue the fight, now that intercession by the 'yellow brother' (China) from the North and the 'white ones' (United States) from the South was imminent." This then became the subject matter of the next lot of leaflets and broadcasts from the Indian side.

The Indian Army issued fresh leaflets through which all ranks of the Pakistani Army in the East Pakistan were told to disregard the lies coming from GHQ Pakistan Army in West Pakistan, and advised them to surrender as no "brothers", either "white or yellow", would be coming to provide them with succour. All these messages and leaflets concluded with the assurance from General Manekshaw that they would be treated fairly. This promise was eventually honoured in letter and spirit. On 11th December 1971, Major General Rao Farman Ali, Pakistan's Military Governor of East Pakistan, appealed to the Pakistani Representative at United Nations, on telephone, to seek an immediate ceasefire, on the declaration of which Pakistan's entire Defence Forces and civilian employees in East Pakistan would be withdrawn under United Nations auspices. But before the appeal could be passed on to the UN Secretary General, it was vetoed by the President of Pakistan, General Yahya Khan. Nevertheless, damage had been done as the appeal indicated that the war was going badly for Pakistan in the East.

According to Lieutenant Colonel Depinder Singh, Military Assistant to General Manekshaw, a telephone call was received by him at the COAS Secretariat, Army HQ, at about 1600 hrs on 15th December 1971 from Porter King, the genial Defence Attaché (DA) at the United States Embassy in New Delhi. The call was to request for an urgent and immediate meeting with General Manekshaw. Since the Chief was free, King was given an appointment to meet Manekshaw and promptly arrived within fifteen minutes. The message that Porter carried was from General Niazi, the Commander of the Pakistani forces in East Pakistan, seeking a cease-fire.

About the same time, the UNDP representative in Delhi, Dr. McDermot, also called with a similar message received through his channels. General Manekshaw contacted Mrs. Indira Gandhi and apprised her of these messages. After obtaining her approval, Manekshaw confirmed to King that the cease fire offer was acceptable, provided it was unconditional. Furthermore, Indian Armed Forces would cease firing at a stipulated time later that evening. A similar message was relayed to General Aurora, GOC-in-C Eastern Command, as also to Admiral Sardarilal Mathradas Nanda, Padma Vibhushan PVSM, AVSM, Chief of the Indian Navy and Air Chief Marshal Pratap Chandra Lal, DFC, Chief of the Indian Air Force, respectively.

Pakistani Army Surrenders

Within two hours, HQ Eastern Command called to say that General Niazi had accepted the terms but had sought a slight extension to allow his headquarters to inform all subordinate headquarters and units. This was approved and later that night the guns fell silent on the Eastern Front. On the following day, 16th December 1971, at 1630 hours the Surrender Ceremony was held at the Maidan in Dacca (now Dhaka). Not only had a magnificent military victory been achieved, but on the political plain the map of South Asia was altered with the emergence of a new nation, Bangladesh.

It is universally known that victory has many parents and here, too, quite a few staked their name to fame. The chief architect of India's victory was without question General (later Field Marshal) Manekshaw.

While congratulations poured in, the Chief, true to style, turned away from the maps of the East to pore over those of the North and West. Considerable pressure was exerted on the Chief to fly to Dhaka to receive the formal surrender. He refused, stating that this was GOC-in-C Eastern Command General Aurora's show and he along with all ranks of Eastern Command must bask in the lime-light and glory.[119]

Following the conclusion of the surrender ceremony at Dhaka, Prime Minister Indira Gandhi conveyed to General Manekshaw the government's decision to offer a unilateral ceasefire to Pakistan.

Operations on the Western Front

Army Headquarters had gauged that the Pakistan Army would retaliate by launching operations against the 11 Corps Sector, which covered the whole of the Punjab and Rajasthan border with Pakistan. Midway through the war in East Pakistan, General Raina was apprised of his next operational task — to prepare for a new mission on the Western Front.

While the troops of 2 Corps were achieving victory and glory in East Pakistan, Tappy Raina was already busy planning for his next operational task on the Western Front. He was now to take over the responsibility from GOC 11 Corps under Western Command. His new operational responsibility extended from Ferozepur in Punjab to Ganganagar in Rajasthan. This necessitated his absence from his Corps Sector in East Pakistan, with a view to liaise with GOC 11 Corps, Lieutenant General N.C. Rawley, MC, and familiarise himself with the proposed area of operational responsibility to be taken over by 2 Corps.

---

[119] Soon after the surrender ceremony at Dacca (now Dhaka), a photograph of this historic event appeared in all newspapers and television, where Lieutenant General Aurora and Lieutenant General Niazi are seen surrounded by commanders who led their forces to victory. However, General Raina, GOC 2 Corps was conspicuous by his absence. General Raina assisted by Lieutenant Colonel (later General) Sunith Francis Rodrigues, GSO 1 (Ops) HQ 2 Corps was away to 11 Corps Sector, busy in recce and planning the taking over of his new operational role in Western Command.

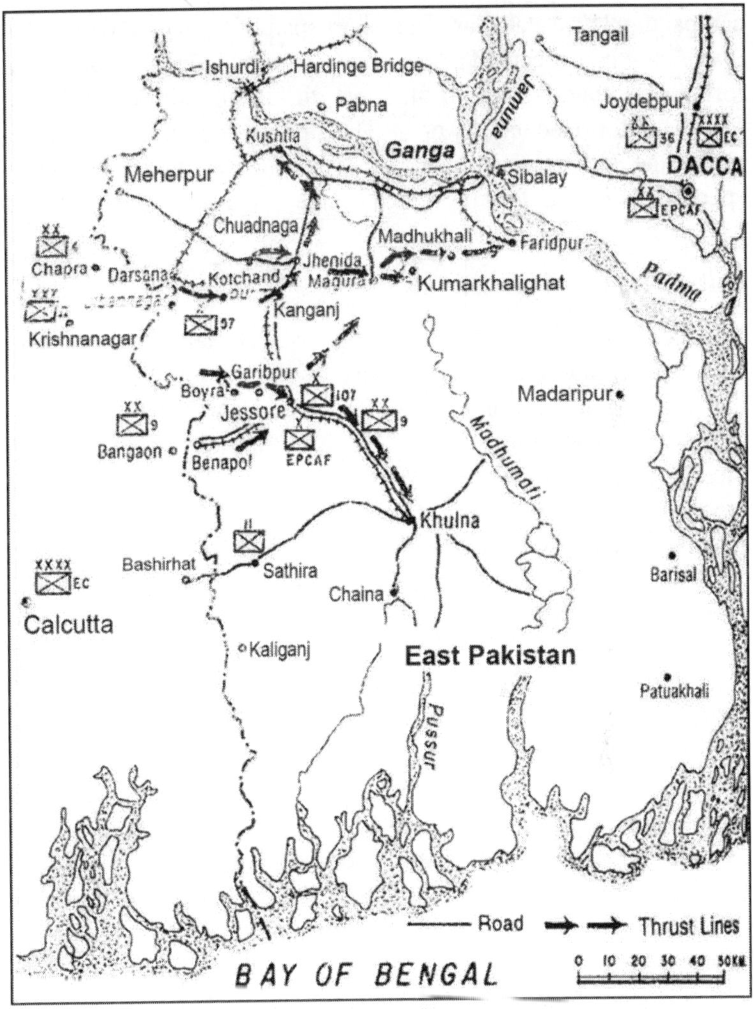

(The external boundaries of India depicted in this map are neither correct nor authentic)

Map 13: Operation of 2 Corps in Western Sector of East Pakistan.

The most remarkable aspect of the Indo-Pakistan War of 1971 was the speed with which Indian Army successfully concluded the campaign in East Pakistan. In a short span of thirteen days the Indian Army had executed a seemingly impossible task: decimated a formidable enemy army in the most difficult terrain, taking more than 93,000 prisoners of war.[120] The strategy was somewhat similar to the German blitzkrieg across France in 1940: the same speed, ferocity and flexibility had been applied.

Joint Services Operations

Whether the Indian Army fought against Pakistan in the Eastern, Western or Southern Fronts, it was, of course not alone. The Indian Air Force, the Indian Navy, the Mukti Bahini, the Indian central police organisations, like the Border Security Force, the people of Bangladesh and West Bengal, in particular, and the Indian government headed by a clear-headed, strong-willed and determined prime minister helped to fashion this victory.

Whenever a government has understood the "military viewpoint", the defence forces in turn have appreciated the political constraints. A clear "Political Aim" resulted in a focused military plan. For once, to their credit, the civilian bureaucrats worked in tandem with staff officers of the Armed Forces to fashion a decisive victory in an incredibly short time, underscoring the principle that "War is a continuation of policy by other means". The success of the army was due to its adoption of a clear-cut strategy, innovative tactics, flexibility of plans, unorthodox methods, and the infused determination of the rank and file to finish the job as quickly as possible. The people of Bangladesh were also largely responsible for this victory.

Totally alienated by the brutality of Pakistan Army, its open massacre and torture of unarmed civilians, the people of Bangladesh cooperated fully with the Indian Army, moving weapons over difficult terrain, pushing vehicles stuck in the mud, ferrying men, weapons and equipment across rivers, acting as guides and

---

[120] The *Sunday Times* of London which had reporters on all the fronts reported, "It took only 12 days for the Indian Army to smash its way to Dacca, an achievement reminiscent of the German blitzkrieg across France in 1940."

providing critical information. Most of all, they were a simple, courageous people who welcomed the Indian Armed Forces as friends and worked together to get rid of what they saw as a cruel oppressor.

The collapse of the Pakistani Army in the east could also be attributed to its debasement during its "occupation" of East Pakistan (now Bangladesh). An army that does not have self-respect or knows that it is not fighting for a "Right Cause", cannot fight. The conduct of the officers and men of the Indian Army was the opposite. There were also strategic reasons why the war in East Pakistan had to be concluded within a quick time frame.

- Firstly, the Mountain Divisions earmarked for the Chinese front had to quickly finish their job so that they could revert to their primary role in case a Chinese threat developed following the war on the Eastern Front.
- Secondly, from the attitude of the Government of the United States, it seemed possible that the US might intervene politically and militarily to rescue their pampered protégé and therefore, the war needed to be successfully concluded as quickly as possible.

The Eastern Army Commander, General Aurora, who was aware of the need for speed, realised that success of his operations in the riverine terrain of East Pakistan (Bangladesh) demanded new innovative concepts of strategy and tactics that would surprise the enemy and keep him off balance. General Aurora was ably assisted by his Chief of Staff, Major General (later Lieutenant General) Jack Farj Rafael Jacob, and the three Corps Commanders, besides all other formation commanders, who fully understood the expediency of "Military Aim" in East Pakistan.

Pakistan Army's highest ranking commander in East Pakistan, Lieutenant General A.A. Niazi, deployed his troops on the "Fortress Concept", expecting the Indian Army to follow the time-worn classic approach and battle procedure of attacking and capturing objectives and carrying on the advance only after regrouping and reorganising. General Aurora anticipated this and planned his operations so that he would not fall into Niazi's trap and get bogged down for months in the quagmire of natural obstacles and strong points on which General Niazi had built his defences.

Tactical Concept

The Eastern Command's tactical concept was as bold as it was simple. Only by adhering to innovative methods could it hope to get through the inner defence line of the Dacca Bowl, before Pakistani defenders from the "fortresses" could get there. This meant jettisoning established concepts and methods and using the principle of surprise and flexibility to fashion new ones, to confuse the enemy and contain strongholds. Simultaneously, it meant bypassing these strongholds and heading for defences in depth. This became the new commandment of the Indian Army in the Eastern Command theatre with inherent focus on speed.

Formation commanders like Lieutenant General Raina, GOC 2 Corps and other Corps Commanders were given a free hand to execute their tasks, provided they kept the above principles in mind.

Chapter 24

Operation Cactus Lilly

Indian Army was fully mobilised when Pakistan attacked some airfields in the Western Theatre in the late afternoon of 3rd December 1971. HQ 2 Corps, was raised primarily for operations in the Eastern Theatre for the liberation of East Pakistan. However, even before the fall of Dhaka, and much before the Cease Fire and surrender by the Pakistan Army, GOC 2 Corps had been assigned a fresh operational task in the Western Theatre. It reflected General Manekshaw's confidence in Tappy Raina's ability to comprehend and manage this dual responsibility on two fronts.

While the formations under the command of 2 Corps continued to operate in capturing their objectives in East Pakistan as per the operational plan of 2 Corps, Tappy Raina, along with his GSO-1 (Ops), Lieutenant Colonel (later General and COAS) Sunith Francis Rodrigues, visited 11 Corps Zone. It was then commanded by Lieutenant General Navin Chand Rawlley, deployed along the Indo-Pakistan Border in Punjab and Rajasthan. Army Headquarters had ordered GOC 2 Corps to take over part of the operational responsibility of 11 Corps, extending from Ferozepur Sector in Punjab to Ganganagar Sector in Rajasthan, thus relieving GOC 11 Corps of the extended defence of this Sector.

After understanding his fresh operational task, a quick reconnaissance and familiarisation of the terrain in his proposed Corps Zone, General Raina quickly prepared the plan for the deployment and occupation of defences by 2 Corps on de-induction from the Eastern Front. He issued Warning Orders to his formations and troops accordingly.

While the war for liberation of East Pakistan was underway, it would be worthwhile discussing how the Indian Army defeated Pakistani intentions in the Western and Southern theatres of operation.

Southern Front

Lieutenant General (later General and COAS) Gopal Gurudas Bewoor was in charge of Southern Command and was responsible for the Rajasthan-Gujarat front. He had two Divisions under him and commanded them directly.

This was the first time that major operations were undertaken in the desert terrain of Southern Command. Considering the difficulties, hazards involved, and the results achieved, operations in Southern Command under Lt. General G.G. Bewoor, GOC-in-C, were very successful and proved that mobile operations in the Desert terrain had considerable potential and needed to be taken up seriously for future operations.

Western Front

It was assessed that the Pakistan Army in the West consisted of ten Infantry Divisions, two Armoured Divisions, two Independent Infantry Brigades, and two Independent Armoured Brigades. Of these, seven were in the holding role, thus giving Pakistan the ability to launch two Corps sized offensives in the plains of Punjab and the Jammu and Chhamb sectors in the state of Jammu and Kashmir, together with a Division sized subsidiary offensive along with one of the Corps offensives. Pakistan also had the capacity of reorganising its defences in Pakistan Occupied Kashmir (POK), to be able to launch a third offensive in Jammu and Kashmir. It is believed that the two Corps size offensives by Pakistan, each of which consisted of an Infantry Division and an Armoured Division, were earmarked as Northern Reserve and Southern Reserve, respectively.

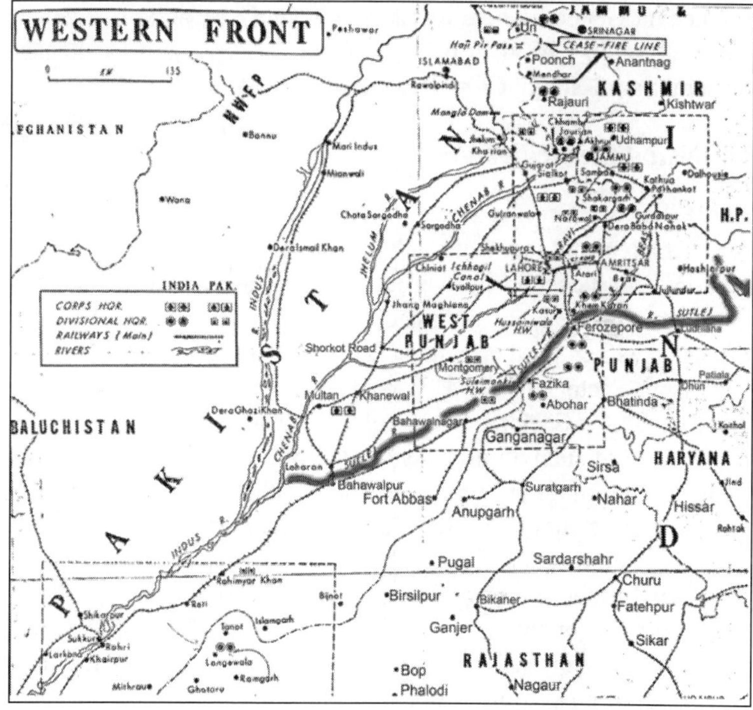

Map 14: Operation Cactus Lilly the Western Front.

From the dispositions of the Pakistani forces, the Indian Army High Command further assessed that the most likely sectors for Pakistani offensives would be, firstly, in the Jammu Sector; with the aim of cutting-off either the Jammu-Poonch or the Pathankot-Jammu Road links to isolate Indian forces. Secondly, a thrust in Southern Punjab.

The Indian forces were organised for the defence of the Western Sector under two Army Commands. Lt. General K.P. Candeth commanded the bulk of the forces on the Western Front, besides holding the responsibility for the Northern Front facing China. His responsibility extended from Ladakh in the North, right down to the borders of Rajasthan. His three Corps Commanders were:

Lieutenant General Khem Karan Singh, GOC 1 Corps, Lieutenant General Navin Chand. Rawlley, GOC 11 Corps, and Lieutenant General Sartaj Singh, GOC 15 Corps.

Opposing Strategies

Pakistan

It was appreciated that Pakistan's strategy in the West would aim at securing significant territory in Jammu and Kashmir, which it could retain after the war. Pakistan had the options of launching its main offensive either in the Jammu-Pathankot Sector, the Pathankot-Gurdaspur Sector, the Dera Baba Nanak-Amritsar Sector, the Amritsar-Ferozepur Sector, or the Fazilka-Ganganagar Sector.

The aim of such an offensive in the plains would be, firstly, to secure some important territory which could later be used to bargain against territory lost by Pakistan in the East and, secondly, to cause maximum destruction to India's mechanised forces.

It was further assessed that the "Second Reserve" of the Pakistani army, if not committed to the defensive battle, could be used as a subsidiary offensive, or for a diversionary attack, or for reinforcing an offensive, or for opening a new front.

The Army HQ assessed that the Pakistani 7 Infantry Division could be used in combination with holding forces for an attack in the 15 Corps Sector in Jammu and Kashmir, with a view to capturing Tangdhar, or Poonch or Naushera. It could also be used for an offensive against Chhamb. Although various options open to Pakistan were considered, confirmation of likely intentions could only be made once the Reserves of the Pakistan Army were located as that would have indicated the likely location of the enemy offensive. However, as it turned out, the Indian Army was not able to locate Pakistan's 1 Armoured and 7 Infantry Divisions right till the end of the war.

India

In the Western theatre, Indian strategy was, "Offensive Defence", i.e. to remain on the defensive and go on the offensive only on orders of Army Headquarters and, that too, for limited objectives.

Much depended on where Pakistan would launch its offensive. The main Indian counter-offensive was to be launched by 1 Corps in conjunction with some formations of 15 Corps. Depending on the situation, the 10 and 26 Infantry Divisions of 15 Corps and the better part of 1 Corps were to participate in this counter-offensive. The 10 Infantry Division was to advance towards Gujarat (in West Pakistan) while the 26 Infantry Division headed towards Marala. 1 Corps was to advance towards Pasrur. These counter-offensives were planned to ensure the security of Jammu and Kashmir. 11 Corps was to be prepared to launch a limited offensive opposite its sector, provided the situation permitted. 1 Armoured Division was located in the 11 Corps Zone and was to be made available by Army Headquarters if an offensive was decided upon.

11 Corps Zone

11 Corps was responsible for the defence of Punjab and the Ganganagar District of Rajasthan. These were considered strategic areas and an offensive by the Pakistani Army in this Sector would threaten the important towns of Gurdaspur, Amritsar, Ferozepur, Fazilka, Abohar and Ganganagar as objectives, as also objectives in depth like Jalandhar, Ludhiana and Bhatinda. The main routes through this sector also led to the heartland of India, and on to Delhi. The effective defence of this Sector was therefore vital. The Sector in Pakistan across the international border was also important because the strategic communication centres of Lahore, Kasur, Sulaimanke, Bahawalpur and Multan were located there, besides several important objectives in depth in what is the heartland of Pakistan.

The 11 Corps, under Lieutenant General Rawlley, had three Infantry Divisions, an ad hoc Sector HQ, with an independent Infantry Brigade Group, under command. HQ 11 Corps was located at Jalandhar, but due to the vastness of this sector, an advance HQ was established at Kotkapura in District Faridkot. 14 Independent Armoured Brigade (Army HQ Reserve) was located in the Corps zone. The 163 Infantry Brigade was moved to the Corps zone in anticipation of an offensive by Pakistan.

As it turned out, during the Indo-Pakistan War of 1971, there was neither any offensive launched by the Pakistani Army against the Indian Army's 11 Corps, nor did the Indian Army launch any major offensive into Pakistan. However, some important combat took place at Dera Baba Nanak, Ferozepur, and Fazilka.

As each converging thrust on Dhaka, East Pakistan, fulfilled its mission, the Indian Army started to thin out and move troops to the Western front. Consequently, by the time hostilities ceased in the East, a fairly substantial reserve had been built up behind the Western Front, poised for offensive operations.

2 Corps in Western Sector

As already narrated earlier, midway through the progress of operations in 2 Corps Sector in East Pakistan, Tappy Raina received orders from Army Headquarters that 2 Corps had been earmarked to partially relieve 11 Corps on the Western Front. He, therefore, took over the operational responsibility of 11 Corps Sectors from the river Sutlej in Punjab to Ganganagar in Rajasthan, facing the Pakistani towns of Kasur, Sulaimanki Headworks, Bahawalnagar, Fort Abbas, Bahawalpur and Rahim Yar Khan.

On arrival from the Eastern Front, Kotkapura (Distt Faridkot) which was the Advance Tac HQ of 11 Corps became the location of HQ 2 Corps. The Sector HQ responsible for the areas of Fazilka and Abohar now came under the Command of HQ 2 Corps. The other two formations, 4 and 9 Mountain Divisions which were part of 2 Corps in the war for liberation of Bangladesh, also moved to the Western Front and were redeployed in the 2 Corps Zone. Furthermore, 1 Armoured Division, the AHQ reserve, already in location in the 2 Corps Zone, was also placed under the command of GOC 2 Corps.

The truncated War Establishment (WE) of HQ 2 Corps was now upgraded to Standard WE Corps HQ, with three Infantry Divisions, an Independent Armoured Brigade, Corps Artillery Brigade, two Engineer Brigades and other Arms and Services. Additional officers were posted by Army HQ on the Staff of Corps HQ, to fill all the existing vacancies. Major General Benjamin Franklin (Ben)

Gonsalves, Artillery, arrived as the new Chief of Staff (COS) and the author of this book was appointed Deputy Assistant Military Secretary (DAMS) to GOC 2 Corps. While the main Corps HQ was at Kotkapura, the heads of services were located at Faridkot.

Within one year of its raising, 2 Corps under Lieutenant General Tappy Raina had successfully fought in the riverine terrain of East Pakistan and now was deployed for an operational role in semi-desert operational environments! The new operational role of 2 Corps required combat skills for fighting across linear water obstacles. General Raina, therefore, issued Special Training Instruction for intense training of units and formations for their new combat role in the new environments in 2 Corps Sector. This was necessary to meet the likely threat from Pakistan since the Pakistani Army was still smarting from the humiliating defeat and loss in East Pakistan,

It may be recalled that in reply to the Pakistani attack on India on 3rd December 1971, Army HQ had ordered Operation Cactus Lilly, the code name given for operations against Pakistan, on 4th December 1971. The war for liberation of East Pakistan, leading to the creation of Bangladesh, was over on 16th December 1971. The deployment of troops on the Western Front, thereafter, continued till well after the summer of 1973, when Operation Cactus Lilly was called off. Orders for de-induction of troops were received from Army HQ.

While all formations and units under the command of 2 Corps had some military station to fall back upon. HQ 2 Corps, which had been raised at Krishnanagar in West Bengal in October 1971, did not have a designated station to fall back to? Army HQ, therefore, decided that as an interim measure, HQ 2 Corps would be located at the newly developed military station, Chandimandir[121], District Ambala (now District Panchkula) in Haryana State, adjoining the Union Territory of Chandigarh, the joint capital of the two states of Haryana and Punjab.

---

[121] Army HQ realised that the location of HQ Western Command at Simla was not a suitable tactical location for effective operational control of the Western Army deployed on the Western Front.

Chandimandir Military Station

The experience of the Indo-Pakistan War of 1965 highlighted the need for shifting the location of HQ Western Command from Simla to a location in the plains of Punjab. When land for HQ Western Command was to be acquired for its permanent key location, known as Key Location Plan (KLP), the Government of Punjab offered the undeveloped and barren terrain between old Panchkula and Pinjore on the National Highway, connecting Ambala with Simla. This area was known as Chandimandir and it was accepted as the future KLP of HQ Western Command. This was later approved by the Government of India and construction commenced. The decision to earmark Chandimandir as the Interim Location Plan (ILP) for HQ 2 Corps was approved by HQ Western Command sometime in the summer of 1972.

General Raina directed the Corps administrative staff to assess the progress of HQ Western Command's KLP Project, so that preliminary action and plans for allotment to various components of HQ 2 Corps and Corps Troops could be decided. This, naturally, would be after ensuring that Chandimandir Military Station was fit in all respects for occupation and habitation by all ranks and their families. This news brought much cheer to all ranks of HQ 2 Corps and its troops.

General Raina made numerous trips to Chandimandir to review progress. A Board of Officers recommended the suggested allotment of buildings and training areas. There was an Advance Landing Ground (ALG)[122] at Chandimandir which made it convenient for the Corps Commander to utilise the Air OP fixed wing aircraft for his trips from Kotkapura to Chandimandir and back. It was decided that the following formations and units would be located at Chandimandir:

- HQ 2 Corps.
- HQ 2 Corps troops, including Signals, ASC, AOC, EME and other allied services.

---

[122] The ALG has been converted into a fairway of the present Shivalik Golf Course and a helipad has been constructed on its southern end.

- Engineer Brigade with all units under command.
- Infantry Brigade with 3 Infantry Battalions.

Orders for thinning out troops from 2 Corps Zone were issued in early 1973, so that allotted accommodation to the units could be taken over from MES and the development of areas allotted to units could commence. Except for a few trees, the entire area was undulating and full of scraggy bushes.

The expectations of the troops were somewhat belied when it was discovered that the status of Chandimandir, being developed as KLP of HQ Western Command, was only that of a military station, and not a military cantonment under the Cantonment Act! Neither were there were any conservancy services, nor any shopping areas for the daily needs of all ranks and their families. An ad-hoc Station HQ was created under Brigadier (later Major General) Rajeshwar Singh, Artillery, Brig i/c Adm, and a statement of case for authorising certain essential conservancy staff for collection of refuse and rubbish from married family quarters and for maintaining cleanliness of roads, was submitted to HQ Western Command.

Until some staff could be spared from other cantonments under HQ Western Command, Tappy Raina organised mobile shops for fruit and vegetables, general provisions and milk supply with Corps Troops transport. To enable children to reach their schools in Chandigarh, the unit transport was authorised to be used for their conveyance.

Arboriculture Plan of Chandimandir

Ironically, while there was ample married accommodation available at Chandimandir for all ranks of HQ 2 Corps and its Corps Troops, there were no suitable houses for the Corps Commander and Chief of Staff. Fortunately, the MES Inspection Bungalow (MES IB) had been constructed and was functional. One of the corner rooms of the IB was generally occupied by the Corps Commander whenever he visited Chandimandir. After the calling off of Operation Cactus Lilly, when all ranks of the Corps HQ arrived at HQ 2 Corps ILP, General and Mrs. Raina chose to make this one room at MES IB their temporary home.

General Raina had ordered the Chief Engineer, Brigadier H. K. Kapur, to prepare an Arboriculture plan for the whole Military Station at Chandimandir. After the approval of the Arboriculture plan, area-wise responsibilities of formations and units were delegated. This task was diligently carried out daily by the troops in the afternoons, only after their Parade timings, except on holidays. The responsibility of obtaining the planting material was entrusted to the Brig i/c Adm in collaboration with the Horticulture and Forest Departments of the Government of Haryana. The existing roads in the Chandimandir military station were named after famous battles that were fought by 2 Corps in the liberation of Bangladesh.

The South East corner of the spur in the MES IB, was converted into an "Observation Post"[123] (later named "Tappy Corner") for viewing the planting activities in the station. The mortality rate of saplings was monitored and, where required, replacements were replanted.

Today, the Military Station at Chandimandir[124] has a very high density of trees, well laid out parks, recreation and sports facilities, besides a shopping market, thus making the station a compact area, full of green cover.

Operational Preparedness

As all ranks of HQ 2 Corps settled down to enjoy a well-deserved peace time routine and family life, Tappy Raina was engaged in preparing Operational Plans, as per the new role allotted to 2 Corps. He was constantly monitoring the training of formations, as per the directive issued, based on the operational role of 2 Corps. At about this time, there was a change in the appointment of ADC to GOC 2 Corps. Captain Chandra Prakash Kala, 14 Kumaon

---

[123] To commemorate the memory of late General Raina, a triangular park was developed on the same spur by Lieutenant General Srinivas Kumar Sinha, PVSM, the then GOC 2 Corps. It was named Tappy Corner and was inaugurated by Mrs Ninette Raina.

[124] It is among the few modern military stations built in independent India whose history does not date back to the British Indian Army.

(Gwalior) replaced Captain Swantantra Kumar Sapru, who reverted to 14 Kumaon (Gwalior), for Regimental duties.

A very high standard of infantry-tank cooperation in assault across water obstacles like canals, and capture of objectives in semi-desert terrain, were practiced. It also included the employment of engineers, using the latest bridging equipment in support of assaulting formations. Similarly, the entire artillery of the Corps was put through training in support of the operations of war that 2 Corps was responsible for as per operational plans. A number of war games and live collective training exercises were conducted to familiarise and test the troops and their equipment.

Just when 2 Corps was honed for the special operational role assigned to it, Army Headquarters announced Tappy Raina's promotion and appointment as General Officer Commanding-in-Chief Western Command to succeed Lieutenant General Mohan Lal Thapan, who had been appointed Vice Chief of Army Staff at Army HQ. After having commanded 2 Corps for two years, General Raina handed over the command on 16th October 1973, to Lieutenant General A.M. Vohra,[125] who arrived on promotion from Army HQ. General Raina established a new tradition for handing / taking over the command of 2 Corps, when he relinquished the command. At a solemn ceremony in the office of the GOC, Tappy Raina handed over the silver Khadga which was displayed in the GOC's office[126] to his successor and long-time friend, Lieutenant General A.M. Vohra.

It may be recalled that this silver Khadga had been presented by the former Raja of Krishnanagar to the GOC 2 Corps when this weapon of Goddess Durga was adopted as the Formation Sign of 2 Corps. The Corps was raised in October 1971 in Bengal during the festival of Durga Puja and this symbol was considered very auspicious.

---

[125] Lt Generals Tappy Raina and Vir Vohra had been friends since their college days at Lahore (*see* Chapter 2).

[126] GOC's Secretariat was then located in the building which is presently the HQ Western Command Library.

Chapter 25

General Officer Commanding-in-Chief, Western Command

On 17th October 1973, Tappy and Ninette Raina accompanied by Captain Kala, the ADC, flew by helicopter from Chandimandir to Annandale Helipad at Shimla.[127] They were ceremoniously received by Major General (later General and COAS) Kotikalapudi Venkata Krishna Rao, Chief of Staff, HQ Western Command[128] and Mrs Radha Krishna Rao. After inspecting a smart Guard of Honour presented by the contingent from 14 Gorkha Training Centre, Subathu Cantonment, the party drove to Command House (Official Residence of GOC-in-C), where the two ladies stayed back, and the newly appointed Army Commander proceeded to HQ Western Command. The Command Headquarters was located in a historic building which was once

[127] The author who was DAMS to GOC 2 Corps, also proceeded to HQ Western Command on temporary duty to officiate as AMS to GOC-in-C, till the arrival of permanent incumbent, Lieutenant Colonel RN Mahajan, VSM, former CO 14 Kumaon (Gwalior) & first CO of The Naga Regiment, raised on 1st November 1970. Ravi Mahajan led this young Battalion in the War for liberation of East Pakistan.

[128] As was the protocol then in practice, the incoming Army Commander arrived in station, only after his predecessor left the station on the previous day, after due ceremonial send off. Accordingly, Lieutenant General M.L. Thapan, PVSM, predecessor of Lieutenant General Tappy Raina, proceeded to AHQ, New Delhi, to take over the appointment of VCOAS, a day prior to the arrival of his successor.

the General Headquarters (GHQ) when Simla (now Shimla) was the summer capital of the British Government in India.

After introduction to senior Staff Officers and heads of Arms and Services, Tappy Raina got busy with briefings by Staff Officers. It did not take the Rainas much time to settle down in the well-appointed Command House, their new residence.

The atmosphere of Shimla, the Capital of Himachal Pradesh (HP), was unique. Vehicular traffic on the Mall was extremely restricted and therefore, walking was the best mode to reach anywhere. Vehicular traffic was only permitted on Cart Road, but there was a paucity of parking space. Therefore, it was common practice for all ranks posted at HQ Western Command, to walk to and from their offices at Command HQ. Traditionally, on Wednesdays and Saturdays, all ranks of HQ Western Command attended office in civil dress, as these days were observed as half working days. At the end of the office hours on those days, families of officers used to meet up outside Command HQ and were seen walking back home happily in small groups. Some would stop at the Gaiety Theatre, also known as Amateur Dramatic Club (ADC), for high tea with friends, before returning home. On most mornings, General Raina also walked from Command House to Command HQ, accompanied by his ADC, Captain C.P. Kala.

Ninette Raina was happy with her new home and its salubrious surroundings of majestic pine trees and a lovely garden full of flowers. While she was busy growing strawberries and mushrooms, the General was busy preparing his Army under Western Command for any eventual threat from Pakistan. The Pakistani army officers were still smarting from their defeat in East Pakistan, and there was a lot of murmur of seeking revenge!

General Raina's span of command and duties increased manifold after he took over this new appointment. Moreover, he was also Colonel of the Kumaon & Naga Regiments, which was an additional responsibility. Clearly, he needed someone from the Kumaon or Naga Regiment as his confidential Staff Officer who could also assist him in dealing with regimental matters. Consequently, the author, who was Deputy Assistant Military Secretary (DAMS) to General Raina at HQ 2 Corps, and was carrying out similar duties, temporarily moved on attachment as officiating Assistant Military Secretary (AMS), HQ Western Command, as a stop gap arrangement.

Lieutenant Colonel Ravi Mahajan,[129] who earlier was posted as an Instructor at DSSC, Wellington, was chosen by Tappy Raina to fill the appointment as AMS, HQ Western Command. Ravi received his posting order in October 1973. However, there was some delay in his arrival from Wellington, and he finally reported at HQ Western Command, Shimla at the end of December 1973. He took over the duties as AMS from the author in early January 1974 and the author reverted to regimental duties.

Tappy Raina set himself a hectic schedule. First and foremost, he had to mould the Command Headquarters so that its staff responded to his service values and work ethos. He had, overall. a very competent team of staff officers and advisors, headed by his Chief of Staff, Major General Krishna Rao, himself a first rate, battle-hardened commander and staff officer. Each section of the General Staff (GS), Adjutant General (AG) and Quarter Master General (QMG) Branches and the Heads of supporting Arms and Services were officers of the rank of Brigadier[130].

General Raina made it a point to be present at all weekly and enlarged conferences at his Headquarter. He would always go well prepared and he attentively absorbed what was presented by various section and department heads. His instructions to them were always clear and concise. Minutes of the conferences were prepared and distributed overnight, acted upon and progressed, on file

---

[129] Ravi Mahajan had been in the Regiment for over twenty years and served in 14 Kumaon (Gwalior) at Amritsar when Tappy was the Battalionn 2IC, and later at Ferozepur when Tappy was the CO. He had seen combat in the Indo-Pak War of 1965 in the Sialkot Sector and had been in the thick of counter-insurgency operations in Nagaland as CO 14 Kumaon (Gwalior). Thereafter, he was selected to raise the Naga Regiment, which was affiliated to Kumaon Regiment. Ravi led his newly raised Battalion in action during the War for liberation of East Pakistan as part of 2 Corps, which was commanded by Lt. General Tappy Raina.

[130] As a result of Cadre Review in 1980, these were upgraded to the rank of Maj Gen.

or in the next conference. All related instructions issued to subordinate Headquarters by the Command Headquarters were placed before the General for his information. His staff soon knew what was expected of them: professionalism, dedication, dispatch. What motivated them was his personal example and zest.

Forward planning came naturally to Tappy Raina who, after years of experience of important Command, Instructional and Staff appointments, always planned well ahead for any event. He toured extensively and visited formation headquarters, units, and installations in his Command. Before going on these tours, he would go through the brief history, the state of equipment, accommodation and the records of service of the officers he was to meet in the formations and units he visited. He paid special attention to personnel and logistical issues which at times were not addressed at the proper levels or with the desired speed. Overall, he was very particular on the state of operational readiness, which had somewhat suffered due to prolonged mobilisation during Operation Cactus Lilly in 1971 and 1972. During visits he listened attentively to briefings of the Commanders being visited. His queries were always pointed. Those visited would get the impression that their problems had been understood at the highest level and would be resolved. Such, indeed, should be the whole purpose of visits by a higher Commander.

The evenings of such visits were set aside for informal social get-togethers with officers. Ladies, too, would be present on such occasions. Tappy moved easily amongst them and made it a point to particularly chat with the ladies and young officers for they otherwise felt neglected at times on such occasions. Tappy Raina drank alcoholic beverages sparingly. Often, he would hold only a glass of lime-cordial and soda in his hand.

After each such visit, the Staff Officer accompanying the Army Commander was expected to put up the draft Tour Notes for his approval within twenty-four hours of the conclusion of the tour. These notes set down with precision the action that was required on the directions and points made by Tappy during the visit: action whether by the visited formation or installation, as also by the staff at the Command Headquarters.

Tappy had a sharp eye for observing improprieties. Once he drove up to a conference hall to address senior officers at Ambala Cantonment, many of whom were of the rank of brigadier. A number of jeeps were parked outside the Hall, each with a star plate, displaying one star as is authorised to a Brigadier. Tappy's opening remarks were: "One of the brigadiers present has the star on his jeep's star plate, upside down". Enough to state that this made all the brigadiers present quite edgy during the address; each hoped that he was not the culprit!

If ever Tappy was unhappy or angry, he never raised has voice. However, the recipient of his disapprobation received from him a cold stare, and remarks such as: *"*I cannot congratulate you for that.*"* Any remark predicated by *"*Sweetheart*"* meant that displeasure or censure was to follow. On the other hand his remark: *"*That was well done!*"* made the recipient ecstatic! Let it be said here that in any gathering he had a "presence" that was not attributable only to his high rank.

When Tappy Raina assumed his appointment as GOC-in-C Western Command, his son Captain Jyoti Raina was serving with his father's former Battalion, 14 Kumaon (Gwalior) at Jalandhar Cantonment. The Raina family had a family reunion over Christmas in December 1973 at their home in Shimla. In the New Year, when everything in their lives was moving smoothly, when their cup was full, fate delivered a cruel blow to the unfortunate parents. At that time Tappy had been GOC-in-C Western Command for barely five months.

On 5th March 1974, Joe was seriously injured, an unfortunate victim of a hit-and-run road accident[131] just outside 14 Kumaon (Gwalior) Officers Mess at Jullundur (now Jalandhar) Cantonment.

---

[131] The accident took place just near the "In-Gate" of 14 Kumaon (Gwalior) Officers' Mess, situated on The Mall, Jalandhar Cantt, when Joe was returning from the Unit lines of his Battalion on his motor bike. As Joe was turning into the "IN" Gate of his Mess, he was hit by a speeding car, resulting in severe head injury to him. He was rushed to the Military Hospital, where the doctors found his state critical; he had to be put on ventilation support immediately!

Gen Tappy Raina, MVC, COAS, along with Army Commanders, calls on Prime Minister Morarji Desai after the lifting of the Emergency in 1977. Left to right: Lt Gen Harish Rai, Lt Gen Inder Gill, Lt Gen Jacob, Lt Gen Vir Vohra, Gen Tappy Raina, Shri Morarji Desai, Lt Gen J.S. Nakkai and Lt Gen O.P. Malhotra.

Army HQ PSOs meeting Tappy (not in the picture) informally in his of ce after taking over as COAS on 2nd June 1975. Left to right: Lt Gens Vir Vohra (VCOAS), Jaswant Singh (DCOAS) "Rocky" Hira (AG), A.N. Mathur (QMG), S.D. Gupta, (MGO), Kundan Singh (MS).

Presentation of Guidon to 61 Cavalry by acting President B.D. Jatti; Col Cdt Gen Raina is on his right.

General Raina inspecting the guard of honour as honorary CoR at Guards Training Centre, Kota.

Early morning on 6th March 1974, General and Mrs Raina along with Lieutenant Colonel Ravi Mahajan, took off in a helicopter from Shimla and rushed to Jalandhar Cantonment. Lieutenant General (later General) Om Prakash Malhotra,[132] GOC 11 Corps, received the Rainas and escorted them to his residence where he and his wife, Saroj, offered General and Mrs. Raina comfort, strength and solace to bear the shock of the reported accident which had come as a bolt from the blue. Later, at the Military Hospital, the parents stood silently near their beloved son as his young body on the hospital bed convulsed and heaved with the ventilator. They listened stoically, holding each other's hand, as the attending doctors calmly explained Joe's condition and the treatment that was being given.

There was no change whatsoever in Joe's condition over the next twenty-four hours. He seemed brain-dead. Even on the night of 7/8th March, there was no change in Joe's condition: Lieutenant Colonel Ravi Mahajan and Major Ian Da Costa, both from Joe's battalion, spent that night near the ICU. They were desperate to carry news of even a little improvement in Joe's condition to the devastated parents, but that was not to be. Next day the Rainas said a private good-bye to their son. The ventilator had fallen silent. Joe died on the evening of 9th March 1974. The small Raina family, Tappy, Ninette, and Joe's sister, Anita (fondly called Annu), was devastated.

Captain Jyoti Narain Raina, the beloved son of Tappy and Ninette, was cremated with full military honours the next day. The funeral arrangements were supervised with military precision by Lieutenant Colonel Inder Sethi, Commanding Officer, 14 Kumaon, the Battalion with which Joe had spent his childhood years while his father was its Commanding Officer and into which he was later commissioned. The procession route from the Battalion Officers' Mess up to the cremation ground was lined by Kumaonis, personnel from other units in Jullundur and a crowd of civilians who had gathered on either side of the route to bid good-

---

[132] He later succeeded Tappy Raina as the COAS on 1st June 1978.

bye to the Army Commander's son. Whereas sons light the pyres of their father, tragically, here a father lit the pyre of his only son. Stoic, sombre, and composed, the General stood erect and, as the Battalion buglers sounded the "Last Post", he saluted his son. Joe's fellow officers from his Battalion shed tears unabashedly as the flames rose from the funeral pyre and as they watched Jyoti (literally, the Eternal Flame) consigned to the flames!

Joe had endeared himself enormously to all those he had served with. In all operational situations — counter-insurgency operations in Nagaland, war for liberation of East Pakistan (Bangladesh) and thereafter, Joe had earned the professional respect and admiration of not only his fellow officers, but of all ranks who came in touch with him.

The next day, before his return to Simla, the General asked to visit, privately, Joe's living quarters in the single officers' accommodation. Captain Sherry Sapru (later Brigadier) was detailed to escort him. Sapru recounts how the General entered, gazed around the room slowly and then sat down on a chair, still and silent for quite a while, deep in thought. It was as if he was communicating with his son, with whom he had maintained a formal relationship. A little later, he asked to see Joe's belongings in the cupboard. On opening the cupboard, he was surprised to find an extremely tidy row of shelves which was most unlike Joe. Among other things, Joe had collected linen, a variety of household items, curtain material and so on. It was as if Joe was planning to settle down in the near future.

The General choked with emotion. For a man who had had an austere childhood, who had been seriously wounded twice during World War II, who had braved the onslaught of the Chinese Army in Ladakh and never flinched under any adversity or pressure, this moment seemed to temporarily overwhelm him. "I never fully understood Joe," he confessed. "I did not realize that he could plan for his future in such detail."

The pain of the blow and the anguish of the parents has been best described by Ninette Raina in the words of an anguished mother, a brave and courageous army wife:

> In Shimla we enjoyed our garden and acquired more pets. We had three dogs, one parrot and a collection of birds. Our house was lovely and the climate was fine. Of course, Tappy was not always there but there was somehow plenty to keep busy with. I remember the bright and happy Christmas that we celebrated that year in December of 1973! Alas, it was to be our last reunion as a complete family!!
>
> The winter of 1973-74 at Shimla, passed off quickly, with Tappy getting more and more involved with his official work. February 1974, had been very wet, rainy, windy and cold, which forced me to remain indoors a lot. Our dogs, too, did not like to go out in the rain and preferred going out at night, when the rain changed to snow. So in the middle of the night, bundled in Tappy's "Parkha coat" and with snow boots on my feet, I would stroll them in the garden. The sentries standing guard at the Command House always looked surprised to see me at that odd hour! They may even have thought that the "memsahib" sleepwalked!
>
> We came down from Shimla to Delhi Cantonment, to celebrate our Silver Wedding Anniversary on 25th February. Our son, Joe, came on a very short leave from his Battalion, whereas our daughter, Anita, also left her University for a couple of days, to be with us on this occasion.
>
> That night we had a family celebration and were very happy. The following morning was the dispersal and parting of com pany with our children. I vividly remember that someone had talked about a boy, who had been knocked down on the road by a car and been crippled, and we went on talking about the danger that traffic posed nowadays. Suddenly, Joe said out of the blue, "If I die — I die"! We were shocked![133]

---

[133] Within a week Joe was dead!

Next day, after seeing the children off, we left for Shimla. En-route, we stopped at Chandigarh for a short duration, where Tappy had some official engagements. We were back home on the 5th of March 1974. After dinner the telephone rang. Tappy took the call in his unhurried way. After receiving the phone call, he was silent for a few minutes, and then he gently told me, "Joe has been involved in an accident and he is in hospital". He was afraid to tell me, because he knew how I would jump! Then several phone calls came, one after the other and it transpired that my boy was quite badly injured!

At midnight, a helicopter flight was arranged for us to fly at first light to Jalandhar and a neurosurgeon was flown from Delhi at the same time. My darling boy had suffered a severe head injury.

We arrived in Jalandhar early next morning, to find our son deeply unconscious, and he had, by then, undergone an emergency operation. But he never came out of it. A second operation helped him somewhat but the unconsciousness persisted! For four days it was a desperate battle but the injury was far too severe and Joe died in the evening of 9th March 1974.

Joe was only 24 years old. The "catastrophe" of Joe's death was only the tip of the iceberg! The whole Raina family was crushed. Amongst three brothers and one cousin brother in Tappy's family, our son was the only male issue.

If only . . . if only, the car driver had stopped, it would not have been so revolting. But the culprit driver drove away after switching off his car's headlights. There had been witnesses. Yet nobody helped!

The accident had happened at about 7.30 p.m. on 5th March 1974, when Joe was coming back on his motorcycle, from his Unit Lines to 14 Kumaon (Gwalior) Officer's Mess, after meeting the Battalion Second-in-Command, Major Ian-da-Costa, in connection with a forthcoming function to be arranged in the Battalion. As Joe was turning into the Officer's Mess gate, a speeding car hit him and his motorcycle was badly smashed, and Joe's helmet went out of shape with the impact. He had also been hit in the back, twice, as the driver tried to manoeuvre the car to escape from the site of the accident. The car was later found after a full manhunt and the law took its course. But what was the use of this to the family? I must add that in Western countries, manslaughter also happens a lot, but the crime of running away from a victim, is heinous and considered as good as murder! But here in India, perhaps human life did not count so much?

For us, life was never the same again; the only anchor for us was that there was another child — our daughter, Anita. But overnight it was a vacuum: only a feeling of having lived and worked in vain! Our life had suddenly become a "blank"! Luckily, we had that second child, though Tappy had originally been quite satisfied with only one. It helped retain our sanity. What would have happened to both of us if we had not had our lovely daughter Anita, after the loss of our beloved son, Joe?

Here at Shimla, there wasn't much to be done now, inside or outside the house. There were no troops nearby, nor any direct welfare activities; nothing to keep me busy! I again started going for long walks with my dogs as I had done in Wellington twenty years ago. But somehow, I wasn't so resilient now and did not have that much stamina. But it had to be done, if only to overcome this new insidious question: what for? So, I accompanied Tappy on most of his tours. We roamed all over the Western Command; I visited outlandish places such as isolated valleys, villages out of Himalayan Expeditions stories, had my first meeting with a yak (from near) tasted my first (and last) "chhang" or barley beer, bathed in hot sulphurous springs and ate all sorts of strange food!

I remember those long helicopter trips, following the River Sutlej in the heart of the mountains, flying parallel to the road that had been cut in the living rock and looked most of the time an open-sided tunnel. We also went up to the border of Tibet. Imagine a bleak, desolate terrain, coloured only by various rocks, iced peaks and rushing and foaming torrents. Villages were the colour of the surrounding mud, interiors dark and smoky, but the pearly smiles of the locals were always bright. The simpler the people are, the more lovable.

When Anita came for the summer holidays in 1974, we invited all her friends to the house. She also needed company and a couple of her teachers in the University who had insisted that she stay with them after her brother's death, came with their three boys. We also had other youngsters with us. A few families of young officers also visited, and we kept very active, very desperately so, collecting mushrooms (we had a shed of them), gathering strawberries and making jam, all of us with an apron tied around our middle.

When we left Shimla, there were enough mushroom tins to last us for a year. But the strawberry jam did not die of old age; it was swallowed there and then, amidst laughter and cries of delight! We also had very long walks, away from the crowds, following small and little used paths in the forest and up the hillsides. Some relatives also came to swell the ranks and our garden received more attention than ever from us.

And there were the fights between our dogs and the monkeys. The latter were wild and all over Shimla. We had acquired a new dog and a parrot and also "munias" (small chirping birds). The fish in the aquarium became fat from crumbs. I needed to keep myself occupied — anything to keep me busy, and to keep away from brooding!

There were dozens of monkeys all around and they could be a real nuisance. Our dogs hated them. They tried all the time to invade our garden, but the dogs kept them at bay. So, they perched on trees and bombarded the dogs with cones and twigs. I even saw them teasing the dogs. One day, a stray dog passing in the road below our house joined the chorus of our dogs in yelping at them. That was one too many for the monkeys. One of them came down, jumped on the road and soundly cuffed the dog which ran away howling. After that my own dogs took great care to "tease" the monkeys only when we were around for safety!

And now that sympathy on the sad demise of our son had been conveyed to us from all sides, life had to go on, so we were left with the inescapable fact that the battle was now our very own and we were alone to fight it!

What do you do when your only son dies at the age of 24, suddenly, at the beginning of his life, so brutally and needlessly? To have gone through a war, Joe just had to die on an obscure road, without any purpose! How does one react when everything one had, has crumbled to dust? When every room reminds you of some action, some words, some images? When his clothes and things come back to you? That is very cruel!

How does one reconcile to the fact that one has worked so long, suffered when the child was ill, planned and sacrificed with so much joy and suddenly all that turns into dust? You have shaped a human life. You have seen the child grow and develop; becoming a projection of yourself in the future, some sort of immortality! Overnight there is void. This happens to everyone, but in different degrees! No one can change this rule of life and death, but it is devastating, and no wonder, that it kills many people! But it would not kill us; it would never kill Tappy; and so, we resolved! He gritted his teeth and went on doggedly in his work and duty.

And the greatness of Tappy was that he went on, now, for the gain of others, the men that he commanded. The vision was there, even clearer. The planning was there but I think in the end, his frame could not take it anymore. His spirit wore it out.

There was once that humble man in Mhow who had told him: "My family, all are dead! So I am also a living dead"! Tappy had admired his loyalty, but when his own turn came, he did not consider himself as dead. He was not alone either, he still had us; I and Anita! He hardened visibly and became stronger than before, his vision clearer. Was he trying to compensate for the life thrown to waste? His own life became a greater achievement. Perhaps, he died too early to get to the very top of his destiny, but he had somewhat achieved an enormous amount. He used to say, "At last, my commitments are over".

There are some children who come to nothing. They vegetate in life or at times they turn to idling or to drugs. Some are derelicts. Others survive accidents or illnesses to remain crippled or diminished, and still others, though healthy and strong,

> are suddenly cut off in their prime! I wonder which is the hardest to bear. But everyone has a "Cross" to bear. Lucky are those whose "Cross" is lighter.
>
> A blow like that may shatter you like glass. It may harden you like steel. But ultimately, the blow tells and the strain is there. Tappy was one of those who would never admit defeat; instead, he would go down fighting. And fittingly, he did just that"!

Back in Shimla, spring was in the air. Wild flowers waved merrily on the hill slopes. The snows on the distant mountains melted and their waters cascaded down the Rivers Beas and Sutlej. The great Gobind Sagar Dam had filled up. But the chill in the hearts of the Rainas was never to thaw. Yet, the outside world only saw their calm demeanours and wondered.

Gaiety Theatre at the Ridge in Shimla is a landmark building dating back to the late 19th century. Gothic in style, it is a cultural complex that has been the social hub of this fine hill station and erstwhile capital of British India. It had select membership, which was desperately sought-after by the elite of Shimla. It was the centre of multi-faceted activities, a meeting place for social interaction, recreation, card games and, above all, as its name implied, it was a show place for the performing arts. Rudyard Kipling, K.L. Saigal and the great Prithvi Raj Kapoor had performed there. However, its overall state had been allowed to deteriorate; its interiors had become shabby and the staff was lethargic. Suffice to say that it had become quite pedestrian and uninspiring, and required resuscitation.

In 1974, the general body meeting of Gaiety Theatre was due. It was important to elect a governing body whose members had intellect and taste, and who would breathe new life into the fine institution. General Raina was determined that the management be changed. He urged all officers of the Armed Forces who were members of the Theatre, to attend the meeting. They did so in large members. Thus, a new governing body was elected with an overwhelming vote. The new dispensation very diligently restored the Theatre to its pristine glory, under the patronage of General Raina.

That same year, at the height of the tourist season, the Western Command Women's Welfare body under Mrs. Ninette Raina's direction, held a *mela* (fun fair) to garner funds for family welfare. General Raina made it known that he desired the event to be a thumping success with the twin objectives of raising the prestige of the Army and, equally important, generating maximum money for the welfare of families: this generally meant army widows and their children. The *mela* was a great success: both its objectives were achieved.

The Prime Minister's Visit to the Sino-India Border in Himachal Pradesh

The operational responsibility of HQ Western Command included the vast district of Lahaul and Spiti in Himachal Pradesh, sharing a common border with Tibet. Through it lay the old major route when trade flourished before the Chinese occupation of Tibet in 1949. It was also linked with Ladakh from time immemorial till it was annexed by the British and bifurcated from Ladakh. Because of its strategic location, Prime Minister Indira Gandhi decided to visit this district on the morning of 3rd June 1974.

Mrs. Gandhi landed at Annandale helipad, Shimla, and picked up General Raina in her helicopter. They flew to Sumdo in Lahaul and Spiti District, which is the second largest election district in India. For the first time, the Congress Party had wrested this prestigious seat. The winner was the legendary and handsome Mrs. Lata Thakur. By visiting her constituency, Prime Minister Gandhi was, in a way, bolstering the party's and Mrs Thakur's positions, besides familiarising herself with the operational situation along this portion of the Indo-Tibetan Border.

A viewpoint for observation of important "land marks" had been chosen at a site above the helipad, where the local Battalion commander indicated the landmarks, mostly on the horizon. The panoramic view of the country's northern border with China was impressive, as also of the Ladakh region slightly to the north-west. Thereafter, General Raina briefed the Prime Minister on the strategic importance of the area and the outline plan to defend it against any incursion from the north by the Chinese.

After visiting Sumdo, the Prime Ministers' party flew back to land at 14 Gorkha Training Centre, Subathu[134], located only about 20 kilometres off the Kalka-Shimla highway. This impressive cantonment town and hill station is the home of two famous Gorkha regiments: the 1st and the 4th Gorkha Rifles. Both regiments have a combined training centre here, known as 14 Gorkha Training Centre (14 GTC). The training centre was established here in 1960 after two centres were moved from Dharamshala and Bakloh (Dalhousie), respectively, and merged here.

Prime Minister Gandhi met the officers and their wives at the officers' mess of the Regimental Centre. She mixed easily with everyone and inquired about the life in Subathu. The fare served at lunch was simple and vegetarian. After lunch, she departed for Chandigarh, where General Raina saw her off. Never once during her visit did General Raina address Indira Gandhi as "Madam" as seemed to be the practice. For him, she was "Prime Minister". Tappy Raina was always correct in his discourse, whether with the high and mighty or with the rank and file. And, for him, there was also no question of supplication.

In his long career, Tappy Raina had gained wide experience. He had fought wars in desert and jungle, in high mountains and the golden (*sonar* in Bengali) plains of erstwhile East Pakistan. He had been an instructor at the premier training institution of the army. As a General Staff Officer grade-2 (GSO-2) in Military Operations Directorate at AHQ, he was involved in operational planning at the highest level during the Indo-Pak operations of 1947-48 in Jammu and Kashmir. Later, he was the Brigadier General

---

[134] Subathu was once under Gorkha rule of Amar Singh Thapa. Perched 4,000 feet above sea level, Subathu was once a thriving trading post on the Indo-Tibetan trade route.

Staff (BGS) at HQ 33 Corps, operationally responsible for Sikkim, Bhutan and North Bengal. After successfully commanding 25 Infantry Division, he was appointed Chief of Staff (COS), HQ 15 Corps, where he was responsible for operational and logistic planning of all troops and formations deployed in Jammu and Kashmir, from Ladakh in the north to Pathankot in the south.

As a lieutenant colonel, Tappy Raina had handled intricate personnel issues of all officers of the army, when he was Assistant Military Secretary in the Military Secretary's Branch, Army Headquarters. Later, he held the appointment of Deputy Adjutant General at the Adjutant General Branch in the Army Headquarters, in the rank of major general. He had travelled abroad and had a good understanding of global situations.

Tappy had an inquiring mind and an absorbing interest in military matters. As a young officer in 1/19 Hyderabad Regiment[135], he had received a sound grounding under British officers. From them he had imbibed only their better attributes of character and professional conduct. All this experience and qualities he brought to bear for the betterment of his command. It also must be added that, having seen the misery of the survivors of wars — wounded soldiers, widowed wives and their bereft children, and being himself visually handicapped, he naturally, had special empathy for his less fortunate colleagues and subordinates. He therefore always endeavoured to understand and alleviate their problems.

Colonel of the Kumaon and Naga Regiments

Despite his responsibility as GOC-in-C Western Command, Tappy found time to attend to regimental matters as the Colonel of the Kumaon and Naga Regiments which he had been guiding since

---

[135] 19 Hyderabad Regiment became the Kumaon Regiment on 27th October 1945. Thus 1/19 Hyderabad Regiment became 1 Kumaon (Para). The Battalion was later transferred to form a part of the Parachute Regiment, and is now designated as 3rd Battalion, Parachute Regiment (Kumaon).

1971. His numerous and important contributions to the Kumaon and Naga regiments are narrated in Chapter 35.

A long outstanding desire of all ranks of The Kumaon Regiments was to get its nearly 200 years of history compiled in the form of a book. General Raina as Colonel of the Regiment, took upon himself the task of getting the regimental history of The Kumaon Regiment, written. It was, indeed, an onerous task: some of the battalions in The Kumaon Regiment were more than one hundred and fifty years old and had seen action in theatres spanning Europe, Africa, the Middle East, Burma and the Far East.

General Raina chose Major K.C. Praval, a seasoned chronicler of regimental histories, as the author. Praval had already written the history of The Parachute Regiment. Tappy met him a number of times and guided him to study relevant historical records and meet regimental personalities, both serving and retired. Some of these had seen action in the Second World War and in Jammu and Kashmir in 1947-48. Others had also participated in counter insurgency operations in the East. Based on the motto of the Kumaon Regiment, i.e *Parakramo Vijayate*, the title of the book was chosen as: *Valour Triumphs: A History of The Kumaon Regiment.*

General Raina frequently went on official tours accompanied by Ninette Raina and one personal staff officer. They would travel by staff car from Shimla to Kalka. Not a word was normally exchanged during these journeys! The General was always deep in thought. In his mind, he was perhaps analysing and defining the problems at his level and how to solve them. Or, how to get things done within the existing system of the Ministry of Defence! Whenever he met ex-servicemen, the General intently listened to their problems, isolated the main issues and sought their resolution. His wide experience, sharp intellect and the habit of deep contemplation always came to his assistance. So also did the counsel of few friends and former colleagues. Notable among them were Generals Vir Vohra, Zoru Bakshi[136] and Rocky Hira, all from the Gorkha Regiments. Zoru and Rocky, like Tappy, were winners of the Maha Vir Chakra for valour in free India's wars. Another regimental officer and a fellow commanding officer of Tappy's vintage, whose opinion and advice he greatly valued, was Brigadier Teg Bahadur Kapur, AVSM.[137]

Tappy Raina always treated his personal staff, whether, an officer, JCO or OR, with great consideration and care. Ravi Mahajan,

---

[136] Lieutenant General Zorawar Chand Bakshi (retd), fondly known as "Zoru", one of India's highly decorated Generals, passed away in New Delhi at the age of 97 years on 24th May 2018. Born at Rawalpindi (now in Pakistan) in 1921, he was educated and graduated in 1942 from Gordon College, Rawalpindi. After joining the Army, he was commissioned in the Baloch Regiment in 1943. As a YO, he saw action in Burma (now Myanmar) during 2nd World War, while fighting against Japanese, where he was Mentioned-in-Despatches.

After the partition of India, Maj Zoru Bakshi was transferred from Baloch Regiment to 5th Gorkha Rifles in the Indian Army. He saw action in Indo-Pakistan War of 1947-48, and was awarded VrC for gallantry. He was once again decorated with the MVC for gallantry, during the Indo-Pakistan war of 1965, when his Brigade captured the strategic Haji Pir Pass on the Pir Panjal Ranges, which was vital for the Uri — Poonch link-up. As GOC 26 Infantry Division he saw action in Jammu — Sialkot Sector. Later, he was awarded the PVSM for distinguished services. Those who knew him said he was strict disciplinarian who remained an icon and source of inspiration to the past and present generations of officers.

[137] Brigadier Tegh Bahadur Kapoor, popularly called "Tegi" was Director Ceremonial & Welfare (CW) in AG's Branch, AHQ. He had already served three COAS, General Kumaramangalam, General (later FM) Sam Manekshaw, MC, General G.G. Bewoor, PVSM, before the appointment of General T.N. Raina, as COAS! He was considered an authority on the subject of ceremonials and Welfare in the armed forces, whose advice was often sought by MOD. The Amar Jawan Jyoti at India Gate was the brainchild of Brigadier Kapoor. It was inaugurated by Mrs. Indira Gandhi on 17th January, 1972. Untill the creation of the National War Memorial in the nearby lawns of India Gate inaugurated by Prime Minister Narendra Modi on 25th February 2019, Amar Jawan Jyoti remained the only memorial to the Indian soldier.

A veteran of World War-2 & J&K operations (1947-48), he had commanded 4 Kumaon in UNEF in Gaza. After commanding the Northern Ladakh Sector he was appointed COS of the International Control Commission in Indo-China.

was known to Tappy Raina, from the day he joined 4 Gwalior Infantry as a Second Lieutenant when, the then Major T. N. Raina was the 2 I/C of the Battalion. Ravi came from a large middle class family, which had been uprooted and displaced by the Partition of India, just like Tappy. Sensing that Ravi had no property to inherit, and considering that in his service, Ravi had already been in wars twice, Tappy advised him, for the sake of his family, to build a house. Ravi had acquired a plot of land in a "Defence Sector" at the newly constructed town of Chandigarh. "Beg, borrow or steal, but make a house," so Tappy admonished Ravi! Tappy himself, when he was a Lieutenant Colonel, posted at AHQ, had made a house at New Delhi. Ravi did just that, but he did not steal: only begged and borrowed and built a house! While the house was under construction, Tappy afforded him every opportunity to visit Chandigarh from Shimla. Ravi's house at Chandigarh was ready before he got relocated to AHQ at New Delhi, in 1975.

Since his college days, Tappy had been fond of Urdu and sought relaxation and inspiration in Urdu poetry.[138] His favourite poets were Faiz, Zauq, Mirza Ghalib and Iqbal. He often quoted Iqbal: "*Khud hi ko buland kar itna ke har taqdeer se pehle khuda bande se khud pooche bata teri raza kya hai?*" Translated, it means, "Elevate yourself so high, that even God, before issuing every decree of destiny, will be compelled to ask you, what is your desire?"

Tappy's relationship with senior bureaucrats was always correct and formal. Once, as GOC-in-C Western Command, he was visiting Delhi on an official tour, when a message was received from the Principal Secretary to the Prime Minister that he would like to meet the Army Commander, at his office. Feigning an urgent engagement, Tappy ignored the message and flew back to Shimla. The Principal Secretary was informed, only after Tappy had reached Shimla!

---

[138] When Tappy was en route to Leh, to take over as Commander 114 Infantry Brigade on promotion to the rank of Brigadier in 1962, Ravi met him at Jalandhar Railway Station. He noticed that, even then Tappy had with him a book of Faiz's poems!

Much later, Ravi enquired from Tappy about his abrupt decision to ignore the message to him from the Principal Secretary to the Prime Minister Tappy replied:

> Look, Ravi, I knew the decision about the selection of the next Chief was soon to be taken. Had I acquiesced and met him and later was appointed the COAS, he could claim his influence in the decision and I would have remained forever obligated to him; but he would have lost nothing had I not been selected"!

On 15th March 1975, Tappy Raina was visiting HQ 11 Corps at Jalandhar Cantonment, where Lt. General Eric Vas was the GOC. On this particular trip, Ninette had not accompanied Tappy, for she still could not bear to go to the place where their beloved son, Joe, had died a year earlier!

On conclusion of his visit to HQ 11 Corps, Tappy was having lunch in the Officers' Mess, when the Officer's Mess telephone rang and an officer of the Corps HQ received the call. He then conveyed to the Army Commander that there was an important call for him from Army HQ. Everyone was agog with anticipation, because the appointment of the new Army Chief was to be made known any day! However, after receiving the phone call, Tappy returned to the dining table and continued with his interrupted lunch in an absolutely calm manner. After finishing his lunch, Tappy took leave of his hosts, and left Jalandhar Cantonment for Kalka, where his wife, Ninette, was to join him from Shimla.

That afternoon of 15th March, Ninette left Shimla after an early lunch, and drove down by car escorted by Captain C.P. Kala, the ADC, who was equipped with a transistor radio. A commentary on a hockey match between India and Pakistan being played somewhere abroad, was being broadcast on the radio. During the entire journey, they were hanging on to the radio commentary and by the time they reached Kalka, Ninette was elated because India had won the match!

Soon thereafter, Tappy too arrived at Kalka from Jalandhar Cantonment. Ninette vividly recalled her meeting with her husband, as under:

When we met at Kalka in the early evening of 15th March 1975, Tappy told me very quietly, "I have been selected to become the next Chief! But keep quiet about it!"

That was typical of Tappy; let others broadcast the news! We looked at each other in silence. Our son would certainly have been very proud that day but all that joy and elation somehow felt hollow for us! And while the telephone rang and rang and people came crowding, to offer their felicitations, we smiled in acceptance and kept a semblance of brave face, but we were both deeply sad in our heart.

That same night, Tappy and Ninette Raina left Kalka for Delhi by the Railway Saloon for the GOC-in-C Western Command, which was attached to the Kalka-Howrah Mail. Tappy Raina was scheduled to attend some meetings at Army HQ and also inspect units at Delhi Cantonment. After a couple of days at Delhi Cantonment, they returned to Shimla, where Tappy's staff officers at HQ Western Command and other civil dignitaries were waiting to felicitate him on his forthcoming promotion and appointment as Chief of Army Staff.

Part V

The Indian Army under General T.N. Raina, MVC

GOD, give us men! The time demands
Strong minds, great hearts, true faith and ready hands;
Men whom the lust of office does not kill;
Men whom the spoils of office cannot buy;
Men who possess opinions and a will;
Men who have honour; men who will not lie.
~ Gilbert Holland

Chapter 26

COAS Indian Army

COAS (Designate)

General Tapishwar Narain Raina, MVC, Padma Bhushan, was to become the eighth Chief of the Army Staff (COAS) of the Indian Army, at the young age of 54 years and four months! He was the first General Officer to become COAS, who was neither from the Royal Military College, Sandhurst (UK) nor the Indian Military Academy, Dehradun! Instead, he received his Pre-Commission Training, during the 2nd World War, at the Officers' Training Academy (OTA), Mhow (MP), when the training period had been curtailed due to the exigencies of War.

He was also the first Chief of the Indian Army who hailed from a humble and conservative Indian middle class family unlike most of his predecessors who were from affluent families. He was also amongst the last Chiefs who had taken part in active operations during World War-2, both, in the Middle East as part of the PAI Force (Iraq Theatre) and Burma (present Myanmar) as part of 36 British Infantry Division. He was the first Chief of the Army Staff who carried independent India's second highest gallantry award, the Maha Vir Chakra (MVC).

General Raina was the third officer from the Kumaon Regiment to attain this exalted rank. His other distinguished predecessors from the Regiment were General S.M. Shrinagesh and the legendry General K.S. Thimayya, DSO.

Once the Government of India announced his appointment as COAS in March 1975 to succeed General Gopal Gurudas Bewoor,

PVSM, General Raina got busy with clearing the pending official work at HQ Western Command. At the same time, his mind was furiously thinking of major issues that would require his attention immediately on assuming his new responsibility as Chief of the Indian Army.

Much before his appointment as COAS General Raina had decided to focus on the need for drastic improvement of operational readiness of the Indian Army. For preparing all ranks of the Army for their role in service of the Nation, the following aspects, in particular, received his attention:

- Battle worthiness
- Fighting capabilities
- Operational readiness
- Living conditions of troops
- Rank structure
- Terms of service
- Welfare
- Re-organisation of the army
- Vision for the army in 2000.

While General Raina was busy preparing himself for his new responsibility, Ninette Raina too got busy with packing, as their home in Shimla, Command House, had to be vacated. Her feelings at the thought of moving from Shimla to New Delhi were as under:

> Our last weeks in Shimla were very hectic. The weather had become warm, clear sky, and all the flowers were blooming. But in conformity with army life, one had to keep ready to move at short notice! In this case of Tappy's transfer, we were lucky! We had two and a half months' notice. But the time passed very quickly. I also felt a passing pang at the absence of my father-in-law, late Rai Sahib A. N. Raina. If he had been alive, he would have been extremely proud of his son, Tapu. Unfortunately, he had passed away in 1966 and did not live to see his youngest son's triumph; but, at the same time, the dear old man was at least spared the agony of seeing his darling grandson, Jyoti, go!

Packing had to start again! Pack, when the weather was so good; when the thrushes sang so beautifully, every morning and evening. They sauntered the whole day on the roof, black and navy blue with a yellow beak. Pack the household, when the hills resounded with the call of birds and monkeys . . . it was a sad task indeed!

Our dogs, seeing everything disappearing into crates and trunks were worried, then alarmed, and our golden retriever would hide herself behind some curtains and whine! At night all three dogs would sleep at the side of our beds and nose us during the night, to make sure we did not run away and abandon them.

Never in my life did I want to see boxes again! I would have got rid of them all, but for our daughter, Anita, who could not bear to part with anything of her father and who would need them one day.

On Saturday, 31st May, when Shimla was at its most beautiful and inviting, we went down the hill to the heat and dust of the plains, like a travelling circus — Budgerigars[139] in the car, parrot and dogs in a vehicle behind, with the cages and the luggage! The whole crowd went, screeching and barking, all the way down to Delhi. It rained cats and dogs that night and it saved us a lot of discomfort from the heat.

When the time came for finally saying goodbye to Shimla, there were three options before the Raina family for their move to Delhi; to travel by road, by air or by rail in a saloon.[140] The rail

---

[139] A small, brightly coloured, chirping bird often kept as a pet in Britain.

[140] GOC-in-C Western Command had at his disposal a Saloon provided by Northern Railway. The saloon was originally made for the Prince of Wales. Fortunately, the colonial era comfortable furniture, fittings and tapestry had been retained. It's a whole rail Bogey (Wagon), compartmentalised into four: a lounge-cum-study, a large bedroom with twin beds and attached bathroom, a coupé for personal staff officer and a pantry. The attendant travelled in a coupé of the adjacent bogey. The saloon seemed to have special suspension as the movement was smooth, cushiony and quiet, thus a great deal of important official secretarial work could also be done.

option was the most luxurious mode of travel, but it was overruled for various logistic reasons. Anita, of course, wanted to go by helicopter as she had never gone up in one. Rule books were scoured to find if she could. To everyone's amusement it was found that while the general's dog could go in the helicopter, his daughter could not! Thus, the road mode was chosen. Because of being summer, an early start was made from Shimla to New Delhi on 31st May 1975. The Rainas made a quiet entry into the Army House.

Shortly after the formal announcement of Tappy Raina's promotion and appointment as the next Chief, Lieutenant Colonel Ravi Mahajan, was sent to Army Headquarters to familiarise himself with the internal working of the COAS Secretariat, as Military Assistant to the Chief of Army Staff (designate). Lieutenant Colonel (later Brigadier) Umesh Saxena, MA to COAS, General G.G. Bewoor, welcomed Ravi and briefed him on the nuances of functioning of the COAS Secretariat. The organisation of the Secretariat and charter of duties of its staff were explained to Ravi Mahajan, who found the Civilian Staff Officers (CSOs) of the Secretariat very experienced, mature and competent in their duties. He also familiarised himself with the processing of cases, both, within the Army Headquarters and the Ministry of Defence; as also the handling of complaints/petitions and minutes of various periodic conferences, that were held at AHQ, including the Chiefs of Staff Committee. Thus, the take-over of the new Chief's Secretariat on the relinquishment of the post by General Bewoor, was seamless.

Chief of the Army Staff, Indian Army

General and Mrs Bewoor very thoughtfully had vacated the Army House, the official residence of COAS, much before the arrival of Rainas from Shimla. When the Rainas arrived at the Army

House,[141] on 31st May 1975, Ninette found it to be a spacious old Lutyens Bungalow on Rajaji Marg (formerly King George's Avenue), which had been improved in instalments over the years by successive occupants. The bungalow consisted of some original rooms, built around an enclosed courtyard and covered veranda. It took her a full week to familiarise herself with its numerous nooks and corners and find her way in that maze! Her first impressions of living in the Army House were:

> The garden and the lawns were a dream. So here, at last we were going to open all our personal possessions, accumulated in our life-time, knowing that at last, this time, these should stay put in the same place for some time. But still the house looked bare, the rooms were so big.
>
> I must recall here something quite hilarious. Did you know that an Army Officer's wife, as the Lady of the House— popularly known as LOH, has no private life? You can't organise your bedroom as you wish because the devoted *sahayak* (helper) would tidy it his own way. And always the only beneficiary of this order would be the "Sahib"! If the LOH's slippers had been mislaid by him, well, that's just too bad! He would bring them to you with a debonair smile but his sole interest was the officer!
>
> Life for us became very serious now. Tappy's appointment as COAS Indian Army came about during a delicate period of post-independence history of India. However, for me, as the President of Army Wives Welfare Association (AWWA), I

---

[141] Prior to General (later FM) K.M. Carriapa's appointment as first Indian C-in-C on 15th January 1949, the British C-in-C used to live at Teen Murti House. General Carriapa was already occupying the house on King George's Avenue, when he was GOC-in-C Western Command. On his promotion and appointment as C-in-C Indian Army, he opted to continue staying in the same house. It thus became the Army House, official residence of all his successors. Teen Murti became the official residence of Prime Minister of India. Mr Jawahar Lal Nehru occupied this sprawling house, which came to be known as Teen Murti Bhawan. After Mr Nehru's death in May 1964, Teen Murti Bhawan was converted into a Memorial of first PM of India!

could keep myself busy in welfare activities relating to problems of many war widows and families of all ranks of the Army.

COAS Secretariat

To assist the COAS, a small secretariat was authorised. The organisation and establishment of the COAS Secretariat included Officers, JCOs and ORs who formed the military component. In addition, some civilian gazetted and non-gazetted staff was also authorised.

The secretariat was headed by an officer of the rank of Lt. Colonel, appointed as the Military Assistant (MA) to COAS, assisted by an officer of the rank of Major as Deputy MA to COAS. The COAS was also authorised two ADCs in the rank of Captain and a JCO ADC in the rank of Subedar Major. The other Military Staff included a JCO PA and two Clerks GD (SD) belonging to Army Service Corps (ASC). In addition, one Despatch Rider (DR) was attached from the pool of AHQ (SD Branch).

The civilian gazetted staff included two Civilian Staff Officers (CSO) as GSO -2, a PS to COAS and one PA. The civilian non gazetted staff comprised of a PA, four Clerks one Record Sorter/Daftry and Jamadar each, and four peons.

Lieutenant Colonel Mahajan, who had been AMS to the GOC-in-C Western Command, was now appointed Military Assistant (MA) to COAS[142]. Major Yogesh Prasad also belonged to 14 Kumaon (Gwalior) and was a former ADC to the General, was appointed Deputy Military Assistant (Dy. MA). Captain (later Brigadier) Dara Jahangir Govadia, a Gold Medal winner from OTS Madras (Chennai), commissioned in The Naga Regiment, was

---

[142] Ravi Mahajan, who the reader must be familiar with, was known to Tappy Raina from the time he joined 4th Battalion, Gwalior Infantry as 2nd Lt at Amritsar, where Tappy was the Bn 2 I/C. Ravi again served under the Command of Tappy as CO, at Ferozpur. On promotion as Lt Col, Ravi again had the opportunity to serve as CO of The Naga Regiment, during Indo-Pak War in East Pakistan in 1971, as part of 2 Corps Commanded by Tappy.

selected to be the ADC. He was soon joined by Captain Swatantra Kumar Sapru,[143] popularly known as "Sherry", who was not only from 14 Kumaon (Gwalior) (later 5 Mech) but had also been ADC to the General when he was GOC 2 Corps. Sapru's father, late Lieutenant Colonel G.N. Sapru, and Tappy Raina had been batchmates at OTA, Mhow, in 1941-42. Sapru was also known to Captain Jyoti Raina, the deceased son of the General. Sapru had been Joe's senior in "I" Sqn at NDA Khadakvasla, and later he was Joe's Senior Subaltern in 14 Kumaon (Gwalior).

Thus General Raina had on his personal staff officers who belonged to the two Regiments, whose Colonel, he was. Moreover, these officers were well known to him and he could trust them as members of his family. In addition to the above staff, the COAS was also authorised a JCO (Sub Maj) ADC. Subedar Major (later Honorary Captain) Dalip Singh, 11 Kumaon was selected as the JCO ADC to COAS.

Two civilian staff officers (GSO-2) were authorised on the strength of COAS Secretariat. Shri Hari Krishan and Shri Ukil were two highly efficient CSOs, who were already posted in the COAS Secretariat. Shri Hari Krishan was later replaced by Shri R.G. Nair. These two CSOs not only presided over the clerical staff but also kept the files moving not only within the Army HQ but also with the Ministry of Defence and Cabinet Secretariat (Military Wing).

Taking Over as COAS

It was customary for the outgoing COAS to vacate the "Chair" of his appointment in the afternoon of the last day of his service and prior to the arrival of his successor. General Bewoor was bid a ceremonial farewell by Lieutenant General Vohra, the then VCOAS along with the PSOs of Army HQ on 31st May 1975.

General Raina assumed the appointment of COAS on 1st June 1975, but was formally received at Army HQ the following day, i.e. on Monday, 2nd June 1975. Since 1st June was a Sunday, the

---

[143] He was born on 15th August 1947, the Independence Day of India!

new "Chief" did not want to disturb all concerned at Army Headquarters.

Exactly at 9.00 a.m. on 2nd June 1975, General Raina left the Army House for Army HQ, located in South Block of the Central Secretariat. The newly appointed ADC to COAS, Captain Dara J. Govadia of The Naga Regiment, sat ramrod straight on the co-driver's seat in the staff car, trying his best not to show that he was overwhelmed by the occasion.

Lieutenant General Vohra, VCOAS[144] accompanied by Colonel Teg Bahadur Kapur, Director C&W AG's Branch, received General Raina, and escorted him to the saluting dais. Meanwhile, as soon as the Chief's staff car came level with the alighting point, on the lawns outside South Block, the Guard of Honour by the 8th Battalion, The Maratha Light Infantry[145], already standing at attention (*saavdhaan* position), smartly presented arms (*salami shastra*), while the brass band played the "General Salute". After inspecting the Guard of Honour, General Raina complimented the officer commanding the guard of honour for its smart turnout and excellent drill.

Thereafter, Lieutenant General A.M. Vohra introduced General Raina, to the PSOs[146], E-in-C and Military Secretary[147] of Army HQ. The introduction to these stalwarts was a mere formality, as the General knew each one of them well. The ritual only marked the ceremony of taking over by the new Chief. Thereafter, the

---

[144] The VCOAS, in addition to overseeing the Directors (now Dir Gen) of Military Operations and Intelligence, also represented the COAS in his absence.

[145] This Battalion was selected for duties at Rashtrapati Bhavan. Lt. Col. Keshav Puntambaker was the CO.

[146] DCOAS, AG, QMG, MGO and E-in-C were the Principal Staff Officers at Army HQ to assist the COAS in their respective area of responsibility. Each one of them had direct access to the Chief and to the Ministry of Defence on many matters.

[147] The Military Secretary (MS) is the confidential advisor to the COAS on all matters pertaining to posting, promotion and other matters pertaining to all officers of the Indian Army. The Military Secretary manages the corps of officers including their career progression, assignments and complaints.

VCOAS guided the new Chief to his office on the first floor of South Block. The lift[148] was waiting for the Chief; it carried him to the first floor of the South Block, which housed the COAS, Staff Officers and secretarial staff of his Secretariat.

The secretariats of the VCOAS and the DCOAS were located in adjoining rooms to the COAS Secretariat. The Defence Minister's set-up was only separated from that of Chief's, by the office of the Defence Secretary and a Conference Room. The Secretariat of the Chief of Naval Staff (CNS) was a few rooms away from the COAS's office.

It was a co-incidence that on the day General Raina, took over the appointment of COAS, Shri D.R. Kohli, ICS[149] succeeded Shri Govind Narain, ICS, as the new Defence Secretary in Ministry of Defence.

As the new COAS entered the portal of his office, the Stick Orderly[150] gave a smart salute. The mundane task of opening the highly polished and heavy teak door belonged to the stately "Daftari" (a civilian post higher than that of a peon), who on that day, was turned out in his starched "whites" and turban. As soon as General Raina arrived in his office,[151] there was a battery of photographers and press reporters, led by Major (later Colonel) P.N. Khera, AEC, PRO (Army), who captured that historic mo-

---

[148] During Tappy's entire tenure as COAS, he mostly walked up the stairs to the first floor, where the COAS Secretariat was situated.

[149] Shri Kohli remained in the post of Defence Secretary during most of the tenure of Gen Raina as COAS and Chairman, Chiefs of Staff Committee.

[150] The Stick Orderly is a soldier who is drawn from the Chief's regiment. He is always in the regimental ceremonial dress. The stick that he carries is really a small silver-knobbed baton which has a silver scroll on which are inscribed the regiment's battle honours. Outside the Chief's office, he has only one function: to look smart and show the Chief's pride in his regiment and *vice versa*.

[151] Unlike the present practice, outgoing and incoming Chiefs did not carry out personal handing/taking over of the charge, nor did the wives and family members attend the solemn ceremony. It was conducted in a crisp and matter of fact military protocol and procedure.

ment with their cameras. This was followed by questions from eager accredited press reporters.

As soon as the initial excitement was over, Ravi placed before General Raina the Red Folder which was used in the COAS Secretariat for papers requiring the Chief's signatures. That morning it had only one sheet, the "Order of the Day" issued by Tappy on assuming his new appointment as COAS. The special "Order of the Day" contained Tappy Raina's first direct communication to the Indian Army as COAS which would go down to every soldier through the channels of the chain of command of the Indian Army. He then briefly addressed the press.

The same day, General Raina attended the Chiefs of Staff Committee (COSC) meeting, which was followed by courtesy calls by Shri SC Katoch, Financial Advisor (Defence) and Shri Har Mandar Singh, IAS, Joint Secretary (G), MoD. Later he met some PSOs and Directors of Arms and Services. In the afternoon he recorded his message for broadcast to the Indian Army as a "Special Order of the Day", followed by an interview for All India Radio (now Akash Vani).

Being his first day in office, Tappy Raina did no real office work. Next day, at 0930 hours, he presided over his first PSOs conference, which traditionally was held in the COAS's office. The MA to the COAS, as the Secretary, recorded the minutes of the conference.

At 1200 hours, the General donned his Summer Ceremonial Dress No 2, with full medals, Sam-Browne Leather belt with sword, went to make a courtesy call on Shri Fakhruddin Ali Ahmed, President of India and Supreme Commander of the Armed Forces at Rashtrapati Bhavan. Later that day, Shri D.R. Kohli, ICS, the Defence Secretary made a courtesy call on COAS. The next day Tappy Raina called on Sardar Swaran Singh, the Defence Minister (Raksha Mantri), who incidentally had been the longest serving cabinet minister; for one score and four years. A few days later he formally called on Prime Minister Indira Gandhi at her office in South Block.

Just a few days after his formal call on the Prime Minister, Tappy Raina sought an official appointment to meet the PM and, soon thereafter, met her at her office. Prior to that, he had already discussed the subject matter of this meeting with the Prime Minister, with the Defence Minister (Raksha Mantri) Shri Swaran Singh.

Briefly, and in his typically succinct manner, General Raina explained to the Prime Minister the Indian Army's defective peacetime posture which created a difficulty in the mobilisation of the army. This difficulty resulted in unacceptable delay despite the super-efficient railways. Tappy Raina gave his own example as GOC 2 Corps during Indo-Pak War of 1971. While the war in East Pakistan was still going on, he had received orders for 2 Corps to take over a new operational responsibility in the Western Theatre. This was even before the surrender by the Pakistan Army had taken place. His troops, deployed in the Eastern Theatre, were suddenly required to switch for a fresh deployment in the Western Theatre to meet the threat from Pakistan. This switch was almost simultaneous with the surrender of the Pakistani Army in East Pakistan.

While the switch from East to West had taken place with speed, but complete demobilisation from the East and fresh mobilisation for deployment in the West took many months. This had caused immense privation to troops who were bivouacked in the open and remained separated from their families left behind in earlier peace time duty stations. The attendant administrative problems, as also the cost to the exchequer, had been horrendous. The PM was quick to understand the problem.

Following General Raina's meeting with the Prime Minister, the Cabinet Committee on Security (CCS) assembled at the Army HQ Operations Room, a few days later. Here, Tappy Raina gave a brief introduction after which the details of the proposed Mobilisation Plan of the Indian Army were presented by Major General (later General and COAS) Arun Vaidya, DMO, and Lieutenant General A.N. Mathur, QMG. This was followed by a lucid summing up by Tappy Raina. His plan to redeploy Indian Army formations and units to new peacetime locations[152] was accepted in totality.

Improvement in the Army's Posture

During Tappy Raina's tenure as the Army Chief, three historical events took place. The chronological order of these events is as under:

1. Improvement in the Army's operational posture.
2. Imposition of the National Emergency by the Government of India under PM Indira Gandhi, on the night of 25/26th June 1975.
3. Establishment of the soldiers' welfare structure in the Indian Army.

General Raina then began planning his tours and visits to each of the Army Commands to familiarise himself with the ground situation. At the same time, he explained his proposed plans of improvement in the posturing of the army and other welfare measures that were being initiated.

---

[152] The British had located the then Indian Army to suit their strategic interests along the border with Afghanistan, to meet the threat from Soviet Russia. However after the partition of India in 1947, and despite the war in Kashmir (1947-48), the Indian Army remained on a low priority of the Government of India, on the misplaced belief that a "non-aligned" and "non-violent" country like India would not face any security threat to its border from its neighbours!

The wake-up call provided by the war with China in 1962 and Pakistan in 1965, respectively, resulted in the expansion of the Indian Army establishment, as also of the other two Services. However, the peacetime locations of units and formations remained *ad hoc*.

The defeat of Pakistani Army and the resultant break-up of Pakistan, and the birth of a new nation, Bangladesh in 1971, demanded a reorientation of the government policy of billeting the Armed Forces.

Defence Ministers (Raksha Mantri)

It may be pertinent to mention here that General Raina's dynamism was adequately matched by an equally understanding and zestful Defence Minister, Swaran Singh. The latter, however, relinquished his portfolio on 1st December 1975, and Mrs. Indira Gandhi[153] herself took over as Defence Minister.

On 21st December 1975, Indira Gandhi relinquished charge of the Ministry of Defence and inducted Bansi Lal,[154] a close confidante and a former Chief Minister of Haryana. Earlier, Bansi Lal had been appointed Minister without Portfolio in Mrs. Gandhi's cabinet on 1st December 1975.

To assist him in his new duties, Bansi Lal had brought along Shri S.K. Misra, IAS, popularly called "Chappy Misra". This officer of the Indian Administrative Service of the Haryana cadre was considered by other bureaucrats in the Ministry of Defence as a "bull in a China shop". However, Chappy Misra had done wonders as Secretary, Tourism Department, in the Government of Haryana. A new ad-hoc appointment as Joint Secretary (Policy and Planning), was created and a room adjoining the Defence Minister's Office was provided to Chappy Misra.

Though, Chappy Misra was appointed as a Joint Secretary, equated to the rank of major general (and equivalent ranks of the Navy and Air Force), but due to his close proximity with the Defence Minister, it appeared that he wanted to become close to and familiar with the three Services Chiefs. He started with hosting dinners to which the three Service Chiefs were invited. General Raina politely declined such invitations.

To the credit of Shri Bansi Lal, it must be said that once he was convinced of the case put up by Army Headquarters, he took upon

---

[153] Indira Gandhi held the charge of Defence Minister from 1st to 21st December 1975. She once again held this charge from 14th January 1980 to 15th January 1982.

[154] He was Chief Minister of Haryana from 1968 to 1975 and came to be known as the architect of modern Haryana before his induction into the Cabinet of Indira Gandhi on 1st December 1975.

himself to use his influence with various State Governments and Ministries, to get the Army's requirement of land and other civil-military liaison matters, resolved. However, the case for allotment of funds was a harder nut to crack because the Army's requirement now looked considerable. It virtually became a battle of attrition. The gap between the requirement and what was being offered by the government was too wide. Since the army's needs were genuine and since General Raina was not a person to give up, a few detailed and strongly worded notes, with the COAS's signature, eventually got the Army a fairly large allocation approved for the long term plan. The effect of that long term plan, and of the determination that led to its approval, is visible today on ground.[155]

Southern Command

On 25th June 1975, Tappy and Ninette Raina went on the General's first planned official tour to Bikaner in Southern Command, where Lieutenant General (later Gen) O.P. Malhotra was the GOC-in-C. General Raina was accompanied by Lieutenant Colonel Mahajan and Captain Govadia. The day temperature at the end of June was not particularly exciting, as there was dust and a hot wind (locally called the "Loo") blowing in the town.

On arrival at Bikaner Airport, they were met by Lieutenant General and Mrs. Malhotra and few other senior officers and their wives. Ninette Raina felt that it must have caused a lot of trouble to the army wives to come out of their cool darkened houses in that stupendous heat. She remembered how she herself was gasping and yet, they were scheduled to stay there for a couple of days. But that did not happen.

After lunch the Chief came to the room and told his wife, "Pack up, we are going back to Delhi immediately"! Surprised, she asked, "Why so suddenly"? He shrugged and answered, "I have been recalled".

---

[155] New military stations have sprung up and there is great improvement in the accommodation situation all over in various military stations and cantonments.

General and Mrs Raina, along with their entourage, left Bikaner by the IAF aircraft within the hour while everybody at Bikaner was mystified. On the drive home to Army House in Delhi, Ninette vividly remembered that the streets of Delhi were deserted. Perhaps, due to the heat and the strong sun, hardly any traffic or people were seen!

Ninette recalled that later in the afternoon that same day, soon after they reached home, a high civil official of the Government came to Army House and had a brief meeting with the General. This was followed by a meeting at the Prime Minister's house the same evening. Ninette Raina believed that there must have been some urgent work that had cropped up, for which her husband had to cut short his trip. The rest of that evening the Rainas spent some leisure time at home with their dogs.

Chapter 27

National Emergency, 1975

Early the next morning, i.e. on 26th June 1975, Tappy and Ninette Raina were enjoying their morning cup of tea and listening to All India Radio (now Akash Vani), when the news about the declaration of "Emergency"[156] having been promulgated in the country by the Government of India, was announced. Years later, Ninette could still remember how Tappy was left holding his cup of tea mid-air, staring at the transistor radio! The Emergency remained clamped for the next twenty-one months, i.e., for nearly two thirds of Tappy Raina's tenure as the Chief of the Army Staff. It now dawned on the Rainas why they had been recalled from Bikaner.

A lot has been written about the third and the most draconian Emergency which quite clearly had been declared, not to safeguard the country but to protect Indira Gandhi's position as Prime Minister.

On 26th June 1975, Shri Fakhruddin Ahmad, President of India, on the advice of Prime Minister Indira Gandhi, exercised his powers conferred on him by Article 352 of the Constitution of India to declare Emergency in the country because the security of India was threatened by internal disturbances. The Government of India immediately assumed extraordinary powers. More than 600 leaders of opposition parties were arrested under security legislation, rigid press censorship was imposed, twenty-six organisations

[156] A controversial period of incipient authoritarianism in India, that lasted from June 1975 to March 1977.

deemed to be of "extremist ideology" were banned and the judicial protection of the Fundamental Rights granted by the Constitution stood suspended.

Parliament, with a massive majority of the Indian National Congress, formally approved the imposition of the Emergency and, subsequently, confirmed various Presidential ordinances. Parliament also initiated sweeping constitutional amendments designed to diminish the power of the judiciary relative to that of the legislature and to further enhance executive power. Indira Gandhi and her supporters sought to justify the Emergency by the disorders that had preceded it. Her critics accused her of using the Emergency to remain in power despite a ruling against the validity of her election in 1971 by the Allahabad High Court on 12th June 1975, and state election results adverse to Congress.

What about the Indian Army? "We didn't even feel that Emergency was implemented", said a former COAS, General Shankar Roychowdhury, PVSM, who at that time was a middle-level officer in the Armoured Corps. But what about the corridors of power, the South Block? Said Lieutenant Colonel Ravi Mahajan: "Nothing happened there too, at least not in the corridors, inside South Block of the Central Secretariat!"

Ravi recalls that he came out of his office twice. Once he walked past the Defence Secretary's office towards the Defence Minister's Secretariat. Later, during the lunch break, he ventured further afield towards the Foreign Ministry and PM's offices, located in South Block; nothing there too! Inside the Army Chief's Secretariat, too, things ticked normally.

Air Chief Marshal O.P. Mehra, PVSM, the Chief of Air Staff (CAS) and Chairman, Chiefs of Staff Committee, dropped in briefly in the afternoon to meet General Raina. But such calls, especially by the Air Chief were quite normal; he was the only Service Chief whose office was not housed in the South Block. Air HQ was located at a distance from South Block near Central Vista. He, therefore, often dropped in to have a chat with Tappy whenever he visited South Block.

At Army Headquarters, normal routine continued to rule. The Principal Staff Officers met at the Chief's office for the weekly

PSOs conference. Enlarged monthly Director's conferences were held as usual. Not a word was ever uttered about the Emergency, nor, as the Minutes of these meetings will no doubt show, recorded.

The army's assistance was sought to enable the holding of political rallies on "Defence Land" in various Military Stations and to provide succour to the public at Shrimati Indira Gandhi's mammoth political meetings. Such requests were politely and firmly refused. Similarly, the PM's younger son, Sanjay Gandhi's dictum that army officers in uniform should attend the Saragarhi[157] Memorial Day at Ferozepur Cantonment, was ignored by the Army.

Only on one occasion did Shrimati Indira Gandhi, quite uncharacteristically and publicly, display bad judgement. During a visit to J&K, while addressing troops of the Jammu Garrison, she had the then President of Indian National Congress, Shri Devakanta Barua[158], allowed to be seated on the dias!

The Emergency made absolutely no difference to the Rainas and their life went on as usual with a whirling routine of meetings, socials, welfare and official tours. They did notice some impact of it in the daily life of the average citizen. Traffic on the roads became orderly, the public was more disciplined and public transport was punctual. Who would complain about such improvement in the daily life of people, especially in a metro city like New Delhi?

---

[157] In 1897, at a small outpost called Saragarhi, 40 miles (65 km) away from the British garrison town of Kohat, in what is now Pakistan, 21 Sikh soldiers of the 4th Battalion of The Sikh Regiment stood their ground against an onslaught of approximately 10,000 enemy tribesmen. Their gallantry in fighting to the bitter end cemented their reputation as brave and devoted to duty soldiers of the Indian Army. A festival is held at Saragarhi Memorial at Firozpur Cantonment on 12th September in memory of the valour of Sikh soldiers who died in action at Saragarhi in NWFP.

[158] President of the INC during the Emergency (1975-77), chiefly remembered for his sycophancy to Prime Minister Indira Gandhi, encapsulated by his proclamation that "India is Indira. Indira is India"! He later parted ways with her and joined Congress (Urs), later renamed as Indian Congress (Socialist). He was the Governor of Bihar from 1st February 1971 to 4th February 1973.

To those who were already living in disciplined and orderly environments like those of the Armed Forces of India, the imposition of Emergency did not make much difference. Like most ordinary citizens and as an army wife, Ninette Raina, appreciated the change from a disorganised to an orderly way of life in the day to day activities of the average citizen. People had become punctual and polite. They proved themselves capable of leading an organised life. During that period, it was proved that Indian people could compare with any other highly organised and disciplined society.

Two and a half years later, on 18th January 1977 Indira Gandhi announced relaxation of Emergency Rule in preparation for parliamentary elections[159] to be held in March 1977. After the Emergency was lifted, allegations were made about the "excesses" in the implementation of family planning programmes. In Indian Army, family planning education had been introduced soon after independence. As a result, most families of Armed Forces personnel voluntarily restricted their family to two children. Ninette Raina, as President AWWA, and her team were constantly monitoring the impact of Emergency on the Army families. About the impact of that period on her own life Ninette Raina recalled:

> At times, I could tell that Tappy was tense! Since the death of our son, "Joe", he was working much harder and his nerves took the brunt of it. And when you direct and control such a vast army like ours, you are bound to feel the pressure. Problems were unending. He could also be very direct and outspoken. Both the Prime Ministers, whom Tappy served, fully realised that Tappy was very direct, honest, truthful and tough person! I am sure that politicians, of whatever political ideology, did not find Tappy easy to bend to their whims!
>
> Tappy never minced his words. To disabuse the minds of the public regarding the role of the Armed Forces in general and the Indian Army in particular during "Emergency", Tappy de-

[159] The Indian National Congress Party led by Indira Gandhi lost these elections to the newly formed Janata Party.

cided to address a Rotary Club meeting at Hotel Imperial, New Delhi. There he publicly declared that the Indian Army was an apolitical organisation, serving the cause of the country's defence and national security, both external and internal. This was reported next day in bold headlines of most newspapers published from Delhi, despite the press censorship that was imposed!

Yet, Ninette was worried for Tappy who was deeply engrossed in trying to better the lives of all ranks of Indian Army and their families. As she later recalled:

> I never talked "shop" with Tappy. On the one hand, I wanted his mind taken off work at home, and, on the other hand, I did not want to appear to be prying! He never told me anything that was confidential. In fact he got very annoyed at such talking by some senior officers' wives. He maintained that if ever there was a security leak, it was the husbands whom he blamed "for opening their mouths too wide".
>
> Tappy did not have many illusions about people but he loved them just the same because he said they were only human, and he was one of them.
>
> There were sometimes hectic days and trying ones also! From June 1975 to March 1977 Tappy functioned for most of his tenure as COAS, under the Emergency when Shrimati Indira Gandhi was the Prime Minister of India. From March 1977 to May 1978, before his retirement from Army Service, Tappy functioned under another Prime Minister, Shri Morarji Desai of the Janata Party. It made no difference whatsoever to Tappy's work or his life as COAS. He was totally apolitical and his sole concern was the Indian Army. Only his staff officers could say what really happened during those years. He never spoke about it at home; besides we had a busy social life, and there was no time for any long conversations between us! I very often went to sleep while he was still closeted in his Study at home, and sometimes, when I woke in the morning (and I was an early riser!), I would find that Tappy was already gone!

For days we lived side by side, without having much time for ourselves! Once I asked him, "Are we married or simply pretending?" And he only roared with laughter! He never told me anything confidential about his work and I did not ask! We were disciplined people, and a little more discipline did not make any difference.

Chapter 28

Operational Readiness of the Indian Army

"No alarm. No complacency. We are aware of the efforts of Pakistan to seek accretions to her Army by acquisition of military hardware from abroad. Any such military accretions which augment the offensive potential of a neighbouring country and, in particular, those which are on a large scale and disproportionate to the essential operational requirements, are a matter of deep concern to us."

~ Gen T.N. Raina, MVC, COAS
Indian Army in January 1976

Immediately after taking over as Chief of the Army Staff, General Raina undertook the long felt need for improvement in the Operational Posture of the Army and, consequently, of its state of readiness for war. This implied moving various fighting formations and units of the army, with all their vehicles and equipment, from their erstwhile peace time locations to their respective operational sectors and areas in the event of future mobilisation for war.

Simla Agreement, 1972

The surrender of the Pakistan Army[160] in East Pakistan, led by Lieutenant General A.A.K. Niazi to Lieutenant General J.S. Aurora, GOC-in-C Eastern Command, Indian Army, at Dacca on 16th December 1971, left both the political and military leadership in West Pakistan shell-shocked. Zulfiqar Ali Bhutto, who had taken over as Prime Minister of Pakistan accepted the terms of the Simla[161] Agreement-1972,[162] as a result of which the Indian Government agreed to hand over all military POWs and CIs (civil internees) to Pakistan. It was also agreed to re-demarcate the Cease Fire Line as agreed under the Karachi Agreement, 1949, which came to be known as the Line of Control (LOC) in J&K and POK.

However, once Pakistan received back all her POWs, the younger officers of the Pakistani Army itched for a showdown with India to avenge the defeat in East Pakistan and the creation of Bangladesh. They blamed India for that.

Pakistan's Aggressive Posture

General Raina, even as GOC-in-C Western Command, had been aware of developments in Pakistan which could lead to aggression by the Pakistani Army. The prevailing military situation was best analysed by Dr K. Subrahmanyam, Director, Institute for Defence

---

[160] Approximately 100,000 prisoners of war and civil internees were brought from East Pakistan to India and detained in various POW Camps.

[161] Simla or Shimla, a hill town at an altitude of 2,100 meters (approximately 6,900 feet) in the lap of Himalaya, is the capital of Himanchal Pradesh. It was the official summer capital of the British Government of India from 1864 to 1947. Shimla was the location of many important meetings and conventions throughout this period.

[162] The Simla Agreement on bilateral relations between India and Pakistan was signed by India's Prime Minister Indira Gandhi and Prime Minister of Pakistan, Z. A. Bhutto, on 2nd July 1972 at Simla. It remained a benchmark in Indo-Pak relations for some time.

Studies and Analyses (IDSA), New Delhi, who summed it up in an article published in the *Onlooker* magazine of 15th May 1975:

> Pakistan's Armed "Might" is today stronger than ever before. It has made up all losses of the 1971 War. From China, it has acquired sophisticated missile boats. With the U.S. ban lifted, it will seek modern aircraft. Yet, another military reverse will shake the unity of Pakistan. And Pakistan knows India is still stronger. Rationally, it (Pak) shouldn't start a war. What India has still to guard against is irrational behaviour from the Pakistani ruling elite!

India, therefore, had once again started worrying about the possibility of another war with Pakistan. Such an apprehension was not borne out of a sense of paranoia, but out of a series of events which revived memories of the past. The Pakistani Armed Forces had by then made good the losses they suffered in 1971 War. In fact, they had exceeded their former strength. Not only that; their entire military force could now be concentrated on India's western borders, improving Pakistan's ability to deploy a force much bigger than it could deploy in the previous twenty-eight years. The Pakistani Army by then had fourteen Infantry Divisions, two Armoured Divisions and three Armoured Brigades. Their Air Force and Navy had also been modernised and strengthened.

As GOC-in-C Western Command, General Raina was fully alive to these developments in Pakistan, since he was the operational Army Commander responsible for most of the Western border with Pakistan. From the moment, in mid-March, when Government of India announced his name as the successor of General G.G. Bewoor, due to retire[163] on 31st May 1975, General Raina started applying his mind to the overall capability of the Indian

---

[163] General G.G. Bewoor, PVSM, took over as COAS on 15th January 1973 from General Sam Manekshaw, MC. General Bewoor who reached the age of superannuation of 58 years in 1974, was granted extension of tenure up to 31st May 1975.

Army to meet the lurking threat from across the border. According to the noted defence analyst, Dr K. Subrahmanyam:

> India had undisputed superiority in numbers in the Air — IAF had around 33 combat squadrons as against the PAF's 16 or 17 squadrons. The Indian Navy too, both quantitatively and qualitatively, was far superior to Pakistan's navy. But in the case of land forces, the Indian Army had a very small margin over the Pakistani Army, and the Indian and Pakistani forces, in terms of deployable forces, had a near-parity.

Logistically speaking, because of Pakistan Army's interior lines of communications and shorter mobilisation time, they had certain advantages over Indian Army in being able to deploy their combat formations and units in battle positions in a much shorter period. Therefore, if the Pakistani Army were to start a war and achieve surprise, they could grab and hold some territory in a short war, which could be used for strategic bargaining. After all, in both the wars, in 1965 and 1971, the Pakistan Army's General Staff had planned to do exactly that!

It was well appreciated that Pakistan could not fight a long war with India. At best it could only fight a war of some three to four weeks. But the history of the 1965 and 1971 wars could persuade the Pakistanis to believe that if they got some initial advantages in a short, quick war, its multiplier effect on India would be tremendous and traumatic, somewhat like what happened in 1962. The Pakistanis were encouraged to believe that they could achieve such a quick and easy victory in 1965. In 1971, presumably, they calculated that even if they lost East Pakistan, they would, to some extent, psychologically compensate their loss, by a quick victory on the Western front.

In understanding the defence needs of India and operational preparations at that juncture, there were certain basic facts which the Indian Government and Army had to bear in mind.

- India's efforts at normalising its relations with its neighbours in the North and in the West had limited success. Though Chinese support of dissidents on India's eastern border regions continued, dissidents trained and armed by China were increasingly becoming disenchanted. They started to return and join the mainstream of national life in India, in response to an offer of conciliation.

- Both China and Pakistan had increased their troop deployments close to India's borders. The troop strength of China's PLA in Tibet was well over 300,000, of whom not less than 180,000 were front troops. This was besides approximately 200,000 or more road building experts lodged in Gilgit area of Pakistan Occupied Kashmir (POK) for building the strategic Karakoram Highway[164]. They would also be available for any military action in that theatre in support of Pakistan. For its part, Pakistan, too, had stepped up its defence efforts significantly, and publicly disclosed the defence budget for 1975-76, showing an increase of over 25% over the previous year's budget.
- The increase in the manpower of Pakistani Army and the arms build-up achieved by them since 1972, were also taken note of. True to the promise he made on assuming power, Prime Minister Bhutto had not only made up Pakistan's equipment and troop losses of 1971, but had also raised at least three new Infantry Divisions and one Armoured Divisions, in addition to

---

[164] The Karakoram Highway (KKH), also known as Friendship Highway in China, built by the governments of Pakistan and China, was started in 1959 and completed in 1979. Pakistan initially favoured routing through Mintaka Pass. In 1966, China citing the fact that Mintaka would be more susceptible to air strikes recommended the steeper Khunjerab Pass instead. It is reported that about 810 Pakistanis and about 200 Chinese workers lost their lives, mostly in landslides and falls, while building this highway. Over 140 Chinese workers who died during the construction are buried in the Chinese cemetery in Gilgit. The route of the KKH traces one of the many paths of the ancient Silk Road.

The highway, connecting the Gilgit-Baltistan region to the ancient Silk Road, runs approximately 1,300 km (810 miles) from Kashgar, a city in the Xinjiang region of China, to Abbottabad in Pakistan. Owing largely to the dispute between India and Pakistan over the State of the Kashmir, the Karakoram Highway has strategic and military importance to these nations, particularly Pakistan and China, who are linking the Karakoram Highway to the southern port of Gwadar in Baluchistan.

modernising Pakistan Air Force. The Pakistani Navy, which had sustained serious losses in 1971, was not neglected. Sizeable bodies of reserve and para military forces had also been created. While most of the reserves would probably be used for internal security duties, at least 150,000 would be available as reinforcements for the regular forces.

The public in India was understandably concerned at this build-up of forces across the Indo-Pak border. This was especially so because Pakistan continued to be unwilling to normalise its relations with this country and planned to settle its differences with India by talking from "a position of strength".

The Government of India was not unaware that Mr Bhutto had internal compulsions for maintaining strong police and military forces. Although Mr Bhutto had claimed that in the past four years he had accomplished almost all foreign policy objectives that he had set for himself and his country, his domestic policies had not won for him many friends in the bifurcated Pakistan, especially in Baluchistan and the North West Frontier Province. Due to his disposition for authoritarianism, Bhutto had succeeded in alienating many leaders in Punjab, some of whom had been his trusted lieutenants. Even the local leadership of Sind, his home province, was not solidly behind him.

Counter-Insurgency

Before the liberation of Bangladesh, the insurgency in North East India derived active support from former East Pakistan and China. It raised its head in the Naga Hills and the Tuensang areas of Assam, followed by Mizoram and some parts of Assam. The Indian Army played a major part not only in defeating the hostile elements but also in winning the hearts and minds of the people, which led to the creation of the states of Nagaland and Mizoram, carved out of Assam state.

In the past, the Indian Army had been deployed in Nagaland and Mizoram, essentially in aid of the Civil Authorities, to ensure that the writ of the lawfully constituted Government of India was obeyed. Any acceleration of the process of normalisation whereby the Army could cease active participation in the maintenance of law and order and concentrate on its primary task of deterring external aggression, was to be welcomed. To the extent it could be perceived then, the revised role of the Army in Nagaland after the return of normalcy would be as in other states of India where the Army could be located as part of the overall deployment pattern, to move to battle locations in the event of hostilities breaking out. While so located, the Army is available to aid the civil authorities if and when necessary and requested.

The Government of India was not insensitive to the aspirations of the Nagas for autonomy. As a result of discussions with representatives of the Naga People's Convention, Prime Minister Nehru announced in the Parliament on 1st August 1960 that the Naga Hills and Tuensang Area (NHTA) would be re-constituted as a state called Nagaland. Thus, Nagaland was formally inaugurated as the 16th State of India on 1st December 1963 in accordance with the Sixteen Point Agreement which was signed with Prime Minister Pandit Nehru on 26th July 1960.

As per Clause 14 of the agreement, the Government of India accepted the demand for raising a separate Regiment in the Indian Army to be known as The Naga Regiment.[165] It was appreciated that a settlement in Nagaland would also have a salutary effect in Mizoram. This was because the genesis of insurgency, notwithstanding the diversion of aspirations expressed, had a commonality at the grass-root level, especially in contiguous areas such as Nagaland and Mizoram.

As far as the Pakistani Army was concerned, their cantonments were located close to the international border. The field formations of the Indian Army, however, had their peace time locations thou-

---

[165] Army HQ approved the raising of The Naga Regiment drawing its nucleus manpower from erstwhile "hostiles", who had surrendered and had been kept in rehabilitation camps. The new Regiment was affiliated to the Kumaon Regiment and its raising commenced on 1st November 1970, with class composition of 50% Nagas and 50% Other Hill Tribes (OHT) comprising of Kumaonis, Garhwalis and Gorkhas. The young Regiment took part in war in 1971 and again in 1999.

sands of miles in the hinterland. A number of India's existing cantonments, though geographically closer to borders, were actually occupied by regimental training centres of the various arms and services. These training establishments had been in those locations for several years, some even from the time when the British Indian Army was mainly fighting along the Durand Line in the North West Frontier Province. The various regiments had come to regard these as part of their private regimental estates with deep-rooted regimental traditions and sentiments. Some of these had even acquired land and other immovable assets with their regimental funds.

Lodged and located in this way, the movement and deployment of our field formations over such long distances, with the meagre resources of rail and road transportation, was time consuming and highly unrealistic. It was a nightmare for logistic staff at Army Headquarters. It was also a potentially dangerous and embarrassing situation for an action orientated Army Chief like General Raina.

Such an unrealistic and operationally unfavourable situation had been allowed to continue for various reasons, including the cost involved in setting up of new Military Stations, (instead of Cantonments)[166] in forward areas. Due to a misplaced belief that there would be a long enough warning period, there was reluctance to disturb the Regimental Training Centres on the ground of tradition, sentiment and even opposition by various senior serving and retired officers, including the Colonels of those Regiments.

When General Raina was the GOC-in-C Western Command, he was concerned and unhappy with the peacetime location of the formations and strategic units under his command. He expressed his views in no uncertain terms, particularly in the light of the experience of 1971, when we were spared such humiliation in October 1971, since Pakistan delayed opening the Western Front by

---

[166] The Government of India decided not to create new Military Stations under the Indian Cantonment Act 1924, which has been repealed by the Cantonment Act 2006.

almost four to six weeks, the period required for completion of the total mobilisation of Indian Army. However, in spite of such a close shave, the status quo remained.

That is why as soon as his appointment as COAS was formalised, General Raina immediately applied his mind to this major lacuna in the Army's Mobilisation Plan and the Operational Preparedness. During one of his visits to Army HQ as COAS (designate), the General one day walked into the office of the QMG and, with his characteristic smile, asked the latter's views on the existing operational mobilisation and deployment plans of the Indian Army. Lieutenant General A.N. Mathur, PVSM, who was from the Corps of Signals and a very competent and worthy QMG, had done his homework with some details, and personally shared General Raina's concern on this matter. He thus expressed his views on the matter with utmost frankness.

Appreciating this forthright exchange of views; General Raina impressed upon the QMG that, like good surgeons, their main concern should be for the patient's safety and health. If surgery and transplanting of various organs of the Army were required in the best strategic interest, then he as COAS would have no inhibitions regarding the shifting of Regimental Centres. "Operational Readiness" could not be subordinated to any traditions or sentiments. He, therefore, asked General Mathur to prepare a detailed alternative plan for peace-time location of the Indian Army's Field Formations and Training Centres. He was also to prepare related plans for operational movement and deployment within the time frame indicated by General Raina. The revised detailed Mobilisation Plan needed to be presented within a fortnight of Tappy Raina taking over as COAS.

For obvious reasons, the plan had to be prepared with utmost secrecy, with only a few people involved in its formulation. General Raina's priorities and aims were very clear: regimental sentiments and traditions had to be subordinated to operational compulsions of national importance.

As scheduled, soon after he took over as Chief of Army Staff, the revised proposed plans of the Indian Army's "Operational

Readiness & Posture" were duly presented to him by the concerned PSOs. These presentations were in great detail and lasted several hours. Because of General Raina's analytical mind, he raised several penetrating and pertinent questions. At the end of the briefing and discussion, he approved the plan in principle but directed his QMG to confirm certain details on the ground. This was to be done by actual visits to various locations in forward areas and Regimental Centres, without giving any indications or details of the proposed plan. Only then could the plans be processed further.

The revised plan involved moving several Regimental Training Centres to locations in the hinterland. At the same time, combat formations and units would move forward to stations vacated by these Training Centres, and to some new forward areas where new military stations, unlike Cantonments of olden days, would be built up from scratch.

Once, all the loose ends had been tied up and the finalised plan approved by General Raina, a time frame for the implementation of plan was decided upon. The completion of all moves and changes of location were visualised in the plan. To some in the Army and Government it seemed a tall order, a tremendously uphill task. However, it had to be done.

To implement this plan, Government approval and sanction of funds for the large-scale movement of troops, shifting of locations and creation of new Military Stations, for which land had to be acquired, had also to be obtained. The plan had major financial implications. There was also apprehension that to ascertain the exact financial implication would necessitate detailed surveys and calculation. That would be time consuming and could hold up the entire exercise, causing a delay of months. Something had to be done to get the plans approved on a war-footing for reasons of inescapable operational compulsion. This had to be accomplished without getting involved in "paper battles", so fondly fought by the bureaucrats in the Ministries of Defence and Finance.

General Raina personally and convincingly presented his proposed plan to Defence Minister Swaran Singh[167] and Prime Minister Indira Gandhi. The Prime Minister was so impressed by General Raina's lucid and well-reasoned logic that she at once agreed and asked for the proposal to be put up to her for formal approval.

The proposal was formalised and put up to Swaran Singh who forwarded it to Indira Gandhi. The file came back within a few days with the shortest and most direct noting by the Prime Minister, "Approved" and signed by Indira Gandhi herself.

The entire exercise was completed within a record time of a few weeks. This amply demonstrated the determination, zeal and drive that General Raina possessed. The tremendous professional rapport that he enjoyed with the Defence Minister and the Prime Minister spoke of the confidence they had in him as Chief of the Army.

No sooner was approval of above plan received that detailed coordination at the highest level with the concerned Command HQs was carried out. Draft time-bound Road and Rail Movement Tables had already been prepared and kept ready for action. The major role played by the Indian Railways in the implementation of this movement plan of the Army must be recorded here. Within the limitations and restrictions of security, the concerned members of the Railway Board were taken into confidence. They reacted

---

[167] Sardar Swaran Singh was India's longest-serving Union Cabinet Minister. He was best known for his role as India's External Affairs Minister, when he led the Indian delegation to the UN General Assembly in 1971 and highlighted the root cause of the conflict as the "brutal repression" of the populace in East Pakistan by the Pakistani military Government, the forced flight of East Pakistani refugees to India, and the Indian Army's subsequent victory in East Pakistan leading to the birth of Bangladesh.

After the declaration of the National Emergency on 25th June 1975, Indira Gandhi entrusted Sardar Swaran Singh with the amending of the Constitution in the light of past experiences. Based on recommendations of the Swaran Singh Committee, the Government incorporated several changes to the Constitution including the Preamble, through the 42nd Amendment of the Constitution of India, passed in 1976 which became effective on 3rd January 1977.

admirably and agreed to meet the Army's requirement with very few minor modifications. Detailed instructions were then issued to the concerned Command Headquarters. There were just no hold ups in the release of funds or in any other manner, by any official, once the Prime Minister's approval had been accorded. Actions were taken and works sanctioned and executed for addition and modification to existing buildings in various stations. Land was acquired on an emergency basis in forward locations.

The entire plan was executed and completed on schedule. The Regimental Centres though initially averse to the idea of moving out of their present stations, soon settled down with speed in their new surroundings. They were eventually happy as they were suitably compensated for their assets left behind. Thus, a seemingly impossible task was smoothly achieved.

It is, indeed, a tribute to the zealous leadership, tact, dynamism and drive of General Tappy Raina that the "Operational Readiness and Posture" of India's Army was considerably improved within a matter of months after his takeover as COAS. Here was a unique example of close and harmonious working with the Defence Minister, the Prime Minister and other officials involved. It demonstrated how direct liaison at the highest level between Army Headquarters, the Ministries and the Railway Board enabled the dispensing of otherwise lengthy procedures in the case of an operationally vital scheme.

Chapter 29

Innovative Planning for the Future

Pakistan's fatal obsession with Kashmir had resulted in three wars, 1947-48, 1965, and 1971.[168] All these wars were initiated by Pakistan, including the 1971 war. Although the causes of the 1971 war lay in East Pakistan, ultimately, as always, it spilled over into Jammu and Kashmir as well. After each war, the Indian Army endeavoured to review organisations and structures, concepts and practices, weapons and equipment to institute any change that was warranted. Notwithstanding the desire to be better prepared for future conflicts, finance as well as lack of knowledge of military affairs, indifference and lethargy on the part of the bureaucracy, have acted as brakes, stalling even minor change. They have often prevented the Indian Army from being fully prepared and equipped to fight a modern war.

It was only in 1975 that a definitive step was taken to overcome the *status quo*. Efforts were made to reorganise and re-equip the Indian Army within the framework of a long-term Perspective Plan based on realistic threat perceptions and technological advances.

Experts Committee

Soon after assuming charge as the Chief of Army Staff, General Raina constituted what came to be known as an Experts Committee, to look into the future strategy for the defence of the country.

[168] Pakistan followed up with aggression in Kargil and Dras in Ladakh in 1999.

Having already initiated plans to improve the Operational Mobilisation Posture, the General addressed the reorganisation and modernisation of the Army. With the approval of Government of India, an Experts Committee to examine this vital matter was constituted.

Between 1947 and 1975, the Army had grown considerably in all fields: combat, combat support as also combat service support. However, such growth had been reactive, due more to external compulsions as also to counter insurgencies, rather than due to any systematic effort. We must not forget that soon after the war with Pakistan in Kashmir in 1947-48, when the Cease Fire Agreement was signed at Karachi in 1949, the Government had toyed with the idea of downsizing the Army. This idea was based on the mistaken belief that a non-violent and non-aligned peace-loving nation did not require a powerful Army.

The result of such a defective policy on National Security resulted in the humiliation at the hands of China in 1962. One consequence of this was the hurried expansion of the Indian Army. The Army's teeth to tail ratio had also become somewhat skewed.

General Raina selected Lieutenant General K.V. Krishna Rao, PVSM, GOC of a Corps, as the Chairman of the proposed Experts Committee. He had not only succeeded Tappy Raina as Commander 114 Infantry Brigade in Ladakh, but was also his former Chief of Staff at HQ Western Command, Shimla. To assist Lieutenant General Krishna Rao, two promising and distinguished officers,[169] Major General M.L. Chibber, PVSM, and Major General

[169] All three rose to very high positions. After the recommendations of the Experts Committee were accepted by the government, Lieutenant General Krishna Rao found himself as DCOAS at Army HQ, to coordinate the implementation of the Experts Committee Report. Subsequently, he himself became Chief of the Army Staff and was able to see through most recommendations of the Expert Committee Report.

K. Sundarji,[170] PVSM, were detailed as Members. Brigadier A.J.M. Homji was appointed as Secretary.

Why the Expert Committee?

The basic purpose in constituting this committee was to carry out an analysis of the changing global scenario. Within that context, defence preparedness to maintain credibility in the world was vital. The committee would also focus on the escalating defence budget, the greater sophistication in weapons and equipment, the concurrent increase in manpower costs, the *ad hoc* manner in which defence matters were dealt with, and the need for ensuring maximum cost effectiveness. All this had to be done while endeavouring to improve the fighting capacity of the Defence Forces in general, and Indian Army in particular.

The high-level Experts Committee was required to examine these matters in greater depth and to suggest measures required for the future build-up necessary for Defence. Based on this, detailed terms of reference were issued by Chief of the Army Staff, asking the Committee to recommend various measures necessary for attaining and maintaining a credible Defence Posture in the future.

Within six months of General Raina taking over as COAS, the Experts Committee commenced its deliberation on 1st November 1975. It was scheduled to submit its report within nine months from that date. The Committee was mandated to prepare and present a twenty-five year perspective plan, from 1975 to 2000. It had to evaluate national security threats, propose a strategy against it, visualise the future battlefield, determine the size of the army and suggest an incremental build-up of forces.

The Experts Committee met a cross-section of experts and departments at every level, ranging from the COAS to the Directing Staff and students of the DSSC, Wellington, and the College of Combat (now War College), Mhow. The Committee took the

---

[170] Major General (later General and COAS) K. Sundarji, after having commanded an Infantry Division was selected to be the first infantry officer as GOC of an Armoured Division in the Indian Army.

benefit of opinions of senior staff officers at the Army and Command HQs, Naval and Air Force Headquarters, R&D cum Defence production establishments of the Ministry of Defence, former Chiefs of Army Staff and selected retired Army officers. In addition, views of military commanders and civil officers deployed in border areas and island territories were also taken.

The committee also held discussions with the Policy Planning Committee, the Bhabha Atomic Research Centre, the Indian Space Research Organisation (ISRO), the Vikram Sarabhai Space Centre and the Planning Commission (now Niti Aayog).[171] Such interaction ensured that the Experts Committee was able to collate a wide cross-section of views prior to making its recommendations. These changes were aimed at improving the Army's teeth to tail ratio, thus making it organisationally lean, even as it pursued modernisation. This Report enlarged the scope and follow up on the limited mechanisation of the Army that had commenced in 1969, with the induction of Topaz and Skot armoured personnel carriers (APC)[172], mainly for employment as "Battle Taxis".

General Raina's vision and the Experts Committee recommendations laid the foundation for the transition of a Second World War Army into a modern Indian Army[173] with reliance on fast-paced operations and tenets of manoeuvre battle. Besides, the specific challenge of intelligence gathering and, more importantly, its evaluation, it was equally important to integrate it as a part of the Army's long-term strategic Intelligence assessment. These assessments become the basis for "Perspective Plans", which in turn

---

[171] The Planning Commission established on 15th March 1950, was replaced by a new organization called NITI AAYOG on 1st January 2015 by PM Narendra Modi.

[172] As a result of the recommendations of the report, this received an impetus with the raising of the Mechanised Infantry Regiment on 2nd April 1979, equipped with BMPs.

[173] This was facilitated by the raising of the Army Aviation Corps in 1986, induction of 155 mm Bofors guns, and re-designating an infantry division as an air assault division, and the raising of the Reorganised Army Plains Infantry Division (RAPID), with an enhanced component of armour and mechanised infantry.

would indicate the nature of organisational changes needed to maximise its benefits. This was best illustrated by the process of Army's mechanisation, which was accompanied by a thrust towards adopting tenets of modern warfare. The planning for the same commenced in 1975 and catered for the period till 2000.

The Experts Committee chose to adopt the following approach:

- Determine the Vital National Interests,
- Assess the international environment,
- Evaluate threats to the national vital interests, both external and internal, and determine the strategy to meet such threats,
- Visualise the battlefield of the future,
- Determine the future size, shape and structure of forces,
- Ascertain the availability of financial and other resources as well as indigenous capabilities and possible internal savings,
- Plan for the build-up of forces, including equipping, in different time-frames,
- Consider various aspects of preparedness.

The voluminous Experts Committee Report produced in 1976 covered all important aspects of defence preparedness. The recommendations of the Committee Report resulted in considerable improvement of the Teeth-to-Tail ratio and the ultimate attainment of a reasonable deterrence capability, a saving of manpower of approximately 1,00,000 personnel and 20,000 vehicles of all types within the Army. Most of the savings were to be ploughed back into modernisation projects. Basically, the thrust of recommendations was towards enhancing Firepower, Mobility, Night-fighting and Electronic-warfare capability; thus developing adequate deterrence capabilities. Separate papers were given on Nuclear Warfare and Higher Defence Organisation and the need of a Chief of Defence Staff (CDS).

Reforms after the Experts Committee Report

After having guided the Experts Committee for nearly two-and-a-half years and after a very meaningful and satisfying tenure of three years as Chief of the Army Staff, General Raina was to retire at 57 years and 5 months on 31st May 1978. To ensure that the Experts Committee Report would be implemented properly, Lieutenant General K.V. Krishna Rao, the Chairman of the Committee, was appointed Deputy Chief of Army Staff (DCOAS)[174] at Army Headquarters. Thus, the recommendations of the Experts Committee began to be implemented so as to be dove-tailed with the Five Year Plan 1979-84, and the subsequent Five Year Plans. This plan[175] was to be updated every five years. General Raina thus seemed to have set the roadmap for continual modernisation of the Indian Army for the future.

Conventional War

Long range planning commenced for the first time in the mid-1970s for meeting India's "National War Aims" keeping in view the national vital interests and the threats to these. Perspective plans, once made, needed constant review and up-gradation, otherwise these lapsed by default. While visualising the battlefield of the future, care had to be taken to distinguish between the conventional and nuclear scenarios.

Changes in the conventional battlefield were appreciated generally in the area of enhanced effectiveness of weapons, capability of fighting by night, mobility on the battlefield, survivability, better command, control and communications, and intelligence ac-

---

[174] The net effect of the measures taken by Lieutenant General Krishna Rao as Deputy Chief of Army Staff was that the teeth-to-tail ratio was improved and the amount spent on modernisation went up. Later, General Sundarji, when he was VCOAS, got the sanction of Government for the Additional Directorate General of Perspective Planning, designated as ADG (PP), with requisite staff, to look ahead with a perspective of twenty-five years. Major General R.N. Mahajan was selected as the first ADG (PP).

General Sundarji was thus able to put out "Plan 2000" on the day he became Army Chief on 1st February 1986.

[175] About thirty years on, another effort was made to reorganise and update the Perspective Planning, which has come to be known as "Shekatkar Committee Report".

quisition. Planning for a future conventional war therefore had to consider advancements in technology that would result in greater destructive capacity of weapons and speed of communication.

Other aspects that needed consideration were the enlargement of the battlefield and the need for decentralisation of command, control and decision-making, intensity of operations and a larger number of casualties. Armoured and mechanised forces with integral armed helicopters and close air support by the Indian Air Force would need to be employed extensively in offensive operations. Attacking forces would need to have tremendous firepower, cross-country mobility and matching logistic. Heliborne forces would need to be used for vertical envelopment in conjunction with air-borne forces, for capturing objectives in depth.

As far as defensive operations were concerned, the defender would have large stretches of territory to defend and would be compelled to ensure that his defences had depth, and that reserves were organised to counter-attack and to prevent unacceptable penetration. Keeping in view the likely battlefield scenario in a conventional war, the following conclusions emerged in respect of the long-term needs of the army:

1. Adequate infantry formations would be required to hold the defences, absorb the initial brunt of the enemy's attack, contain his thrusts, and inflict maximum attrition. Therefore, sufficient mobile reserves would be needed. In the plains, these would have to be based on Armour and Mechanised Infantry, supported by sufficient integrated strike capability in terms of Armour, Mechanised Infantry, Air Defence, Artillery, Assault Engineers and Armed Helicopters which would need to be developed.
2. Adequate vertical envelopment capability would also be required with the "Strike" formations, including close air-support, integrated for both offensive and defensive operations. Adequate air transport for airborne operations as well as for the strategic movement of troops would be required. Also vital was amphibious capability for carrying out limited amphibious operations.

3. Electronic warfare capability to include acquisition and surveillance, guidance of weapons and communications as well as electronic and counter-counter measures and satellite surveillance. Enhanced night fighting capability to make night fighting as efficient as by day; equally important was Logistic support to match mobility of the forces.

Chapter 30

Welfare and Improvement in Service Conditions

Accommodation

While concentrating on the improvement of operational readiness of the Army, General Raina did not forget the welfare and betterment of service conditions of all ranks. With new raisings and change in locations of field formations and units, there was now the added burden of land acquisition and construction of accommodation. Some new cantonments had to be built closer to the International Borders (IB). All this could not be done within a short time. At the same time, the General Raina appreciated that the Army could not continue to drift along with a trickle of funds made available for this purpose in the annual defence budgets.

A detailed long-term plan was, therefore, prepared to cover the anticipated requirement of funds for this purpose over the next fifteen to twenty years to meet the Army's entitlement in various cantonments and military stations. The plan took into account the formations and units proposed to be raised in the 6th and 7th Five Year Plans, as well. Accordingly, a detailed proposal was submitted to the Government for approval. This, however, ran into rough weather! Even for the most immediate requirement of land, the concerned state governments were generally averse to parting with land where the Army needed it. The concerned Army Commanders and QMG at Army HQ tried their best but their efforts produced limited results. Unlike the earlier case of re-location of formations, this particular case-file kept gaining weight, because of "notings" and "counter notings" between the bureaucracy and the QMG Branch at Army HQ. But General Raina had evolved a system that whenever any important case was getting delayed in the bureaucratic wrangles, he would raise the matter with the Defence Minister. The case for the acquisition of land was thus expedited through this channel.

The Army was woefully short of all types of accommodation for various requirements, like, the accommodation for troops, for their vehicles and equipment, married and other than married (OTM) accommodation for all ranks. These shortages were compounded progressively by limited allotment of funds for this purpose by the Government on the one hand, and on the other hand, by an increase in the Army's strength after 1962. This increase took place, as several new formations and units were raised. Over the years, the question of accommodation had received inadequate attention. A much larger allocation of funds was required for both the acquisition of land and for the construction of accommodation.

New Military Stations

One of the major problems facing the Army was the question of new cantonments. Most of India's cantonments dated back to pre-Independence era and owed their origin to the pre-World War 2, or earlier period. The situation that faced Army Headquarters now was quite different. While the Army had to ensure the continued use of what assets it possessed, it was necessary that any new locations would keep in view the prevailing operational requirement. This was a problem being tackled by the army as a long-term plan in view of the large financial outlays involved.

Training Areas

The other problem was the question of training areas. A modern field force needed extensive areas for its training, in particular areas where it could carry out Field Firing and Battle Inoculation under realistic battle conditions. The problem was being tackled by a phased programme of acquisition of necessary areas with the assistance of central and state governments. As the land in the country has very rightly been utilized for extensive agriculture, the period during which the manoeuvres could be conducted by field formations and units tended to be restricted. The problem was overcome by drawing up training schedules meticulously and making full use of the available time.

Modernisation

The continued modernisation of the Army was another major problem. Not only had personnel costs mounted, the cost of sophisticated modern equipment, too, had escalated steeply. Since very large financial resources were involved, it was necessary in the climate of financial strain to ensure a high degree of cost effectiveness in the spheres of Army activity. This was a problem which was kept under constant review by the Army.

Health and the Army Hospital (Referral & Research), Delhi Cantonment

Gen Raina, during his entire service, held the Army Medical Corps in very high regards. He was aware of his own experience as a young officer, when he was injured during the Second World War in Iraq. The way he was treated in the Field Hospitals; not only his physical injuries received medical care, but also continuous encouragement from Doctors and the Nursing staff, which helped him to get back to his normal professional and personal life. He continued serving with distinction, at every appointment as he grew up in his profession, and rose to the rank of General and became the Chief of second largest Army of the world.

General T.N. Raina, MVC, COAS, while addressing the 7th Annual Conference of the Neurological Society of India at the Armed Forces Medical College, Pune, in February 1978, compared the two professions, which no nation should neglect. He elaborated that there are two main noble professions in the world:

> One is my profession — the profession of arms, and the other is the profession of medicine, which does the greatest service to humanity.

As part of the welfare of troops, General Raina was keen to improve the services of the Army Hospital in Delhi Cantonment. Even while sanctioning numerous projects for the existing Army and Base Hospitals in Delhi Cantt, General Raina revived the proposal for a new Army (Referral & Research) Hospital[176], to replace the existing Army Hospital at Delhi Cantonment. Army and Base Hospitals had been built during Second World War and many *ad hoc* facilities had been added since then.

A project proposal for a new and large Army Hospital Complex for Delhi Cantonment had been gathering dust in Army Headquarters for many years. In the meantime, the existing Base and Army hospitals had grown as untamed wild monsters, proving a nightmare to manage for the Commandants of each hospital!.

The proposal envisaged the construction of a modern hospital complex, designed to meet the requirements of the highest quality medical care for the three Services. It was to be equipped with the latest facilities and equipment for the most efficient referral treatment and medical research in problems peculiar to the environment of the Armed Forces. The Army (R & R) Hospital was conceptualised on the pattern of the All India Institute of Medical Sciences (AIIMS), New Delhi. The equipment and facilities of Army (R&R) Hospital were planned to be world class. The emergency and trauma services were to be at par with international standards and there would be super specialty centres for cardiology, oncology, neurosciences and orthopaedic surgeries, like knee and hip replacements.

---

[176] The Army Hospital (Referral & Research) was finally ready for functioning in 1998, when General V.P. Malik, PVSM, AVSM, was the COAS.

The Army Hospital (R&R), developed for Emergency, Trauma and Specialty care of all ranks of the three services is spread across several acres of land. It is home to some of the best doctors from the Armed Forces. Equipped and run like an upscale private hospital, it is open only to service personnel and their families who are referred from military hospitals across the country.

Post-Retirement Resettlement

A baffling problem which the Army had been facing was about the post-retirement resettlement and rehabilitation of all its ranks. By the very nature of things, the Army could not offer a full life career to its personnel. A man had to be retained in service only as long as he was relatively young, physically fit, and mentally tough to bear the stresses and strains associated with military service.

Lateral Induction

There was, therefore, a high degree of outflow from the Army of personnel who could have a much longer useful career ahead of them. In the 1970s, the Indian Army was retiring approximately 50,000 personnel every year, including 800 officers. The question of resettlement after retirement from the Army had an unsettling effect on even the serving personnel. The number of men who could go back to till their lands, as was the case in olden days, was now much smaller.

Informally, efforts were made to absorb some of the retired personnel in Central Police Organisations (CPOs), like CRPF, BSF, ITBP, CISF, SSB, Railway Protection Force (RPF), and so on. A certain percentage of vacancies were also reserved in Government departments for the retirees and these were availed of.

Post retirement, rehabilitation training in various skills was also imparted to personnel about to retire to make them fit to avail of self-employment opportunities. Notwithstanding all these efforts, there were large numbers who had to fend for themselves. Whenever the occasion arose, General Raina always took the opportunity of appealing to the private corporate sector to accord preference in employing personnel who retire from the Army. He used to convincingly put across the merits of ex-servicemen; they were honest, hard-working, disciplined and had been trained to inculcate a spirit of dedication and pride in their work.

General Raina was of the firm view that CPOs would greatly benefit from lateral induction of trained personnel from the Army. He therefore recommended that officers, JCOs and other ranks that were surplus to the Army's requirement could be laterally transferred to such CPOs / Para Military Forces like Assam Rifles, so as to provide them with trained leadership and manpower. Such lateral induction from the Army to CPOs[177] could be of great benefit to those organisations and also financially advantageous to the Government.

Teeth to Tail Ratio of the Army

A critical review was frequently carried out at Army Headquarters of the organisation and composition of the existing units, formations, establishments and installations of the Army, the weapon system, equipment scales and manning patterns. This was to ensure more effective utilisation of manpower and equipment while effecting economies wherever possible. Based on such periodic reviews, re-organisations in the establishments were carried out aimed at improving the teeth-to-tail ratio and cost effectiveness.

The efforts at improving the teeth-to-tail ratio had brought about an improvement of approximately 10 per cent since the 1960s, and of about 4 to 5 percent in the previous three years, or so. Further, studies were in hand to bring about organisational and equipment improvement so as to build additional punch into the Army as then constituted.

Erosion in the Indian Army's Status

Another important proposal taken up for government approval was to arrest the "Erosion in the status of Armed Forces" in general and of Indian Army in particular. The major thrust of the proposal was to prevent Central Police organisations from adopting the badges of ranks in use by Indian Army, including the display of flags and star plates. Unlike in the army, where the rank of officers and JCOs were pre-fixed to the name, police officers did not carry

---

[177] The proposal for lateral transfer from Army to CPOs was submitted to the Government of India and was approved in principle. However, after the fall of Indira Gandhi's government in 1977, the Janata Party Government headed by Shri Morarji Desai sat over this proposal like it did over many other decisions of the previous government.

any rank. They were recognised by the "appointment", which was suffixed to their name.

Since independence, the central government has been pushing the growth of various central police organisations (CPOs) for purposes of policing the international border, for law and order, and for industrial security. Until the partition of India, the British government had created only the Central Reserve Police Force (CRPF) for maintenance of law and order in the provinces. After India became a sovereign republic on 26th January 1950, however, there was an expansion of police forces at a huge cost to the national budget. It led to the practice of police forces imitating Indian Army by adopting army badges of rank and using flag and star plates as formation commanders in Army did. This caused confusion in the mind of the public about Army's image. These police organisations also began adopting the practice of pre-fixing the appointments of their officers, as if these ranks were similar to those of commissioned Army officers.

The government of Prime Minister Indira Gandhi had agreed to the above proposal in principal. However, Mr. Ashwani Kumar IPS, the then DG BSF, and one of the most senior serving police officers, called on Tappy Raina and virtually beseeched him not to go ahead with this proposal. As he explained, it would cause loss of face to senior IPS leadership. Tappy Raina calmly advised Mr. Ashwani Kumar that police forces in most advanced countries of the world had distinct uniforms and badges of ranks. Therefore, he did not see any problem in Indian police forces giving up the current practice of imitating the army. Sadly, this proposal of Army HQ met the same fate as several other proposals at the hands of the new government. It then remained buried in the files by successive governments and did not see the light of day.

Primary Need of the Army

The primary need of the Army was an overall qualitative improvement. This implied a continuous improvement in the quality and training standard of officers and men, and the updating of weapons and equipment to keep pace with modern developments. Qualitative improvement was ensured by proper selection, initial and in-Service training and regular training exercises under realistic battle conditions of all units and formations. Measures to ensure a high state of well-being and morale were kept foremost in mind.

As regards weapons and equipment, General Raina believed that what the Indian Army had was commensurate with the prevailing situation. However, keeping in mind the future improvements required he instituted the regular updating of equipment and initiated projects of development to cater to the Army's needs over time.

Self-Sufficiency in Armament Needs

Indian Army had a high degree of self-sufficiency regarding its armament needs. There were, however, areas where inputs and components had to be imported, but as time went on an increasing degree of indigenisation was being ensured. But there would be areas where the requirements in numbers were small and, therefore, uneconomical for indigenous production. Viewed from this angle, even the most advanced countries did not necessarily aim at hundred percent self-sufficiency in armament.

Electronic Warfare

Electronic equipment is used for communications, surveillance, guidance of weapons, and many other purposes in the Army. An enemy, therefore, can adversely affect the efficiency of the defence forces by interfering with the waging of electronic warfare.

General Raina was fully aware of the dangers of electronic warfare being conducted against our forces in the event of war. In fact, the threat in this field was assessed continuously. In making the assessment, new technological developments, which had taken place in the field of electronic warfare and to which an enemy was likely to have access, were carefully considered. Based on such assessment, steps were taken to negate the threat.

Chapter 31

Indian Army since Independence

In an interview with the Chief Editor of *Sainik Samachar*[178] on the eve of Army Day 1978, six months before his retirement, Chief of the Army Staff General Raina highlighted some significant achievements of the Indian Army in three decades, since 1947. When India was partitioned into the two Dominions — India and Pakistan, de facto both Dominions remained under the rule of British Crown! Only when it (India) became a Sovereign Republic on 26th January 1950, did India become a truly independent nation, as the Republic of India, under its own Constitution. The President of India was now head of the Nation and Supreme Commander of the Armed Forces of India.

General Raina warmly complimented the role of the Indian Armed Forces in general and the Indian Army, in particular, during the preceding three decades. Some of the most significant achievements he highlighted were:

> In the perspective of our long history, the Indian Army has been continually engaged in Military Operations to restore unity, as well as meet external threats in the last three decades. It had undertaken operations in Junagarh and Hyderabad, fought a war in Jammu and Kashmir during 1947-48, liberated Goa in 1961 and fought three major wars in 1962, 1965 and 1971.

---

[178] Courtesy *Sainik Samachar*, Vol. XXV No-3, 15th January 1978.

In every test, our Army acquitted itself admirably and emerged victorious except against the Chinese Aggression in 1962. However, the 1962 war was an eye-opener for the Indian Government and the Army. It taught us that a modern war cannot be won without updating our weapons and equipment, and that national security should not be jeopardised by taking undue risks in the size of our force levels as compared to our adversaries. The lessons of 1962 stood us in good stead during the 1965 and 1971 wars.

But there was always an ever-present danger in a democracy, to get carried away by the transient easing of tensions with potential adversaries, and we need to remain watchful of such a trend towards complacency.

The conduct of operations by the Indian Army during the Indo-Pak War-1971, became a subject of study amongst the professional military circles throughout the world. The Indian Army had successfully forced a quick military decision in East Pakistan (now Bangladesh) and won a complete victory within 14 days, operating over terrain which had been considered almost impassable! In West Pakistan also, it overcame the Pakistani Military forces and attained its aims successfully.

The Army has always remained the pioneering light in the sphere of national integration. Religion, caste, language and regional distinctions have been successfully synthesised into a homogenous Indian community, bearing arms in the defence of the country.

Professionalism and Discipline

Further, when we look at the record of political events in practically all the newly independent States in Asia and Africa during the last thirty years, it goes to the credit of the Indian Army that it has remained completely and utterly apolitical. This is attributed to the professionalism and discipline instilled in the Army as also the wisdom of our statesmen who have made this possible.

During the last three decades, the Indian Army has brought the country a good name, high prestige and reputation by undertaking successful Peace-keeping missions throughout the world, whether, in Korea, Indo-China, Congo, the Middle East, Cyprus and Lebanon, under the aegis of the United Nations.

Teeth to Tail Ratio in the Army

In the history of the Indian Army, "October 1962" was a turning point! Till then the Army had remained sadly neglected, but after the Sino-India war in 1962, we have constantly endeavoured to rectify the imbalance in our force levels and modernisation. The Army has progressively improved its fighting potential by a more purposeful utilisation of manpower and equipment. This is evident from the fact that the ratio of teeth elements to the overall force level has been enhanced from 59 to 67 per cent, since 1960.

Counter Insurgency

The Army has been involved in counter-insurgency operations in Nagaland and Mizoram over an extended period. Except in one country, nowhere else in the world have counter-insurgency operations by any army attained such success, in spite of the fact that our army has exhibited utmost restraint and discipline in these operations.

Adventure and Sports

The Army has produced sportsmen of international standing like Milkha Singh and its teams have excelled in games like hockey. Army wrestlers have made a mark in international competitions. One recalls the name of Lila Ram who won a Gold Medal at Cardiff (Commonwealth Games). Among others I can think of are: Hanorary Lt. Chand Ram (Athletics), Subedar Sajjan Singh (Wrestling) Nb. Subedar G. Ram Singh (Athletics) and Subedar Chand Ram (Swimming).

Recently our mountaineers have been crowned with success in their assault on Mt. Kanchenjunga in North Sikkim.[179] Earlier, Army personnel had taken part in various expeditions to Mt. Everest and even skied down Trishul Peak in Central Himalaya.

Thrust on Self-Reliance

The Indian Army is aware of the present day technological developments taking place all over the world and the consequent changes in the defence forces of various countries. It is keeping pace with such developments.

It is well to remember that we spend only about 3.5 percent of the GNP on our Armed Forces which rates amongst the lowest in the world. For example, even Pakistan spends over 9 percent of her GNP on her Armed Forces. Within these fiscal constraints, we are doing our best to keep pace with the various technological developments.

Our thrust has always been on self-reliance based on indigenisation. This has proved to be a sound and right approach, although at times we are left behind others in certain trends towards modernisation.

Operational Training

Considering the widely different types of terrain and climate in the Indian sub-continent in which the Army has to operate, it places great demand on the "Fitness and Mental Robustness" of all ranks of units and formations, to adapt themselves for their respective operational roles.

As stated above, the Indian Army has to operate in different types of terrain and climate, such as the Rann of Kutch in Gujarat and the desert of Rajasthan, the green flat plains of Punjab, which are interspersed with numerous rivers, canals and smaller water channels, high altitude and snow-bound areas in the North and North East and dense forests in the East.

---

[179] The concept of adventure training in the Indian Army and establishment of a training cell at Army Headquarters has been well described in Chapter 32.

Keeping the strategic importance of the Andaman & Nicobar Islands in the Bay of Bengal, the Indian Army is trained in maritime operations along with the Indian Navy and is now deployed to ensure the security of these Islands.

The Army has to be adept in operating in all these diverse conditions, which demands an Army in top physical state, and mentally robust condition. This places different and conflicting demands on professional training. Of course, the ideal would be to have different Forces for each different type of terrain and climate, which would require a vast Army. Our country obviously cannot afford such vast Armed Forces. We have, therefore, laid stress on the youthful profile of the Army, and on physical fitness and mental alertness which is ensured by vigorous training. Since the same units have to be ready to fight in such diverse types of terrain and climate, they are trained in different types of warfare suited to such regions.

This does mean a strain but that has to be accepted. With physical, mental and professional training that we insist on, I am confident that the Indian Army will fight efficiently in all these types of terrain and climate, if and when the need arises.

In the 1965 and 1971 Wars (with Pakistan), our combat troops have proved their ability to operate effectively in different terrains and climatic conditions. Even in 1962, one might recall that troops rushed from the plains and from South India, and, yet, gave a good account of themselves in the operations in Ladakh at a height of 14,000 to 16,000 ft above sea level.

Higher Technical Competence

Sophisticated weapon systems with increased precision, guidance and lethality are being progressively introduced in our Army within the constraints imposed by resources and finance. This trend is contributing to increased combat effectiveness of the Army.

Sophisticated weapon systems are very expensive and involve increased capital investment. Similarly, to counter the effect of acquisition of these weapons by our adversaries, it demands better protective measures and higher scales of resources. Both these effects have financial implications and we need to take note of this aspect in our Defence planning. To keep pace in this field will, naturally, cost us more every year.

Any step towards modernisation in weapons and equipment calls for a parallel effort in improving the quality of the Service Personnel, who operate these systems under battle conditions. The introduction of more lethal and sophisticated weapon systems demands that our officers and men acquire higher technical competence than hitherto fore. In order to attract such quality of manpower, improvement in the existing service conditions of the Armed Force personnel becomes imperative.

In the light of development in weaponry, training imparted to officers and men was suitably modified to give it a better technical orientation.

The advent of "Smart" weapon or Precision Guided Munitions (PGM) had called for increased mobility in the battlefield. Army HQ took various measures to augment the battlefield mobility of our field formations. This again costs more money.

The above logical analysis of the state of the Indian Army by General Raina raises doubt about the ability of the nation to bear the required cost. One should also bear in mind that even if the Indian Army had the resources to go in for all the sophisticated weapons developed abroad, there was always the question of the willingness of other countries to sell these to India. And, most important, would they continue this supply un-interrupted during a war? Hence, General Raina's emphasis on developing technologically advanced weapons, indigenously.

Aid to Civil Authorities

It is a well-known fact that Indian the Army had been called upon to render "assistance to civil authorities" on a number of occasions in various parts of the country, during the tenure of General Raina as COAS. Such assistance encompassed a wide range of commitments during the preceding years, such as combating floods and mounting rescue and relief operations in a total of thirty-three places in the states of Jammu and Kashmir, Punjab, Haryana, Delhi, Rajasthan, Gujarat, Madhya Pradesh, West Bengal and Assam. General Raina highlighted some important type of aid rendered:

- Establishing radio communications, providing medical items and water supply detachments in the cyclone devastated areas of Tamil Nadu and Andhra Pradesh, till such time as the State Governments were in a position to mobilise their own relief organisations.
- Maintenance of public-utility services which were considered vital for the life of the community and declared as essential by the Government, as a result of strikes by the employees of such services. Army technical personnel were provided to assist in the running of Electricity and Power Supply Stations in Uttar Pradesh, running of milk plants in Maharashtra and providing assistance to civil hospitals in Bombay (now Mumbai) city.
- Rescue, relief and medical assistance during the two major rail disasters at Udalgiri in Assam and at Naini near Allahabad in UP.
- Providing assistance for the prestigious Kumbh Mela at Allahabad, which included the construction of a 2000 feet long pontoon bridge over the River Ganga and other allied assistance.

General Raina further highlighted that the prolonged deployment of troops and military equipment, when providing assistance to the civil authorities, does encroach upon the time required to train for operational preparedness and the life of the equipment used. However, in an emergency, the Armed Forces must come to the assistance of their countrymen. As long as the Civil Administration draws up its plans in advance and takes necessary steps for meeting emergencies with its own resources, and calls the Army only as a last resort when its own resources have been exhausted would it be legitimate. Troops and equipment would then remain committed but only for a short duration. The time thus lost in rendering assistance could be made up by putting in extra hours of work and effort in training and maintenance of equipment.

Welfare and Better Service Conditions

Married Accommodation

General Raina explained that, as per authorisation, there was an overall requirement of approximately 2,54,000 units of married accommodation. Against this only 1,43,000 units were available; thus, there was a shortfall of 1,11,000 units, which was a matter of grave concern to him. He outlined the steps that were being taken to meet the shortage of accommodation:

- **Additional Funds.** Measures were being taken to alleviate this hardship to the troops. Recently, the government had approved the enhancement of the allocation of money for married accommodation. This would make up the shortfall in about 12 years. As per earlier plans, it would have taken 24 years!
- **Hired Civil Accommodation.** As an interim measure local Army authorities had been authorised to hire private houses for all ranks to make up deficiencies, up to authorised scales. To make up for an increase in rents, ceiling for rents for different categories was under review.
- **Compensation in Lieu of Quarters (CILQ).** The other ranks are also permitted to arrange accommodation under their own arrangements and are paid Compensation in lieu of Quarters (CILQ). Rates of compensation were revised upwards in 1976. The percentages for permitting this compensation also had been revised and were now authorised up to 25%, 50% and 100% of the strength for OR, NCOs, and JCOs, respectively.
- **Separated Family Accommodation (SFA).** In 1963, it was decided to provide accommodation for separated families of troops posted to Field Areas (Non-Family stations), at peacetime Military Stations and Cantonments. Nearly 8,438 units of this type of accommodation had already been constructed.

Some more welfare measures pertaining to Insurance, Children's education and Housing were under consideration, General Raina told *Sainik Samachar* and he was hopeful that these would be finalised by Army Day 1978.

Rehabilitation and Resettlement

There were very few job opportunities for the retiring personnel of Army, whether in the public or the private sectors in rural areas. General Raina directed the Adjutant General and Director General (Resettlement & Rehabilitation), to make a two-pronged attack on this problem. It was aimed at taking employment for our retired personnel to the villages, instead of their coming to cities. Therefore, the Army encouraged economically viable co-operative schemes for them in villages, while offering all possible help in these ventures. For instance, a pilot project for weaving bandages was established at The Kumaon Regimental Centre, Ranikhet. More projects on similar lines were also considered for fruit canning, pickle making, and so on which enabled ex-Servicemen to have gainful work in rural areas. Some of the important steps taken by Tappy Raina were:

- **Pre-Release Training.** Pre-release training of soldiers in industrial training institutes and various other courses were introduced to enable servicemen to become self-employed after retirement in various occupations, like bee-keeping, poultry, piggery, dairy and mechanised farming, animal husbandry, tailoring, welding, carpentry, book binding, tractor repair and maintenance, insurance, and so on. Provision was made for allotting tractors on payment to ex-servicemen from the reserve quota by the Directorate General of Resettlement.
- **Ordnance Factories and Defence Production Units.** Siting and locating defence production units and ordnance factories in rural areas was also proposed to the Ministry of Defence, as it would certainly help in the rehabilitation of ex-servicemen. But here other considerations were involved, like the availability of raw material, communication facilities, and so on. Such units would encourage ex-servicemen to setup small scale industries to produce ancillary goods and components to supply to industrial and other establishments set up at the nearest industrial hub.

According to Tappy Raina, the single most significant achievement of the Army during his tenure was the "Change in Training Philosophy" of the Indian Army:

> In a large Armed Force like ours, there cannot be a single most significant achievement. A number of very important steps have been taken in the period 1975-1978, towards improving the Army to achieve its task. Some of these contributed directly to the modernisation of the forces, and others, to the improvement of the man in uniform, so that he would be in a better state of body and mind, to carry out his tasks. A few of these achievements are:

- **Mobility of the Army** has been improved and along with this, as I have already mentioned, the proportion of "Teeth to Tail" ratio has been enhanced in these three years from 63 to 67 percent.
- The Training philosophy has undergone a dynamic change so as to prepare ourselves for a future war, should it ever come, and not think in terms of the last war.
- **Service Conditions**. Though a great deal more is required in the improvement of service conditions of the Army, some steps have been taken in this direction. These include increasing the ages of retirement, changing the pattern of the length of Colour service of other ranks, introduction of the scheme of Army Group Insurance and so on.
- **Indian Army is Apolitical.** It is to the credit of the Indian Army that, unlike in many other countries, it has remained completely and utterly apolitical, thanks to the professionalism and discipline instilled in it, as also the wisdom of our military leaders and statesmen who have made this possible. Besides giving a good account of itself in all the military operations, beginning with the Kashmir operation (1947-48), the Indian Army has always proved to be an instrument of "National Integration" and has brought the country a good name and reputation by its conduct in United Nation Peace-keeping missions, throughout the world.

Chapter 32

Adventure Training in the Army

In the overall training policy evolved after the war with Pakistan in 1971, General Tappy Raina was of the view that the Army should train itself by undertaking adventure challenges in the field of mountaineering, trekking and sailing, during peacetime. One of the officers whose opinion he sought in 1976 was Colonel Narinder Kumar (nicknamed Bull) of the Kumaon Regiment. As Bull remembers, the question posed to him by General Raina was — “More than half of our Army is deployed at high altitudes. Why can’t we organise some adventure activity for our soldiers, like a big mountaineering expedition?”

When the human spirit soars higher than Mount Everest, we get a person like Colonel Narindar Kumar, PVSM, KC, AVSM and a Padma Shri awardee. True to type, Bull Kumar took up the challenge first, and then started thinking of the implication of Tappy’s statement.

According to Bull Kumar, General Raina’s most important contribution to mountaineering and adventure training in the Army was, the setting up of an Army Adventure Cell at the Military Training Directorate of Army HQ. The honour of setting up this Cell went to “Bull” Kumar. And so began the pursuit of Peacetime challenges: of conquering the mind and directing the energy of All Ranks while deployed in difficult terrains.

Ascent of Kanchenjunga

The first such venture undertaken by the Army Adventure Cell was a mountaineering expedition to climb the Himalayan peak, Kanchenjunga, in West Sikkim on border with Nepal. This is best described by Bull Kumar himself, as the leader of this expedition:

> By this time, I had been on deputation as Principal of the Himalayan Mountaineering Institute at Darjeeling for five years and was Principal of the National Ski Institute at Gulmarg, for another five years under the Department of Tourism. General T.N. Raina, who was also the Colonel of my Regiment, never called me by my rank or name. He always called me "Shri Bull"!
>
> Sometimes in 1974-75, while I was Principal of National Ski School, I was invited to the Raising Day of 7 Kumaon in the Kashmir Valley, where the Chief Guest was General Tappy Raina. All the officers of this battalion were smartly dressed and trying to catch the General's eye. Of course, it was their day. So, I stood in a corner, and enjoyed my glass of beer before lunch.
>
> During the evening cocktails, as General Raina walked up to me I stood to attention and greeted him with compliments of the day. In response, he put his hand on my shoulder and told me to relax. Then he said, "Shri Bull, you better get yourself permanently absorbed in the Department of Tourism as you have no future in the Army".
>
> He was right because I lacked the qualitative requirement for becoming even a Colonel. I replied, "Sir, I will be happy to stay on in the army, even as a Major, but I cannot stick to this job even for another year". I was completing my tenure as Principal of the NSI for the sixth year — a period of two extended tenures.
>
> He enquired, "What's happened, are you in any trouble"? I replied, "I don't fit into this bureaucratic culture". He tried to calm me and said, "Come, my boy, what has happened?" I said, "Sir these bureaucrats, say something, do something else, and write something else. Their main aim is not the progress of the

work (in this case the Ski School). They just want to catch you and put you in a corner and not punish you, but only keep a sword dangling over your head so that you can dance to their tunes." I felt I had done all I could for the Institution.

The General thought for a while and asked me, "Where can I fit you in the Army?" Without hesitation, I said "Commandant High Altitude Warfare School, Gulmarg". He looked piercingly at me with his only eye and said, "Let me see", and moved on.

A few days later I received a personal DO letter from the COAS, informing me that my case had been examined by the MS for a posting to HAWS, but, unfortunately, I did not fulfil the Qualitative Requirement (QR), because I had neither commanded an Infantry Battalion nor successfully attended the Junior Commanders course at Infantry School (now War College), Mhow. So, General Raina wished me the best of luck, and that was it.

I was indeed touched that the COAS was personally concerned about a young army Major; but just then some developments took place.

Major H.P.S. Ahluwalia[180] (popularly known as "Ahlu"), a renowned mountaineer, had come up with the idea of sponsoring an expedition to ski down Trishul, in the Kumaon Hills. It so happened that long time back I had discussed this idea with Ahlu when I was Principal of HMI, Darjeeling, and Tenzing Norgay was my Director of Field training. I had proposed to the Ministry of Defence that I would like to organise an expedition

---

[180] Born on 6th November 1936, Major H.P.S. Ahluwalia, EME, a world class mountaineer and an experienced skier, had climbed Mount Everest on 29th May 1965. As an instructor at HAWS, Gulmarg, while engaging Pakistani infiltrators in 1965, he suffered a bullet injury which left him paralysed from his waist below. This did not quell his spirit of adventure in mountaineering. Though wheelchair borne since then, he is Chairman of the Indian Spinal Injuries Centre, New Delhi, which was setup in 1993. A Padma Bhushan, Padma Shri and Arjuna awardee, he has authored many books on the subject of mountaineering, including his autobiography, *Higher than Everest.*

for skiing down Trishul, the mountain my team had climbed in 1958.

I received a very short and curt reply from the MoD, "You are Principal of a mountaineering institute not a skiing institute". That was the end of my dream project!

However, the idea lay dormant in my mind all this while. So, when I received Ahlu's proposal to organise and lead this expedition, I naturally jumped with joy. I knew that Ahlu who was based in Delhi had the ability and contacts to gather resources for the expedition and to make such an idea possible.

As Principal of the Skiing and Mountaineering Institute, I knew my department could not say no, but bureaucrats have many weapons at their command. This time the Finance Ministry did not agree. So the team members and I decided to take leave of absence from duty to be able to undertake the proposed expedition. My friend, Ahlu, raised all the money from Mr. Krishnamurthy, who was head of the public sector giant, BHEL. As I had been an Instructor at HAWS earlier, I decided to invite them also to join the expedition. I announced that there would be selections for the Ski Trishul Team, sometime in March-April 1976 depending upon the snow conditions. This gave everyone a full season to train and prepare.

The three months of the skiing season of 1976 were spent in training the team, to build their stamina for climbing. It was tough training but the boys worked hard. The final selection was done in the first week of April and the team finally left for Joshimath.

The success of the expedition generated tremendous publicity, like never before. We had set a world record and that was indeed a cause for celebration. My expedition team returned to Joshimath, triumphant and in high spirits. To our good luck, General Tappy Raina also flew to Joshimath the same day on a visit to the mountain brigade located at Joshimath.

That morning, the *Times of India* carried my picture on the front page with a small caption: "Ski down Trishul, makes history — takes 10 days to climb and 45 minutes to come down!"

During the day I received a message from the Brigade Commander that since the COAS and Colonel of my Regiment was in the station, I was invited to dinner being hosted at the Brigade Officers' Mess in honour of the visiting dignitary. Having been out on expedition, I had not carried any formal clothes with me, and did not want to look shabby and un-presentable. My beard was unkempt and face badly sunburnt, therefore I declined the invitation due to lack of a formal dress for dinner. Back came the reply from the Brigade Commander that my regret was not accepted and it was desired that I should attend. I made all efforts to wriggle out because I did not want to be improperly dressed in the august presence of General Tappy Raina. I simply couldn't afford to take such a chance with my Colonel of the Regiment.

The Brigadier immediately sent three officers of different sizes to me — tall, stout and thin — with clothes for me to select. The outfit that I finally chose fitted me better than any of my own clothes. A barber was quickly arranged and I had my hair cut and beard shaved. Still my face was a sight; a patchwork of several shades. Finally, I landed in the Brigade Officers Mess to attend the dinner.

During pre-dinner drinks, General Raina cornered me and said, "Bull, every time a big expedition goes to the mountains I see an Army officer leading it and another Army person scales the summit, yet the newspapers do not give any credit to the Army. Names of ministers and bureaucrats hog the headlines, whereas it is actually the Army which trains and prepares you for all this."

It was a truth that could not be denied. Very slowly I responded, "Sir, may I ask you a question?" Normally a Major or a local Colonel would not dare to ask a question from the COAS. He said, "Shoot". And very quickly I asked him "Who climbed Everest first?" and, he very spontaneously replied "The British". I gave a little pause and very slowly replied, "Sir, the British had only sponsored and organised the expedition. It was actually an Indian and a New Zealander who climbed the mountain." He got my point and asked me to organise a big expedition for the Army. I said "Yes sir, but first please get me released from the Department of Tourism and let me revert to the Army."

Expedition to Kanchenjunga

Despite many hurdles by the Department of Tourism, Colonel Bull Kumar was relieved. He reverted back to the Army and was attached to one of the Sections of the Military Training Directorate, Army HQ, New Delhi. Thus, was sown the seed of the Indian Army Adventure Cell at Army HQ, New Delhi. Bull Kumar was given the task of organising a big Army mountaineering expedition. After much thought and consideration, he chose the challenge of climbing Kanchenjunga in North Sikkim from the difficult North-East Spur. This route to the elusive but mighty and majestic Kanchenjunga Peak is situated in North Sikkim and borders Nepal. The preparatory period and the success in climbing Kanchenjunga is best narrated by Bull Kumar himself:

> I received all possible support from the COAS. He said, "I will sign two letters on your behalf. Just let me know to whom these have to be addressed." I said, "One to the Prime Minister, Mrs Indira Gandhi, asking her to be the Patron of this expedition and the other one to the senior most officers in the customs department as this will enable me to import some mountaineering equipment." He did that immediately and after that I was left to fend for myself.
>
> While the preparations were in progress, General Raina received a letter from Shri H.C. Sarin, ICS (retired), Chairman of the Indian Mountaineering Foundation (IMF), saying that Bull Kumar was a good leader and climber but the Indian mountaineers were not yet ready to tackle the route along the North East Spur.
>
> The second point made by Chairman IMF, was that four months were not enough to organise an expedition of this magnitude. General Raina made a note in red ink, "Shri Bull to speak." So I was summoned to the office of COAS and point-

edly asked, "What do you have to say about this letter from Chairman IMF?" I too decided to hold back no punches, and told the COAS, that Shri HC Sarin, ICS was not a mountaineer himself, and that his opinion was based on the mala fide advice given by other mountaineers. IMF should be asked to name one mountaineer who had achieved half as much as I had. He got the point and nodded.

As regards the second point that there was not have enough time to prepare, I had a very good answer, "Sir, if Pakistan attacks you tomorrow, would you request them to give you time to prepare?" General Raina spoke to his Vice Chief, Lt. Gen. A.M. Vohra, and told him to convey to Shri H.C. Sarin that the expedition would go on and that he had given his last advice as Chairman of IMF.

As part of preparations, we had put together everything possible but we still had no foreign exchange to purchase some important items. Only the year before, India had pledged its gold reserves with the International Monetary Fund to avoid a debt payment crisis. As it turned out, for an expedition like Kanchenjunga-North East Spur, all major mountaineering equipment companies of the world were willing to give their goods for free!

The expedition turned out to be an outstanding success. A big reception awaited us at Gangtok, the capital of Sikkim. Lt. Gen. O.P. Malhotra, PVSM, who had relieved Lt. Gen A.M. Vohra as Vice Chief, came to accord a warm welcome and a grand reception to the entire expedition. We flew to Delhi in a special IAF aircraft, and upon landing at IAF Technical Area, Palam Airport, our expedition was received by none other than General Raina, along with all his PSOs.

A press conference was held at Army House, where General Raina explained the object of launching an Indian Army expedition to Kanchenjunga, which successfully climbed the peak along an untried route for the first time. This achievement of the expedition laid the foundation of the proposed Army Adventure Training Cell.

The successful launch of the maiden project of climbing Kanchenjunga brought glory not only to the Indian Army, but also to Indian mountaineering across the world. This naturally made me and all members of my Kanchenjunga expedition, feel very proud. We were taken to meet Defence Minister Shri Jagjivan Ram,[181] and the Prime Minister Shri Morarji Desai, to brief them about the importance of our Kanchenjunga expedition and what its success meant to the Army.

A few days later, General Raina hosted a dinner in honour of the members of Kanchunjunga expedition at the Army House. There, a "Pipping" Ceremony took place and this Substantive Major and local Lt Col Narinder Kumar was promoted to the rank of Colonel, along with my posting orders to High Altitude Warfare School, Gulmarg, in the appointment of Commandant.

In the meantime, Shri H.C. Sarin, ICS (Retd), Chairman IMF started receiving congratulatory messages from various climbing clubs from all over the world! They all acknowledged that the climb of Kanchenjunga from its North East Spur was one of the most difficult climbs yet done.

The Germans, who had gone up to 26,000 feet on this route but had missed the summit, had been awarded the Olympic Gold Medal. But since this was the first major Indian expedition that had been done without the help and sanction of the Indian Mountaineering Foundation, the IMF failed to adequately acknowledge this unique achievement and did not even recommend me or any member of the Kanchenjunga expedition for any national award. This was despite the fact that there were

---

[181] Babu Jagjivan Ram's inspiring leadership as Defence Minister galvanized the entire nation and the Armed Forces to deal with the crisis in East Pakistan. It was indeed a saga of unparalleled valour, as nearly one lakh soldiers of Pakistan Army laid down their arms before the Indian Army. In fact, the creation of a new nation, Bangladesh brought about a watershed in the geo-politics of South Asia. The historic and decisive victory of 1971 bears testimony to the confidence, patience and immense courage of Babu Ji. It was during his tenure as the Defence Minister that India entered into the Indo-Soviet Treaty of Peace, Friendship and Cooperation.

three Padma Bhushans being awarded to mountaineers that year, but Kanchenjunga remained ignored by the Indian mountaineering circles!

The Indian Army, however, did not fail us. I was awarded the most distinguished service award of Param Vishist Seva Medal (PVSM) for organising and leading this expedition successfully. Similarly, many other members of my expedition were decorated with various honours and awards.

Race to Secure Siachen Glacier

Soon after assuming the appointment of Commandant HAWS, Gulmarg (J&K), Colonel Bull Kumar, through his mountaineering fraternity, learnt about some foreign expeditions being allowed by the Pakistani Army to Siachen Glacier,. This was an intrusion into Indian Territory. The matter was reported to Army HQ. To verify the matter of intrusion by Pakistan Army in the garb of mountaineering expeditions, Commandant HAWS was tasked by Army HQ to obtain confirmation of such activities of the Pakistani Army. Bull Kumar decided to lead an Advance Mountaineering Course for the purpose and soon got down to forming an expedition to Siachen Glacier through Nubra Valley, a task described by him as follows.

> My biggest task as Commandant HAWS was getting Siachen Glacier back to India. The nation should thank General Raina, COAS, for taking bold decisions. It was at his initiative that I had been given the Command of HAWS in the rank of Local Colonel, so that the Indian Army could benefit from my experience and that of my team members in the art of high altitude and snow warfare.
>
> Sometime later I was asked to lead an expedition to Siachen Glacier to plant the Indian tricolour to let the world know that the glacier belonged to India.

Having given his blessings to the proposed expedition to Siachen Glacier, General Raina laid down his appointment as COAS of the Indian Army. The historical expedition to Siachen Glacier led by Bull Kumar[182] turned out to be a game changer and resulted in India occupying this strategic glacier. Siachen Glacier continues to be defended by the Indian Army to ward off the evil design of the nation's adversaries.

---

[182] The plucky mountaineer and gallant soldier and founder of Indian Army Adventure Cell, Colonel Narindar Kumar, PVSM, KC, AVSM, a Padma Shri and MacGreggor Medal awardee, died on 31st December 2020, at about 10.00 AM at Army Hospital (R&R), Delhi Cantt, leaving behind his shattered and grieving beloved wife and supporting inspiration, Mridula, and daughter Shailja.

The family was yet not over their grief on the sudden passing away of their son, on 16th September 2020, when the legendary Bull Kumar too went departure to meet his Maker.

Chapter 33

Higher Defence Organization

Chief of Defence Staff (CDS)

The Higher Defence Organisation of a nation is concerned with the "counsel and wise management" of its defence forces. An efficient and rational defence high command is the base on which the whole edifice of national defence rests. The importance of this base in the context of national security cannot be overemphasized. It is now an accepted truism that a modern war must be fought by all the three Services acting under a unified command and, unless this is done, chances of success will be slender.

During the Second World War, the concept of a unified command in a theatre of operations under a Supreme Commander got firmly established. In the post War days, the concept of Higher Defence Organisation got incorporated in most countries, democratic, socialist or developing — except India! Many nations introduced a professional coordinator or head, who was a top-ranking officer, for the three Services. He was known by different designations in various countries, but a fairly common designation used was Chief of Defence Staff (CDS). In India, however, there was a strong lobby which was opposed to the idea of a Higher Defence Organisation. The civil servants saw in the CDS a rival to their power. Even some Service Chiefs viewed this appointment as an erosion of their respective authority.

In the seven decades since India's independence on 15th August 1947, the Indian Armed Forces have continued to serve the motherland steadfastly and in a totally "apolitical" manner. Despite having fought wars against Pakistan in J&K in 1947-48, 1965, 1971 and 1999, and not forgetting the Sino-India war in 1962, an impression existed until a few years ago that the political leadership in India harboured a lurking fear of a military coup!! Despite the Indian Army's role in saving the State of Kashmir (now J&K) during 1947-48 and its role in defeating the rulers of Hyderabad and Junagarh States, the then political leadership could not be convinced of the mind-set of the Indian military leadership. The ethos, values and philosophy of the Indian Armed Forces, in general, and the Indian Army, in particular, as also the temperament of its military leaders, did not ever contribute to such a misadventure, in contrast to the neighbouring countries.

Subsequent to the Partition, in the Indian Dominion, General Sir Rob Lockhart, KCB, CIE, MC was the first C-in-C of independent India's Army (15th August 1947 to 31st December 1947). He was succeeded by General Sir Roy Bucher, KBE, CB, MC (1st January 1948 to 14th January 1949). It was in the latter's succession that Lieutenant General K.M. Cariappa, OBE, on promotion to the rank of General, became the third C-in-C of Indian Army, and the first Indian to be appointed to this exalted post on 15th January 1949.[183] General Cariappa remained in this appointment for four years, from 15th January 1949 to 14th January 1953. He was succeeded by General Maharaj Rajendrasinhji, DSO as C-in-C Indian Army, for a period of two years. Shortly before his retirement, however, the Government announced the abolishment of the appointment of C-in-C. Instead, each Service would be headed by a Chief of Staff. Thus, General Satyavant Mallanah Shrinagesh became India's first Chief of the Army Staff (COAS). Similarly, heads of the Indian Navy and the Indian Air Force were

[183] Ever since then, Indian Army observes 15th January as Army Day each year.

respectively designated as Chief of the Naval Staff (CNS) and Chief of the Air Staff (CAS).[184]

This decision of the Government of India was a fall-out of the Prime Minister's perception of the Indian Army. Pandit Jawahar Lal Nehru kept the Army leadership away from matters concerning national policy, despite the fact that the Indian Army had been moulded as an "apolitical" one. It seemed that the new leaders of independent India harboured scepticism about the Army's loyalty, possibly because they perceived it as a creation of the erstwhile British rulers. The fact that the civil service and police were equally, if not more, involved in the governance by British Raj, was ignored!

After the end of Second World War, the Indian Army was in the process of re-organisation when the British decided to quit the Indian sub-continent, and partitioned it into two Dominions of the British Empire — India and Pakistan. This also necessitated the division of the British Indian Army between the two nations. The Partition of Indian sub-continent created near civil war conditions in both Dominions, and the Indian Army ensured that migration of people from one Dominion to the other was carried out with minimum bloodshed.

Soon after the country's partition, when the Indian Army needed time for consolidation and re-organisation, it was compelled to get operationally committed in the states of Kashmir, Hyderabad and Junagadh. Despite this role played by Indian Army in the consolidation of India, the political leadership continued to ignore the importance of its Armed Forces in general and the Army in particular. Some of the first steps were the introduction of a New Pay Code (NPC) for Indian Commissioned Officers (ICOs) and the downgrading in the Warrant of Precedence of the status of officers

---

[184] General Maharaj Rajindersinhji, DSO became the first Indian Army General Officer, who after holding the appointment of C-in-C till 31st March 1955, then became COAS for 45 days, from 1st April to 14th May 1955. His successor, General S.M. Shrinagesh, de-facto was the first COAS appointed under the new orders of Government of India, and held this appointment from 15th May 1955 to 7th May 1957.

of the Armed Forces. In addition, the government also wanted to reduce the strength of Indian Army! Within one month of hoisting the national flag on 15th August 1947, Pandit Nehru directed that the strength of Indian Army be reduced to 150,000. In no case was it to be beyond 175,000! The view of the political leadership was that after the war in Kashmir, and the annexation of Hyderabad and Junagadh states, the nation did not need to have a large standing army for the newly independent India.

With the doing away of the appointment of C-in-C in 1955, every function of the three Defence Services was now duplicated in the Ministry of Defence (MOD), where civilian bureaucrats not only exercised financial and administrative control, but also usurped the power of decision making. The Defence Forces accepted the supremacy of the elected Civil Government of the day but, certainly, that did not imply the supremacy of the civil bureaucracy.[185] Pandit Nehru's advisers only added to his phobia of a possible military coup. It is believed that Nehru even consulted Mountbatten in early 1961, in connection with a coup canard. Lord Mountbatten was convinced of the falsity of such reports and advised Nehru that an appointment of the Chief of Defence Staff should be created and given to the then COAS, General K.S. Thimayya. But Mr Nehru's innate distrust of the military as an instrument of the State remained firm. Even after the humiliation at the hands of China during the Sino-Indian conflict in 1962, Nehru's scepticism about the military remained undiminished as he believed that the danger of a military mentality was spreading in India and Army's power increasing; and that bothered him! Until recently, the government shied away from filling up the much needed appointment of Chief of Defence Staff (CDS), despite force levels of the three Services having increased and that too in

---

[185] The Defence Forces implicitly accepted the supremacy of civilian authority; they however felt that civil supremacy did not imply supremacy of the civilian bureaucracy but of the elected representatives of the people. The system also did not cater for statutory structural consultations and interaction between the Defence Services and other departments of the Government at the policymaking level.

the present nuclear and cyber warfare environment and the threat from its two neighbours, China and Pakistan. Even the role of Armed Forces in the liberation of East Pakistan and the creation of a new neighbouring nation, Bangladesh, did not convince successive governments of the need for a Higher Defence Organisation for India headed by a Chief of Defence Staff.

Over the past few decades, thus, the three Armed Forces have grown as three separate entities, with little commonality. Indian Army, Indian Navy and Indian Air Force, each have their own branches, each separately doing the same things, whether in the field of communication, maintenance, logistics or operations, thus incurring avoidable expenditure annually unlike the way other modern-day armed forces have evolved. Nearly sixty-five years ago when the appointment of C-in-C was abolished, successive Indian governments continued with the ad-hoc arrangement of having a Chiefs of Staff Committee without a permanent Chairman.

Since 1955, the successive governments in India followed an ad-hoc arrangement of higher defence organization in India, by creating the appointment of Chairman, Chief of Staff Committee (COSC), instead of a full time Chief of Defence Staff (CDS), with its own secretariat. To spread the message and wider understanding about the need for a CDS, United Service Institution of India (USI) organized a seminar at Vigyan Bhawan which was attended by a large number of senior serving and retired defence officers, bureaucrats and some of senior journalists. Colonel Pyara Lal, AVSM, the then Secretary USI, was the main co-ordinator for organising this seminar with a far reaching message for the need of an HDO for India with a CDS to head it. Colonel Pyara Lal and his team worked directly under the direction of General T.N. Raina, MVC, who was not only the COAS, Chairman, Chiefs of Staff Committee, but also Vice Patron of the USI. The views and recommendations of this seminar were further reinforced in the USI Paper No 7, titled Higher Defence Organisation in India (June 1980) by late Lt. Gen. S.K. Sinha, PVSM, the then Adjutant General, Army HQ, New Delhi.

Chairman Chiefs of Staff Committee

The chairmanship of the Chiefs of Staff Committee rotated among the three Service Chiefs, with the senior most Chiefs Of Staff in tenure presiding over its meeting. On 1st March 1976, Tappy Raina took over the additional responsibility of great national importance when he succeeded Admiral S.N. Kohli, PVSM, CNS as Chairman COSC.[186] He held this position with his typical imagination and vision till his retirement on 31st May 1978.

Tappy Raina knew exactly what he wanted to achieve as COAS and Chairman COSC and pushed his ideas and proposals with phenomenal energy and drive. This was done with transparent sincerity backed by his personal charm and rapport with the higher ups. The latter included the Prime Minister, Defence Minister (Raksha Mantri), Cabinet Secretary, other Secretaries in the Departments of Defence, Finance, and Home, and the Prime Minister's Secretariat (there was no PMO then). Tappy's determined, unbiased and honest approach achieved quick government clearance and approval. This resulted in the implementation of various important proposals and projects affecting not only the Army but all the three Services. One of the far reaching decisions taken was the transfer of the existing arrangement of maritime air reconnaissance responsibility from Indian Air Force to Indian Navy. This, of course, was to the great satisfaction of Admiral Jal Cursetji, PVSM, CNS, but with reluctance on the part of Chief of the Air Staff, Air Chief Marshal Hrushikesh Moolgavkar, PVSM, MVC.[187]

About the same time, the Army's proposal for the creation of an Army Aviation Corps was also almost approved, but by that time there was a change of government at the Centre, and a new Janata

---

[186] Air Chief Marshal O.P. Mehra, PVSM, Chief of the Air Staff was Chairman COSC until his superannuation on 31st January 1976. He was succeeded by Admiral S.N. Kohli, PVSM, CNS as COSC from 1st February to 29th February 1976.

[187] He was a fellow student of Tappy Raina at the first DSSC course held at Wellington (Nilgiris). ACM Moolgavkar had earned the second highest gallantry award of Maha Vir Chakra, during war in J&K (1947-48). He remained CAS during most of Tappy's tenure as COAS & Chairman COSC.

Government under Morarji Desai as Prime Minister came to power. Unwisely, the new Government put on hold most of the important decisions affecting national defence and security of the previous Government. Thus ACM Moolgavkar succeeded in preventing the transfer of the assets of the IAF to the proposed Army Aviation Corps[188].

Finally, the Indian Government accepted the operational necessity for a Chief of Defence Staff and Prime Minister Narendra Modi himself announced to the nation from the ramparts of the historic Red Fort, Delhi, on 15th August 2019, that the Armed Forces of India would soon have a Chief of Defence Staff (CDS).

The Government subsequently issued orders and appointed a four star General as the first CDS. General Bipin Rawat, PVSM, UYSM, AVSM, YSM, SM, VSM, the outgoing COAS was selected to be India's first Chief of Defence Staff. Relevant government orders were issued on 24th December 2019 and General Rawat assumed his new appointment on 1st January 2020. This new organisation, envisaged several decades earlier will, undoubtedly, continue to evolve and fine tune its functioning over time. Its prime task will be the integration of the three armed forces of India. The CDS will be the Principal Military Adviser to the Defence Minister (Raksha Mantri). He will, however, not exercise military command over the three services.

The government approved the appointment of CDS in four star rank with twin hats: Secretary to a new Department of Military Affairs (DMA) in MOD and also Permanent Chairman, Chiefs of Staff Committee (PC-COSC). In fact, no one expected a CDS quite in the manner the Modi Government announced a Service Chief was elevated to the post of CDS to serve till the age of 65 years of age. Nor did anyone visualise a new Department of Military Affairs, unique to India, under the CDS. It takes away from the civilian Defence Secretary, a bulk of the charter of his work.

---

[188] Army Aviation Corps was finally created in the Indian Army on 1st November 1986. About the same time, the Regiment of Artillery was further bifurcated by the creation of Army Air Defense Corps on 12th January 1994.

Chapter 34

Farewell to Arms

Once General Raina reached the top rung of the promotion ladder, by and large he seemed more relaxed. The major decisions he had planned for better operational readiness and welfare of all ranks of Indian Army, all stood approved. Notable among them were the Army Group Insurance (AGI) and the Army Welfare Housing Organisation (AWHO), among many other such projects. Some other measures such as scholarships for meritorious children of servicemen from AG's Welfare Funds, the setting up of Army Public School at Dhaula Kuan, Delhi Cantonment, as a precursor to a chain of such schools throughout the country in all Military Stations, was also implemented during his tenure as COAS. Many other welfare schemes that were in the process of being formalised when Tappy Raina demitted office on 31st May 1978 came to fruition over the next couple of years under his able successor, General Om Prakash Malhotra. Having been closely associated with the formulation of these schemes, General Malhotra ensured that the Army Welfare Societies started functioning with full steam before the end of his own tenure.

Obtaining the approvals of various Ministries and State Governments that were required for these schemes, considering their legendary sloth in taking decisions, was quite creditable for Tappy Raina. This success was a tribute to meticulous staff work, especially by the PSOs at Army HQ, namely Lieutenant Generals Jaswant Singh, who was later succeeded by K.V. Krishna Rao, as DCOAS, R.D. Hira, AG, A.N. Mathur, QMG, S.D. Gupta, MGO, with the coordination and guidance by Lt. General A.M. Vohra,

VCOAS, who was later succeeded by Lt. Gen. O.P. Malhotra. In addition to the team of PSOs, there were some key appointment holders for the execution of General Raina's plans. They were, Lieutenant Generals Kundan Singh, Military Secretary, J.S. Bawa, E-in-C, R.P. Sapra, SO-in-C and other directors of Arms and Services, not forgetting the part played by Maj. Gens. A.S. Vaidya, M.L. Chibber, the then Directors Military Operations, S.K. Sinha and Hriday Kaul, as Directors Military Intelligence.

Also at play was General Raina's personal rapport with Shri S.C. Katoch, IA & AS, Finance Advisor (Defence). It has to be conceded that General Raina's clarity in presentation of his plans, sincerity of purpose and direct contact with the Prime Minister and Defence Minister helped in obtaining prompt decisions. Also, it was the timing: the political leadership of India had been most impressed by the performance of the Armed Forces and was therefore amenable to accepting these proposals.[189]

General Raina had recommended improvement in the pay and pension of all the ranks of the Indian Army; instead, a case for "cadre-review" was suggested from some quarters. This was not acceptable to Tappy because he believed that the Indian Army was structured in such a way that the rank and appointment of each individual was specific to the nature of responsibility. He was in favour of upgrading certain appointments based on functional necessity, both in staff and instructional duties.

During his tenure as COAS, more than 300 need based appointments of officers were upgraded. After General Raina's retirement, however, the Indian Army along with the other two Services succumbed to the temptation and adopted a cadre review, which upset the Army's traditional rank and appointment structure. Such upgradations led both to avoidable dilution of each rank without appropriate appointments and also to professional satisfaction.

---

[189] The other two Services were quick to follow and their equivalent welfare societies were formed very soon after, on lines similar to that of the Army.

Farewell to the Indian Army

After putting in more than thirty-six years of distinguished service, and on completion of his three-year tenure as Chief of the Army Staff, General Tapishwar Narain Raina, MVC and Padma Bhushan awardee, proceeded on retirement on 31st May 1978, at the age of 57 years and 5 months.

On the eve of handing over his charge as COAS, General Raina, in his Special Order of the Day, conveyed the following message:

> As I lay down my office as COAS, I thank you all, from the senior most officer to the newly joined recruit, and also all civilians in the Defence Services for the cooperation, loyalty and support you have given in my tenure.
>
> I retire from the Army with a feeling of immense satisfaction and utmost admiration for the service, which both nurtured and matured me. I shall always remember with a deep sense of gratitude the spirit of comradeship and fellow feeling which cannot be matched elsewhere.
>
> I shall take away many impressions into the evening of life, but the one which I shall treasure above all, is the picture of the Indian soldier — staunch and tenacious in adversity, humane and gentle in victory — the man to whom the Nation has time and again, in the hour of trial, looked upon to ensure its safety and honour. I will conclude my military service by paying homage to him — my friend and comrade-in-arms during the last thirty-six years.
>
> I also take this opportunity to wish good luck, success and all happiness to my successor, General O.P. Malhotra. I am confident that all of you will continue to discharge your duties with the same zeal and dedication as you have done during my tenure as your Chief.

On the last day of his army service, General Raina arrived at Army Headquarters in South Block where he was met and escorted by Major General Aban Naidu, PVSM, GOC Delhi Area, to the COAS Secretariat. There he was received by Lieutenant General O.P. Malhotra, PVSM (COAS Designate) and Shri S. Banerjee, IAS, Defence Secretary, Ministry of Defence. At a brief ceremony, General Raina formally handed over the appointment and the office of the COAS to his VCOAS, General Malhotra, after which General Raina was accorded a warm ceremonial send-off from Army Headquarters. That same day General Raina also relinquished his responsibility as Chairman, Chiefs of Staff Committee, which he had held creditably since 1st March 1976. Air Chief Marshal H. Moolgavkar, PVSM, MVC, Chief of Air Staff, assumed the Chairmanship of the Chiefs of Staff Committee.

A guard of honour was presented by the contingent of 3 Kumaon (Rifles) on the lawns of South Block. After inspecting the smart Guard of Honour, General Raina complimented Lieutenant Colonel (later Brigadier) K. George, the Commanding Officer of the Battalion. Thereafter, the General took leave of his successor, General Malhotra, and all PSOs and Heads of Arms and Services of Army Headquarters who had lined up to bid farewell to their outgoing Chief.

That evening a social farewell function was held at the Defence Services Officers' Institute (DSOI), Dhaula Kuan, Delhi Cantonment. After meeting the officers and ladies, General and Mrs. Raina, were given an affectionate and touching send off by all officers of Army Headquarters, Delhi Area. At the end of the evening, General Raina was carried by his fellow officers on their shoulders, lustily *"That he was a Jolly Good Fellow"*! General Malhotra and his gracious wife, Saroj, escorted General and Mrs. Raina to the waiting staff car in the porch of DSOI, where they took their leave of the Malhotras and drove straight from DSOI Dhaula Kuan to their own home in Greater Kailash I, New Delhi.

Part VI

Dedication to the Regiment

"Whatever a great man does that, other men also do; whatever he sets up as the standard, which the world follows."
~ Bhagavad Gita. 3.21

Chapter 35

Colonel of the Regiment

Colonel of the Regiment (COR) is a key element in the regimental system of the Indian Army, inherited from the days when it was a part of the British Indian Army. With its roots going back to the 18th century, when "Colonels" owned and equipped their regiments, whereas Colonel of the Regiment of today is the head of the family and responsible for the protection of the best interests of the regiment. He is almost always of the rank of a General officer, who has at some time served in the regiment.

The last British soldier left India with the Somerset Light Infantry shortly after India's independence, but Indian Army regiments continued to have British Generals as Colonel Commandant or Colonel of the Regiment for years thereafter. The post-Independence army of India wisely decided to retain the practice that the British had introduced of selecting one of the senior serving officers of the rank of General Officer as Colonel Commandant or Colonel of the Regiment. He would have served in the Regiment, and preferably commanded one of its battalions. Such a figure is the binding force that ensures harmony amongst the units constituting the regiment. This appointment bestows additional responsibility on the selected senior officer in guiding all ranks of the regiment, as its "father figure" on matters affecting the regiment. In discharging his onerous duty to the regiment, the COR is greatly assisted by the respective commandants of the Regimental Centre.

During his tenure as COAS cum Chairman Chiefs of Staffs Committee, General Raina was also Colonel of The Kumaon and Naga Regiments, Colonel of 61 Cavalry, and Honorary Colonel of the Brigade of Guards. Despite his pre-occupation with matters of higher command, he still found time to discharge his duty towards all these regiments as their Colonel. But the strain of this began to be felt by him towards the end of his tenure as COAS.

Colonel of the Kumaon Regiment

At the time of the India's partition, Major General Sydney B. Pope, CB, DSO, was the Colonel of the 19 Hyderabad Regiment (later Kumaon Regiment) for about eighteen years, from 28th August 1931 to 31st May 1949. He is credited with getting the name of 19 Hyderabad Regiment changed to 19 Kumaon Regiment on 27th October 1945. He was responsible for the relocation of The Kumaon Regiment Centre (KRC) from Agra to Ranikhet in District Almora. This was in recognition of the valour and excellent performance by the troops of the Regiment during the Second World War. Soon thereafter, the prefix "19" was dropped and ever since then it has been designated as "The Kumaon Regiment". Each year, 27th October is celebrated as "Kumaon Day" by Kumaon Regimental Centre and all Battalions of the Regiment.

The first post-war Reunion of the Regiment and the Battalion Commanders' Conference was held at the Kumaon Regimental Centre, Ranikhet, on 29th May 1949. Although Lieutenant General (later General and COAS) S.M. Shrinagesh was the senior most officer of the regiment, but in the long term interest of the Regiment and to provide continuity, Lieutenant General Shrinagesh proposed that Major General K.S. Thimayya, DSO, (later General and COAS) be selected as the first Indian Colonel of the Kumaon Regiment. Accordingly, during the Battalion Commanders' Conference, Major General K.S. Thimayya was unanimously selected by the Commandant KRC and Battalion Commanders of the Regiment. This was approved by all other senior officers present, including Major General Yadunath Singh, MVC, Brigadier (later

Lieutenant General) K. Bahadur Singh, MBE and Brigadier (later Major General) K. Bhagwati Singh.

Major General K.S. Thimayya thus became the first Indian Colonel of The Kumaon Regiment on 1st June 1949, and held this appointment for nearly twelve years. He was succeeded by Lieutenant General K. Bahadur Singh, MBE,[190] on 8th May 1961, who held this appointment for the next ten years. On retirement from Army service, Lieutenant General K. Bahadur Singh was appointed the Lieutenant Governor of Himachal Pradesh. Nevertheless, he continued to discharge his duty as Colonel of the Kumaon Regiment till he was succeeded by Major General Tappy Raina on 16th May 1971. Colonelcy of the regiment is the highest honour that a regiment can accord to a regimental officer. On the other hand, the Kumaonis could not have done better. Even before he had accepted this appointment, General Raina had been taking an active interest in the regiment's affairs as one of its elder family members.

General Raina was Deputy Adjutant General in Army HQ at the time of his appointment as Colonel of the Regiment. During that tenure he had played an important role in convincing the then Chief of the Army Staff, General S.H.F.J. Manekshaw to affiliate the proposed new Naga Regiment with the Kumaon Regiment.

Colonel of the Naga Regiment

Shortly after his appointment as Colonel of The Kumaon Regiment, General Raina was approached by the newly raised Naga Regiment to accept the Colonelcy of the Naga Regiment, which he graciously did. He assumed this appointment on 8th Junc 1971, thus becoming the third Indian officer as Colonel of The Kumaon

---

[190] Commissioned from RMC Sandhurst in October 1932 and joined 4/19 Hyderabad Regiment. He held various staff and command appointments. After being Adjutant General for three years, he was founder Commandant of the National Defence College (NDC). He later became the first GOC-in-C Central Command, Lucknow. On retirement from the Army, General K. Bahadur Singh was appointed Lt. Governor of Himachal Pradesh.

Regiment and the first Colonel of The Naga Regiment; a unique distinction in the post-Independence Indian Army.[191]

That same year he also had the unique honour of raising a new Corps to meet the threat of war in East Pakistan. He was appointed GOC 2 Corps on 7th October 1971, as part of Eastern Command, responsible for the liberation of East Pakistan. 2 Corps was operationally responsible for the South-Western Sector of East Pakistan (now Bangladesh). For exceptional leadership of his corps and professional qualities of a high order in the service of the nation, the Government of India awarded Tappy Raina the Padma Bhushan.

After his successful command of 2 Corps, General Tappy Raina moved to Shimla in October 1973 to assume command as GOC-in-C of the largest and operationally most important Western Command of the Army. Earlier, he had earned name and fame when the whole country came to view him as the saviour of Ladakh, during the Sino-India war of 1962. As we saw earlier in the book, under Tappy Raina's command 114 Infantry Brigade had blunted the Chinese attack to capture Chushul, the gateway to Leh, the District Headquarters and former capital of Ladakh.

A popular, respected and battle-tested Army officer, General Tappy Raina had grown to be an inspiring leader. Though sympathetic to the needs of all ranks, he was firm in matters of discipline, duty, and pride in the regiment's customs and traditions.

During his tenure as Colonel of The Kumaon and Naga Regiments, Tappy Raina was responsible for the creation of the following important institutions at The Kumaon Regimental Centre, Ranikhet:

- Regimental Mankameshwar Temple.
- The Bandage Weaving Training Centre (now KRC Woollen Centre).

---

[191] The convention of Colonel of The Kumaon Regiment also holding the Colonelcy of the Naga Regiment still continues. General Raina held these responsibilities with great distinction and benefit to both regiments till his retirement on 31st May 1978.

- War Widows Weaving Training Centre
- Regimental War Memorial.
- Regimental Museum.
- Mankameshwar Mandir.
- Refurbishing of KRC Officers' Mess (Heritage Building).
- Promotion of Sports.
- Regimental Reunion — 1976.
- Regimental Colours to 18 Kumaon and The Naga Regiment.

Weaving Training Centre for War Widows

The wars of 1947-48, 1962, 1965 and 1971, as also the counter-insurgency operations in the Northeast of the country, resulted in a large number of casualties. Thus there were numerous bereaved families of army personnel. General Raina, as Colonel of the Regiment, obtained the government's approval to establish a vocational training centre for the rehabilitation of war widows of the regiment where they could be taught skills to enhance their earning capacity.

Accordingly, a Bandage Weaving Training Centre was set up in 1977 at the Kumaon Regimental Centre, Ranikhet with the assistance of the Directorate General of Rehabilitation, Ministry of Defence. The scope of the project was later enlarged from weaving only bandages to also include preparation of woollen shawls, tartans and tweed cloth.

The finished product was initially marketed from the sale counter of the weaving centre, at a nominal profit to individuals of the Kumaon Regimental Centre. The income from the sale proceeds was utilised for giving stipends to the trainees and for meeting the cost of wool and other ancillary charges. Based on the success of this project[192], the earnings of trainees increased from Rs. 300 per month to Rs 1,800 per month, in just five years since the establishment of the weaving centre in 1977.

---

[192] To rehabilitate more widows and their dependents, another training-cum-production centre for weaving woollens was set up at KRC Ranikhet in another old deconsecrated church in 1984.

War Memorial

At the end of the World War 2, Major General Sydney B. Pope, Colonel of the Regimental Centre, as well as all battalion commanders and other senior officers of the 19 Hyderabad Regiment, felt the need for commemorating the deeds of valour, triumph and sacrifice of the brave martyrs of the regiment by erecting a suitable war memorial. The decision, however, remained deferred, till well after 19 Hyderabad Regiment was re-designated as The Kumaon Regiment and a permanent home for the Kumaon Regimental Centre (KRC) provided at Ranikhet in May 1948.

Many Kumaoni and Naga soldiers had shed their blood and lost lives in the three major wars with Pakistan, respectively, in 1947-48, 1965 and 1971 as also the Sino-India War in 1962, and counter insurgency operations in the Northeast of the country, and in Jammu and Kashmir. While the nation remembers its soldiers and their sacrifice only in the hour of national crisis, a regiment enshrines the memory and deeds of such martyrs forever. A war memorial, therefore, is the sacred symbol and testimony of their blood, fortitude and sacrifice that a proud regiment takes inspiration from before its soldiers set forth to the battlefield.

Once again it fell upon the shoulders of General Raina to give shape to the unfinished task of setting up a regimental war memorial at the home of The Kumaon and Naga Regiments at KRC, Ranikhet. Tappy Raina could not have found a better Centre Commandant than late Colonel P.C. Mehta, AVSM (formerly of 4 and 2 Kumaon), ably assisted by the then Adjutant KRC, Captain (later Lieutenant General) Arjun Ray (8 Kumaon) to give shape to this project.

The late Ms. Shona Ray, the architect who was engaged for this project suggested that instead of the common universal design of war memorials in the shape of a vertical column, the war memorial at Ranikhet should express the theme of the fallen martyrs having gone back to the lap of Mother Earth — ashes to ashes, dust to dust. The design of the proposed war memorial agreed upon was in the shape of two arched walls, depicting the lap of the mother. Once the design was approved by Colonel of the Regiment, the Commandant, Colonel P.C. Mehta set into motion the construction of Kumaon Regimental War Memorial in February 1974. It was located at the entrance to the main Recruit Training Area cum Drill Square on Som Nath Ground[193], Dulikhet. The memorial, merging into the cedars, lifted high the scroll of martyrs on its central curves. Set in golden Jaisalmer stone, the monument appeared to rise from the womb of Mother Earth into the icy blue skies above.

Regimental Museum

Ever since Kumaon Regimental Centre moved from Agra to its permanent home in Ranikhet in 1948, a need was felt for starting a museum to enshrine the regiment's rich heritage of over 160 years. In the absence of a suitable building, old historical objects, weapons, equipment and records were kept in different places at the regimental centre.

The concept and location of the museum was discussed in detail with Mr Siali, Chief Architect, E-in-C Branch, Army HQ. The interior design was planned and executed by a renowned company of architects and designers based in New Delhi. The approval of Army Headquarters had been accorded for its construction, and funds accordingly provided. The foundation stone of the museum was laid during the 7th Post War Reunion on 29th October 1976. The museum building was completed by April 1978 and all artefacts selected for display were moved and arranged in it in accordance with the period of the regiment's history, i.e. from 1788 to 1971. The design and layout of the museum was quite distinct to other government buildings. The collection of objects and artefacts on display are awesome, varied and numerous. They take the visi-

---

[193] The main training area of the Kumaon Regimental Training Centre was named Som Nath Ground in memory of Major Som Nath Sharma, the first recipient of the nation's highest gallantry award, the Param Vir Chakra. Major Sharma laid down his life in the Battle of Badgam in 1947.

tor through a journey of the annals of the regiment, its rich history of valour and triumphs, of dedication and devotion to duty.

The foundation stone was laid on 29th October 1976 by General Raina and Kumaon Regiment Museum inaugurated by him in May 1978 just before his retirement on 31st May 1978.

Mankameshwar Mandir

Tappy Raina believed that religion universally signifies the quest for the Divine Truth that every culture and every individual around the world seeks. No conviction is more universal, no theory more fundamental than this. Life must have its origin in the Divine Spirit of God. Goddess Durga in the form of Kali Mata is the deity of Kumaon Regiment. She is enshrined not only in the Regimental Centre temple but in all battalions of the Kumaon Regiment.

The Mankameshwar Temple at the Kumaon Regimental Centre, Ranikhet was initially constructed in 1972 with *shramdan* (troop labour) as a matter of faith. Presently the temple is dedicated to Goddess Kalika, Lord Siva and Shri Radha-Krishna.

KRC Officers' Mess — Heritage Building

After taking over as COR, General Raina took the initiative to improve and restore the character of the Officers' Mess building, which was being threatened with demolition by MES engineers. Thanks to General Raina's efforts, the KRC Officers' Mess and the attached Annexe, now called The Kumaon Lodge, were declared as heritage buildings. KRC managed to thwart many proposals by MES engineers to demolish and rebuild these two buildings. Subsequently, steps were taken to strengthen the buildings without altering the character.

Until 1975, the original KRC Officers' Mess building had an open verandah, running in the front and to its southern side. Keeping in view the vagaries of the weather, the fog, snow and sleet, General Raina directed Commandant KRC to ensure that the entire verandah and the Band Stand of the Officers' Mess were properly glazed well before the regimental reunion in 1976. It has been a boon for the mess building[194] to have become climatically controlled and insulated, where some of the trophies could be dislayed.

Sports

General Raina raised the matter of promoting sports and games within the Regiment at the Battalion Commanders' Conference at KRC in October 1972. It was decided that the KRC would play a pivotal role in training regimental teams in boxing, basketball and long distance running. Battalions located in peace stations would train the regimental teams in hockey, football, swimming and athletics. This policy paid rich dividends when sportsmen from The Kumaon and Naga Regiments started earning laurels in various all India sports meets. This was particularly so in the case of Boxing where under the coaching of Havildar (APTC) Om Prakash,[195] young boxers, including those from amongst recruits, were able to successively win the All India YMCA Boxing Tournament held at New Delhi. Similarly, individual sportsmen in long distance running also started winning in national level meets.

Battalion Commander's Biennial Conferences

It is customary for battalion commanders of infantry regiments to assemble at their respective regimental centres to resolve such important regimental matters as raised by the battalions. Army Headquarters had sanctioned that each Regimental Centre can host such a conference once every two years, and a Regimental Reunion for ex-servicemen and war bereaved families, every four to six years at the respective Regimental Centres. During General Raina's tenure as COR, he presided over the 11th, 12th and 13th

[194] A new library building was constructed across the drive way, at the time of Bicentenary Reunion in 1988.

[195] Hav (APTC) Om Prakash later became a national coach for boxing.

Battalion Commanders' Biennial conferences in the years 1972, 1974 and 1976, respectively.

The 7th Post War Reunion cum 13th Biennial Battalion Commanders' Conference of Kumaon & Naga Regiments was held at KRC Rainkhet from 26th to 29th October 1976, to coincide with Kumaon Day on 27th October. Lieutenant Colonel (later Lieutenant General & COR) D.D. Saklani, the officiating Commandant KRC and his team of officers, JCOs and NCOs left no stone unturned in organising each and every event in great detail.

Regimental Reunion, 1976

For every serving and retired soldier, a Regimental Reunion is an occasion to look forward to. It is also an occasion to recall and remember the times and experiences of bygone days. The Kumaon Reunion in October 1976 was particularly memorable for those who attended it. To begin with, it was the first reunion that General T.N. Raina, COAS, hosted as Colonel of The Kumaon & Naga Regiments. The chief guest was another distinguished former officer of the Regiment, General Tan Sri Ibrahim Bin Ismail, PMN, SPMJ, SPMK, SPDK, PNBS, DIMP, PIS, Chief of the Armed Forces Staff, Ministry of Defence, Malaysia. The latter was accompanied by his wife, Puan Sri Zakiah Ibrahim. Like the Prime Minister of Malaysia, the Hon'ble Datuk Hussein Onn, General Tan Sri Ibrahim Bin Ismail had also served with 19 Hyderabad Regiment during World War 2.

General Ibrahim had a strong love for his old Regiment, and he shared many nostalgic memories of his days with such famous personalities of the Regiment as General S.M. Shrinagesh (former COAS), who was his company commander at IMA, Dehra Dun, and General K.S. Thimayya, DSO, (also a former COAS), who was his company commander at 19 Hyderabad Regiment Training Centre, Agra. General Tan Sri Ibrahim Bin Ismail was proud of the fact that he had served under both. As a gentleman cadet, Gen Ibrahim Bin Ismail did his training at IMA, Dehradun with another illustrious son of the regiment, late Major Som Nath Sharma, PVC.

This was perhaps the first occasion in the Regiment's history that a former Colonel of the Regiment also came all the way from Kotah (Rajasthan) to attend a regimental reunion. It was a great gesture on the part of Lieutenant General Kanwar Bahadur Singh, MBE and the "Rani Saheba", to grace some of the functions. Also for the first time two retired British officers of the regiment, now members of Kumaon Regiment Dinner Club, London, were present at this reunion. Lieutenant Colonel A.T.B. Craig (former CO 3 Kumaon (Rifles) and 7 Kumaon) had come from his home in Broadstairs, Kent (UK), and Lieutenant Colonel Robert Going had come from Killarney, Ireland.

Valour Triumphs: A History of the Kumaon Regiment

When he was GOC-in-C Western Command, Lieutenant General Tappy Raina, in addition to his duties as Army Commander, made time to attend to various regimental matters as the COR, including publishing the history of The Kumaon Regiment. After finalisation of the structure of the proposed history, the author, Major K.C. Praval got busy in preparing the draft manuscript of the book.

The preparatory work of compiling the material for the book, and the offering of assistance to the author, required close linkage between the author and Colonel of the Regiment. Major Praval would send the draft of each chapter to Shimla by post. Lieutenant Colonel Ravi Mahajan, AMS, HQ Western Command, would already have studied the particular period covered by the draft in the well-stocked HQ Western Command library, as also in the regimental records, available in the secretariat of the Colonel of the Regiment. Such corrections or suggestions in the draft manuscript, would then be returned to the author, by post.

On some occasions, the author was invited to Shimla, for personal discussions to resolve certain issues. This practice continued even after General Raina's move to AHQ, New Delhi, when the author would come to discuss and finalise some important issues specially pertaining to the Indo-Pakistan War in 1971. The pictorial sections of the book were also finalised during these sessions. It was then decided that the proposed Regimental History of the Kumaon Regiment would be printed and published by Thompson Press, Faridabad.

An event that added to the uniqueness of the Regimental Reunion in 1976 was the release of the book, *Valour Triumphs: A History of The Kumaon Regiment*, authored by Major Karam C. Praval. The book[196] was released by General T.N. Raina, MVC, at the Reunion Dinner held at KRC Officer's Mess, Ranikhet on 27th October 1976. It was a proud moment for the author[197] and for Kumaon Regiment. The project that had begun soon after General Raina took over as Colonel of the Regiment in May 1971[198], was, finally, successfully concluded.

It was a mammoth task to faithfully compile the deeds of about one score battalions of the Regiment, spanning nearly two centuries; and it was a lasting tribute to General Raina's dedication to the Regiment in which he had the honour to serve.

---

[196] Speaking on the occasion, General Raina emphasized, that there could be no triumph without valour, hence the title of the book *Parakramo Vijayate* (valour triumphs). This is also the Motto of the Regiment that inspires the younger generations to display valour and seek triumphs!

[197] Major Praval retired from the Army in 1969, after 34 years of service. He lived through a good bit of the period which he narrates in this book. During the Second World War, he served in North Africa where he won the Indian Distinguished Service Medal (IDSM). He had varied experiences in the Army and contributed to various journals. He is the author of *India's Paratroopers*, published in 1974.

[198] When the draft manuscript was sent for printing, Lieutenant Colonel Ravi Mahajan, MA to COAS, would proof-read at the press itself, to speed up the process. Later, the proof-reading was completed by his successor, the author of the present book.

General T.N. Raina presenting credentials as India's High Commissioner in Canada.

Amar Jyoti Trophy presented by Gen and Mrs T.N. Raina, to 5 Mech Inf Bn (Kumaon), in memory of their only son, Capt Jyoti Narain Raina, who died on duty. Joe had served meritoriously in the battalion which was formerly 14 Kumaon (Gwalior) and earlier commanded by Gen Tappy Raina (1957-1959).

Capt Joe Raina during the war for the liberation of Bangladesh in December 1971.

Visit to Nepal: Gen and Mrs Raina being received by Gen and Mrs Shamsher Guna Bahadur at Tribhuvan Airport, Kathmandu.

Visit to USA: Gen Raina visits the Indian Embassy in USA. On his left are Ambassador Nani Palhkhivala, Lt Gen "Rocky" Hira, Maj Gen M.L. Chibber, Maj S.K. Sapru Deputy MA to COAS and Brig D.S.C. Rai, Defence Attache.

Reunion. Three former of cers of 19th Hyderabad Regiment (now Kumaon Regiment) reunited at Kuala Lumpur. Left to right: General T.N. Raina, COAS Indian Army, Hon'ble Datuk Hussein Onn, Prime Minister of Malaysia and Gen Tan Sri Ibrahim Bin Ismail, CAFS, MOD, DF Malaysia, 18th April 1977.

General Raina in cordial discussion with Gen Gholam Reza Azhari at Tehran during his visit to Iran in November 1976.

Senior army of cers serve as Tappy Raina's pall bearers at the electric crematorium, Nigambodh Ghat, Delhi.

Ninette at home, surrounded by memories of Tappy and Joe.

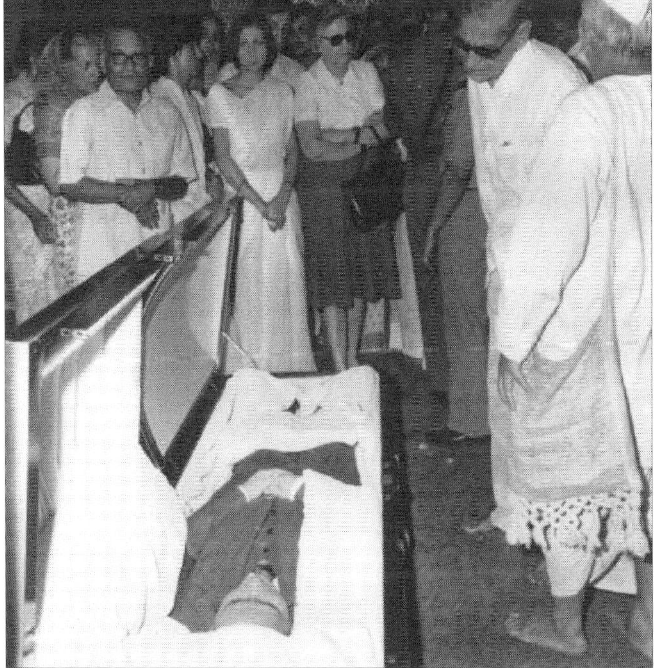

Farewell Tapu. Elder brother Suraj Raina emotionally gazing at his younger brother. Ninette and Anita Raina standing by somberly.

1st Chief's Conclave, 4th October 2003. Sitting from L to R: Dr (Mrs) Ranjana Malik, Mrs Swaroop Sharma, Mrs Radha Krishna Rao, Mrs Ninette Raina, Mrs Piroja Kumaramangalam, Mrs Radhika Bewoor, Mrs Raj Kumari Shrinagesh, Mrs Rita Vij, Mrs Bimla Thapar, Mrs Saroj Malhotra, Mrs Vani Sundarji, Mrs Jean Rodrigues, Mrs Krishna Roychowdhury and Mrs Roopa Padmanabhan.

Standing from L to R: Gen V.P. Malik, Gen S.F. Rodrigues, Gen K.V. Krishna Rao, Field Marshal S.H.F.J. Manekshaw, Gen N.C. Vij, Gen O.P. Malhotra, Gen V.N. Sharma, Gen S. Roychowdhury and Gen S. Padmanabhan.

Highlights of the Reunion

The presence of two Chiefs, General Tan Sri Ibrahim Bin Ismail, Chief of Armed Forces staff, Ministry of Defence, Malaysia, and General Raina, Chief of Army Staff, Indian Army, besides a large number of ladies, among them, Puan Sri Zakiah Ibrahim and Mrs. Ninette Raina, lent a good deal of colour and grace to each and every function connected with this historic Reunion.

For General Raina it was particularly heartening to see such a large turnout of pensioners who had come from the states of UP, Rajasthan, Madhya Pradesh, Haryana, Manipur and Nagaland. They were there in hundreds. Most of them looked fit and sprightly. Some were bent and shrivelled with age, their clothes hanging loosely upon them. But one thing was common to them all; the flame of the Kumaoni spirit burned in their hearts with equal warmth whether they were Kumaonis, Ahirs or Rajputs. Their faces lit up every time the Colonel of the Regiment, General Tappy Raina appeared amidst them. And when he spoke to them or shook hands with them, it looked as if their life's ambition had been fulfilled. Such are the bonds that tie a regiment together as one family. The mental pictures of the various events organised at this reunion remained etched in the minds of all those who were fortunate to be part of this grand event.

Every reunion at The Kumaon Regimental Centre is not only a great occasion for the Kumaon and Naga Regiments, but it is also a tremendous attraction for the people of Kumaon Hills in general, and of Ranikhet, in particular. The spectacle and the many colourful ceremonies that form part of the Reunion always bring cheer to them. They flock to Som Nath Ground[199] to witness every event with great eagerness. The Kumaon and Naga Regiments will,

---

[199] The main Parade Ground in Dulikhet, originally known as "Dulikhet Maidan," also doubled up as a Race Course and Polo Ground, right up to 1947, when British troops were located here. After the arrival of KRC from Agra in 1948, this Ground became the training area for the recruits. It was named after Major Som Nath Sharma, PVC (posthumous).

however, have to wait for many years to witness a reunion of the kind and scale that took place in October 1976. It was unique!

Colour Presentation to 18 Kumaon and The Naga Regiment

The origin of the custom of carrying Colours in the Army goes back in time, when a man fixed his family emblem to a pole and held it up in battle. This served the dual purpose of indicating his position and, at the same time, also acted as a rallying point. Major victories in battlefields were emblazoned on the Regimental Colours. With the advent of regimentation in British Indian Army, each regiment was presented Colours by the king or ruler of the country. In the case of India, Colours are presented to the armed forces by the country's President.

Regimental Colours symbolize the spirit of those who serve under them. Representing all that is noble and honourable, they are a call to loyalty and chivalry, demanding the best service and the noblest quality in man. They are the pride and living spirit of every battalion for they recall all those who laid down their lives in the battles that earned the Battle Honour emblazoned on the Colour. It is customary to stand up and salute the Colours whenever these are paraded on ceremonial occasions. Prior to being put to use, the Colours are consecrated at a religious ceremony. They are, in fact, a portable silken regimental history that inspires reverence and pride in soldiers, both serving and retired.

After India became a Sovereign Republic, the King's Colours of Indian Armed Forces were laid to rest at Indian Military Academy, Dehradun, on 23rd November 1950. Ever since then, new Colours have been presented to various regiments of the Indian Army by the President of India. However, battalions in the regiment which are raised later are presented Colours by the Chief of the Army Staff.

Colour Presentation to 18 Kumaon by the COAS

The 18th Battalion, The Kumaon Regiment received the Regimental Colours from Chief of the Army Staff on 5th May 1978, at an impressive parade in Dehra Dun where the battalion was stationed. The parade was commanded by Lt. Colonel (later Brigadier) Pran Kaul, Commanding Officer of the Battalion. The Colours were first consecrated by the Battalion Pandit (religious functionary) and Captain J.L. Sharma received the Colours from General T.N. Raina, MVC, COAS. Thus 18 Kumaon earned the distinction of being one of the youngest infantry battalion at that time to receive the Regimental Colour.

Colour Presentation to The Naga Regiment by President of India

On 6th May 1978, the fanfare of bugles marked the commencement of the Ceremonial Parade with KRC Brass Band in attendance. The parade ground was done up to give it the character of Nagaland culture. The wooden carved gate at the entrance to the parade ground and the colourful *shamianas* (canopy) for the spectators completed the picture of a Naga festive occasion in their traditional environment.

The parade, comprising four contingents, was commanded by Lt. Colonel (later Brigadier) V.S. Dogra, VSM, Commanding Officer of the Battalion. Major (later Colonel) Govind Sajjanhar was Parade Second-in-Command. The Ensign Officer was 2/Lt (later Major General) K.M. Balsara and the Colour Escorts were Naik (later Subedar Major and Honorary Captain) Heni Mao and Naik Imsenkaba Ao. The Colours were brought to the fore and consecrated by Subedar (RT) I.C. Thuma, the Priest of the Battalion Church and Subedar (RT) Jamuna Dutt Kothari, the Pandit at the Unit Mandir.

The Colours were then handed over to Major Govind Sajjanhar, just as the President of India, escorted by two ADCs and accompanied by the Colonel of the Regiment and COAS, General Raina, arrived at the parade ground.

After the march past, the parade formed a hollow square for the actual ceremony of the Presentation of the Colours by President Neelam Sanjeeva Reddy. The Colours were received from the President of India by 2/Lt Balsara on behalf of The Naga Regiment. After the presentation of Colours, the President delivered his address to the troops of the Naga Regiment:

> I am happy to be with you all on this historic occasion. Your smart turn out and the ceremonial manoeuvres which I have witnessed this morning, speak volumes of your competence as professional soldiers. Though still young in years, your Regiment has, by its performance in War and in Peace, earned for itself a proud place in the annals of our Army.
>
> As the Supreme Commander of the Defence Forces, under our Constitution, may I tell you that the presentation of the Colours to your Regiment is a tribute to your loyalty, valour and dedication to the service of our Motherland. None of us, as citizens of this great country, can ask for a greater honour or a nobler cause to serve.
>
> Our Defence Services have over the years established certain fine traditions of "Service before Self" and I am sure that The Naga Regiment, which has now come of age, will not only maintain but also enhance this glorious record of service.
>
> While thanking you all for the opportunity you have given me to come here and get to know you all in person, I wish you a bright and prosperous future. May God be with you always in peace or in Battle.
>
> Jai Hind.

General Raina issued the following special message to The Naga Regiment on the occasion of the Presentation of Colours:

> The excellent integration that has taken place in your Regiment is praiseworthy. Men of different communities, religions and states get together here and work together. Hardly had your raising been complete, when the Regiment was put through its

> acid test in the 1971 war for the liberation of Bangladesh. The Regiment acquitted itself creditably and justified the confidence that was reposed in it.
>
> During the short span of life of the Regiment, it has had the opportunity of serving in field and peace areas. Wherever The Naga Regiment has served, it has earned a name and fame for itself by its sheer DEDICATION, DEVOTION AND VALOUR. Your capacity for sacrifice, suffering hardship and willingness to undergo risks is commendable. Nothing great in this world is achieved without sacrifice and suffering, and our Army is a symbol of that great principle.
>
> It is in recognition of meritorious services and sacrifices of the Regiment that it has been chosen to receive the Colour from the President of India. It is my fervent hope that the Colour will inspire you to greater deeds of valour and sacrifice and bring honour and glory to our country.

The presentation of Colour to The Naga Regiment made the nation aware of this elite regiment, its steady growth and worthy performance since its raising nearly eight years earlier. More importantly, all ranks of the regiment were full of a sense of pride, self-confidence, a sense of achievement and a feeling of total integration with the motherland. This was also the last occasion for General Raina as Colonel of the Naga Regiment to visit and see The Naga Regiment take its own rightful place in the great Indian Army.

Colonel Commandant 61 Cavalry

61 Cavalry was raised in November 1953, after the merger of Indian Princely States with the Union of India. It includes all those glorious horse cavalry units such as Jodhpur Lancers and Mysore Lancers that played a big role in the great victory at Haifa. Also included in it are similar units of some of the princely states like Gwalior, Jaipur, Bikaner, Patiala and Saurashtra.

The 61 Cavalry has the distinction of being the last operational horsed cavalry regiment in the Indian Army, and for that matter, perhaps, in the whole world. Their incomparable mobility in keeping watch on vital installations, patrolling and counter insurgency against dismounted personnel is still indispensable. Each year on 23rd September, 61 Cavalry Regiment celebrates Haifa Day as their Battle Honour Day. Customarily, the Chief of Army Staff, by virtue of his appointment, is also the Colonel Commandant of 61 Cavalry.

The regiment today is employed for both ceremonial and operational duties. In its ceremonial role, the people of India are all familiar with the famous mounted bodyguard unit at Rashtrapati Bhavan, known as the President's Body Guard (PBG). 61 Cavalry is located at Jaipur and one of its squadrons is located at Delhi Cantonment. The regiment has also been detailed every year to provide a contingent of mounted squadron for the Republic Day and Beating Retreat ceremonies. Both these are a unique privilege for this regiment.

61 Cavalry has also produced some world-famous horse polo players. Among them are Lieutenant Colonels R.S. Sodhi who was Commandant at that time, and V.P. Singh, H.S. Sodhi and Farooq Bijli.

To commemorate the completion of twenty-five years since the raising of the regiment, General Raina, in his capacity as Colonel Commandant of 61 Cavalry, invited the President of India to present the Guidon[200] to this elite cavalry regiment. The event took place on 23rd September 1977 at Jaipur, to coincide with the 59th anniversary of the Battle of Haifa[201] and the Silver Jubilee of the

---

[200] Guidon (originally a French word) is a Standard and the equivalent of the Regimental Colour for the Cavalry. It is swallow-tailed shape, 27 inch × 30 inch, on an 8-foot 6-inch long pole. It is much smaller than an infantry Colour, so that it can be carried by a soldier on horseback.

[201] The Teen Murti Memorial erected at the crossing of roads in front of the Teen Murti House (former residence of late Pandit Jawahar Lal Nehru in New Delhi, is commemorative of the great victory of the port town of Haifa in Palestine on 23rd

Regiment. The only cavalry regiment of India was thus thrice blessed on that day in 1977, when Shri B.D. Jatti, the Acting President[202] of India, presented the Regimental Guidon. This was followed by celebrations of Haifa Day and the first reunion of serving and retired cavalrymen.

It was an impressive ceremonial parade commanded by Lieutenant Colonel R.S. Sodhi, where officers, risaldars and all ranks were turned-out in their ceremonial dress on their "chargers". Shri B.D. Jatti, escorted by General Raina, COAS and Colonel Commandant 61 Cavalry, presented the Guidon to the elite 61 Cavalry Regiment. The Acting President accompanied by the Colonel Commandant of 61 Cavalry, inspected the impressive parade of the cavalry men, all skilled horse riders. The chargers, chestnut brown and some white, added to the attraction of this unique Parade.

After presentation of the scarlet guidon and inspection of the parade, Shri Jatti, Acting President of India, addressed all ranks of the 61 Cavalry, and complimented the Regiment for their Steadfastness, Loyalty and Devotion to duties in the service of India. The Guidon, he added, would remain the pride of their Regiment, and expressed his confidence that 61 Cavalry would maintain the highest traditions of bravery and courage set by their predecessors. He reminded all ranks of 61 Cavalry that the capture of Haifa was a glorious chapter in the history of this elite regiment. Present on

---

September 1918, during First World War. This battle marked the decisive defeat of the Turkish Army at the hands of the British Indian Army Cavalrymen.

The conquest of Haifa occurred during the last part of the Palestine campaign. A squadron of Mysore Lancers with a couple of machine-guns was sent up to Mount Carmel, from where heavy artillery and machine gun fire had halted the advance of Jodhpur Lancers towards Haifa. It was later reinforced by a squadron of Yeomanry, but there was no sign of any slackening of enemy fire from Mt Carmel. The day of 23rd September was passing fast, and, as such, the Jodhpur Lancers were ordered to attack as scheduled, in spite of the heavy fire.

[202] Due to the death of incumbent President of India, Shri Fakhrudin Ali Ahmad in harness on 11th February 1977, Shri B.D. Jatti, Vice President of India, was sworn in as the Acting President.

this occasion, amongst the veteran cavalrymen, was Captain (Honorary) Vir Singh, then 80 years old, a living memorial of the Battle of Haifa, who took part in it as a "Sowar". Captain Vir Singh was the cynosure of all eyes as he talked to the Colonel Commandant of his Regiment, General Tappy Raina, and narrated the glory of the Haifa victory. It was now 61 Cavalry's proud privilege to celebrate this Battle Honour.

Chapter 36

A Son in His Father's Footsteps

General Raina had the ability to inspire those around him and his son, Jyoti Narain, who everyone called "Joe," was no exception. Joe was born on 20th November 1949 at Bradford-on-Avon in England. The elder child of Tappy and Ninette Raina, the strapping lad endeared himself to one and all by his boundless energy, unflagging courage and a zest for adventure that lured him to explore the unknown.

Ever since he was a young schoolboy, Joe had been encouraged to think for himself, to explore things that aroused his curiosity, and to read widely. His parents encouraged him in his love for music and also in sports. Tappy and Ninette Raina always believed that it was important for their children to have one creative hobby which would bring out the finer, more sensitive aspects of their personality; and, at the same time, some sport was also essential, particularly in the growing up years when expending energy in the right channels was considered healthy and necessary.

Joe was encouraged from a young age to stand up for himself against bullying, which was a common practice in Boys' schools, and to hold his own with his peers. Like his father, he was fiercely independent minded. It was while his father was commanding 14 Kumaon in Ferozepur in 1957, and when he was only eight years old, that Joe declared that he would one day join his father's battalion. That dream remained constant!

Joe joined Sherwood College, Nainital at the age of ten where he made quite a name for himself, both good and bad. No activity escaped his notice and no public school law could subdue Joe's animate critical mass. Stampeding through corridors in "ammunition" Boots, scaling snow-capped peaks, swimming in the forbidding Nainital Lake; he was just unstoppable! As a swimmer he set a record, and also earned straight 'A's in the Trinity College Music exams for playing Piano. He was even offered a scholarship to focus on music. Like his father, Joe had many facets to his personality and wide-ranging interests.

The Chinese aggression of 1962 found Brigadier Raina, in command of 114 Infantry Brigade, operationally deployed in the snowy winters of Ladakh. Some 1,000 miles to the south in Sherwood College, Nainital, Joe was huddled over chemicals and booby traps hidden away in a secret cave laboratory equipped with electric fittings and bottles of explosive chemicals. "I must have a secret place to keep booby traps and chemicals ready for an emergency," explained Joe apologetically to the horrified Principal, Mr. Llewelyn when discovered. The "emergency" Joe referred to, was in anticipation of any invasion by an enemy! He was aware of what was happening on the Ladakh front where his father was — and did not want to take any chances! Adventure held treasures for Joe, be it the fossils he gathered from the remote areas of Ladakh or the hitch hiking trip that took him across Europe to France and back. His love for life and his spirit of adventure were unquenchable.

When it was time to sit for the all-India entrance exam to the National Defence Academy (NDA) in Khadakvasla, Pune, Brigadier Raina decided to take two months furlough and coach his son. Joe was bright but also very playful and not easy to tutor, and his father wanted to ensure that his son was admitted to the NDA. Brigadier Raina set up a gruelling schedule from early morning to late evening. In between classes with his father, Joe was given time to go cycling, play football, meet some friends, or listen to music. Ninette ensured that Joe was kept well fed with wholesome food. With just two months of disciplined work with his father, Joe was able to stand second in the all-India exam. He joined the NDA in 1965.

After a pre-commission training at the National Defence Academy and Indian Military Academy (IMA), Dehra Dun, Joe was commissioned as an officer on 15th June 1969 in the 14th Battalion, The Kumaon Regiment (Gwalior)[203]. Thus his lifelong dream was finally fulfilled when he began his new life in the fine battalion that had once been commanded by his very able father.

Second Lieutenant Jyoti Narain Raina was selected to receive the Regimental Colours for his Battalion from the President of India, Shri V.V. Giri, on 27th October 1970, at a special Colour Presentation Parade at the Kumaon Regimental Centre Ranikhet. Captain "Joe" Raina was true to the "Standard" right through his short, breezy career. The men who served with Joe in 14 Kumaon still talk with admiration of his towering strength and dash in counter insurgency operations and, later, in the War for Liberation of East Pakistan (now Bangladesh). It was a coincidence[204] that father and son fought in the same war, but in geographically opposite Sectors.

Cadet "Joe" Raina at the NDA

After serving for nearly three years in Ladakh Scouts (1963-1966), and perhaps in appreciation of my work in the newly raised Ladakh Scouts, this Author received his posting orders from Army HQ as an Instructor Class "C" at National Defence Academy (NDA), where the author joined duty as a Division Officer (Div O) in May 1966. It was here that I met Cadet Jyoti Narain Raina for the first time. Joe was as one of the cadets under my charge as Divisional Officer in "India" Squadron of No. 3 Battalion. As I settled down in my new duties I learnt that some cadets at NDA, whose fathers were from Kumaon Regiment, as also those in authority at the Academy, automatically expected me to act as their local guardian/Counsellor. We (married officers) were encouraged to invite cadets of our "Divs", to our homes over a cup of Tea. For

---

[203] Now 5th Battalion, The Mechanised Regiment.

[204] Lieutenant General Tappy Raina was leading 2 Corps whereas Captain Joe Raina was Mortar Officer in 14 Kumaon (Gwalior), as part of 181 Infantry Brigade in 23 Infantry Division Sector which was part of the 4 Corps offensive for the liberation of East Pakistan.

us, this was our first home since our marriage, so we used to invite in batches of 4-5 Cadets, for social interaction about their educational, hobbies and family background.

I came to know Joe Raina more closely because of some such visits to our home, and through the periodic Social get-togethers at the Squadron Ante Room. Of course, I used to meet him in various training classes on service subjects as well. I soon realised that Joe had a somewhat different mental makeup, which made him stand apart from the normal run of young cadets. He was a proficient swimmer, who won laurels for his Squadron in Inter-Squadron Aquatics. He was equally proficient in playing several musical instruments, his favourite being the piano accordion. Yet, it was surprising to see Joe often on "Defaulters" Parade!

After completing his first two terms in "I" Squadron, in accordance with policy[205], Joe was transferred to "G" Squadron in No 2 Battalion for the remaining four terms of his training. His squadron officers were generally fond of him as a person but were at a loss to understand why he so frequently defied the Academy discipline. As a result of that he often received the punishments of "Extra-Drills" and "Restriction Parades" on most Wednesdays and Saturdays. Such punishments deprived the defaulting cadets the liberty to visit the town or even any place of entertainment within the NDA campus, like the cafe or cinema hall. Sometimes, Joe used to come to seek advice and guidance, but I found him too proud to ask for help. He also felt he was intellectually superior to most other cadets of his age and batch. Often there were reports of Joe's absence from classes; he would invariably be found in the reference section of the NDA's magnificent library.

In January 1968, I was appointed the Weapon Training Officer in the Army Training Team. Joe was now in his 5th term and I began to see him frequently, because the Army cadets commenced their basic military training after finishing the first four terms. In

---

[205] The then Commandant, NDA, Major General Ranbir Bakshi, MC, had laid down the policy that Cadets, on joining the NDA, were to be kept together in two or three Squadrons, as a Course. After completing two terms they were to be transferred to other Squadrons in a different Training Battalion.

the initial four terms the emphasis used to be on teaching the cadets drill, physical training (PT), equitation, games, map reading and navigation, service etiquette, military geography and military history, besides academics.

The most difficult and important term for cadets used to be Fourth term. Joe successfully completed this and was promoted to the Fifth term. It was also the term when his confrontation with his Squadron and Academy authorities, particularly the Cadet Appointments, came out in the open and assumed serious proportions. I remember once being sent for by Lieutenant Colonel B.D. Malhotra, a pedigree officer of the Brigade of Guards, who was the Officer Commanding No 2 Battalion and also Officer in Charge of the Army Training Team. On reaching his office, I was rudely told by the Battalion Commander that Joe's defiant attitude could no longer be tolerated any more, even though he was the son of a highly decorated and gallant army officer! On enquiring further, it was revealed that Joe had had a serious scrap with a Cadet Sergeant of his Squadron. As a result, his Squadron Commander had put Joe up on a charge-sheet before the Battalion Commander for relegation, if not withdrawal from NDA. The Battalion Commander wondered, if a counselling by me to Joe would help as a last chance for him to improve his sense of discipline. So I asked Joe to come and see me in my office that afternoon during the "Rest" period.

At about 2.30 pm that afternoon, a crestfallen Joe, visibly upset, walked into my office. I offered him a chair to sit and he sat down on the chair across the table. I recall speaking candidly to him on how important it was for him to uphold the good name of his parents and particularly of his father. I tried to appeal to his sentiments on various planes including his school and family background. But so far, I felt that it was a one-way traffic in our dialogue! After about ten minutes, I asked him if he would rather we did not discuss the matter any further.

At this unexpected turn of our meeting, Joe lifted his head and looking straight in my eyes asked me if he could ask me a few questions? Smilingly, I nodded. He asked me if I had been a cadet at this Academy. To which I replied, "No, I had not"; at which he shrugged his shoulders and said that it was no use talking to me then, because I would not understand his problem! On being pressed further, he confided that he was tired of everyone pushing him about for being the son of a decorated senior officer of the Army, exhorting him to live up to his father's reputation! Nobody cared to see him simply as Joe Raina! Why, he asked, could they not see him simply as a cadet without dragging in his father's name every time? I understood, at once, how everyone in authority including the NCO and JCO instructors, in their desire to urge and spur Joe to excel were, in fact, unwittingly suppressing his individuality and personality. Joe resented that. This resentment manifested as a defiant attitude towards their orders. Joe confided that he felt "hunted" and therefore did not know how he could turn the tide of such incidents to make a fresh start!

I saw the sincerity of his resolve and discussed his problem with Lieutenant Colonel "Bunny" Malhotra. The latter had a good laugh and, thereafter, grew fond of Joe. He issued instructions to Joe's Squadron Officers and cadet appointments to show greater understanding of his individual personality.

Throughout my tenure at NDA Khadakvasla, I never received any letter from Joe's father asking for any particular attention or help for his son. For that matter, I doubt if he ever approached anyone else in the NDA, with such a request as a father, Brigadier Raina wanted Joe to find his own feet and progress on his own steam. But poor Joe came to develop a sort of complex because of his father's professional fame and reputation, which had spread widely in the country in general and in the Army in particular. I doubt if the illustrious father was even remotely aware of the effect his fame and name had on his son, who though proud of his parents, was at an impressionable age. At that stage, it was important for him to seek and establish his own independent identity and personality. He had the strong urge to be recognised for what he was and not be perceived just as a mere shadow of his father.

In June 1968 I was posted out from NDA, and headed this time to 6th Battalion, The Kumaon Regiment. The Battalion was deployed in the high altitude area of Kanzalwan in the Gurez Valley in North Kashmir, across the famous Rajdhai Nangan (Rajdhan)

Pass, an area which remained heavily snow-bound and cut off for over six months from the rest of Kashmir Valley.

After reporting to my new unit, 6 Kumaon, we heard that Major General Raina, COS 15 Corps (he had been promoted meanwhile) was expected to visit our Battalion. One fine morning, when the snow was still covering the majestic firs on the slopes of surrounding mountains, General Raina arrived in an Air Force helicopter and landed on the snow-compacted helipad at 6 Kumaon Battalion HQ at Kanzalwan. When I was introduced to General Raina, I was pleasantly surprised to learn that he already knew of me from joe's letters, and wanted to have a longer chat about his son and his performance at the NDA, Khadakwasla. He invited me to visit him at HQ 15 Corps when passing through Udhampur on my way to Pune where I was required to attend a Course at the Institute of Armament and Technology (IAT).

On arrival at Udhampur, I found a message at the Transit Camp that I was invited to Dinner at the COS's residence and that transport would come to take me there. I quickly changed my clothes and at 7 p.m sharp, a shining black staff car arrived at the Transit Camp Officer's Mess, to take me to the General's Residence. That evening spent in the company of General Raina has remained indelibly imprinted on my mind! We sat talking of our experiences of Ladakh and I felt greatly flattered when he told me how closely he followed my actions after I took over "F" Company of the Ladakh Scouts. This Company had the operational responsibility of providing protection to the flank of 114 Infantry Brigade Sector, of which he was the Commander and hero during the Battle of Chushul in 1962!

Never until then had the significance of my missions of patrolling the vast span of my area of operational responsibility from the Siachen Glacier in Nubra Valley to the Karakoram Pass, Daulat Beg Oldi (DBO), Depsang Plateau, Galwan and Cheng Chenmo River Junction where it joined River Shyok, occurred to me! As a Scout Company Commander, my Company's task was to act as the "Eyes and Ears" to gain information about the enemy and his activity. I recall from my memory how during that summer of 1963-64, my Company was kept on the move to gain information about the Chinese activities and deployment along the Line of Actual Control.

Joe as a Young Regimental Officer

After joining his battalion as a young officer, Joe settled down to learning his new responsibilities. Like all young officers, he attended courses of instruction to enhance his professional knowledge. After having had the privilege to receive the Regimental Colours for his Battalion, Joe realised that this had added to his responsibility as an officer.

One had to enter Joe's room in the Battalion Officer's Mess to shake off the fire-eating image that Joe Raina had on the outside. Inside, one discovered an unassuming, camera shunning and glib-tongued gentleman. He lived amidst his fondly nurtured fossils from Ladakh, cupboards of ancient coins, collecting which was a passion, glowing stones, with the strains of the music that he so ardently loved in the background. This was Joe at home with friends!

With great passion and zeal, Joe rode his motorbike, a companion as dear to him as any horse to a cowboy! The machine would splutter, then cough and strain and then pull away, its engines roaring with crescendo as it picked up power and speed after every bend. Alas, he had to part company with his machine and all dear ones on 9th March 1974, when he left us wide eyed and numb!

The nation lost a soldier, the parents their beloved son, Anita, her only brother. And his fellow officers and friends lost a comrade-in-arms. The flame to his memory, as his name, "Jyoti", indicates, continues to burn brightly in the hearts of his family.

Part VII

Military and Diplomacy

"In the end, it is not the years in your life that count,
but the life in your years."
~ Abraham Lincoln

Chapter 37

Armed Forces and International Relations

"You have no idea how much it contributes to the general politeness and pleasantries in diplomacy, when you have a little quiet 'Force' in the background!"
~ George Kennan, well-known US diplomat and political realist.

On the face of it, armed forces and diplomacy and international relations belong to very different realms in India. Yet, they represent two sides of the same coin. If diplomacy is the first line of engagement between nation states, the military is seen as the last option and could involve the use of force.

Military diplomacy does not replace but supplements the overall national foreign and security policy guidelines set by the political leadership of the government in power, in the field of international relations. It is aimed at building greater confidence between nations and preventing conflicts.

Military and Diplomacy during General Raina's Tenure as COAS and Chairman COSC

Not many in India realised that the Chiefs of the three Defence Services play an important role in promoting the government's foreign policy. Heads of foreign armed forces are invited and reciprocal visits to those friendly countries are undertaken by the three chiefs of India's Armed Forces. Visits of service chiefs to other countries are crafted with deliberation and care. Prerequisites to such visits must conform to mutually comfortable politico-strategic environments and hold the potential for beneficial relationships.

In India, political and organisational factors continue to constrain the involvement and effectiveness of military diplomacy. In the opinion of General V.P. Malik, former COAS, few democracies have the kind of overwhelming civilian bureaucratic control over the military as India does. The civilian bureaucracy has never been enthusiastic about giving the armed forces any opportunity for international diplomatic engagements. In addition, the Ministries of External Affairs and Defence, respectively, did not see eye to eye on the objectives of India's military diplomacy. While the Ministry of Foreign Affairs realised the value of military diplomacy to some extent, the Ministry of Defence[206] remained conservative, even suspicious, of its exploitation!

Military interactions are generally conducted through exchanges of Military or Defence Attaches, visits by military delegations, military studies abroad and military assistance to friendly countries. Selected officers of the armed forces get exposed to aspects of foreign relations by their visits as students of the National Defence College (NDC), New Delhi, as part of the NDC students' exchange programme. Such visits in groups are planned to countries of interest, in consultation with the Ministry of External Affairs, Government of India, based on mutual interest in matters concerning defence.

---

[206] The political and financial approvals for military delegations to go abroad were controlled and processed by bureaucrats; and such visits were usually kept to a minimum. The same attitude was adopted when foreign military delegations were invited to India.

After the defeat of Indira Gandhi in the General Election in 1977, the situation became more confused after Mr Morarji Desai became Prime Minister of India, heading a coalition Government.

During his tenure as COAS Indian Army and Chairman COSC, General Raina's visits to some of the friendly countries were programmed when neighbouring countries were eager to gauge India's burgeoning international stance. Sri Lanka, Bhutan, Iran, Nepal, Malaysia, Sweden, USSR, Yugoslavia, and USA were some such countries.

On the invitation of the heads of armed forces of some of these friendly countries, General Raina visited Sri Lanka, Bhutan, Sweden, USSR (now Russia), Yugoslavia, Iran, USA and Malaysia. In reciprocation, General Raina, as Chairman Chiefs of Staff Committee and COAS Indian Army, also invited heads of some foreign armed forces to visit India. Some of General Raina's visits to foreign countries considered important from the national security point of view are briefly described in the succeeding paragraphs.

Sri Lanka

Soon after taking over as COAS, while reviewing the invitations from the heads of foreign armies, General Raina noticed that Sri Lanka[207] had been regularly inviting the Indian COAS. For some unexplained reason, however, no Chief of the Indian Army had ever visited Sri Lanka since 1948. This was, presumably, on the advice of the Ministry of External Affairs. General Raina, therefore, took up the matter with the Secretary, Ministry of External Affairs and only then did the Government give approval for his first foreign visit as COAS to Sri Lanka from 16th to 21st March, 1976. This was at the invitation of Lt. General Don Sepala

---

[207] Ceylon was officially renamed Republic of Sri Lanka In 1972. The new constitution of Sri Lanka formally made Buddhism the country's primary religion. Tamil admissions in universities were cut back. Subsequent civil unrest resulted in a state of emergency in Tamil areas, with Sinhalese security forces imposing many discriminatory laws. As a result, a large number of militant Tamil groups emerged.

Attygalle[208], LVO, SLAC who was Chief of the Sri Lankan Army from 1st October 1967 to 13th October 1977. General Tappy Raina was accompanied by Ninette Raina, Major General (later Lieutenant General) S.K. Sinha, PVSM, the then DMI, and the author of this book, in his capacity as MA to COAS.

On arrival at Colombo Airport, General and Mrs Raina and accompanying members of the delegation were ceremoniously received by General and Mrs Attygalle, along with many other Sri Lankan senior army commanders and their wives. A smart, well-turned out ceremonial Guard of Honour by a contingent of the Sri Lankan Army was presented to the Indian COAS. General Attygalle repeatedly emphasised that though India was the closest neighbouring country of Sri Lanka, ever since independence of both nations from British Rule in 1947 and 1948, respectively, India had ignored the Sri Lankan Army. This was so despite the fact that the two Armies had operated together during the Second World War, and that the Sri Lanka Army continued with the same pattern of organisation as the Indian army. No Indian Army Chief had accepted the invitation to visit this small island nation during all these years. Naturally, therefore, the visit by General Raina was a very special event and it was greatly appreciated by the Sri Lankan Government and its Army.

Once the ceremonials were over, many issues of mutual interest in the areas of training, weapons, equipment and threat perceptions, were discussed. General Raina observed that the void created by the lack of Indian diplomatic interest in meeting the needs of the Sri Lankan Armed Forces had opened a gateway for China to step in. The apathy of the diplomatic staff at the Indian High Commission towards Sri Lanka was noticed by General Raina. He was horrified to find the Indian High Commissioner[209] improperly

---

[208] General Attygalle was a well-known military leader, who also held the responsible appointment as Defence Secretary, MoD, Government of Sri Lanka. Later he was High Commissioner of Sri Lanka in the United Kingdom.

[209] The then High Commissioner of India in Sri Lanka, was found to be casually dressed in a T-shirt, shorts and sandals at the occasion of presentation of Guard of Honour by the Sri Lankan Army, where national flags and national anthems of

dressed at the ceremonial reception at Colombo Airport accorded to the Indian delegation by the Sri Lankan government.

During this visit, the Sri Lankan Army had arranged an extensive tour of its institutions at different locations, including Kandy. The latter was a popular hill station and former HQ of South East Asia Command (SEAC) of Vice-Admiral the Earl Mountbatten of Burma.[210] Also of special interest was the visit to many development projects which were being undertaken by Sri Lankan Army Engineers to assist their civil administration. A visit to the Tamil majority area of North Sri Lanka,[211], however, was excluded. On conclusion of the visit, a detailed report with appropriate recommendations was submitted to the Government of India.

The visit to Sri Lanka by General and Mrs T.N. Raina was followed by their visits to other friendly foreign countries, like Bhutan, Nepal, Sweden, Iran and Malaysia.[212] General Tappy Raina also visited the Soviet Union, the United States and Yugoslavia with an appropriate delegation.

---

both nations were played. Such disrespect by a senior Indian diplomat, was not only pointed out to the High Commissioner by General Raina through Maj. Gen. SK Sinha, PVSM, but was also brought to the notice of the Secretary MEA, Government of India, on return from Sri Lanka.

210 Lord Mountbatten was later appointed Viceroy of India in succession to Field Marshal Wavell in March 1947 just before the partition of the Indian Subcontinent. After the creation of Pakistan as a separate Dominion, Lord Mountbatten became the Governor General of the Indian Dominion in August 1947. He was succeeded by Chakravarti Rajagopalachari in June 1948. Both Dominions continued under the British Crown, until the Indian Dominion became Sovereign Republic of India on 26th January 1950.

211 The LTTE (the Liberation Tigers of Tamil Eelam), popularly known as Tamil Tigers, was formed to fight for an independent Tamil state. At the end of the 1970s, the Sri Lankan Government instituted the draconian Prevention of Terrorism Act. Under its authority, thousands of Tamil youth were arrested.

212 After the change of Government in 1977, when Morarji Desai became Prime Minister of India, the wives of the three services chiefs, though invited, were debarred from accompanying their husbands on official tours.

Bhutan

A tiny and remote kingdom nestling in the Himalayas between its powerful neighbours, India and Tibet Autonomous Region (TAR) of China, Bhutan is situated in the North East of India. Arunachal Pradesh lies to its East, North Bengal to its South and Sikkim to its West. In the North, it has a border with the Tibet Autonomous Region (TAR) of China. Almost completely cut off for centuries, Bhutan had tried to let in some aspects of the outside world while fiercely guarding its ancient culture and traditions.

The Bhutanese name for Bhutan, Druk Yul, signifies "Land of the Thunder Dragon". It only began to open up to outsiders in the 1970s. The Wangchuk[213] hereditary monarchy has wielded power since 1907. Remote Bhutan first allowed the world a peek inside the country only in 1974. Isolation has preserved the heavily Buddhist-influenced culture of the last Shangri-La.

Bhutan had remained mostly isolated except for an invasion by China in 1720, followed by British intervention from 1772 to 1865. Finally, Bhutan entered into an agreement with the British in 1910. Under this Treaty, Bhutan gave the British control of its foreign relations. The Treaty was renewed in 1949, after India became independent. The Treaty guaranteed non-interference in Bhutan's internal affairs, while allowing New Delhi's influence over its foreign relations. It also gave India the responsibility to defend Bhutan from external aggression. (An example of the practical implementation of this aspect of the Treaty was the involvement of the Indian Army at Doka La, also known as the Doklam stand-off, in the summer of 2017). An Indian Military Training Team (IMTRAT), headed by an officer of the rank of Brigadier (now Major General) as Commandant, has been permanently located in Bhutan with its HQ at Ha Dzong.

General Raina accompanied by Mrs. Ninette Raina, Major General A.S. Vaidya, DMO Army HQ, this author as the MA to COAS, Major P.N. Khera, PRO Army HQ and Captain Dara

---

[213] Bhutan became a two-party parliamentary democracy after elections in March 2008.

Jahangir Govadia, ADC to COAS, visited Bhutan from 18th to 21st May 1976. The delegation flew in an Indian Air Force aircraft from New Delhi to the IAF Station, Hasimara which is surrounded by lush green tea gardens in Dooars (North Bengal). Due to inclement weather, however, the remainder of the journey from Hasimara to Thimphu was undertaken by road.

After about an hour's journey by car from Hasimara airfield, General Raina and his delegation entered the gateway of Bhutan through the border town of Phuntosholing. This road journey provided General Raina and his delegation, an opportunity to observe the countryside and various development projects being undertaken by the Indian Government in Bhutan.

On arrival at Thimphu, the capital of Bhutan, General and Mrs. Raina were received by Brigadier Depinder Singh, VSM, Commandant IMTRAT, and Mrs Balli Depinder Singh. Also present was Colonel Makshi Gongma Lam Dorje, the Chief Operations Officer (COO) of the Royal Bhutan Army (RBA). That same evening Colonel Lam Dorje hosted a dinner at Headquarters Royal Bhutan Army Officers' Mess, where General Raina and members of his delegation could meet many officers of the RBA.

On the following day, General Raina was presented a Guard of Honour by the RBA, followed by an audience with His Majesty Jigme Singye Wangchuck, the King of Bhutan. This was followed by discussion with senior members of the Government of Bhutan and RBA. Later, General and Mrs Raina called on Her Majesty, the Queen Mother.

Next day the delegation flew from Thimphu by an IAF helicopter to Paro and watched the joint training in progress there. Later, they visited Ha Dzong, where General Raina saw training being conducted. This was followed by a briefing and discussion with Brigadier Depinder Singh, Commandant IMTRAT, on operational matters. The same evening, General Raina and the accompanying delegation attended a *Bara Khana* for all ranks of IMTRAT.

On 21st May 1976, General and Mrs Raina, accompanied by the delegation, left Ha Dzong by an IAF helicopter for Hasimara Airport, where an IAF aircraft was on location for the return journey to New Delhi.

Iran

Two momentous events preceded General Raina's visit to Iran from 10th to 19th November 1976, and gave his tour an added significance. The first was India's crushing defeat of Pakistan's military power in 1971 in the then East Pakistan and the creation of a new nation, Bangladesh. More important, this dismemberment of Pakistan was executed against considerable sustained resistance by the world's most powerful nation, the USA. The second important event was the nuclear detonation by India at Pokhran in 1974, announcing to the world India's entry into the exclusive nuclear club. This made the world stand up and take notice of a new, strong India which made independent decisions.

By February 1975, there was a tremendous improvement in bilateral relations between India and Iran. The most important aspect of these relations was the concurrence to collaborate in a Nuclear Energy Accord. As a result, Iran and India signed a Nuclear Cooperation Agreement in February 1975.[214]

In the meantime, to establish its ascendancy in the region India took the initiative of inviting General G.R. Azhari, the Supreme Commander of the Iranian Defence Forces, formally the number 2 in the Iranian hierarchy after the Shah of Iran, to visit India. General Azhari came on an official visit to India in March 1976. His visit was marked by an undisguised show of Iranian ascendancy in the region. He was warmly received by India and held wide ranging discussions with General T.N. Raina, Chairman Chiefs of Staff Committee and the Indian Defence Minister, Shri Bansi Lal. Later, General Azhari and his delegation were given an extensive tour of India and many of her important military institutions. In reciprocation, on behalf of the Government of Iran, General Azhari invited

[214] The Minister for External Affairs, Government of India, visited Iran in November 1975 to attend the 5th meeting of the Indo-Iranian Joint Commission. A significant outcome of this visit was the finalisation of the $630 million agreement for the exploitation of Kudremukh Iron Ore Project in the Indian state of Karnataka, which was a landmark in Indo-Iran economic as well as political relations.

General T.N. Raina, COAS & Chairman COS Committee, along with a suitable delegation of officers. Mrs Ninette Raina was also invited to accompany General Raina.

In May 1976 Indo-Iranian relations received an impetus by the visit of the Iranian Prime Minister, Abbas Hoveyda, to India, followed by the return visit of the Indian President Fakhruddin Ali Ahmad to Tehran in June 1976.

General Raina's visit to Iran took place during the second week of November 1976 when the country was still ruled by Emperor Mohammad Shah Pahlavi, who was firmly under US influence. Although the political contours between India and Iran did not quite over-lap, because of geographical proximity both nations were keen for closer understanding on matters of mutual security interests.

General and Mrs. Raina were accompanied by Lieutenant General A.N Mathur, QMG Army HQ, Major General Hirday Kaul, DMO Army HQ, Maj. General P. Puri, Commandant CME, Kirkee, and Captain Dara J. Govadia, ADC to COAS. Colonel Farhadi, Military Attache, Embassy of Iran in India, New Delhi, also accompanied the Indian military delegation.

On arrival at Tehran Airport, General and Mrs Raina were received with great ceremonial protocol. The visit was marked by a series of meetings and in-depth discussions with General Azhari and other senior military commanders. The Government of Iran had placed a special Royal Iranian Air Force Aircraft for the visiting Indian delegation, who were given a complete tour of Iran. The places they visited included Isfahan, Abadan, Air Force Base Dezful, Shiraz and also the main Iranian Naval Base, Bandar Abbas, a port city on the Persian Gulf.

General Raina with his charisma and social dynamics cemented a personal rapport with all shades of Iranian officials. What added flavour was his familiarity with basic Farsi (Persian language) and, to great applause; he recited couplets from the great Iranian poets, Hafez and Sa'adi. Mrs Ninette Raina, too, with her poise and grace, made an impressive impact on her Iranian hosts and hostesses. Her refined and polished French language made for intimate communication with the upper Iranian social order. The visit was a perfect Indian projection in Iran. Politically, Iran was firmly in the US fold while India was aligned to the Soviet Union for its major defence needs. Yet, the excellent rapport created by General and Mrs Raina with the Iranians built a very positive and friendly platform. This visit was soon followed by those of the Chiefs of the Indian Navy and Air Force who also visited Iran soon after.

One direct outcome of General Raina's visit was the agreement to continue the exchange of army officers at the two countries' respective Defence Services Staff Colleges. The first two Indian Army officers who attended the Iranian Staff College were of the rank of Major.[215] After a gap of one year, the same course was upgraded as "Command & General Staff Course,"[216] to be attended by officers of the rank of Lieutenant Colonel. Indian Army officers who were selected for this course had to learn the Persian language for three months, as the medium of instruction on the course was Persian. This course was based on the "Command & General Staff Course" of the US Army.

In retrospect, General and Mrs Raina's visit to Iran generated tremendous goodwill and the willingness on both sides to promote relationships between India and Iran for mutual understanding and stability in the region. This visit by the COAS of the Indian Army was followed by a reciprocal visit by General Gholam Ali Oveissi, C-in-C of the Iranian Imperial Army.

---

[215] Major (later Major General) Vinod Saigal, Armoured Corps, was the first officer from Indian Army to attend this course. Interestingly, the second Indian Army officer to attend the Iranian C&G Staff Course was Major (later Lt General) Surinder Nath, Artillery, who rose to be VCOAS, Indian Army.

[216] At the time of the visit of General Tappy Raina to Iran, Lt Col (later Major General) R.K. Khanna, VSM, The Kumaon Regt, was attending the Iranian CG & S Course. He was followed by another Indian Army officer, Lt Col (later Lt. Gen.) Baljit Singh, Artillery. Lt General Baljit Singh, AVSM, VSM has been writing articles on wild life, mountaineering, historical and military heroes. He is also the author of many books.

Sweden

Despite the brilliant performance by Indian Army in the war against Pakistan in 1971, India remained dependent on foreign suppliers for meeting its critical defence supplies of anti-tank weapons, ammunition, equipment and special clothing for troops deployed in varied terrains along the border. Even when General Raina was GOC-in-C Western Command, he had assessed that the Pakistan Army would, in all likelihood, try to avenge its defeat in East Pakistan. He had, therefore, asked Army HQ to recoup and make up the shortages in arms, ammunitions and equipment. At the same time, he also urged for the build-up of reserves at each echelon, so that the Army could be fully prepared to meet Pakistan's threat.[217]

India had remained largely dependent on the USSR for its defence needs. To some extent it also met its requirement from some European countries, like Sweden and Yugoslavia. It was in this connection that Lieutenant General Carl Eric Almgren, Chief of the Swedish Defence Forces, accompanied by a small delegation, was invited to India in early 1976. As a result of discussions with the visiting Swedish delegation, areas of mutual interest were identified. It was followed by a highly successful reciprocal visit to Sweden by General Raina from 22nd to 28th August 1976. The Indian Army delegation comprised General Raina, Major General S.K. Sinha, DMI and the author of this book as the MA to COAS.

Air Commodore N. Chatrath, VrC, IAF, the Military and Air Attaché at the Indian High Commission, London, was also concurrently Defence Attaché at the Embassy of India at Stockholm, Sweden. He and his wife met General and Mrs. Raina at Heathrow Airport, London, during the six-hour transit halt, due to change of aircraft. Taking advantage of this halt, General Raina asked Air Commodore Chatrath to brief him and the delegation on the detailed tour programme of the visit to Sweden. Air Commodore and

---

[217] With the return of Pakistani Army Prisoners of War by India, as a result of the Simla Agreement 1972, the Pakistan Army not only made up its manpower, but, with further help from USA, it also largely made up the loss of equipment as well.

Mrs Chatrath also accompanied the delegation from London to Stockholm. At Arlanda Airport, Stockholm, General and Mrs. Raina were informally received by Lieutenant General Carl Eric Almgren, Mrs Lisa Almgren, Major General Claës Skoglund and Captain Rainer Trübenbach (Swedish Army Liaison Officer).

The next day began with a visit to the Military Staff Building, where a Guard of Honour was presented to General Raina, followed by a briefing on the Swedish Army by Lieutenant General Carl Eric Almgren. After the lunch hosted by the C-in-C of the Swedish Army, the Indian delegation paid a courtesy call on the Minister of Defence, before visiting the Staff College of the Armed Forces. Next day, General Raina and the accompanying delegation visited Bofors[218] to witness the demonstration of the products of AB Bofors.

On Wednesday August 25th, the delegation visited Skövde,[219] where briefings on the Military Command, and West-Regional Command Organisation were explained. The same day, before departing by helicopter for Eskilstuna, where the Swedish National Industries Corporation was located, the Swedish Army Armour School was also visited. The next two days were spent in visiting a Signal Regiment, the National Home Guard Combat School, an infantry regiment and the National Defence College, before visiting the Supreme Commander of the Swedish Armed Forces at the Military Staff Building at Stockholm.

The Swedish Army had prepared a separate programme for Mrs. Ninette Raina, President, Indian Army Wives Welfare Association, which included visits to a hospital, a home for the aged, a

---

[218] Bofors is a Swedish company. The name has been associated with the iron industry for more than 350 years. Located in Karlskoga, Sweden, the company was founded in 1646.

[219] There are several military units in Skövde, Skaraborg Regiment and the Logistic Regiment with the Swedish Armed Forces Logistics and Motor School and the Land Warfare Centre. The Logistics School is a joint armed school that develops the skills of students and staff from the Army, Navy and Air Force within disciplines of military science, military technology, leadership and individual combat fighting.

textile work-loom, a day nursery and a factory worker's home. She also had useful discussion with Mrs Lisa Almgren, wife of the Swedish Army Chief, on various welfare activities of Swedish Army families.

Historically, by virtue of its geographic location Sweden had remained a neutral country, despite the wars fought in its neighbourhood in Europe, including Second World War. Up to that point Sweden had not fought any war for almost 160 years! Yet, the nation maintained a high degree of operational preparedness in manpower, weapons and equipment. On further inquiry, it was learnt that all citizens of Sweden between the ages of 18 and 45 years had to perform compulsory military service, after which they remained on the list of Royal Swedish Army as reservists. Their deployment and defensive positions are kept prepared close to their homes. Similarly, plans for all major buildings like hospitals, and high-rise commercial and office and residential blocks were prepared to meet any threat, including nuclear, by building underground shelters.

On inquiry by General Raina with regard to major threats to Sweden at that time, General Almgren replied, *"If and when two elephants fight, smaller beings also get trampled"*! He explained that the two elephants were, the Warsaw Pact Block, led by USSR and the North Atlantic Treaty Organisation (NATO) led by USA. In the event of a war breaking out between these two power blocks, Sweden feared a threat from either, or both!

The Royal Swedish Army comprised approximately twenty-five percent Regular all ranks and the remaining seventy-five percent were reservists. All reservists were, periodically called upon to perform their military duty in rotation. Sweden therefore had remained a major source of "state of art" weapon systems, armament and equipment, without itself participating in any of the world wars. However, the Swedish army generously provided manpower for the UN peace keeping role.

General Raina's delegation was shown various training establishments, where Royal Swedish Army soldiers were undergoing training with the latest infantry weapons and equipment that had been introduced.

Another important visit was to the Royal Swedish National Defence College (RSNDC). The National Defence College was the most important institution where civil and military personal were trained for leading positions in "Total Defence" in Swedish society, which comprised military defence, civil defence, economic defence and psychological defence.

After a week-long, meaningful visit to Sweden, General and Mrs. Raina and the Indian delegation were given a warm send-off by Lieutenant General and Mrs. Almgren at Arlanda Airport, Stockholm.

Nepal

Nepal shares a long 1,593 kilometre border with India on its south, east and west, and a shorter border to the north with the Tibet Autonomous Region (TAR) of China. Nepal's main rivers drain into major Indian rivers and feature several multipurpose or hydroelectric projects, heavily assisted by the Indian government. India has been a major donor of economic assistance to Nepal, along with international lending agencies, including the United Kingdom, United States and China.

More than eighty percent of Nepal's population, including its hereditary rulers and aristocratic class, were closely linked to that of North India by historical origin, linguistic similarity, educational background, and religious affiliation. Nepal was proclaimed a Hindu kingdom in 1962. The Indo-Nepal border is open and Nepali citizens enjoy the legal right of working and living in India on the same basis as Indian citizens.[220] The major human capital of Nepal traditionally has been the Gorkha soldiers, who have long been an important component of the Indian Army and also serve with the British and Malaysian armies.

Official relations between India and Nepal are based on the "Treaty of Peace and Friendship" which was signed in 1950, and later renewed and amended as "Trade and Transit Treaty". Nepal

---

[220] The estimated number of Nepalese in India in the 1970s was approximately 10 million, whereas the total population of Nepal was approximately 15 million.

is a founder member of the South Asian Association for Regional Cooperation (SAARC), and Kathmandu is the headquarters of its permanent Secretariat.

Indo-Nepal relations have always been of great importance because of Nepal's dependency on India for most of her economic and other material needs. Being a land-locked nation with its border with China on one side and India on the other, Nepal's access to the rest of the world has been through India. Being the only Hindu nation[221] in the world it had remained culturally very close to India.

The economy of Nepal received a considerable contribution by way of pay and pension earned by Nepalese soldiers, who form a sizable contingent in the Indian army. For a long time, the Indian army maintained a large training team for joint training with the Royal Nepal Army[222]; besides a Military Attaché (MA) at the Embassy of India at Kathmandu. The Indian Army also maintains a Pension Paying Office (PPO) at Pokhra.

At the invitation of General Rt. Hon. Guna Shamsher Jung Bahadur Rana[223], Tri.Sha.Pa, C-in-C Royal Nepal Army, General

---

[221] Prior to the abolition of the monarchy in Nepal, it was officially known as His Majesty's Government. Now the Federal Democratic Republic of Nepal, with a Head of State, assisted by the Executive, Legislative, Judiciary and Cabinet, rules Nepal; and the Government is the Executive Body and the Central Government of Nepal. The President is the Head of State, and the Prime Minister holds the position of the Head of Executive. The role of President is largely ceremonial as the functioning of the government is managed entirely by the Prime Minister, who is elected by the Parliament. The heads of constitutional bodies are appointed by the President on the recommendation of Constitutional Council, with the exception of the Attorney General, who is appointed by the President on the recommendation of Prime Minister.

[222] At the behest of China, which had started exercising pressure to reduce Nepal's dependency on India, the Indian training team was withdrawn at the request of the Government of Nepal.

[223] Born at Sagar in Madhya Pradesh on 18th August 1923, and educated at Sagar, Kathmandu and Patna, Bihar, in India. Commissioned as a Captain in RNA in 1939, he rose to become COAS, RNA, in May 1975, about the same time as Tappy Raina's appointment as COAS Indian Army.

T.N. Raina, MVC, accompanied by his wife, Mrs Ninette Raina, Lieutenant General Eric Vas, Adjutant General, Army HQ, and Major Yogesh Prasad, Deputy MA to COAS, visited Nepal from 4th to 7th April 1977. Colonel (later Major General) Ashok Krishna was the Military Attaché and Major (later Lt Gen) Tej K. Sapru was his Deputy, at the Embassy of India. Nepal was still ruled by King Birendra and Shri Tulsi Giri was the Prime Minister.

Some of the salient issues that were discussed during this visit by General Raina were:

- **Weapons and Equipment for the Royal Nepal Army.** The Nepalese Chief pointed out that the supply of weapons and equipment from India was slow. On return from the visit, General Raina ensured timely supplies of the requirements of the Royal Nepal Army.
- **Pension Payment Office (PPO), Pokhra.** General Raina projected the requirement of land required for the setting up of the Pension Payment Office (PPO) at Pokhra, to facilitate the payment of pension to Nepalese ex-servicemen from the Indian Army. The required land was allocated on priority by the Royal Government of Nepal. On his return to India, General Raina prevailed upon the GOI to allocate an additional amount of Rs. 89 lakh, towards the envisaged costs of the project.
- **Honorary Rank of General of Royal Nepal, Army.** At a special ceremony held in the Royal Durbar, His Majesty King Birendra, conferred the honorary rank of "General of the Royal Nepal Army," on General T.N. Raina, MVC, COAS Indian Army. Soon after the investiture ceremony at the Palace, General Raina thanked the King for the allocation of land at Pokhra. He availed the opportunity to request the King to allocate land for setting up of another PPO at Dharan.
- General Shamsher Jung Bahadur Rana and General Raina agreed for further close cooperation between the two armies in training and other matters of mutual interest.

General Raina met ex-Servicemen at Pokhra and presented gifts to them and noted with concern their problems. Lieutenant General Eric Vas, AG Army Headquarters, took note of the needs of the ex-servicemen, and on his return to India, took prompt action to resolve the issues.

Reciprocal visit by COAS Royal Nepal Army

To further strengthen the relations between India and Nepal, General Raina invited General Shamsher Jung Bahadur Rana to visit India. Thus, a Nepalese delegation led by General Rana, arrived at New Delhi on 6th December 1977, on an eight-day visit of India.

On arrival at the Indian Air Force Technical Area at Palam Airport, New Delhi, an impressive Guard of Honour by the 3rd Battalion, The Kumaon Regiment (Rifles), carrying their Regimental Colours, was presented to General Rana. On the following day, after laying a wreath at Amar Jawan Jyoti, at India Gate, General Rana called on General Raina, at Army HQ, where the Skill at Arms Silver Trophy for the Royal Nepal Army was presented. Next day both host and guest called on Shri Jagjivan Ram, Defence Minister and Shri Morarji Desai, the Prime Minister. Later, the Nepalese Army Chief was conferred the Honarary Rank of General of the Indian Army, by the President of India, Shri N. Sanjeeva Reddy.

During the remaining duration of his visit, the Nepalese Chief visited IMA Dehra Dun, College of Combat, Mhow, and also the training centres of Rajputana Rifles and 39 GTC at New Delhi and Varanasi, respectively.

Malaysia

Malaysia being a fellow member of the Commonwealth, and located in South East Asia, it had enjoyed friendly relations with India. Even during the Second World War, selected officers of Malaysian Army came for training to India, at the Indian Military Academy. Some of those former officers rose to high positions in independent Malaysia after the War.

Hon'ble Datuk Hussein Onn who was the Prime Minister of Malaysia in the 1970s trained at the IMA Dehradun before serving in the 19 Hyderabad Regiment (now Kumaon Regiment). Similarly, General Tan Sri Ibrahim Bin Ismail[224] had also served with the 19 Hyderabad Regiment (now Kumaon Regiment), during Second World War. General Ibrahim had a strong love for his old Regiment, and he shared many nostalgic memories of his association with such famous personalities of the Kumaon Regiment as General S.M. Shrinagesh (former COAS) and General K.S. Thimayya, DSO, (also a former COAS) under whom he had served.

To revive the past association of such illustrious leaders of the Malaysian Government, General Raina invited General Tan Sri Ibrahim Bin Ismail, Chief of the Armed Forces Staff, Ministry of Defence, Malaysia, and his wife, Puan Sri Zakiah Ibrahim, and one staff officer, to visit India. He was to be the Chief Guest at the 7th Post War Reunion[225] held at the Kumaon Regiment Training Centre, Ranikhet in October 1976. During the visit, General Ibrahim also held discussions at Army HQ New Delhi, with his host. Later, a visit was also arranged to Para Brigade at Agra, where General Ibrahim had spent time as a young officer at the 19 Hyderabad Regiment Training Centre.

To further cement the relations between the armies of Malaysia and India, the Malaysian Government invited General Raina to visit Malaysia. For General Raina, the visit to Malaysia was as significant as that he had made to Sri Lanka. The importance of maintaining close relations with neighbouring nations and littoral states could not be over emphasised.

General and Mrs. Raina, accompanied by Brigadier R.N. Mahajan, (former MA to COAS and who was then Commander of an Infantry Brigade) and Captain S.K. Sapru, (ADC to COAS) embarked on this visit from 17th to 23rd April 1977 at the invitation of General Tan Sri Ibrahim Bin Ismail, Chief of the Armed Forces

---

[224] Gen Tan Sri Ibrahim Bin Ismail PMN, SPMJ, SPMK, SPDK, PNBS, DIMP, PIS, is the author of a book "Have You Met Mariam?" This is the story of the author and his country, before and during 2nd World War. At the age of 22 years he infiltrated into Japanese-held territory, for which he was awarded the MBE. He retired as Chief of Malaysia's Armed Forces Staff in 1977.

[225] The details of the grand celebration of the 7th Post War Reunion at KRC Ranikhet have been described in Chapter 35.

Staff, Malaysia. Colonel K.L.K. Singh, Artillery, Defence Attache, High Commission of India in Malaysia, joined the Indian Army delegation on the arrival of General Raina at Kuala Lumpur.

This visit by General Raina further cemented ties not only between two armies but also between the two nations. This was because the Hon'ble Datuk Hussein Onn, SMN, DK, Prime Minister of Malaysia and General Ibrahim had also served along with General Raina as subalterns at the 19 Hyderabad Regiment Training Centre, Agra, during the Second World War in 1942. This relationship of illustrious contemporaries from two different nations meeting after nearly three decades was well received by the people of Malaysia.

The visit commenced with the presentation of a smart Guard of Honour at the Armed Forces HQ, Kuala Lumpur (KL), by a contingent of the Malaysian Army, attired in their national dress and head gear. Later in the day, General Raina accompanied by General Tan Sri Ibrahim Bin Ismail paid a courtesy call on Hon'ble Datuk Hussein Onn, Prime Minister of Malaysia, in the latter's office. That evening General and Mrs. Raina and the delegation were the guests at a formal banquet hosted by the Hon'ble Prime Minister of Malaysia.

Next day the delegation visited the Malaysian Army Staff College, which had been tailored and organised by the Australian Army albeit, with a curriculum on the lines used by Indian Army. It was during this visit that a decision to nominate Indian officers to attend the Malaysian Staff College was taken. Later that day, General Raina visited the Counter Insurgency (CI) School, established just outside Kuala Lumpur, where the training by troops of the Malaysian Army was witnessed.

On 20-21st April, General Tan Sri Ibrahim Bin Ismail, and his wife, Puan Sri Zakiah Ibrahim accompanied General and Mrs Raina and the Indian Army delegation to Johor Bahru, where they were the personal guests of the Sultan, Sir Ismail Al Khalidi Ibni Al-Marhum Sultan Ibrahim Al-Masyhur, KBE CMG, KBE of Johor Bahru. The penultimate day was a trip organised to Penang, after which the delegation returned to Kuala Lumpur, prior to their return to India.

During this visit it was amply visible that despite Malaysia being an Islamic country, it was very progressive and liberal in outlook. This was evident by the fact that the diverse ethnic groups' i.e, Malays, Chinese and people of Indian origin, reflected the secular fabric of the country. It was also heartening to note that women constituted a major portion of the work force both in the civil services and the armed forces.

The Union of Soviet Socialist Republics (USSR)

The Union of Soviet Socialist Republics (USSR) was seven times the size of India and before its break-up, consisted of fifteen constituent republics. It had an estimated population of 253.3 million, comprising 120 nationalities, and was ruled by an elected president as the head of state, a vice president and twenty members of the presidium. Premier Leonid Brezhnev was Chairman of the Presidium & General Secretary of the Communist Party and Aleksei Kosygin was Chairman of the Council of Ministers.

Government of India had been trading with the Soviet Union for a long time, because the two nations had a Rupee Trade Agreement. At the time of war with Pakistan in 1971, when the US had threatened to bring its naval fleet into the Bay of Bengal, the Indo-Soviet Friendship Treaty acted as a deterrent to American military intervention. Therefore, traditionally, a majority of defence requirements were obtained by India from the Soviet Union. Keeping in view the threat perception from Pakistan, the Indian Army was seeking state of the art equipment, comprising tanks, armoured personnel carriers (APC) and attack helicopters (AH), to neutralise the threat of the Pakistani army's two armoured divisions, supported by infantry.

Indian Army sources had learnt that the Soviet Armed Forces had developed a new tank,[226] T-72, and a combat infantry

[226] The T-72, which entered production in USSR in 1971, was first seen in public in 1977. The T-72, though introduced in the early 1970s, was not a further development of the T-64. Rather it was a parallel design chosen as a high-production tank, complimenting the T-64. The T-72 retains the low silhouette of the T-

vehicle,[227] the BMP-1, for operations by its mechanised forces. It was known to Indian military intelligence that a Squadron of T-72 tanks had been secretly taken to Libya in North Africa for trials in desert terrain. The BMP-1 catered to mobility, firepower and protection (speed and good armament), and afforded all squad members the ability to fire from within the vehicle. The armament could provide direct support for dismounted infantry in attack and defence and destroy comparable light armoured vehicles. Firepower of this infantry combat vehicle (ICV) consisted of the innovative combination of the 73 mm gun and a launcher for the anti-tank wire-guided missile (ATGM).

General Raina projected to the Ministry of Defence his assessment that any future combat with Pakistan in semi-desert and desert terrain would require maximum employment of mechanised forces[228] equipped with state-of-the-art tanks and ICVs. It was,

---

54/55/62 series, featuring a conventional layout with integrated fuel cells and stowage containers which give a streamlined appearance to the fenders. While the T-64 was deployed only in forward-deployed Soviet units, the T-72 was deployed within the USSR and exported to non-Soviet Warsaw Pact armies and some other friendly countries.

[227] The Red Army mechanized infantry tactics during the 1950s were similar to 2nd World War methods, in which APCs were used as "Battle Taxis", to keep the infantry in close proximity to the tanks during movement, but once in enemy contact, these would unload their infantry before retreating to safer areas. This was in contrast to the German doctrine of "Infantry Fighting Vehicles", where the vehicles were supposed to remain with the tanks and engage lighter targets, both to take a burden off the tanks, as also to support their infantry squads.

[228] The Army's Mechanised Forces constitute the cutting edge of the nation's strategic deterrence. It was, therefore, imperative that our Mechanised Forces continued to modernise, incorporating emerging technologies, that were advancing at an exceptionally fast pace and emerging as a dominant factor in warfare. Countries that could exploit emerging technologies and who synergised the same with innovative operational doctrines and organisational infrastructure would achieve a higher level of Military effectiveness. The Mechanised Infantry component of our Forces, then equipped with APCs for the Infantry's carriage into battle and fight dismounted. Therefore, there was dire need for ICVs for the Mechanised Infantry of the Indian Army.

therefore, proposed to acquire T-72 tanks and BMP-1 ICVs from the USSR. The Government of India approved this proposal and General Ivan Pavlovsky, C-in-C of the Soviet Ground Forces and Deputy Defence Minister of the USSR, was invited to visit India. General and Mrs Pavlovsky and their delegation visited India in early 1977. Immediately after this visit, a reciprocal invitation by General Pavlovsky was extended to General Raina.

General Tappy Raina, accompanied by Lieutenant General Gurbachan Singh, popularly called, "Butch," MGO, Army HQ, Major General Harish Datta, Commandant, College of Combat, Mhow (MP), and Brigadier A. Kaul, Artillery, and this author as MA to COAS, visited the USSR from 31st August to 8th September 1977. The delegation left Delhi at 7.00 am (IST) on 31st August 1977 by an Air India flight to Moscow, with a technical halt planned in Tehran, the capital of Iran. However, on reaching Tehran Airport, it was discovered that the aircraft had developed some technical problems.

Despite the late arrival in Moscow, a message was received from the Soviet hosts that the planned Guard of Honour[229] by the Soviet Army would nevertheless be presented to the Indian COAS on arrival! This now required all members of the delegation and General Raina to be dressed in full ceremonial uniform on deplaning.

An officer of the rank of Major General of the Soviet Army, who was detailed as the Liaison Officer (LO) to accompany General Raina during his entire tour, came on board the aircraft and presented himself to General Raina and briefed him on the rescheduled programme due to the delayed arrival.

On inquiry about the presentation of Guard of Honour at that belated hour, the English-speaking Liaison Officer explained that, in accordance with Soviet military protocol, when a dignitary is honoured as a guest, especially one from a friendly country like India, it did not matter whether it was day or night!

---

[229] Traditionally, in the Indian Army, no ceremonial Guard of Honour is presented after sunset, when all flags are lowered at Retreat. They are again raised at sunrise, when the Reveille is sounded.

The programme of the visit as received from Brigadier J.S. Dutta, the Defence Attaché at the Embassy of India, Moscow, did not indicate, whether the T-72 Tank and BMP-1 would be shown for evaluation of its suitability for the Indian Army during this visit of General Raina. Without that, the visit seemed futile.

Next morning, when General Raina and his delegation called on General Pavlovsky, Commander-in-Chief of the Soviet Ground Forces and Deputy Defence Minister, the above-mentioned shortcoming in the programme was pointed out. Thereafter followed a courtesy call on the Marshal of the Soviet Union, Dmitriy Fedorovich Ustinov, the Defence Minister of the USSR.

In the Soviet Union, at all official meetings and receptions, it was customary to propose toasts with glasses of vodka, to continued warm and friendly relations between India and the Soviet Union. In response to a very warm welcome address by the Defence Minister, Marshal Ustinov, lauding the Indo-Soviet Friendship Treaty of 1971 and the deep friendship between the two nations, General Raina expressed his personal appreciation for the overwhelming warmth extended to him and his delegation, from the time they had touched down on Soviet soil. However, General Raina expressed his disappointment that the "state of art" tank T-72, which had already been introduced in the Soviet Army, had not been included in his programme for this visit. He further added that, from all available accounts, he believed that no other nation in the world could match the characteristics of the T-72 tank and BMP-1 ICV, and, therefore the main purpose of this visit would remain unfulfilled without seeing these two combat platforms.

On hearing this statement coming straight and frank from General Raina, Marshal Ustinov adjourned the meeting for a coffee break. All, except Marshal Ustinov, General Raina and General Pavlovsky along with two interpreters, adjourned to the adjoining room where coffee and vodka were served. A revised programme was then prepared which now included a visit to the nearby Vystrel Academy, where the T-72 tank would be demonstrated that same afternoon. In addition, it was also decided that General

Raina and his delegation would be taken to Minsk,[230] where a unit of the Rogachov Motorised Division was carrying out field firing. They would witness an exercise with the Soviet troops, employing T-72 tanks and BMP-1 ICVs supported by attack helicopters in a river crossing exercise at battalion group level.

The visit to Vystrel Academy was very rewarding. Not only was the T-72 tank shown but all its technical capabilities were also demonstrated. General Raina and members of his delegation were invited to sit inside the tank, where its operational capabilities were explained. The major advantage the T-72 Tank was that it required a crew of three instead of four as in tanks of the Indian Army. This implied a saving of manpower in each armoured regiment.

Next day, the whole delegation was taken by a Soviet Air Force aircraft from Moscow to Minsk. The visit to Minsk was one of the most rewarding experiences for the Indian delegation. Not only were T-72 tanks and BMP-1 ICVs supported by attack helicopters, seen in combat action, but the delegation also witnessed a tactical exercise, where employment of the Soviet Army's T-72 tanks, BMP-1 ICVs and attack helicopters were seen in a live tactical combat situation. At the end of the day, the delegation also took the opportunity to meet some of the field commanders and crew members of the tanks and ICVs.

After visiting Minsk, the delegation went to Leningrad[231] (St Petersburg), USSR's second largest city. In its long history, Leningrad was remembered as the cradle of the Great October

---

[230] Capital of the then Byelorussian Soviet Socialist Republic from 1919-1991. An important communication centre on the route from Moscow to Warsaw (Poland), both by Road and Rail, it became the independent Republic of Belarus, after the breakup of the USSR.

[231] From 1712 until 1918, St. Petersburg was the capital of the Russian Empire. Peter I (the Great) began the construction of the city as his "Window on the West" in 1703. During the subsequent three centuries, St. Petersburg was identified with the three major forces shaping Russian history: Westernisation, Industrialisation, and Revolution! The city was renamed Petrograd in 1914, at the beginning of World War I, because it sounded less German, it was then named Leningrad, after the death of Vladimir Lenin in 1924, and again became St. Petersburg in 1991, when the Soviet Union collapsed.

Socialist Revolution which ushered in a new era in the history of Russia. During the Second World War, the city suffered one of the longest and most horrific of sieges[232] by the Nazi German Army. Lasting from 1941 to 1944, it was also known as the 900-day siege! The city was awarded the "Order of Lenin" in 1945.

The Soviet Army Command at Leningrad arranged the visit by General Raina and his delegation to some important military centres. This included the Klinin Artillery Academy and the Kirov Military Academy. This was followed by a visit to the Leningrad Military District, commanded by Colonel General M.I. Sorokin, where important discussions of mutual interest were held.

The next destination was Tashkent, capital of the Soviet Socialist Republic of Uzbekistan, an important crossroad of culture and of strategic location, approximately 3,400 kilometres from Moscow. Here the delegation experienced different time zones within the same country!

At Tashkent Airport, General Raina and his delegation were received by Colonel General S.Y. Belonozhko, Commander-in-Chief of the Turkestan Military District. Being an Asian part of the USSR, there was immense warmth, even by the local residents, for India. The reader will recall that after the Indo-Pak War in 1965, the Peace Agreement between India and Pakistan was reached, with Soviet intervention, at Tashkent. It later came to be known as the Tashkent Peace Agreement[233]. Also included in the programme was a visit to Samarkand.

---

[232] The siege of Leningrad (the modern-day St. Petersburg) during the 2nd World War, lasted almost two and half years and cost the lives of an estimated 1,000,000 city residents! The seige began on 8th September 1941, when German troops completed their encirclement of the city. As his blitzkrieg rushed towards Moscow, Hitler made the strategic decision to by-pass Leningrad and hoped to strangle the city into submission, rather than commit valuable resources in attacking it directly.

[233] The Agreement was signed on 10th January 1966, between Indian Prime Minister Lal Bahadur Shastri and Pakistani President, F. M. Ayub Khan, at Tashkent. Unfortunately, after signing the agreement, Lal Bahadur Shastri suffered a fatal heart attack during the same night and died at Tashkent.

After Uzbekistan, the delegation returned to Moscow for final discussions and meeting with Soviet military leaders and for farewell calls, before departing for India. During the farewell courtesy call by General Raina on Marshal Ustinov, the latter made an interesting observation. Marshal Ustinov stated that the Soviet Armed Forces held their Indian counterparts in very high esteem for their professionalism, high integrity and character. However, when it came to settling military deals, it was not the men in uniform from India who signed and approved the deals. Instead, it was a civilian bureaucrat and a politician of the Government of India, who would invariably bargain and reduce the requirement of spares and so on from five to seven years, to one year!

In the Soviet Union, no discussion at any conference table or official banquets could progress without the hosts proposing and drinking numerous toasts with vodka, followed by reciprocal toasts by the guests. Half-way through the visit, General Raina jokingly remarked to this author that if he died in the USSR, it should be said "that he had died drinking for his country"!

During the entire tour General Raina felt a genuine desire at all levels of his Soviet hosts to maintain and strengthen cordial relations between our two nations. The delegation formed a very high opinion of the dedication of the Soviet soldier and his professionalism.

The visit led to positive results. It was the first time that the USSR had provided an opportunity to see the T-72 tank and offered the 152 mm Howitzer ML-20M with high angle capability. The visit also helped in establishing personal contact with various echelons of the Soviet Land Forces, thereby promoting understanding and good-will.

Yugoslavia

General Nikola Ljubicic, Federal Secretary for the National Defence of Yugoslavia, had visited India in 1970 at the invitation of General Sam Manekshaw (later Field Marshal) then COAS, Indian Army. Greatly impressed with India and its Armed Forces, he was particularly keen on Indo-Yugoslav defence co-operation and wanted to put it on a practical and "on-going" basis.

General T.N. Raina visited the Socialist Federal Republic of Yugoslavia (Jugoslavija), at the invitation of General Ljubicic, from 31st October to 9th November 1977. He was accompanied by Major General Krishnaswamy Sundarji, GOC 1 Armoured Division, and Captain Dara J. Govadia, ADC to COAS.

General Raina and his delegation commenced their programme with a visit to the Higher Military School and Centre, Belgrade. This was followed by the call on General Nikola Ljubičić, Federal Secretary for the National Defence. Later on, the same day, they visited the permanent Exhibition of Armament and Military Equipment.

From Belgrade the delegation proceeded to Zagreb by special aircraft, where General Raina was received by Colonel General Dušan Ćorković, Commander 5th Army. He visited the Republic HQ of Territorial Defence, followed by a visit to an Armoured Brigade. Later, he also witnessed a mountain battalion exercise.

Other highlights of General Raina's trip to Yugoslavia included a visit to some important training institutions, such as the Military High School, Higher Military Academy and the National Defence School.

A visit of special interest was the one to the Infantry Training Centre and School, Sarajevo. The school was commanded by an officer of the rank of Major General and was meant to train NCOs and officers of all echelons of infantry command from platoon commander to battalion commander. The school conducted a basic two-year course for young officers' and various other courses for company/battalion commanders. It also offered specified courses of 20 to 30 working days. The NCO course was run for four years to make candidates fit to command a platoon. Most of the training in this school was practically political. Political education constituted 3 to 5 percent of the syllabus. It is believed that the wing for morale and political education was also located at this school.

On 4th November 1977, during the visit to one of the Yugoslavia Army Training Establishments, Captain Govadia, ADC to COAS learnt about the air crash[234] of an Indian Air Force aircraft, involving Morarji Desai, Prime Minister of India. Captain Govadia recalls the incident as follows:

> I also recollect that while we were attending a briefing at a Training Establishment, I was informed about the miraculous escape of our Prime Minister, Shri Morarji Desai, in an air crash

---

[234] On that fateful day, 4th November 1977, Prime Minister Morarji Desai left Palam Airport, New Delhi at 17.15 hours in an India Air Force Tupolev 124 jet aircraft of VIP (Comn) Sqadron, with crew comprising, Wing Commander Clarence D'Lima (Captain), Squadron Leader Mathew Cyriac (Co-Pilot) Wing Commander Joginder Singh (Navigator), Squadron Leader V.V.S. Sankar (Flight Engineer), Flight Lieutenant O.P. Arora (Flight Signaller) and Flight Lieutenant P.K. Raveendran (Trainee Flight Engineer), on a six-day tour to the North East region of India, Jorhat, in Assam, was his first destination. The Prime Minister's entourage included his son, Kantilal Desai, former Chief Minister of Arunachal Pradesh, P.K. Thungon and former DIB, Shri John Lobo, among others. The ill-fated aircraft was scheduled to return to base at Palam Airport New Delhi, the same night. On that day, it was known that the weather in Jorhat was not conducive to air travel. It is a mystery as to why the Prime Minister's aircraft was allowed to fly to Jorhat in such conditions.

While approaching Jorhat Airfield, the aircraft crashed in an adjoining paddy field. The captain of the aircraft and the crew showed extreme presence of mind, even after the aircraft had hit tree-tops and nose landed the plane, knowing full well that the cockpit would take the full impact and put them (crew) at grave risk!

All the VVIPs emerged unscathed, except Kantilal who suffered some injuries, because he had not fastened his seat belt. Just before the aircraft was preparing to land, Flight Engineer (UT), Flight Lieutenant Raveendran, had been asked by the Captain of the aircraft to move out of the cockpit and go to the rear of the aircraft. It was a providential escape for Raveendran, for all five members of the crew died while saving the Prime Minister's life.

Despite the tragic crash, Raveendran and another airman showed great presence of mind to evacuate the Prime Minister and his entourage from the rear door which had come open due to impact. The residents of the village Takela Gaon played a heroic role in evacuating the Prime Minister his entourage to the safety of the village headman's house, till help arrived from Jorhat Airbase.

near Jorhat airfield, in the state of Assam in the Northeast of India. I had scribbled a note behind the copy of the Tour Program and passed it on to the COAS. The General had a quick glance and drafted a small message of prayer for the safe survival of the Prime Minister.

General Raina and his delegation also visited the Defence Industrial Hub at Pretis near Sarajevo, where a complex of factories produced a wide range of ammunition, fuses and propellants, apart from assembling Volkswagen cars and manufacturing items for civil consumption. The factory at Pretis specialised in ammunition for armour and artillery such as the 76 mm guns for T-55 tanks. The premises were located in a shallow valley, the upper part of which narrowed appreciably, to make it a difficult aerial target.

After a courtesy call on the Prime Minister and Defence Minister of Yugoslavia on 7th November 1977, General Raina and his delegation held a final discussion with Colonel General Stane Potodar, Chief of the General Staff, Yugoslav National Army.

That same day, Shri N. Krishnan, the Indian Ambassador in Yugoslavia, hosted a lunch at his residence, in honour of General Raina. Captain Govadia, ADC to COAS and who was part of the delegation, recalled that Major General Sundarji and he were both also invited for the lunch by the Indian Ambassador:

> When Major General Sundarji and I reached the residence of Ambassador, our gracious hostess Mrs Krishnan welcomed us in the absence of her husband, who, we were told, had gone to Belgrade Airport to receive the Indian Foreign Minister. Shri Atal Bihari Vajpayee, after an official visit to the Soviet Union, had flown impromptu from Moscow to Belgrade. After receiving Vajpayee at the airport, Ambassador Krishnan invited him to join the luncheon party being held at his residence, so that he too could meet General Raina.
>
> 7th November 1977 was a cold and cloudy day in Belgrade. The guests, mostly officers of the Indian Embassy and their wives, were accepting only non-alcoholic drinks, knowing the aversion of Prime Minister Morarji Desai towards alcoholic

drinks. I seemed to have made an innocent fauxpas by accepting a glass of beer! However, when Foreign Minister Vajpayee arrived at the luncheon party, feeling cold, he asked the hostess if he could have a glass of whisky, much to the surprise of everyone! Thereafter some other guests present also switched to hard liquor drinks!

The United States of America (USA)

Barely six months after his visit to the Soviet Union in September 1977, General Bernard Rogers, Chief of Staff, United States Army invited General Raina to visit the United States. Perhaps this visit was a precursor to the proposed visit by Prime Minister Morarji Desai to the United States in June 1978. The visit was, possibly, also a balancing act by India between two world powers, the Soviet Union and the United States. It was also foresight on the part of the Indian government to keep all avenues in defence cooperation open, rather than put all eggs in the Soviet basket.

General Raina visited the United States from 6th to 15th March 1978. He was accompanied by Lieutenant General R.D. Hira, MVC, GOC 11 Corps, Major General M.L. Chibber, DMO Army HQ, and Major S.K. Sapru, Deputy MA to the COAS. The delegation travelled from New Delhi to New York by Air India *via* Paris and London.

General Raina and his delegation were received at John F. Kennedy International Airport by Brigadier General Robert L. Herriford (Sr), Commander, Defence Contract Administrative Services Region, New York, on behalf of the Chief of Staff, Colonel James H. Bremer, Jr. The Defence Attaché, Embassy of the United States of America in India at New Delhi, was detailed as the Liaison Officer with the delegation for the entire duration of the visit. Brig DSC Rai, Armd Corps, the Defence Attache at the Embassy of India was also present to receive and then travelled as part of Gen Raina's Delegation.

On the day after their arrival in New York, the Indian delegation visited the famous United States Military Academy, West Point, where, they were received by Brigadier General Charles

Wilson Bagnal, Deputy Superintendent United States Military Academy, and a Guard of Honour was presented to General Raina. After a briefing about the Academy, the delegation visited the training classes, barracks and the Academy Museum. A "Guest Lunch" was organised very efficiently with approximately 4,000 cadets also in attendance. Among them were some lady cadets, too, for whom the entry to the Military Academy at West Point had been opened only the previous year.

The next day was spent in Detroit visiting the Headquarters of the United States Army Tank and Automotive Material Command. During the briefing, the development of the M-60 tank programme was also explained. This was followed by a visit to the Arsenal Tank Plant,[235] where the production of the M-60 Tank was in progress. From here the delegation flew to Fort Knox, Kentucky and visited the US Army Armour Centre and School of which Major General Thomas Lynch was Commandant. A static display of equipment and also air cavalry operation were organised. The delegation was introduced to the Cobra attack helicopter and a demonstration of its flying capability. General Raina and members of his delegation were also given the experience of flying in this attack helicopter and the firing of machine guns and rockets from the air.

Throughout the visit, the hosts were forthcoming and frank in providing inputs and information to General Raina on equipment in service of the US Army, including those items that were in the final stages of development. This included details about the XM-1 tank, IFV fitted with TOW missiles, advanced attack helicopters fitted with Hellfire third-generation anti-tank missiles, Black Hawk utility helicopters, CLGP (Canon Launched Guided Projectile) and thermal imaging night sights. On the basis of the above inputs, General Raina felt that the acquisition of the Laser Range Finder (LRF) sights and TOW missile systems for augmenting its anti-tank resource, would be of interest to India.

---

[235] Concurrently, the development of the XM-1 tank was in progress; the first XM-1 was expected to roll out by February 1980.

The delegation then proceeded to Fort Benning, Georgia where a visit to the US Army Infantry Centre and School was followed by discussions on the Mechanised Infantry Doctrine. The next halt was at Fort Bragg, North Carolina, where General Raina expressed the desire to visit the home of a US Army officer in the garrison. This gesture was much appreciated by the American hosts, who escorted General Raina and his delegation to one of the houses in the garrison. It was the home of a Major, where General Raina interacted freely with the officer, his wife and children and enquired about their welfare.

General Raina's assessment at the end of his visit to the United States was that there would be a positive response from the US government should India wish to purchase any equipment from them for the Indian armed forces. In order to diversify India's source of supply of defence equipment, General Raina's recommendation was for India to exploit this opportunity and make a beginning with relatively simple bids, for training devices and for TOW missiles.

What greatly impressed General Raina and his delegation during the visit were the magnificent memorials to war heroes and Army museums found in almost every military station. These played a significant role in the national integration of US citizens as a large number of children were taken to visit such memorials and cemeteries. General Raina, therefore, strongly recommended that India, too, should emulate this practice. On 15th March 1978, the General laid a wreath in a most sombre and dignified ceremony at the Tomb of the Unknown Soldier, located at the Arlington National Cemetery in Virginia.

General Raina was fairly impressed by the free and frank discussion not only with the Chief of Staff of United States Army, but with all officers at various levels who expressed their professional opinions unhesitatingly and freely.

Major S.K. Sapru, member of this delegation, recalls that en route to Fort Knox, because of the deteriorating weather conditions, the aircraft carrying General Raina was diverted to a neighbouring military airfield. From there the General and his entourage drove to Fort Knox, KY.

That evening, an early and quiet dinner was organized for the Indian delegation at the VIP Guest House. Also present on the occasion was General Eugene Forrester, Commander, US Recruiting Command. General Forrester had developed a close bond with Major General M.L. Chibber when both had attended the RCDS Course, UK. Sapru recalls the following episode:

> As the evening progressed the conversation between the four Generals present (Raina, Chibber, Hira and Forrester) veered to their families. General Chibber mentioned how he had lost a young daughter who had been unwell. General (Rocky) Hira recalled his only son who had died not long ago in a tragic road accident in Delhi. The mood was already sombre when General Forrester softly added that his wife who had been a licensed pilot and fond of adventure had disappeared, never to be found again, while flying solo from Tasmania to a Pacific Island in a single engine aircraft. General Raina spoke of his son, Joe, who had died recently. A long, eerie silence followed!

Four outstanding military professionals, befitting their rank, character and personae, sat in quiet reverie, united by the tragedies that define human existence.

At the US Army Armour Centre and School, Fort Knox, Kentucky, tank officers, without hesitation, gave their assessment of the Soviet T-72 Tank, which they considered to be an excellent weapon system having numerous attractive features. Clearly, the US Army firmly believed that motivated human capital of the nation was the primary instrument for war. Therefore, no efforts were spared for enrolling suitable officers and other ranks for their army and then training them to become motivated members of the US armed forces.

The induction of women into various branches of the US Army, at that time, was still being debated. That the US Army was playing a very useful and effective role in racial integration was evident by the high percentage of black Americans amongst the officers and those below officer ranks.

The US Army maintained a high degree of operational readiness for a short war, working on an 18-hour notice for mobilisation. Other major highlights and observations of the visit were:

- The Army in the US was organized around functional commands rather than geographical commands, keeping in mind the global role of US military.
- Extensive opportunities and facilities were provided to officers during their career for acquiring post-graduate degrees including doctorates in science and the humanities. Well educated officers were considered an asset, not only to the armed forces but to the nation as well.
- The standard of cadets at West Point and the professional competence of the soldiers of the US Army were found to be nearly at par with those of gentlemen cadets and soldiers of Indian Army.
- The tactical doctrines practiced for the next war constantly laid emphasis on the "combined arms" concept.
- The tactical doctrine of the US Army for combined operations of Infantry, Armour and Army Aviation Corps was what the Indian Army needed to adopt. It was of interest to note that the US Army Aviation Corps[236] had a larger number of aircraft than the US Air Force; whereas India had yet to accept its induction in the Indian Army for combined mechanised operations against our adversaries.

On 14th March 1978, General Raina arrived in Washington and was received by General Bernard William Rogers, Chief of Staff of the US Army. That evening, General Rogers hosted a dinner in honour of General Raina and his delegation. It was attended by senior officers of the US Army, including General Lyman Louis Lemnitzer, Chairman, Joint Chiefs of Staff (retired), Major General Surinder (Sindi) Bhaskar (of Indian origin), who headed the Dental Corps of the US Army, representatives of the National Se-

---

[236] As already mentioned earlier in Chapter 27, Army Aviation Corps was finally created in Indian Army on 1st November 1986.

curity Council, the State Department and Mr. Nani Ardeshir Palkhivala, the Ambassador of India to the United States.

The next day, Ambassador Palkhivala hosted a lunch in honour of General Raina and his delegation. It was attended by General Bernard W. Rogers, other senior US Army officers and selected representatives from the United States Congress, the State Department, the Department of the Army and the officials of the Indian Embassy.

Although, it was not included in the programme, General Raina also called on Mr Clifford Alexander Jr., Secretary of the Army, along with General Rogers. Thereafter, General Rogers escorted General Raina to an adjoining room where other senior Generals in the Pentagon were already present. It was here that on behalf of the President of the United States of America, General Rogers presented the medal of "Legion of Merit"[237] to General Raina in a simple ceremony held in front of the national flags of India and the United States.

The description of the various interactions during General Raina's official foreign visits serves to highlight the aims and objectives of military diplomacy. These are, broadly speaking:

1. Strengthening of diplomatic ties with other countries;
2. Joint training of the military of both countries;
3. Improving knowledge and awareness of weapons and military technologies;
4. And, very importantly, establishing a sphere of influence. It enables direct interaction with foreign military organisations to learn about their weapons, tactics, doctrines and strategies.

In the contemporary context, as the prospects of conventional conflicts among major powers is reduced and the focus has shifted to terrorism, internal conflicts and civil wars, military diplomacy

---

[237] This medal is meant only for foreign dignitaries and is presented to distinguished commanders from friendly countries.

has emerged as a new international priority. Almost every country in the world has institutionalised it. China is known to use military diplomacy extensively and calls it "Foreign Affairs work performed by defence institutions and Armed Forces"! On the contrary, until recently, India did not make much use of it: Whether this was deliberate or a result of bureaucratic and political inertia is not clear. It is obvious that with greater utilisation of military diplomacy, India can enhance the pursuit of its national interests.

Chapter 38

The Last Post

After General Raina relinquished his appointment as COAS of the Indian Army and Chairman of the Chiefs of Staff Committee, the Rainas settled down in their own house in Greater Kailash I in South Delhi. Ninette Raina recalls that period:

> Our house in M-Block, Greater Kailash, Part-I, New Delhi, had been renovated, cleaned and spruced up, well before Tappy's retirement on 31st May 1978! We moved into the house along with our dogs and birds and soon felt settled. At last Tappy was happy to have time all to himself! We began to enjoy a relaxed life in our own home.
>
> At the crack of dawn Tappy would set out in the peaceful surroundings (at that hour only!), with our three dogs, walking at a breakneck pace. He had thought of lots of projects and made plans for what was left of our lives. However, on Independence Day 1978, he realised that everything was not all right with him. He fell ill, and after a long stay in Army Hospital for suspected tuberculosis in his lung, he was transferred to Military Hospital, Pune, where he was finally diagnosed with cancer of the lung. That had to be operated upon. After his treatment at Pune, he returned home, looking a different person to what he was at the time of his retirement!

Within a few months of retirement and recovery from his illness, Tappy Raina was offered an ambassadorial post, that of India's High Commissioner to Canada. Before accepting the offer, however, Tappy informed the President and Prime Minister of India that his state of health might interfere with this new posting. He was advised to proceed just the same; equally, the medical facilities there would be excellent. And so, another exercise of packing got underway. Ninette Raina never thought she would have to ever pack after Tappy's retirement from the army. Neither did she think that during his assignment as a diplomat, her beloved husband, would not return home alive.

On 1st February 1979, Tappy and Mrs. Raina left Delhi. They stopped in London to equip themselves for the severe winter that was to be met with in Canada. At the time of his retirement, the General had got rid of most of his heavy woollens and now he had to buy some of those same items again!

The Rainas landed in Toronto on 3rd February and everywhere it was white with snow. The very next day they experienced a blizzard but their hotel room was warm and smug. At Ottawa, a house awaited them with all the trimmings, but the General decided to proceed to Ottawa only on Monday, 5th February 1979, because he did not want to disturb the staff during the week-end and that too, in such weather!

The Soldier Diplomat

On reaching Ottawa General Raina immersed himself immediately in his new duties. Ninette Raina spent time getting acquainted with the staff of the Indian High Commission and others who were from a non-military background.

Presentation of Credentials

On 8th March 1979 General Raina, MVC, former COAS of the Indian Army and now High Commissioner of India in Canada, was invited to present his credentials to the Governor General of

Canada,[238] It was a very formal and cordial occasion. While General Raina, was escorted in state by members of the Royal Canadian Mounted Police in their famous red coats and wide felt hats. Mrs Ninette Raina and the other ladies of the High Commission followed separately in their private cars.

Mr G.B.S. Sidhu, First Secretary (Economics & Consular) at the Indian High Commission in Canada, who accompanied the General to the Governor General's House remembers how the Governor General and other Canadian officials present at this ceremony were greatly impressed with General Raina's eloquent speech made without reference to any written paper or notes. Upon their return to the High Commission, there was a "vin d' honneur" at General and Mrs Raina's residence, for senior officials and the entire staff of the Indian High Commission that same evening.

Canada and India have much in common. Both nations were former British colonies, belonged to the Commonwealth, and had English as an official language. From the point of view of the resources index, however, the two were on opposite ends: Canada was amongst the wealthiest and most developed of nations, whereas India was amongst the developing and poor countries of the world. Both nations had a history of mutual respect and cooperation. Past Canadian prime ministers, notably Lester Pearson, had very warm relations with the former Prime Minister of India, Pandit Jawaharlal Nehru. Canada had made significant contributions to India's development in virtually every field. Canadians of Indian origin were numerous: they were highly educated and

---

[238] General Raina along with some other diplomats presented his credentials to the Governor General of Canada, Mr. Edward Richard Schneyr. Popularly known as Ed, at the age of forty-three, he was one of the youngest governor generals of Canada. A seasoned politician, he had been the premier of Manitoba. Subsequently he had some unusual appointments for an ex-Governor General: he was appointed Canada's High Commissioner to Australia. Strangely, even after occupying such high federal posts, he wanted to return to active politics but was defeated in the elections. As Governor General of Canada, he was accused of seeking political popularity.

affluent and wielded political influence disproportionate to their numbers. They formed only four percent of the population then.

India's nuclear explosion at Pokhran in 1974 had somewhat strained its relations with Canada, as it was believed that the nuclear fuel used in the Indian bomb had been produced using Canadian technology. After a period of drought, relations between both nations were somewhat restored. It was at this juncture, that General Raina, was chosen as the High Commissioner of India in Canada. The General was known to be suffering from cancer and so his appointment was somewhat controversial, even though he was passing through a period of remission. On taking over his duties, however, he was fully functional.

As luck would have it, when the General assumed charge as High Commissioner for India in Canada, Brigadier Ravi N. Mahajan, VSM, was the Military and Naval Attaché at the Indian Embassy at Washington DC, USA. He was also concurrently the Defence Attaché for Canada. As already brought out in earlier chapters, Brigadier Mahajan's association with Tappy Raina went back twenty-five years to their time together in Amritsar in 1953. They were to spend many hours together in Ottawa. During Brigadier Mahajan's short official tours to Canada, the Rainas always insisted that he stay with them.

The High Commissioner's official residence at 585 Acacia Avenue, Ottawa, was large and located in a very exclusive neighbourhood. It had a vast reception area and a dining room that could seat two dozen guests. There were at least half-a-dozen bedrooms. The Indian government had acquired this building in 1950, although it had been built much earlier. Thus, in 1979, it looked well beyond its years. The floors and the stairway were wooden and creaked with age. Overall, the place needed urgent repairs and refurbishing. Much work was also needed to restore the large garden to its pristine glory. It may be recalled that in India, too, strict economy was in force at that time as far as maintenance of government accommodation, both offices and residences, was concerned. The same measures were in force for the country's properties abroad. Sadly, the office of the High Commissioner was also in a decrepit state. It had creaking stairs and an elevator that lurched precariously. Its plumbing and heating were outdated. Ten years earlier, another former Indian Army Chief, late General Jayanto Nath Chaudhuri, OBE, had served as the High Commissioner there.

One of General Raina's major achievements in Ottawa was the construction of the new High Commissioner's office at 10 Spring Field Road. The construction of the new building had been pending for years. The General with his characteristic drive and energy was able to get the Ministry of External Affairs to release funds and complete the new office.

The High Commissioner's residence was also refurbished to a considerable extent. It was a corner mansion, which, on one side shared a garden fence with Mr. Pierre Trudeau, who was at that time the Leader of the Opposition in the Canadian Parliament. He was a French Canadian and became quite friendly with the Rainas. After a brief period, Mr. Trudeau was re-elected as prime minister. His "over the garden fence" neighbourly acquaintance with the Rainas was informal.

The Role of a Diplomat's Wife

As far as the pace of social life was concerned, General and Mrs. Raina did not find it different from Delhi. Their social life at the Army House had been hectic. The crowd in Canada, however, was different. They met numerous people from all over the world, and that was a very educative and interesting experience. Mrs Ninette Raina recalled her experience as a diplomat's wife, as follows:

> I enjoyed my role as a diplomat's wife after having been an Army wife for nearly three decades. It was good to be living in a bilingual country, as I was at home in both languages. Our home soon became the meeting place of both English and French cultures in an Indian surrounding. The house and its decorations were entirely Indian and, of course, so was the food, which our visitors expected! The official residence of the High Commissioner was an imposing house in a huge plot of land in an area of big houses, forests and a lake. Everything was

orderly, silent and private. But there were some ludicrous situations to begin with! The men coming to repair the house did so in cars that were much swankier than our staff car! They seemed quite amused to see the difference.

The furniture in the High Commissioner's Residence was old, and I spent days finishing my stock of Araldite, to stick broken legs and split furniture pieces. The wall to wall carpet had seen better days. Originally, it would have been a light grey but it had taken on all the hues of the rainbow! The problem for me was how to camouflage the stains, till such time as we could replace the worn out items. The simple replacement of these items ran into high figures and renewal was a headache. We had to stick to a budget. We were not a rich country, but when I looked at the other embassy's spotless residences, I felt very embarrassed.

Some chairs in the house were rather askew, and some incongruous pictures were hung on the walls, where they could not hide the most glaring stains and scuffs. Tappy and the household staff huffed and puffed in the basement, making everything shipshape! The High Commissioner's house was to be organised just like in the Army, when everything was neatly put in its place, repaired or replaced! The floors had been scrubbed and everything was tidy, and whatever was redundant, was removed. Tappy being a soldier, transformed the house to our mutual satisfaction.

Our first winter in Ottawa was severe. In February of that year the temperature went down to 25 to 35 degrees Centigrade below zero, and when the wind-chill factor was added, it was very low indeed. Going outdoors on foot was out of the question for us. I saw other people doing so, only on skis on the road before the house. Houses were comfortably warm and cosy and we had piping hot water at the turn of a tap. The electric equipment in the kitchen buzzed or rang when the food was ready in the oven and the freezer held a month's supplies of food. The electric washer, although on its last legs, offered sterling service. Any time, any day, we were functional. Windows were double-paned and very tight. Life was really like a dream.

There was colour TV the whole day and movies galore. I never went to cinema in Canada. There was a film every afternoon in French and many others in English. There was music broadcast the whole day from stereo radio stations.

On 7th February 1979, I recorded in my Diary, the prevailing condition of the Indian High Commissioner's residence. It was impossible to camouflage the upstairs curtains which were in shreds. Why? Because, one morning the TV room was aired in my absence! Tappy was looking very sheepish. All the potted plants in that room were drooping, burnt by the cold. This was Canada and not India; opening a door or window in the winter of Canada was to invite disaster.

The whole basement was full of garden implements but nothing was in working order. By and by some new utensils came for the kitchen, which was quite empty. I had to go out and buy a frying pan and teaspoons, because eight guests were expected for Tea next day. The official set of twenty-four, had saucers but only six cups! The staff advised Tappy, "Do like your predecessors, just improvise"! I also chanced to find that there were eight dozen glasses in the basement, not even washed. They still contained dry tea and sugar! Among the "refuse and condemned items" I found a huge lace table cloth that was badly stained with coffee stains. Someone had probably upset several coffee pots on it! With much toil and patience I managed to clean it and spent hours re-embroidering the holes in it.

Oh, my goodness! Did I miss "Army House" and its impeccable order? I got new cups but these were not crested and didn't match the existing ones. Outside, the snow had now turned to rain.

The housework was very heavy to start with; the vacuum cleaner was out of order. After repair it was pressed into service and its humming was always heard in the background. Two men could not keep three floors plus a basement under control and I had to get down to it also in between my engagements. Washing, ironing, darning, polishing cutlery and crystal ware, spit and polish everywhere kept us all happily occupied. The washing alone was tremendous. The washer hummed several hours a day. Climbing and running all over the huge house — up and down and down and up, gave me a good exercise and a huge appetite.

The season changed, the end of the winter also brought some thaw six weeks late. We could at last see our garden. Organising of the garden started, with Tappy in command. Two of our household staff were ex-servicemen from the Indian Army and so was the High Commissioner's driver. They set to the task, with a strong will, just like the old days of the Army, for them. What was a joy was the fact that the dusty atmosphere in which I had lived for years in different places in India wasn't there. The air here was clear and clean and the furniture stayed graciously shiny after polishing. No dust! Dusting once a week was more than enough. By mid-May, the painting and distempering of the house was done. Now it looked clean.

We had spread some of our personal carpets on those floors and the result was quite pleasing and, oh bliss, it was decently neat. Tappy said over and over again, "If I stay long enough here I will give my country an official residence, of which one can be proud"!

The first spring in Canada was an enchantment, with lilac in the garden. The whole hedge was white with these and bushes in the garden were pink, mauve or red. The sweet fragrance could be had from far away and a lovely copper maple suddenly got covered with bronze leaves. Among the dark fir trees, it was striking.

By now we had come to know many people and met many Indians too. Our social life began to be very hectic, either the official one or the private one! Indians in Ottawa are mostly the elite professionals like, professors, engineers, doctors, architects and so on. Many were Canadian civil servants too. It was a matter of joy to see their houses as spick and span as any Canadian's but better decorated too.

Canadians are practical people and go for comfort above all, whereas most Indians in Canada, went in for beauty or appearance! Many were connoisseurs and had lovely artistic houses. It was amusing to learn the point of view of people living in such a cold country, where comfort at home came first. Priorities were in that order: a house in town, a house in the country (even a shack), a car and a boat! That meant spending lots of money, and they worked hard for it.

Historically, Canada was comparatively a new country, of which the Canadians could justifiably be proud. However, living in this country required a lot of grit! Beginnings must have been terrible in that cold wilderness. But to Indians, it had its amusing sides too; anything that was more than 50 years old, was considered an antique! To people having their roots in Mohenjo Daro and the Indus Valley, that appeared incredible!

We travelled a lot around the countryside in Canada. First, we went to Montreal and later to Quebec. I was very eagerly looking forward to knowing French Canada. The moment we crossed from Ontario into Quebec, all signals and direction on street posts ceased to be bi-lingual in English and French. Here there were only French sign-posts! My knowledge of French was sought for translation and interpretation. But there was hardly any strikingly French character in the region except for the tree lined roads and the old part of Quebec. Not even the food! But everywhere, there was much politeness and calm. One could see that the French people who settled in Canada in olden days, did not have much Latin blood in them. As for the man in the street, I could not understand his "dialect". They had spoken like that in villages of France but that was 300 years ago!

Then, on to our next destination, New Brunswick in East Canada, located in the South of Quebec, which reminded me ot Sweden, on a bigger scale. And finally, we went to Nova Scotia, also on the eastern coast of Canada, situated on the Atlantic Ocean, where I was reminded of Brittany (in France). In both those provinces, I could speak both my languages!

On the other side of Canada, we visited Winnipeg, Calgary, Edmonton, Vancouver and Victoria. Everywhere we met lots of people of Indian origin. In British Columbia, they deal a lot with the timber business and one found them even in quaint places such as in isolated sawmills or paper mills! Everywhere the welcome was warm and generous. In fact they (Canadians of Indian Origin), worked very hard outside their own country, because they have strong incentives, which is a human norm. I had friends of mine in Saigon who never went out of their way to work hard. But when they lived in France, they did work hard! Was it to keep warm, the climate being trying for them, or simply because they receive better pay and facilities? Keep a man happy and you will get his goodwill.

Whenever I went to western countries, there were homes for the "aged". Economic compulsions had a part to play in this state of affairs, but there was selfishness too. These homes provided all possible amenities for old people and they were well looked after on the material side. I visited some of the most modern of these homes, particularly in Sweden. Food was centrally cooked and then distributed, while it was still warm. Even in their own houses, old people could get that food delivered, so as to avoid any stress. Old ladies, if they so wanted, had their own tiny kitchenettes in their small apartments to make jam or cookies or simply chat over a cup of coffee. Gadgets were designed to be operated with only one hand if the person was handicapped. There were buttons for alarm bell everywhere, on the floor level, the furniture, the bed, the kitchen, in case of accidental fall or seizure. They had a lot of company and many hobbies. Yet, I saw many of them just sitting and staring into space! Surely they would have much preferred to live in India, where we have far less comfort but mostly live with our loved ones in the family. They simply wanted to feel wanted. My friends readily admitted that the Indian way was better.

After experiencing the Canadian spring, we started to have a taste of the Canadian summer. Now hot, damp and humid winds blew from the Great Lakes. At times, I felt that Canada could be as hot as India! Through the change of seasons, Tappy went on working, and keeping official appointments, relating to his diplomatic duties. I heard some comments during social gatherings and parties outside, that he was very good at his job.

> On 18th July, a very big party for several ambassadors was hosted at our residence, which finished very late. The huge lace table cloth that had once been badly stained, and which with much toil and patience, I had managed to clean, repair and restore, looked gorgeous by candlelight on our long dining table. The Canadian ladies kept on asking about it! They all wanted one like that. There were many beautiful things that had been spoilt and discarded in the basement and my heart pained, for I hated that waste. People did not care for things that did not belong to them. They had no pride in those things at all.

As time passed, General and Mrs. Raina acquired more and more friends. In no time, Tappy Raina became very popular. As a diplomat, he was honest and frank and did not hesitate to say "No" when other people would say "Yes" merely to please. He was also very urbane. Public relations were always an art he excelled in.

When the fall (autumn) arrived in Canada, it was such a beautiful season for the Rainas to experience. As Ninette Raina writes:

> When the sun rays touched the red maples, it was like a burst of rubies everywhere. Travelling around parks and forests was enough to make one cry with joy and happiness; everything was so beautiful! And the grass was always so green by contrast. That was our only "Fall" there.
>
> Travelling in this country gave one the impression of immense space but also of an austere beauty. The countryside could be very empty and the only change at times were the dark blue lines of hills on the horizon and masses and masses of trees, dark and silent. It looked sometimes as if all the innumerable crowds of India had been frozen into trees; they were the same, milling but motionless! I learnt quite a few things. That the wolf, for example, so despised and hated in European lore was considered by most in Canada as a noble animal. I saw a few of them, and to my surprise, they not only howl, but also barked like dogs!
>
> Raccoons are scavengers look like huge squirrels with dark lines round their eyes like glass frames. One sees their red eyes

around the houses at night. Whatever they eat must be dipped into water first. Skunks are a horrid thing. They look very pretty, black with white stripes down their back from head to tail and about the size of a Spitz dog. But they atomise some smelly substance when annoyed or in danger and that is enough to make one choke or vomit.

It so happened one day that our next-door neighbour, Pierre Trudeau,[239] had a family of skunks under his house. One fine morning as the sun was golden and inviting on the grass of the garden, the most dreadful skunk smell wafted to our house and permeated everything. The stench was so strong, that the whole staff ran away. They just disappeared and I also had to run down to hide in the basement, to avoid the worst of the smell!

Tappy and I enjoyed lovely walks along the Ottawa River bank which was lined with the stately tall coniferous trees and maples. The air was crisp and cool in the morning and we had the whole area to ourselves, as the only people one met at that hour of the morning or evening were joggers.

Our children (daughter Anita and her husband) had come to visit us that summer after a week's stop-over in Paris. They landed in Montreal on a torrid day and I collected them, as Tappy was too involved to leave his desk. We had to stop in every locality on our way back to drink some fluids, because it was so hot.

Next day there was such a storm that a big tree was uprooted on the electric wires, breaking them, and we had no power for twelve hours. That was the only time we went without electricity during our whole stay in Canada, indeed a far cry from Delhi. We had cold dinner and no light that night, but it was high summer and no harm was done. And we had a lovely reunion with the children.

There was once an invitation to Tea at the Governor-General's residence. So everybody flocked out for the big gathering on the vast grounds of Rideau Hall. Diplomatic people

[239] Who had lost his premiership that year and lived in the house meant for Leader of the Opposition.

came in formal attire, there were glamorous saris, suits and ties, Achkans (long coats worn by men in India on special occasions), African robes, etc and to our amazement there were also the inhabitants of the town in open-collar shirts or no shirts at all, ladies in short pants or bikinis, and children barefoot! In summer, people needed the sun so much in those latitudes that they uncover to the maximum! And there is no formality in such events. At least they were comfortable while we suffocated in our formal attire!

Since taking over as High Commissioner of India in Canada, the remission from his cancer disease permitted General Raina to be active and effective. On 17th November 1979, General and Mrs. Raina were delighted with the news that came in the morning from India, that they had a grandson,[240] born to their daughter, Anita. This new addition to their family, Gaurav, gave Tappy further incentive and inspiration. He wanted to buy all sorts of toys and asked Ninette to get them for their grandson.

During Brigadier Mahajan's brief stays with the Rainas at Ottawa, he often accompanied Tappy during his walks in the scenic and peaceful neighbourhood of their residence. At times, they came across late Pierre Trudeau cycling with his son, Justin,[241] then a young lad.

During these walks, the General and Brigadier Mahajan often talked about their shared experiences and events. Tappy revealed to Brigadier Mahajan that before leaving India, during his formal call on Prime Minister Morarji Desai, he had asked him: "Prime Minister, I am suffering from cancer, yet you are sending me on this mission?" "I know General, that is also a reason to send you to Canada so that you can get good treatment and get well", replied the Prime Minister, Morarji Desai.

---

[240] Unfortunately, General Raina never saw his grandson, Gaurav.

[241] At age 43, Justin was to become the youngest Prime Minister of Canada.

During one of their conversations, General Raina jolted Brigadier Mahajan when he asked, *"Ravi, should I die here or go back to our home in New Delhi?"* Ravi was later to relate that he had a lump in his throat. He quickly recovered and advised him to remain in Canada, and added, *"Sir, if you go back, you will become a* tamasha*, your house will be inundated with visitors and there will be no peace for you and your family".*

In the spring of 1980, General and Mrs. Raina went on a brief private visit to Washington DC, where they were house guests of Brigadier and Mrs. Mahajan. By now, the General's health had somewhat deteriorated. His gait and speech were still quite steady, and his brain was still razor-sharp. However, his physical co-ordination of the upper extremity had begun to decline, and he had to be helped by his caring wife, Ninette. Overall, it was a relaxed period of bonhomie for the two families, who had shared so much together in good times and bad.

At one point General and Mrs Raina went from Ottawa to Edmonton. At Edmonton Airport, they lost their way inside the huge terminal building. By the time they found their bearings they discovered that the building had been shut and they were locked-in. Luckily for them, a lone airport official, who by chance was passing by, saw their plight and escorted them through some private offices and helped them to get out of the airport. They had been wandering there like lost souls for nearly one hour. This airport was very far from the town and nobody was expected at that time. Then, a car loomed on the horizon, which was quickly flagged by the General. The driver loaded their suitcases in the car-boot and asked them their destination. Once in the car, the General with a smile, addressed him in Hindustani; he had recognised a countryman! According to Mrs. Raina, the driver nearly drove them into the ditch in his surprise! The rest of the journey (and it was very long), was spent in cosy chatting, and the man was so overwhelmed that he wanted to drive them straight to his home for tea. Since the General had a train to catch and they could not afford to be delayed they declined his kind offer. And when it came to paying the fare, Tappy had to argue with the driver to accept the fare because the driver simply refused to take any money. Finally, he could prevail and persuade the good man to accept the payment of fare for the trip.

During one of her visits with Tappy, Mrs. Raina recalls:

> In Vancouver Island we once had lunch in a saw-mill in Port Alberta. While people talked about barking of trees and the making of wooden tiles for house roofs, I was admiring the trees. I had wanted for a long time to see a Douglas Fir tree, and I saw lots of other trees, including a redwood. My hosts were so amused at my liking trees that I was presented with a handbook on trees of British Columbia.
>
> It was a strange feeling for me to contemplate the Pacific Ocean from this part of the world. I had first seen it from the other side of the globe as a child in French Indo-China! Tappy had promised to help me see an animal that I wanted to admire, a white whale, in particular, a Baluga whale. Alas, he did not live long enough for us to go there. I had to be content with the black and white killer whales, only.

Whenever Mrs. Raina was free from other commitments, she would wander in their big garden and observe life around her. Their house was separated from that of their immediate neighbour by only a few trees. No fence as such, as was often the case in the New World! Pierre Trudeau's three sons used to play extensively on their own grounds and the cats of his house often came to Mrs. Raina for a pat. They would follow her from flower bed to flower bed and they became good companions. According to Mrs. Raina:

> One day a ferocious dog set about the cats and they high tailed it up a tall fir tree. Unfortunately one cat could not get down on its own and mewed lamentably from up there! It was their neighbour and former Prime Minister of Canada, Pierre Trudeau himself, who dragged a ladder, set it against the tree, climbed up and retrieved his cat.

> All the time there was hectic activity going on, particularly in the evening. Offices closed early (and started early, too) and people came back and worked in their gardens. We had a lawn mower with a small motor and the bearer ran races round the lawn cutting the grass. But the neighbours had little mowing carts on which they sat and mowed their grass. Till the fall of night, people were busy all over the place. Then lights would go on in the houses and it was dinner time.

The memory that Mrs. Raina had kept of this landscape around was a contrasting image; a white one and a green one. Winters were lovely when the sky would be blue after a storm, and the sun would shine brilliantly, unlike other times when it remained misty and dark, for days! In March, stumpy birds with a thick bill would flutter in the bare branches of the trees and whistle beautifully. Neighbouring dogs would come round and say hello; friendly and trustful. Animals were very much loved and looked after.

The Rainas quietly saw in the dawn of 1980. By the middle of January, their garden was an ice skating rink: they hardly had any snow, but the sudden intense cold had frozen the wet ground. Then, at last, it was spring. Mrs. Raina described it as follows:

> And the spring came again. Whistles and chirrups arose all around. Squirrels stopped knocking at the windows and begging for food. The first crocus burst out of the soil and the snow. Strings of big "V" flying formations overflew Ottawa and resounded with the call of wild geese.
>
> The River that the whole winter we had seen between the bare trees from our bedroom windows was now hidden behind new foliage. Immediately work started in the garden. The new chancery building was being finished, new furniture and carpets installed. Potted plants, bright windows, spacious library and reading room, a dignified atmosphere and yes, it was chic! The old building was sold and immediately pulled down by the new owners.

After the official parties for the inauguration of the new chancery, we hosted a get-together for the High Commission staff on 25th April. That same evening, Tappy took ill.

While the party was going on and everybody was having a jolly good time, Tappy's legs started giving way and he had to sit down. Suddenly he could not hold his glass. We rushed him to the hospital where he was admitted on the spot. In the night, the doctor rang me up to tell me he had suffered a stroke. After three days of anxiety, he was discharged, feeling better. The doctor told me privately that it was not advisable for him to continue working at the pace as he was doing. It was necessary to take him back home (India) by X'mas that year.

I requested the doctor to tell it directly to Tappy; he would appreciate that as a soldier. Once told about his present state of health, Tappy like a true soldier, took it on the chin! He was not afraid in the least and decided he would ask for his recall and leave by the end of summer. He went on working normally, first at home then back at the office.

Due to his backache Tappy had to sleep upon a hard board. He told me many times that on foreign tours he was given very soft beds in hotels and rest houses. He had to sleep on the carpet instead and in the morning his attendants, orderlies or waiters were amazed if not downright concerned to find him there.

Also his old chest injuries, received during the Second World War, made him suffer at times. Some "shrapnel" continued to nag him from time to time because these remained embedded so near his heart, that it had not been possible to extract them. All his life, Tappy carried those little bits of metal in his chest. Many years later, X-rays showed that these had moved up toward the shoulder. At times he was very uncomfortable but he would not let this distract him from his work.

On 6th May 1980, General and Mrs. Raina went for a short holiday to USA and came back to their home in Canada on 11th May Alas, on the 19th of May 1980, the General reached the end of the road of his life. He suffered a brain haemorrhage early in the evening, and passed away at the hospital, without regaining consciousness. It all happened in only two hours.

> *Just as a person casts off worn-out garments and puts on others that are new, so does the embodied soul cast off worn-out bodies and take on others that are new.*
>
> ~ The Bhagvad Gita, II (22)

Ninette Raina was, of course, devastated. After Tappy's sudden death, the packing up of the house was done by the staff as Mrs. Raina could not supervise it. Later, after the bulk of the luggage had gone and only the hand luggage was left and packed, she discovered that a crateful of papers, cuttings, magazines and other material had been carefully collected by General Raina for future reference. During his brief "Last Post" as a diplomat, General Raina had become an even more acute student of the international scene and was probably planning to use this material. Ninette had it destroyed and left behind, as there was nothing personal in it anyway. To Ninette it proved only too clearly that Tappy Raina would never have had a peaceful, relaxed life at all; he would have continued working, even after his final retirement.

> *Je viens à vous, Seigneur, père auquel il faut croire; Je vous porte, apaisé, les morceaux de ce coeur tout plein de votre gloire que vous avez brisé.*
>
> *(I come to you O Lord, our father who we must trust, and offer you the pieces of this heart, so full of thy glory, which you have broken but which is now at peace.)*
>
> ~ Victor Hugo (Les Contemplations)

Tributes by the High Commission Staff

Many years later, Lieutenant General Mahajan recalled that his visits from Washington to Ottawa, had become more of a personal nature, because of the General's illness. According to Mahajan, there was a regime change at Ottawa; Mr Trudeau had once again regained power. So, nothing of great importance perhaps happened during that period in Indo-Canadian relations. All that Mahajan could remember was that it was a period of thaw in the equation between two countries after India's Nuclear Test at Pokhran had somewhat angered Canada. General Raina's presence as Indian High Commissioner in Canada greatly helped in mending the relations between India and Canada.

Most staff members of the Indian High Commission recalled that the time they spent in Ottawa under the leadership of the General and Mrs Raina was a refreshing experience for them. Mr Arjunan Iyer, a senior member of the staff at the Indian High Commission at that time fondly recalled his association with General Raina:

> At the outset I would like to share that the time we spent in Ottawa under the leadership of General and Mrs Raina was the most memorable and rewarding in my bureaucratic career.
>
> He was a good and fair judge of the officers working under him. He knew exactly whom to trust, to what extent, individual capabilities and, above all, the limitations of the officers working under and with him. I got a feeling that he chose to trust me a little more than many others in the High Commission possibly because I also was originally from the disciplined service.
>
> Both General and Mrs Raina were the embodiment of grace and kindness, qualities that were in full play in all the diplomatic gatherings they hosted or graced.
>
> The manner and extent to which General Raina contributed to the speeding up the movement of the High Commission to 10 Springfield Avenue, was well known. Though, I arrived later, I

gathered that General Raina had pursued this task with his quiet efficiency and commitment to discipline and time schedules.

On the political front, the manner in which the Canadian government responded to his passing away culminating in the transport of his body to India, etc., is a reflection of what General Raina had meant for the Indo-Canadian relationship and how much he had contributed to developing and nurturing this relationship.

Death in Harness: A Soldier Par Excellence Departs

Thus, ended the life story of an extraordinary person who retired as the Chief of Indian Army at the young age of 57th years and 5 months after completing his full tenure of three years. He passed away on 19th May 1980, seven months before his 60th birthday.

General Raina is credited with the profoundly laconic statement that the Indian Army is apolitical and his career vindicated it. The image that he left behind was that of the soldier with no other concern than the profession of arms.

The coffin containing General Tapishwar Narain Raina's mortal remains, accompanied by his bereaved wife, Ninette Raina, and daughter, Anita, escorted by Major Dogra was flown from Ottawa to New York by the Canadian government. There it was transferred to a waiting Air India aircraft and flown to Mumbai, from where it was then flown to Delhi in an Indian Air Force aircraft. The remains of General Raina, and the accompanying bereaved family, were received at the Indian Air Force Technical Area, Palam Airport at 05.30 a.m. on 25th May 1980, by his successor, General O.P. Malhotra, the Chief of Army Staff, Eric Gonzalves, Secretary in the External Affairs Ministry and Mr John Haydel, the Canadian High Commissioner in India. Also present were Major General P.N. Kathpalia, Colonel of the Kumaon and Naga Regiments and Brigadier Teg Bahadur Kapur, Director C&W, Army Headquarters, a dear friend of General Raina's, who personally organised all the ceremonial events connected with the military funeral.

The coffin draped in the Tricolour was taken to be laid in State at the Vaughan Club, Delhi Cantonment. A large number of dignitaries, military attaches, serving and retired officers, family, friends and relatives, placed wreaths. Among them was External Affairs Minister, P.V. Narasimha Rao.

The late General's cap, medals and sword were placed on the national flag draped casket by Colonel of The Kumaon & Naga Regiments, Major General (later Lieutenant General) Kathpalia. The casket containing the mortal remains was not opened till a few minutes before the cremation.

Later in the day, the coffin was carried on a Gun Carriage from Delhi Cantonment to the electric crematorium at Nigam Bodh Ghat, Delhi, for cremation with full military honours. Amid booming guns the coffin was mounted on a flower bedecked gun carriage. Four hundred Jawans (troops) their heads bowed and arms reversed, lined the route as the cortege started in slow motion. Detachments from 3rd Battalion of the Parachute Regiment — formerly 1st Kumaon Regiment (Para), and 14th Battalion The Kumaon Regiment (Gwalior) were among the regiments where the late General had served, and were now present to offer him their last salute.

A large number of military personnel, including the three Services Chiefs, friends and relatives paid their last respects to the 59-year old General. Wreaths were laid on behalf of the President, Prime Minister and other dignitaries. Canada's High Commissioner to India placed a wreath on behalf of the government and people of Canada. A wreath was also placed by Lt. Col. D.K. Khanna, GSO-1, on behalf of the General Officer Commanding and All Ranks of 25 Infantry Division.

Among those present on the occasion of General Raina's funeral were the three Service Chief, General O.P. Malhotra, Admiral Jal Cursetjee, and Air Chief Marshal Hrushikesh Moolgavkar, besides all the PSOs, heads of arms and services of Army Headquarters.

There were also many personal friends of General and Mrs. Raina, which included Mrs. Rajkumari Shrinagesh, wife of late General S.M. Shrinagesh, Mrs. Mohini Bhagat, wife of late General P.S. Bhagat, General P.P. Kumaramangalam (Retd), Major General K. Bhagwati Singh (Retd), Lt. General J.F.R. Jacob (Retd), who was Tappy's batch mate at OTA, Mhow, Air Chief Marshal O.P. Mehra (Retd), Admiral S.N. Kohli, former CNS (Retd), Lt. General J.S. Nakai (Retd), Lt. General Har Prasad (Retd), Lt. General M.M. Khanna (Retd), Lt. General K.P. Candeth (Retd), Lt. General N.C. Rawlley (Retd), Lt. General Bhatia (Retd) and Maj General S.N. Antia (Retd), besides many others, both from the Defence Services, Civil Bureaucracy as well as many civilian officials who had worked with General Raina. Among those present were Subedar Major (Clk) Mulk Raj, 14 Kumaon (Gwalior), Subedar Hira Singh, 13 Kumaon (served at Chushul).

Besides this author, Major Yogesh Prasad, Major Swantatra Kumar Sapru and Major Dara Jehangir Govadia and all those who had served at COAS Secretariat, during the tenure of General Raina, were there to bid farewell to him on his last journey.

The brief religious ceremony was presided over by General Raina's elder brother Suraj Raina since General Raina's only son, Captain J.N. Raina had died in a road accident six years earlier. General Raina's wife, Ninette and daughter Anita Raina Thapan were also present. As the body was slid into the crematorium chamber, guns boomed 17 times in salute and the buglers sounded the Last Post. There was many a wet eye in the crematorium premises.

The next day, 26th May 1980, the ashes were collected from the cremation ground by this author along with Late Lt. Colonel Ajay Musharan, AOC (later Finance Minister of Madhya Pradesh), and Arjun Thapan, the son-in-law of the Rainas. The ashes[242] were

---

[242] The ashes of General Raina were immersed in the river Ganga in Hardwar. When the urn passed through Roorkee Cantonment, troops from the local formations paid their last homage to the departed General by lining up on both sides of the road with reversed arms.

then taken from Delhi to Haridwar, where they were immersed in the holy River Ganga with full religious rites.

> *"Weeping may endure for the night but joy cometh in the morning."*
>
> ~ Psalms. 30

The Nation Remembers its Soldier-Diplomat

The news of the untimely demise of General Raina at Ottawa was received with great shock and disbelief. Obituary tributes were published in all national newspapers, whether in the capital or other parts of India.

N. Sanjiva Reddy, the President of India sent a message of condolence to Ninette Raina:

> I was shocked to hear the sudden and sad demise of General T.N. Raina. General Raina was a brave soldier with an illustrious record of service in the Indian Army. His integrity and transparent sincerity captured all those who came into contact with him. His services to the Indian Army as its chief would be long remembered. His untimely death is a loss to the nation.

Indira Gandhi, who had again become India's Prime Minister in 1979, sent a message of sympathy and condolence to Mrs. Ninette Raina in Ottawa, where she described General Raina as a "Distinguished Soldier" and a "Thorough Gentleman with deep dedication to our country's welfare".

The External Affairs Minister, Mr. P.V. Narasimha Rao, sent his condolences to Ninette Raina, saying, "the country has lost a gallant, wise and sage gentleman. General Raina was a great soldier, who also became an eminent diplomat".

In New Delhi, the Canadian High Commission in a message said,

> General Raina brought high distinction to his post of High Commissioner in Ottawa and contributed in many ways to improve understanding between our two peoples.

Soldier Par Excellence

Tappy Raina, as he was known to friends, was a soldier to the core, ever absorbed in the profession of arms. At the very outset of his Army career, while serving in the Middle East, during the Second World War, Tappy had sustained serious injuries at Kirkuk in Iraq; not only did he lose an eye, but some splinters remained embedded in his body for the rest of his life. Time and again they troubled him but that didn't prevent the doughty soldier from making further progress in his career. Tappy even went on to acquire "Wings" as a Paratrooper in 1946, when his battalion, 1 Kumaon, became a parachute battalion. His grit and guts came into full play in Ladakh in 1962, when his brigade put up a stiff resistance to the invading Chinese and took a heavy toll of the enemy. He was rewarded with a well-earned Maha Vir Chakra. Wherever the Indian Army saw action, whether in Burma (Myanmar) during the Second World War, or against Chinese aggression in Ladakh in 1962, or in the war against Pakistan for the creation of Bangladesh, Tappy Raina was in the thick of it.

True to his soldierly disposition, he could take triumph and tragedy in his stride. When he was the General Officer Commanding-in-Chief, Western Command, his only son, Captain Jyoti Narain Raina, who had followed his illustrious father into The Kumaon Regiment, died in a road accident on 9th March 1974 in the prime of his youth. General Raina absorbed the shock and dedicated himself with even greater determination to improving the life and service conditions of the men he commanded.

As an Army Commander and, later, as the Chief of the Indian Army, General Raina showed great concern for the men in his charge, both professionally and in matters of welfare. He promoted the Army Group Insurance (AGI) Scheme and, Army Welfare Housing Organisation (AWHO). He was also instrumental in raising the retirement age of officers, junior commissioned officers (JCOs) and jawans. He brought to an end the antique system of enrolling soldiers on eight years of "active" and seven years as "reservists". This system had put many young soldiers to great disadvantage in their resettlement, while remaining on the "Reserve" list!

The bandage factory at Ranikhet, which catered to the rehabilitation and self-employment for the needy disabled ex-servicemen and war widows, was also General Raina's initiative for self-employment[243].

After fighting a hard battle against the challenges to his health, against all odds, General Raina died with his boots on in the line of duty.

---

[243] *Sainik Samachar*, Vol. XXVII, No. 21 dated 1st June 1980

Epilogue

Those who join the Indian Army are "born twice"; once in their parents' home and, second, when they join the Indian Army and take an oath to serve Bharat Mata or Mother India. All his life, Tappy Raina, who had lost his own mother as an infant, devotedly served his motherland. In this, he was fully supported by his loving wife, Ninette. When Tappy's mortal remains were brought back to India from Ottawa where he was serving as High Commissioner, the Indian Army stood firmly by Ninette and their daughter, Anita, in their hour of grief. The vast family of the Indian Army remained a part of Ninette's life until the end of her days.

One of the biggest strengths of the Indian Army has been its cohesiveness and camaraderie amongst the past and the present heads of the Indian Army family. It is almost a revered practice in the Army to take counsel of the older members of the family, who, though retired, have not outlived their utility. Against this background, the idea of a biennial Chief's Conclave Was conceived and introduced during the tenure of the 21st COAS of the Indian Army, General Nirmal C. Vij, PVSM, UYSM, AVSM. This event brought together former Chiefs and their wives for various cultural, social and ceremonial functions. The former Chiefs of Army Staff were separately given an exhaustive briefing on the current Operational, Administrative and Man-management issues of the Army. Their wives were invited in their capacity as former Presidents of the Army Wives Welfare Association (AWWA).

The first Chief's Conclave was organised on 22nd and 23th October 2004 at New Delhi. It was attended by nine former Chiefs of Army Staff and their wives. In addition, there were five ladies whose husbands, all former Chiefs, were deceased. Heading the list was Mrs. Raj Kumari Shrinagesh, whose husband, General S.M. Shrinagesh was the first General to be appointed COAS, after the appointment of C-in-C was abolished by the Indian Government in 1955. Ninette continued to attend such get-togethers till her own health prevented her from doing so. The tradition of holding the Chiefs Conclave still continues.

Ninette Raina passed away at her home in New Delhi on Thursday, 25th January 2018, leaving behind the fragrance of her wonderful memories for all of us and her daughter, Anita, and two grandchildren, Gaurav and Madhav. Soft spoken and gentle, she was the personification of kindness, compassion and graciousness. She was cremated at the Lodhi Road, Electric Crematorium, New Delhi by simple Arya Samaj rites, in the presence of family and close friends. Wreaths were placed on behalf of the COAS, President AWWA, GOC-in-C Western Command, GOC 25 Infantry Division, GOC Delhi Area, Colonel of the Kumaon & Naga Regiments and CO, 5 Mech Infantry (14 Kumaon).

Ninette was born on 26th May 1923, at Dakar, capital of Senegal (then a French colony) in West Africa. Her father, Charles Kurtz, was a senior officer of the French Colonial Service, and the Kurtz family moved frequently between the three continents of Africa, Europe and Asia. Thus, from childhood, Ninette and her two siblings were exposed to people and cultures of different countries. This gave her a broad-minded outlook. She first saw the Indian army when 20 Indian Division, as part of the Allied South East Asia command, arrived in Saigon to take surrender of the Japanese Army.

The French in Saigon were jubilant to see the Indian Army march through the streets of Saigon. Captain Tappy Raina, a young officer of 1/19 Hyderabad Regiment (later 1 Kumaon and now 3 Para Regiment — SFF), arrived in Saigon in that context. He was 24 years old and attached to the Brigade Headquarter. Ninette and Tappy met in the euphoria of the aftermath of war and were drawn to each other. Even when Tappy went away on duty to Indonesia, their friendship continued to grow through letters and later blossomed into courtship. The Kurtz family returned from Saigon to France on 31st December 1946.

In January 1949, Ninette arrived in India by boat and was married to Tappy on 25th February 1949, at Dehra Dun, by Arya Samaj rites. They began their married life in modest accommodation at the King Edward Road Officers' Hostel in New Delhi, where Tappy was then posted. Throughout their married life, Ninette stood by Tappy in all situations, both in peace and war. As Tappy rose in rank, Ninette shared his responsibilities by engaging in welfare work for his subordinates and their families, especially with those who were war-bereaved. She was a proud Army wife and a loving mother to her two children, Jyoti and Anita.

Tragedy struck when the Rainas lost their son, Jyoti (fondly called Joe) on 9th March 1974. He was 24 years old. Joe, who had followed in his father's footsteps and was a Captain in his father's Battalion, died as result of a road accident in Jalandhar Cantonment. Life for Tappy and Ninette was never the same again.

A cancer survivor herself since 1968, Ninette saw her beloved Tappy succumb to the same illness on 19th May 1980, at the age of 59, while he was High Commissioner for India at Ottawa. Thereafter, Ninette's life centred around her daughter and two adored grandsons, Gaurav and Madhav.

Fate took Tappy away a week before Ninette's 57th birthday in 1980, and she was called away, almost a week before Tappy's 97th birth anniversary in 2018.

Bibliography

Cardozo, Ian (Major General), Ed., *The Indian Army: A Brief History*. Centre for Armed Forces Historical Research, New Delhi 2005.

Fisher, Margaret W. and others, *Himalayan Battleground,* Frederick A. Praeger, New York, 1963.

Grant, N.B. (Brig.), *Retiring Age in the Armed Forces* in USI Seminars, Number Three, New Delhi, 1975.

Jacob, J.F.R. *An Odyssey in War and Peace,* Roli Books, New Delhi, 2011.

Jayal, B.D. (Air Marshal) and others, *A Call for Change: Higher Defence Management in India*, Institute for Defence Studies and Analyses, New Delhi, 2012.

Kapur, Teg Bahadur (Brig.), *Unknown Significant Facts: From a Soldier's Diary*, Minerva Press, New Delhi, 2014.

Malik, V.P. (General), *India's Military Conflicts and Diplomacy — An Inside View of Decision Making*, Harper Collins, India, 2015

Mansingh, Surjit, *Historical Dictionary of India*, Vision Books, Delhi, reprint 1999.

Nanporia, N.J. *The Sino-Indian Dispute*, A Times of India Publication, July 1963.

Narayan, B.K., *General J.N. Chaudhuri: An Autobiography*, Vikas Publishing House Pvt. Ltd., New Delhi 1978.

Praval, K.C. Valour Triumphs: *A History of the Kumaon Regiment*, Thomson Press, 1976.

Singh, Depinder, (Lt. Gen.), *Field Marshal Sam Manekshaw: Soldiering with Dignity,* Natraj Publishers, Dehradun, 2nd Edition, 2003.

Singh, Jagjit, (Maj. Gen), *The Saga of Ladakh: Heroic Battle of Rezangla and Gurung Hill (1961-62),* Vanity Books, 1983.

Singh, Joginder, (Maj. Gen), *Behind the Scenes: An Analysis of India's Military Operations 1947-1971*, Lancer Publishers, January 1993.

Sinha, S.K. (Lt. Gen.), *Changing India: Straight from the Heart*, Manas Publications, New Delhi, 2017.

Sinha, S.K. (Lt. Gen.) *Higher Defence Organisation in India* in USI Papers, Number Seven, New Delhi, 1980.

Sinha, Satyanarayan, *The Chinese Aggression*, Rama Krishna and Sons, New Delhi, 1961.